McGRAW-HILL PUBLICATIONS IN PSYCHOLOGY

J. F. DASHIELL, Ph.D., Consulting Editor

STUDIES IN PERSONALITY

Lewis M. Terman

STUDIES
IN PERSONALITY

CONTRIBUTED IN HONOR

OF

LEWIS M. TERMAN

Card under

mc Nemar

FIRST EDITION

McGRAW-HILL BOOK COMPANY, INC.

NEW YORK AND LONDON

1942

137

S+9

STUDIES IN PERSONALITY

COPYRIGHT, 1942, BY THE
McGRAW-HILL BOOK COMPANY, INC.

———

PRINTED IN THE UNITED STATES OF AMERICA

19034

May, 1942

THE MAPLE PRESS COMPANY, YORK, PA.

PREFACE

Lewis M. Terman, servant of psychology, has labored untiringly to extend the boundaries of our knowledge of human behavior. His achievements and personality have been an inspiration to psychologists everywhere and especially to those who have had an opportunity for work and study under his guidance. It is fitting, therefore, that this series of papers on a topic about which so much of his own research has centered should be prepared for the occasion of his sixty-fifth birthday.

The authors of this book are but a small proportion of his many former graduate students who have been quickened by his leadership and who join with us and with his colleagues everywhere in the hope that his work may be continued for many years to come.

ROBERT G. BERNREUTER
CATHERINE C. MILES
MILES A. TINKER
KIMBALL YOUNG
QUINN McNEMAR ⎫ Editors
MAUD A. MERRILL ⎭
FLORENCE L. GOODENOUGH, Chairman

January, 1942.

CONTENTS

PAGE

PREFACE. vii

CHAPTER

   I. INTRODUCTION. 3
Robert S. Woodworth

  II. AN EXPERIMENTAL STUDY OF THE RESOLUTION OF CONFLICT BY CHILDREN: TIME ELAPSING AND AMOUNT OF VICARIOUS TRIAL-AND-ERROR BEHAVIOR OCCURRING 13
Roger G. Barker

 III. A STUDY OF IDENTICAL TWINS REARED APART UNDER DIFFERING TYPES OF FAMILY RELATIONSHIPS 35
Barbara S. Burks

 IV. THE APPRAISAL INTERVIEW: A CRITICAL CONSIDERATION OF ITS THEORY AND PRACTICE WITH PARTICULAR REFERENCE TO THE SELECTION OF PUBLIC PERSONNEL 71
Franklin Fearing

  V. THE USE OF FREE ASSOCIATION IN THE OBJECTIVE MEASUREMENT OF PERSONALITY 87
Florence L. Goodenough

 VI. RESPONSES BY RHESUS MONKEYS TO STIMULI HAVING MULTIPLE SIGN-VALUES. 105
H. F. Harlow

VII. THE RELATION OF PHYSIOLOGICAL AND SOCIAL INDICES OF ACTIVITY LEVEL. 125
L. P. Herrington

VIII. PERSONALITY AS RELATED TO SOURCE AND ADEQUACY OF SEX INSTRUCTION. 147
E. Lowell Kelly

 IX. PSYCHICAL BELIEF 159
John L. Kennedy

  X. MECHANISMS OF HALLUCINATIONS 175
Heinrich Klüver

ix

CHAPTER   PAGE

XI. PSYCHOLOGICAL STUDY OF A YOUNG MALE PSEUDOHERMAPHRODITE
    REARED AS A FEMALE. 209
                    Catharine Cox Miles

XII. A TECHNIQUE FOR DETECTING ATTEMPTS TO FAKE PERFORMANCE ON
    THE SELF-INVENTORY TYPE OF PERSONALITY TESTS. 229
                    Floyd L. Ruch

XIII. SUCCESS AND FAILURE: A STUDY OF MOTILITY 235
                    Robert R. Sears

XIV. THE PLACE OF INDIVIDUAL DIFFERENCES IN EXPERIMENTATION . . 259
                    Eugene Shen

XV. INDIVIDUAL AND SEX DIFFERENCES IN SPEED OF SACCADIC EYE
    MOVEMENTS. 271
                    Miles A. Tinker

XVI. A NOTE ON PERSONALITY FACTORS AFFECTING THE REHABILITATION
    OF PROBLEM FAMILIES 281
                    Raymond R. Willoughby

XVII. VARIATIONS IN PERSONALITY MANIFESTATIONS IN MORMON POLY-
    GYNOUS FAMILIES 285
                    Kimball Young

BIBLIOGRAPHY OF PROFESSOR TERMAN'S WRITINGS 315
                    Gretchen Ann Magaret and Clare Wright

STUDIES IN PERSONALITY

CHAPTER I

INTRODUCTION

By

ROBERT S. WOODWORTH

Columbia University

It is a great honor to have the opportunity of contributing to this volume a few remarks by way of introduction. It is true one has something of the feeling of a chairman introducing a speaker who "needs no introduction." Certainly Lewis Terman needs no introduction to an audience of psychologists, an audience of educationists, or any audience of well-informed friends of social progress. None of our contemporary psychologists, it is safe to say, is more widely known by the general public. Even those who are not familiar with his name have had some contact with the work he has done. They know of the intelligence tests even when they have perhaps lost sight of the fact that it is to Terman, after Binet, that we owe the development of the tests to a degree of excellence adequate for both practical and scientific use.

True enough, some who know just a little about this work are skeptical of its value. Ten or twelve years ago, I heard a social scientist express the hope that Terman would conduct no further researches, since he had "done enough harm already." This speaker's animus stemmed from a predilection for the environmentalist side of the nature-nurture controversy and so was quite understandable, but he betrayed a decidedly secondhand acquaintance with Terman's actual work and a complete ignorance of Terman's fundamentally judicial and open-minded attitude on this important problem. Fortunately, the hope expressed by our environmentalist friend has proved to be ill founded. Further researches have been conducted, and the past decade has indeed been astonishingly productive. A host of well-wishers will join in our hope that the story of Terman's life and work may be long continued in the coming years.

This life story is remarkable for continuity of interest and persistence of effort. In his brief autobiography Terman himself has traced the origins of his psychological interest back into early school days.[1]

"Whatever the cause, almost as far back as I can remember I seem to have had a little more interest than the average child in the personalities of others and to have been impressed by those who differed in some respect from the common run. Among my schoolmates or acquaintances whose behavior traits especially interested me were a feebleminded boy . . . a backward albino boy . . . a spoiled crippled boy . . . a 'lightning calculator' . . . an imaginative liar. . . . I am inclined to think that the associations which I had with such schoolmates were among the most valuable of my childhood experiences."

Early environment, although thus stimulating an interest in individual differences, did not by any means provide an easy "trail to psychology." It was an uphill road, leading through the normal school and several years of elementary and high-school teaching, with much intensive reading along the way in educational philosophy and psychology, on to Indiana University, where, under the influence of Bryan and Lindley, plans were shaped for a lifework of psychological teaching and investigation. Laboratory experiments of the brass-instrument type were repellent rather than attractive, but experiments on leadership in children, as related to sex and age, were carried through with great enthusiasm, and the whole literature on leaders and great men and on the feeble-minded and degenerate was covered as part of the work for the master's degree from Indiana in 1903. The master's thesis, though now regarded by its author as having no scientific value, is still good reading. Clarity of thought and expression are as conspicuous in this first paper of Terman's as in his numerous later writings. Besides the experimental and questionnaire data on leadership in children, it contains some pioneer observations on dominance order, "pecking order," in domestic herds of horses or cattle. As a biographical document it sounds the keynote of its author's lifelong interest in individual differences, especially in the gifted group, in heredity and environment, and in mental development. "The psychologist, in order to interpret the adult mind with its multiplicity of instincts, reflexes, feelings and

[1] Carl Murchison, ed. History of psychology in autobiography. Worcester, Mass., Clark University Press, 1932. Vol. III, p. 300.

ideational elements, watches their development from childhood and even calls to his aid the mental unfolding in the phylogenetic series."[1]

This last sentence points to the influence of G. Stanley Hall, coming, in part, through Bryan and Lindley. To become a student under Hall at Clark University was the next step, and Terman has borne eloquent testimony to the stimulating environment there, the close contacts with the members of the staff and able fellow students, and the all-important presentation of one's work from time to time in Hall's exciting seminar. It was not Hall, however, or any other member of the Clark staff, that gave particular direction to Terman's own researches. Rather, it was Binet, whose scale of tests was still a thing of the future but whose earlier studies of the intelligence of children were well known to Terman. "Genius and Stupidity: a study of some of the intellectual processes of seven 'bright' and seven 'stupid' boys" was the title of Terman's dissertation. It was an intensive qualitative study, designed to bring out the intellectual processes of brighter and duller individuals, and it also served to reveal the merits of certain now familiar test items such as "ball in field" and the interpretation of fables. A variety of other tests were also tried out. A few sentences from this paper will indicate the direction of Terman's interests at this early stage of his career.[2]

"One of the most serious problems confronting psychology is that of connecting itself with life. . . . It has passed into a proverb that of all men the psychologist is the most helpless before the individual mind. If taken to task, he pleads the doubtful excuse that it is his business to know mind in general and that he has nothing to do with this or that individual mind. . . . The earliest attempt, at least in modern times, at a direct relating of psychology and life, was phrenology. This, science at once disowned. . . . More recently . . . we have the empirical work coming under the head of *mental tests*. . . . Binet, for example, in 1896 expressed the hope that he would soon succeed in devising a series of mental and motor tests which . . . would indicate definitely the child's grade of intelligence. . . . The following study, at least, is undertaken in the faith that psychology and life are not prime to each other, and that even at present some of the common factors may be sought without thereby cheapening either the methods or results of experimental psychology. How extremely little is herein contributed to this end, no one is better aware than the writer; but he would fain co-operate with the pioneers already at work."

[1] *Ped. Sem.*, 1904, **11**, 413–451.
[2] *Ped. Sem.*, 1906, **13**, 307–373.

For the first few years after he obtained his degree, this program could not be actively prosecuted because of poor health, and by the time Terman became professor at Stanford in 1910, Binet had already published his earlier tentative test scales. These Terman at once began to use and to adapt and amplify. In collaboration with his students, he undertook a thorough revision, involving trial of the tests on large samples of children and adjustment of the scoring so as to give the average child of each age a mental age equal to his chronological age, *i.e.*, an I.Q. of 100. This large-scale enterprise resulted in the Stanford-Binet intelligence-test scale of 1916, dedicated "to the memory of Alfred Binet, patient researcher, creative thinker, unpretentious scholar, inspiring and fruitful devotee of inductive and dynamic psychology." These words can safely be taken as expressing Terman's own ideal, and we can as safely assert that that ideal has been fully realized.

The practical success of the Stanford-Binet tests far exceeded anything anticipated by their author. "I knew that my revision of Binet's tests was superior to others then available, but I did not foresee the vogue it was to have and imagined that it would probably be displaced by something much better within a few years."[1] In another place he said, "May we not hope that 10 or 15 test scales will soon be devised, each more perfect than the Binet series . . . tests which will explore every line of efficiency, intellectual, volitional, motor, personal, pedagogical, social, linguistic, etc.?"[2] It is interesting to inquire why these expectations were not realized. Other valuable revisions of the Binet scale made their appearance, and there was considerable activity in providing performance and paper-and-pencil intelligence tests, as well as school achievement tests, with some effort also toward personality measurement. But the Stanford-Binet remained the standard intelligence test for a period of 20 years. One reason was that it provided the advantage of a common standard. Comparability of results was thus promoted, and there was a feeling that the introduction of variants would do more harm than good. The test scale was so much of a unit that it could not very well be revised in a piecemeal fashion. Any adequate revision would be another large-scale enterprise, calling for much ingenuity in the invention of new items, for expert testing and statistical treatment, for patient experimentation in

[1] From the already cited autobiography, p. 324.
[2] L. M. Terman & H. G. Childs. *J. educ. Psychol.*, 1912, **3**, 287.

respect to scoring and placement of the test items, and for a representative sampling of the population such as would yield valid age norms. It was not a task to be undertaken lightly, especially in view of the excellent results obtained with the scale as it was. Yet there was, of course, room for improvement, and the satisfaction was general when it was learned that Terman himself had undertaken the task of revision.

The 1937 revision of the Stanford-Binet test, published by Terman and Merrill after 10 years of work, was certainly a great achievement. Not only was the scale extended downward to the 2-year level and upward well into adult levels but it was actually doubled by the provision of two equivalent forms. And these forms have been well standardized on a large and representative sample of the native-born white population of the United States. Even so, the authors say, "Nothing approximating perfection can be claimed for the results." But their hope is "that this revision of the Binet method will long provide a common standard." From the reception given the revised tests, it appears certain that they will be of immense value both in the appraisal of the individual for educational and vocational guidance and in many important lines of research that will be raised to a higher level by the use of these more precise instruments of measurement.

So much of Terman's research has been cooperative that we can safely regard the cooperative attack as characteristic of the man. An unusual opportunity for such cooperation was afforded by the exigencies of the war of 1917–1918. As a member of the committee that prepared the Army Alpha group test of intelligence and demonstrated its utility, Terman contributed his full share toward this outstanding achievement. Major Terman was attached to the general psychological staff at the surgeon general's office "to conduct inquiries concerning the value of psychological examining, and to improve methods of work," and he was primarily responsible for the valuable historical report on the development of methods of psychological examining in the United States Army.[1] In his autobiography, he says:

"One result of the war experiences was to confirm and strengthen my earlier beliefs regarding the importance of mental tests as an integral part of scientific psychology. Whereas I had thought that only a handful of

[1] *In* Robert M. Yerkes, ed. *Psychological examining in the United States Army. Mem. Nat. Acad. Sci.*, 1921, **15,** 299–546.

psychologists were of this opinion, I now learned that many were. I could return to my work with more confidence than ever that, in the long run, contributions to the field of mental tests would receive the recognition they deserved."

His presidential address at the Madison meeting of the American Psychological Association in 1923 was a clear and convincing defence of mental tests as a major instrument of scientific psychology.[1]

"It is true that the practical usefulness of mental tests is one of their outstanding characteristics. . . . However, when one looks into the history of tests over the last 30 years, one finds that the psychologists who devised and used them were by no means always governed by practical considerations. . . . If the test has been properly constructed and validated it may at once become a tool for the investigation of important scientific problems. . . . I do not believe that anyone interested in the whole science of psychology can weigh lightly such problems as individual and race differences, the interrelation of mental traits, the phenomena of mental growth, the limitations of educability, or the psychology of genius, mental deficiency and insanity. Upon all these, the mental test has thrown light. It is proving itself applicable not only to the problems of intelligence, but also to those of emotion, volition, temperament and character. It has become one of the important methods of psychological research; some would say, the most important. Not the least of its contributions is the fact that it has broadened and intensified our incentive to research, enlarged the public support of our science, and attracted new hosts of workers to the psychological vineyard."

The nature-nurture problem, or the problem of determining the relative importance of heredity and environment in producing differences among men, is certainly a scientific problem as well as one of great social significance; and it is a problem that has been attacked by the aid of the intelligence tests. The objection has sometimes been raised that these tests are not suitable for the purpose because they are based on an assumption that prejudges the case. The supposed assumption is that the tests are measuring native intelligence or native differences in intelligence. No doubt many psychologists have hoped that they were measuring native intelligence and have spoken as if they were. But it is impossible to put one's finger on any step in the whole operation—from the selection of test items and their standardization up through the arrangement of the scale and the determination of age norms and

[1] *Psychol. Rev.*, 1924, **31**, 93–117.

on to the administration and scoring of the tests—where the supposed assumption comes into play and affects the results. Unwarranted assumptions are likely to creep in when the results are interpreted, but the tests themselves are unbiased so long as they are taken to be what they obviously are, a sampling of the subject's present abilities. Of course, they do not get at all abilities, and their limitations need sometimes to be borne carefully in mind. But the best evidence that they do not force the investigator into any foregone conclusion on the nature-nurture problem is the fact that they have been used by investigators with very different predilections who have drawn radically different conclusions—though it must be said that their data do not differ as radically as their conclusions.

Another mistaken objection, concerned with the "constancy of the I.Q.," is that the tests are so standardized as to force the I.Q. to remain constant. The standardization does force the average I.Q. to remain constant—such being the nature and definition of the I.Q.—but there is nothing here to prevent any individual's I.Q. from going up or down to any extent. How much it goes up or down is a question of fact, and the tests are an unbiased instrument for determining the fact. Of course, such tests cannot be absolutely precise. Terman takes pains to point out the probable error of any single determination of the I.Q., a probable error that is quite small. But even with a probable error of only 3 points, we must expect occasional fluctuations of 10 points or more from day to day without any real change in the subject's intelligence. Unwarranted inferences from individual cases may easily be drawn from failure to take account of the probable error. In statistical studies, the more likely error is one of selective sampling. The psychologist is under no obligation to settle the nature-nurture controversy out of hand, but he does owe it to his colleagues and to the world at large to be circumspect and scientific in his methods. Certainly many of us sympathize heartily with Terman when he voices his distaste for "shoddy work" due to poor methodological procedures employed in studies of heredity and environment. And we agree with him when he says, as he has time and again, that full recognition of the value of cultural and educational influences need not in the least blind us to the existence of large individual differences in intelligence and personality.

"The hereditarian can wholeheartedly join with the environmentalist in the demand that more and better educational opportunity be provided for every child, but he has too much respect for facts and too little faith in miracles to expect that equalization of opportunity will result in equality of achievement."[1]

That Terman cannot be accused of overlooking the importance of environment is shown by his early and often repeated insistence that exceptional children should be given exceptional school opportunities to develop their potential abilities. In his 1915 paper on "The Mental Hygiene of Exceptional Children," he pointed to the neglect of such children in the schools.[2]

"Instead of developing a differentiated course of study which would allow dull children to make steady progress without becoming retarded we have too often promoted them to tasks which for them are impossible of accomplishment. The inevitable result is apathy and discouragement, or else overpressure. Bright children, on the other hand, are almost always underpromoted. They are rarely given tasks which call forth their best ability, and as a result they run the risk of falling into lifelong habits of submaximum efficiency."

The study of genius and of the gifted child is one of Terman's lifelong interests, dating from his student days or earlier. In the first volume of *Genetic Studies of Genius* and before that, in a 1922 paper on "A New Approach to the Study of Genius," he traced for us the history of this long-continued investigation. He distinguished three prior stages in the study of genius. In the first, typified by Lombroso, selected cases were used to support some preconceived theory. This error is avoided in the second stage, represented by Galton's inductive study of historical characters by aid of biographical material. Cattell's study of living American men of science who furnished autobiographical data exemplifies the third stage and marks a distinct advance in respect to the reliability of the data within the chosen categories but was necessarily meager in respect to the childhood of the gifted individual. With the coming of the Binet tests, the way was prepared for a fourth stage. Instead of working back from the adult to his formative period, it was now possible to locate gifted children, "geniuses" for their age level, obtain contemporaneous data, and follow these children on into adult life. So we should discover how gifted children turn out, and, on the reasonable expectation that some of them would attain eminence

---

[1] *Yearb. nat. Soc. Stud. Educ.*, 1940, **39,** Part I, p. 466.
[2] *Ped. Sem.*, 1915, **22,** 529–537.

in life, we should possess better information than previously on the childhood of some highly gifted persons. We should learn something of the problem of how to educate a gifted child. And we should "find out what truth there is in the widespread view that gifted children are usually conceited, freakish, socially eccentric, and prone either to illness and early death or to nervousness and insanity."

The answer to this last question came out clearly in the first volume of the *Genetic Studies* and still more surely in the follow-up studies reported in the third volume and in the recent paper[1] on the "Status of the California Gifted Group at the End of Sixteen Years." As children, with few exceptions, these young people were of good health and normal or superior personality. As young adults, many of them are taking high rank, and very few could be found to substantiate the pessimistic view that was formerly held. Some of them are not measuring up to their intellectual potentialities, the reason lying apparently in poor motivation, emotional conflicts, or personality defects, dependent, in some cases, it would seem, on their own family background. The conclusion is that, although most children giving an I.Q. of 140 or over grow into adults of marked ability, great achievement cannot be predicted with certainty even for those with the highest I.Q. The reason for such relative failure may lie in personal difficulties, and it may lie in the inadequate education, stimulation, and opportunity afforded by society.

The promised more complete analysis of these unique data is awaited with great interest, and a further follow-up of these still-young people is something that we should all agree simply must take place. The same can be said of the other large-scale and long-time enterprises so characteristic of Terman—his tests, his studies of heredity and environment, his investigations of sex differences or of masculinity and femininity, and his work *Psychological Factors in Marital Happiness*. No one can say that Terman has picked out the easy tasks, and no one can deny that he has succeeded nobly in his early ambition to establish a direct relation between scientific psychology and the life of the people. He is truly to be numbered among the pioneers, whose example is an inspiration to the younger generation and whose work and influence will long endure.

[1] L. M. Terman & M. Oden. *Yearb. nat. Soc. Stud. Educ.*, 1940, **39**, Part I, 67–89.

CHAPTER II

AN EXPERIMENTAL STUDY OF THE RESOLUTION OF CONFLICT BY CHILDREN: Time Elapsing and Amount of Vicarious Trial-and-error Behavior Occurring[1]

By

ROGER G. BARKER

University of Illinois

INTRODUCTION

Choicelike behavior, *i.e.*, hesitation and vacillation between alternative actions [VTE behavior in the terminology of Meunzinger (6)],[2] may occur in quite different psychological situations. In one of these, a conflict occurs between simultaneously existing but mutually exclusive desires. This is the situation of the gourmet, for example, deciding between favorite delicacies. Choicelike behavior may occur in situations where there is no conflict between desires but where discriminative difficulties arise in identifying the intended action. This is the situation existing in psychophysical experiments where instructions determine the subject's desires, but where the intended action cannot be easily carried out because the limen of discrimination has not been reached. Choicelike behavior may arise, also, when a subject is faced with undesirable alternatives, even though the least undesirable action may be clearly known and discrimination between the alternatives may be perfect. The tension arising from the necessity of engaging in an undesired action in such a situation may give rise to behavior very similar to that occurring in the other situations. Undoubtedly, combinations of these situations frequently exist when choicelike behavior occurs.

In considering problems of choice behavior, it is necessary to be explicit as to the conditions of the behavior under consideration, whether the source is conflict, discriminative difficulties, or tension.

[1] This investigation was conducted in the laboratories of the Harvard Psychological Clinic.

[2] Numbers in parentheses refer to the References at the end of the chapter.

In the present experiments, every effort is made to create conflict situations undisturbed by discriminative difficulties. We have been concerned with the time elapsing and with the amount of VTE behavior occurring during the resolution of conflict under three conditions: (*a*) where the conflicts involve alternatives that vary from those of similar desirability, *e.g.*, orange juice and pineapple juice, to those that differ greatly in desirability, *e.g.*, orange juice and vinegar; (*b*) where the conflicts involve alternatives that vary from those that are desirable, *e.g.*, orange and pineapple juice, to those that are undesirable, *e.g.*, vinegar and salt water; (*c*) where the conflicts are "real" ones—*i.e.*, the consequences of the choice are experienced by the subject—and where the conflicts are "hypothetical" ones—*i.e.*, the subject merely states what his action would be if the conflict were presented to him.

Procedure

Each subject was presented with a sequence of pairs of liquids and was required to indicate the one of each pair he desired to drink. The following seven liquids were used: orange juice, pineapple juice, tomato juice, water, lemon juice, vinegar, and a saturated solution of salt water. Each of these seven liquids was paired with every other one. By the method of paired comparisons, the liquids were placed in preference series indicating the order of desirability for each subject individually. These preference series made it possible to study conflict behavior under two of the conditions mentioned: (*a*) where the alternatives were of similar desirability, *i.e.*, near together in the preference series, and where they were of discrepant desirability, *i.e.*, far apart in the preference series; and (*b*) where the conflicts were between desirable liquids, *i.e.*, liquids at the positive end of the preference series, and where they were between undesirable liquids, *i.e.*, liquids at the negative end of the preference series.

The alternatives were presented under two conditions: in one case, the subject was required to drink the liquid of his choice; in the other, he merely indicated the liquid he would drink if he were required to do so. These two conditions constituted the "real" and "hypothetical" choices, respectively.

Nineteen boys, aged 9 to 11 years, served as subjects. They were given a small cash reward for participating in the experiments. Each boy came to the laboratory by individual appointment. After his ability to read the names of the liquids was tested, seven small glasses, each containing 6 cc. of liquid, were placed before him, and he was instructed to drink each of the liquids, to name it, and to tell how he liked it.   Several subjects who were deficient in reading ability or unfamiliar with some of the liquids were eliminated.

During the experiments the subject was seated in a chair at a small table.   At a suitable distance and height, the names of the liquids were presented in an exposure apparatus; they were exposed in pairs side by side at the same height.   At a convenient reaching distance, a lever extended 6 inches above the top of the table.   The lever was mounted 2 inches below the surface of the table and was so placed and weighted that it came to rest in a vertical position on a line midway between the cards in the exposure apparatus.   The lever could be moved easily to the right or to the left from the vertical position through arcs of 5 inches.   When the lever was moved as far as it would go to either side, a circuit that sounded a buzzer was automatically closed.   The subject indicated the liquid of his choice by moving the lever to the side corresponding to the position of the card with the name of the desired liquid.   Movements from the vertical of less than the 5-inch maximum that sounded the buzzer did not "count," and the subject was free to reverse the movement at any point within the limits of these arcs.   Before each exposure, the lever was returned to the central vertical position, and the subject placed his hand in position upon it.   On a continuously moving tape, an automatic record was made of the time of exposure of the two cards and of all the movements of the lever.   This provided a record of the time from the moment of the occurrence of the conflict until its resolution and of the VTE behavior occurring.

Every pair of cards was presented twice in each sequence of conflicts; their positions were reversed on the two exposures to avoid the influence of position.   Thus, both the "real" and the "hypothetical" sequences involved 42 choices.   The data for a particular choice in a sequence consist of the average of the two determinations. The order of presentation of the paired liquids follows:

1. tomato-lemon	9. vinegar-water
2. orange-pineapple	10. lemon-pineapple
3. vinegar-lemon	11. orange-water
4. salt water-water	12. salt water-tomato
5. orange-tomato	13. pineapple-orange
6. pineapple-vinegar	14. lemon-salt water
7. water-tomato	15. orange-vinegar
8. salt water-pineapple	16. pineapple-tomato

17. orange-lemon
18. pineapple-water
19. water-orange
20. salt water-orange
21. vinegar-tomato
22. tomato-salt water
23. lemon-water
24. water-salt water
25. tomato-pineapple
26. salt water-vinegar
27. vinegar-pineapple
28. water-vinegar
29. lemon-orange

30. tomato-orange
31. water-pineapple
32. pineapple-lemon
33. lemon-tomato
34. lemon-vinegar
35. orange-salt water
36. pineapple-salt water
37. vinegar-orange
38. tomato-water
39. tomato-vinegar
40. salt water-lemon
41. vinegar-salt water
42. water-tomato

The "real" sequence was presented first in the experimental session in the case ot 9 of the subjects; the "hypothetical" sequence followed after a 10-minute intermission. With 10 of the subjects, the sequences were presented in the reverse order.

RESULTS

The verbal comments and facial expressions of the subjects on first tasting the liquids made it clear that in every case the drinking of the liquids provided a series of actions varying from desirable actions (actions of positive valence) through indifferent actions to undesirable actions (actions of negative valence). In the case of every subject, the response to at least two liquids of the seven was positive; *e.g.*, "That's orange juice; I like it—especially in this kind of weather," or, after carefully smelling the liquid, "Oh, this is pineapple juice; that's O.K.," and then, after drinking it, "Can't you give me some more of that?" In the case of every subject, at least one of the liquids was reacted to negatively; *e.g.*, "Say, this is vinegar; do you mean to say I have to drink this?" (very wry face after gulping it down); "Gee, I wish there was sugar in that. Ugh!" Finally, in the case of every subject, there was evidence that some of the liquids were neutral; *e.g.*, "That's water; water is all right when you're thirsty; I'm not very thirsty now, but that much doesn't bother me."

The place of a particular liquid in a preference series varied from subject to subject and, for the same subject, from the "real" to the "hypothetical" sequence. In Table I, the ranking of each liquid by each subject is given. The first number refers to the ranking of the liquid in the "real" sequence; the second number refers to its ranking in the "hypothetical" sequence. Where there was not consistency of choice on the two presentations of each pair of alternatives within a sequence, the two liquids have the same ranking in the subject's preference series. In these cases, if it was necessary to assign a liquid a unique place in a subject's preference series, the order given at the top of the table was arbitrarily followed.

TABLE I

RANK ORDER OF PREFERENCE FOR LIQUIDS*

Subject	Pine-apple	Orange	Tomato	Water	Lemon	Salt water	Vinegar
1	1, 1½	3, 1½	2, 3	4, 4	6, 5	5, 6½	7, 6½
2	1, 1	2, 2½	3, 4	4, 2½	6½, 7	6½, 6	5, 5
3	2, 3	3, 2	1, 1	4, 4	7, 7	5½, 6	5½, 5
4	4, 4	1, 1	4, 3	2, 2	4, 7	5½, 5	5½, 6
5	1, 2	2, 1	4, 3	3, 7	5, 4½	6, 4½	7, 6
6	2, 2	1, 1	3, 3	4, 4	6, 6½	6, 5	6, 6½
7	1, 1	2½, 3½	2½, 3½	4, 2	5, 6	7, 5	6, 4
8	1, 1	2, 2	6, 7	3, 3	4, 4	5, 6	7, 5
9	1, 1	3, 2	2, 3	4, 4	5, 5½	6, 5½	7, 7
10	1, 3	2, 1	3, 4	4, 6	5, 2	7, 7	6, 5
11	2½, 4	2½, 1	1, 2	4½, 3	4½, 5	6½, 7	6½, 6
12	2, 2	1, 1	4, 3	3, 5	5, 4	6, 6	7, 7
13	4, 4	3, 3	2, 2	1, 1	5, 5	6, 6	7, 7
14	1, 1	2½, 3½	4, 3½	5, 5½	2½, 2	6, 6½	7, 7
15	2, 1	3, 2	1, 3½	4, 3½	5, 5	7, 6	6, 7
16	1, 4	4, 2	2½, 2	2½, 2	7, 6½	5½, 5	5½, 6½
17	1, 1	3, 2	2, 4	4, 5	6, 3	6, 7	6, 6
18	2, 3	1, 1	4, 4	3, 5	6, 2	5, 6	7, 7
19	1, 1	4, 4	2, 2	5, 5	3, 3	6, 6	7, 7

* First number refers to the "real" sequence, second number to the "hypothetical" sequence. For subjects 1 to 9 the sequence of "real" conflicts preceded the "hypothetical" conflicts; for subjects 10 to 19 the sequence of "hypothetical" conflicts preceded the "real" conflicts.

The time required for the resolution of conflicts is given in seconds. The amount of VTE behavior has been converted to a numerical value in the following way: Every shifting of the lever followed by a return toward the original position is called a *waver*. Such wavers involved relatively small or relatively large spacial displacements of the lever. Three sizes of wavers have been arbitrarily designated; the smallest wavers have been given the numerical weight of one, the medium wavers a numerical weight of two, and the largest wavers a numerical weight of three. Each subject's VTE score is the sum of his wavers as thus weighted for extent of displacement. These VTE scores are not completely adequate. Some subjects expressed their vacillation by body, head, or eye movements rather than by movements of the lever, and the study of Wells (7) indicates that a great amount of "running back and forth" in conflict situations of this sort is entirely "mental," with no measurable manifestations.

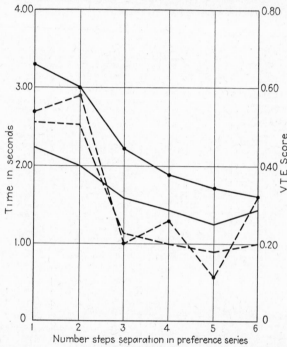

FIG. I.—Initial presentation of conflict. Time elapsing and VTE behavior occurring during the resolution of conflicts between alternatives separated by different 'distances' in the preference series. Mean scores. ●━━● 'real' conflict; ▬ ▬ ▬ 'hypothetical' conflict; ——— time; ─ ─ ─ VTE score.

Furthermore, some of the wavers are "mistakes" in carrying out intentions. The relation of the VTE measure obtained to the total amount of VTE behavior is not known.

In Tables II and III and Figs. 1 and 2, data are given for the resolution of conflicts between alternatives of varying degrees of difference in desirability (valence). The second column of the tables and the first point of the curves refer to conflicts between alternatives separated by a single "step" in each subject's preference series, *i.e.*, they give the average time and VTE scores for conflicts between

liquids 1 and 2, 2 and 3, 3 and 4, etc.   The third column of the tables
and the second point of the curves refer to conflicts between alternatives separated by two "steps" in each subject's preference series,
i.e., liquids 1 and 3, 2 and 4, 3 and 5, etc.   The fourth column of the
tables and the third point of the curves refer to conflicts between
liquids separated by three "steps" in the preference series.   The
solid curves in the figures represent time; the broken curves, VTE
scores.

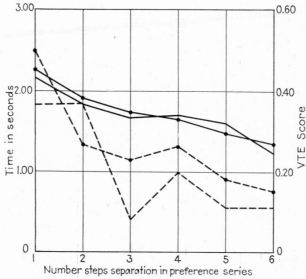

FIG. 2.—Second presentation of conflict.   Time elapsing and VTE behavior
occurring during the resolution of conflicts between alternatives separated by
different 'distances' in the preference series.   Mean scores.   ●━━● 'real'
conflict; ━━━ 'hypothetical' conflict; ——— time; ——— VTE score.

According to these data, in the case of both "real" and "hypothetical" conflicts and on both the initial and second presentations
of the conflicts, there is an inverse relationship between the time
required to resolve a conflict and the "distance" between the
alternatives in the preference series.   A similar inverse relationship
holds for magnitude of VTE scores.   The significance of these
relationships has been tested by subtracting the time and VTE scores
for the alternatives separated by one "step" in the preference series
from those separated by six "steps" and determining the probability
that the obtained mean difference might arise by chance (3).   This
probability is less than .01 for the "real" and "hypothetical" time

STUDIES IN PERSONALITY

TABLE II
Time in Seconds Required to Resolve Conflicts between Alternatives Separated by Different "Distances" in the Preference Series

Subject	Number of steps separated in preference series					
	1	2	3	4	5	6
"Real" conflict, initial presentation						
1	2.36	1.78	1.88	1.64	2.23	1.90
2	1.08	1.24	1.03	.88	1.02	1.23
3	4.81	5.51	3.18	3.09	3.24	2.13
4	4.12	4.72	3.92	3.74	2.71	2.10
5	2.07	1.60	1.32	1.23	.94	1.00
6	3.90	3.70	2.10	1.70	1.40	1.50
7	.77	.74	.72	.65	.58	.57
8	7.10	4.50	2.90	1.80	1.70	2.00
9	3.80	3.20	1.90	2.20	1.60	1.90
Mean.....	3.33	3.00	2.21	1.88	1.71	1.59
"Real" conflict, second presentation						
10	1.50	1.40	1.20	1.20	.80	.90
11	1.24	1.09	1.06	1.10	1.02	1.20
12	1.46	1.42	1.40	1.24	1.12	1.07
13	5.83	4.40	3.54	3.33	2.32	2.08
14	2.43	2.10	1.78	2.32	1.18	1.50
15	2.46	1.99	1.88	1.80	1.57	1.73
16	1.56	1.44	1.53	1.28	1.48	1.25
17	1.35	1.27	1.14	1.01	1.29	.73
18	3.44	2.66	2.55	2.33	3.09	2.20
19	.94	.94	.94	.88	.82	.80
Mean.....	2.22	1.87	1.70	1.65	1.47	1.35
"Hypothetical" conflict, initial presentation						
10	2.90	2.90	1.60	1.50	1.40	1.80
11	1.23	1.16	1.12	1.08	.97	.90
12	1.47	1.46	1.50	1.33	1.35	1.30
13	7.20	6.14	3.64	3.53	2.50	3.20
14	1.57	1.79	1.48	1.32	1.43	1.65
15	1.60	1.45	1.39	1.14	1.25	.73
16	1.42	1.50	1.52	1.46	1.03	1.30
17	1.04	.84	.59	.54	.62	.88
18	3.39	1.98	2.12	1.74	1.44	1.58
19	.72	1.02	.79	.79	.80	.98
Mean.....	2.25	2.02	1.58	1.44	1.28	1.43
"Hypothetical" conflict, second presentation						
1	1.45	1.49	1.34	1.23	1.49	1.33
2	1.19	1.14	.96	.89	1.02	1.10
3	3.89	2.68	1.95	2.81	2.78	1.43
4	3.27	2.70	2.68	3.03	2.62	1.85
5	1.48	1.40	1.51	1.07	.89	.95
6	3.18	2.28	1.98	1.89	1.79	.95
7	.65	.68	.66	.74	.86	.50
8	2.60	2.10	2.10	2.00	1.35	1.50
9	1.55	1.76	1.80	1.35	1.30	1.30
Mean.....	2.14	1.80	1.66	1.69	1.57	1.21

TABLE III
AMOUNT OF VTE BEHAVIOR (WEIGHTED SCORE) IN RESOLVING CONFLICTS BETWEEN ALTERNATIVES SEPARATED BY DIFFERENT "DISTANCES" IN THE PREFERENCE SERIES

Subject	Number of steps separated in preference series					
	1	2	3	4	5	6
"Real" conflict, initial presentation						
1	.20	.10	.00	.00	.00	.00
2	.60	1.20	.50	.20	.50	1.00
3	.25	.00	.00	.00	.00	.00
4	.00	.20	.25	.30	.00	.00
5	.80	1.40	.75	.00	.00	.50
6	.40	.10	.00	.30	.00	.00
7	.70	.90	.10	.50	.50	.00
8	1.30	.80	.20	.00	.00	1.00
9	.60	.50	1.00	1.00	.00	.50
Mean.....	.54	.58	.20	.26	.11	.33
"Real" conflict, second presentation						
10	.00	.50	.20	.70	.00	.00
11	1.20	.70	.00	.50	.00	.00
12	.30	.00	.40	.00	.00	.00
13	.40	.00	.00	.00	.00	.00
14	.50	.30	.40	.50	.00	.00
15	.10	.30	.10	.00	.00	.00
16	.40	.20	.00	.00	.00	.00
17	.75	.60	.00	.00	.75	1.00
18	.60	.00	.60	.70	.50	.00
19	1.25	.10	.60	.20	.50	.50
Mean.....	.55	.27	.23	.26	.18	.15
"Hypothetical" conflict, initial presentation						
10	.60	.60	.00	.00	.00	1.00
11	1.20	.90	.60	.50	.00	.00
12	.00	.00	.00	.00	.00	.00
13	.20	.00	.00	.00	.25	.50
14	.70	.00	.40	.00	.00	.00
15	.00	.30	.00	.00	.50	.00
16	.50	.80	.50	.70	.00	.00
17	1.00	.50	.00	.00	.00	.00
18	.80	.50	.25	.20	.00	.00
19	.30	1.60	.50	.20	.50	.50
Mean.....	.53	.52	.23	.21	.18	.20
"Hypothetical" conflict, second presentation						
1	.10	.20	.00	.00	.00	.00
2	.80	.50	.00	.30	.00	.00
3	.30	.30	.25	.70	.00	1.00
4	.40	.70	.00	.00	.50	.00
5	.60	.20	.25	.00	.00	.00
6	.70	.10	.10	.00	.00	.00
7	.20	.40	.00	.50	.50	.00
8	.00	.20	.10	.30	.00	.00
9	.20	.70	.00	.00	.00	.00
Mean.....	.37	.37	.08	.20	.11	.11

TABLE IV
TIME IN SECONDS REQUIRED TO RESOLVE CONFLICTS BETWEEN ALTERNATIVES THAT ARE IN NEIGHBORING POSITIONS IN THE PREFERENCE SERIES

Subject	Order of alternatives in preference series					
	1-2	2-3	3-4	4-5	5-6	6-7
"Real" conflicts, initial presentation						
1	1.80	2.20	1.55	2.13	2.20	4.25
2	1.20	1.05	.88	.78	1.35	1.20
3	5.20	4.85	5.68	2.20	3.70	7.20
4	2.85	2.65	5.05	2.53	3.33	8.30
5	1.90	.98	1.40	3.33	1.63	3.20
6	4.30	2.60	1.80	2.10	6.70	5.70
7	.77	.65	1.07	.45	.85	.85
8	2.00	4.30	2.80	3.30	5.20	25.10
9	2.60	2.80	3.70	2.00	2.30	9.50
Mean.....	2.51	2.45	2.66	2.09	2.28	7.26
"Real" conflicts, second presentation						
10	1.20	1.80	.60	1.40	2.40	1.50
11	1.10	1.30	.90	.75	1.35	2.05
12	1.42	1.17	1.70	1.45	1.60	1.40
13	3.78	9.75	5.00	4.55	4.05	7.83
14	2.15	2.65	2.90	2.40	1.20	3.30
15	3.18	2.35	2.00	2.58	2.18	2.48
16	1.23	1.25	1.43	1.48	1.80	2.15
17	1.05	2.63	.70	.95	1.00	1.75
18	2.55	2.60	2.03	2.65	4.23	6.60
19	.70	1.13	.83	1.05	.93	1.00
Mean.....	1.84	2.66	1.81	1.93	2.07	3.01
"Hypothetical" conflict, initial presentation						
10	3.60	3.10	4.00	1.50	2.70	2.50
11	.65	1.05	1.45	.85	1.15	2.25
12	1.30	1.50	1.50	1.70	1.20	1.60
13	10.30	4.95	3.73	5.63	9.00	9.60
14	1.68	1.83	1.80	1.40	1.40	1.30
15	1.35	1.73	1.60	2.05	1.28	1.60
16	1.53	1.13	1.35	1.55	1.38	1.55
17	.83	1.70	.70	.73	.85	1.40
18	5.10	1.55	2.55	2.28	2.53	6.30
19	.70	.70	.78	.63	.73	.80
Mean.....	2.70	1.92	1.95	1.83	2.22	2.89
"Hypothetical" conflict, second presentation						
1	1.15	1.68	1.40	1.25	1.50	1.70
2	1.10	1.05	.95	1.15	1.53	1.35
3	2.98	2.95	2.10	2.43	7.88	5.00
4	2.00	1.88	4.58	2.60	3.60	4.98
5	2.35	1.58	.93	1.28	1.43	1.33
6	7.53	1.45	1.95	1.40	3.68	3.08
7	.55	.70	.47	.47	.85	.85
8	3.70	2.10	2.30	1.90	3.20	2.20
9	1.10	1.10	1.60	1.20	2.70	1.60
Mean.....	2.50	1.61	1.81	1.52	2.93	2.45

TABLE V

AMOUNT OF VTE BEHAVIOR (WEIGHTED SCORE) IN RESOLVING CONFLICTS BETWEEN ALTERNATIVES THAT ARE IN NEIGHBORING POSITIONS IN THE PREFERENCE SERIES

Subject	Order of alternatives in preference series					
	1-2	2-3	3-4	4-5	5-6	6-7
"Real" conflict, initial presentation						
1	0	0	0	2	0	0
2	3	0	0	0	4	0
3	0	1	1	0	1	0
4	0	0	0	0	0	0
5	3	0	0	3	2	2
6	2	0	0	0	0	0
7	2	0	4	0	0	2
8	0	0	0	3	6	6
9	0	4	0	0	0	3
Mean.....	.56	.28	.28	.44	.72	.72
"Real" conflict, second presentation						
10	0	0	0	0	0	0
11	2	2	0	5	3	2
12	0	0	2	2	0	0
13	3	0	2	0	0	0
14	0	2	0	0	4	2
15	0	0	0	0	1	0
16	0	0	0	2	3	0
17	0	3	0	2	4	0
18	2	2	1	0	2	0
19	0	5	2	3	2	3
Mean.....	.35	.70	.35	.70	.95	.35
"Hypothetical" conflict, initial presentation						
10	0	0	5	0	1	1
11	1	2	5	0	0	6
12	0	0	0	0	0	0
13	2	2	0	0	2	0
14	0	0	0	0	0	0
15	0	0	0	0	0	0
16	0	0	2	0	2	2
17	0	2	2	0	2	6
18	1	2	0	4	0	3
19	0	0	0	0	2	2
Mean.....	.20	.40	.70	.20	.45	1.00
"Hypothetical" conflict, second presentation						
1	1	0	0	0	0	0
2	0	2	0	0	3	5
3	0	2	2	0	0	0
4	0	2	1	0	2	0
5	2	2	0	0	3	0
6	2	0	0	0	3	3
7	0	0	0	0	2	0
8	0	0	0	0	0	0
9	0	0	2	0	0	0
Mean.....	.28	.44	.28	.00	.72	.44

scores and for the "real" VTE scores. For the "hypothetical" VTE
score, it is between .05 and .02. In the making of these computations, the data of both the initial and second presentations have been
included; thus, $n = 19$. These relationships are in accord with
those obtained by Dashiell (2) for colors and by Wells (7) for
artificial flavors.

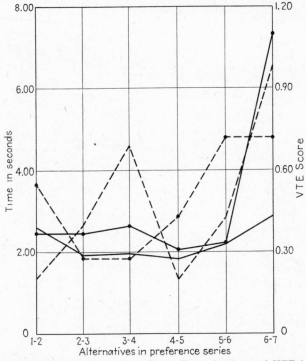

FIG. 3.—Initial presentation of conflict. Time elapsing and VTE behavior
occurring during the resolution of conflicts between neighboring alternatives in
the preference series. Mean scores. ●━━● 'real' conflict; ━━━ 'hypothetical' conflict; ──── time; ──── VTE score.

In Tables IV and V and Figs. 3 and 4, data are given for the
resolution of conflicts between desirable (positive) alternatives,
between neutral alternatives, and between undesirable (negative)
alternatives. Column 2 of the tables and the first point of the
curves refer to conflicts between the first and second liquids
in the preference series, i.e., they refer to conflicts between alternatives that were, on the average, desirable; columns 4 and 5 of the
tables and points 3 and 4 of the curves refer to conflicts falling near

the middle of the preference series, *i.e.*, they refer to neutral alternatives; column 7 of the tables and the last point of the curves refer to conflicts between alternatives 6 and 7 of the preference series, *i.e.*, they refer to undesirable alternatives.

Each item of these tables is derived from a single pair of determinations for each subject. The resulting variability of the individual

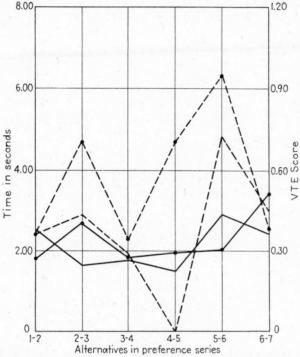

FIG. 4.—Second presentation of conflict. Time elapsing and VTE behavior occurring during the resolution of conflicts between neighboring alternatives in the preference series. Mean scores. ●━━● 'real' conflict; ━ ━ ━; 'hypothetical' conflict; ———— time; ─ ─ ─ VTE score.

scores makes these data less reliable than those just considered. However, there appears to be a general tendency for time and VTE scores to increase when negative alternatives are involved. When the significance of the tendencies is tested by the method described, the probability that the obtained mean differences might have arisen by chance is between .05 and .02 for the "real" time scores, and it is greater than .05 in all other cases. The suggestion that the smallest time and VTE scores occur in the case of the neutral alternatives is not borne out by statistical tests in any case. Wells's data (7) for artificial flavors are in accord with the finding that the time required to resolve conflicts is longer for negative than for neutral or positive alternatives. Dashiell's data (2) do not bear upon this problem.

No crucial comparisons of "real" and "hypothetical" conflicts can be made with the present data. It is not possible to hold both the order of presentation and the subjects used in the two sequences constant; further, the number of subjects in each group is too small to assume equivalence among them. The relevant data, such as they are, will be found in the tables and curves. It will be observed that when the "real" sequence of conflicts is presented first in the experimental session, more time is required for their resolution and more VTE behavior occurs than when the "hypothetical" sequence of conflicts is presented first in the experimental session (this assumes, of course, that the two groups of subjects are equivalent in other respects). This difference appears to be removed when the "real" and "hypothetical" choices are presented second in the experimental session; this may be due to the fact that memory plays an important part upon the second presentation of the sequence.

Discussion[1]

It has been mentioned previously that the boys who served as subjects in this experiment were paid a small cash reward, and it was obvious from their conversation that this was the dominant motive that brought them to participate in the experiments. The situation facing the subjects on coming to the laboratory was therefore essentially as represented in Fig. 5. The subject had entered region A, which consisted of familiar conversation with the experimenter in the reception room while the subject was waiting for the experiments to begin, i.e., waiting to enter region B. An eager interest in region B was indicated by many questions; e.g., "What are we going to do?" "Is it going to be fun?" "How long will it take?" Region B was at this time an unstructured region with both positive and negative components giving rise to minor conflict. Although unstructured, region B was clearly a route to region G, consisting of the cash reward and freedom to engage in all the other activities present in the subject's life-space. The force toward G, $f_{A,G}$, was clearly indicated by the remarks that were made during the interval

[1] In this discussion, the concepts and notations developed by Lewin (5) are followed.

that the subject was in A; *e.g.*, "I'm going to get the same money I got before, aren't I?" "How long will it take this time? I want to go swimming this morning." "When I get through here, I'm going to take my money and go to a movie right away."

On entrance into the experimental room, region B rapidly lost its unstructured character. As the experimenter's instructions increased the definiteness of this structure, there is reason to believe, on the basis of the behavior of the subjects, that region B assumed a dual character. Whereas for the subject coming to the experiment region B was only a means to attain G, it now became to a greater or less degree an activity with its own significance. The evidence for this circumstance is found in such behavior as the following: Subject 11 was clearly absorbed in the procedures of the experiment;

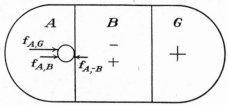

FIG. 5.—Psychological situation of subject upon coming to the laboratory.

both the apparatus and the decision required of him held his attention closely. During the greater part of the experimental session, there was no evidence that the activities functioned as a means to an end. However, on three occasions, the dual character of the activity was clearly indicated when the subject remarked, "Say, I can't take all day at this. This is Saturday, you know." "I'm going to get 15 cents this time, too, aren't I?" "My friend is waiting for me. He will wonder what's happened to me, I suppose."

Elsewhere (1) it has been proposed that behavior of this sort can be accounted for in terms of overlapping situations of differing potencies. It is suggested, therefore, that a more adequate representation of the situation for subjects engaged in the experiments is given in Fig. 6. To some extent, the subject is in situation S^1, where region B (participation in the experiments) is a route for passing from A to G. Simultaneously, he is to some degree in situation S^2, in which region B has the significance of an activity with its own conflicts, rewards, and punishments. The relative potencies of these overlapping situations in determining behavior varied from subject to subject and from minute to minute of the experimental session.

The detailed structure of region B is represented in Figs. 7, 8, and 9. The subject who understood the instructions and was seated before the table with his hand on the lever may be represented as in

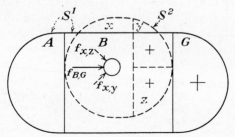

FIG. 6.—Psychological situation of subject while engaged in the experiments.

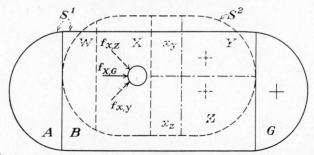

FIG. 7.—Psychological situation of subject presented with positive alternatives.

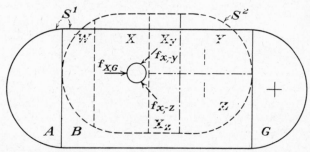

FIG. 8.—Psychological situation of subject presented with negative alternatives.

subregion W, *i.e.*, waiting for the particular alternatives to be presented. When the cards were exposed, he may be represented as having moved to region X, *i.e.*, the region of resolving the conflict, of choosing one of the pair of alternative actions. At this moment, three forces act on him, namely, $f_{x,G}$; $f_{x,Y}$ or $f_{x,-Y}$; $f_{x,Z}$ or $f_{x,-Z}$. The strength of force $f_{x,G}$ is directly in proportion to the valence of

G and to the relative potency of situation S^1. Forces $f_{X,Y}$ or $f_{X,-Y}$ and $f_{X,Z}$ or $f_{X,-Z}$ are also directly proportional to the valences of alternatives X and Y and to the potency of situation S^2. A conflict arises when the directions of the forces in X are opposed, *i.e.*, when both Y and Z are positive (Fig. 7) or negative (Fig. 8). Such conflicts may be resolved in three ways: (*a*) The strength of one of the opposed forces may become so great that the resultant force is sufficient to enforce a decision. (*b*) Force $f_{X,G}$ may increase in strength and reinforce one of the conflicting forces to a point at which a decision occurs. (*c*) In the other case, the conflict between the

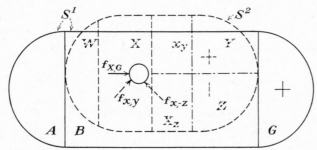

FIG. 9.—Psychological situation of subject presented with a positive and a negative alternative.

opposed forces is not resolved, strictly speaking; the relative potency of S^1 increases to such a degree that the significance of the conflict occurring in S^2 becomes negligible, *i.e.*, as the potency of S^2 approaches zero, the strength of the opposed forces approaches zero.

Other constellations of forces in region X do not lead to conflict, *i.e.*, when the valences of regions X and Y are of different signs (Fig. 9).

These are the basic psychological situations that existed for the subjects in the present experiments. However, to account for the observed behavior, more specific assumptions have to be made, namely:

1. *There is a direct relationship between the length of time a subject remains in a state of conflict in region X and the relative potency of situation S^1.* The behavior of the subjects clearly indicated that the longer they were delayed by an unresolved conflict in region X, the more important the "means" aspect of the resolution of the conflict became; *e.g.*, subject 8, after hesitating before tomato juice and

vinegar for a long time, said, "Well I can't sit here all day. I have to get through sometime." Subject 15, after oscillating between tomato juice and pineapple juice, remarked, "I guess I'm crazy. It doesn't make any difference which of these I take. I can't stay here forever."

As the relative potency of the situation S^1 increases with the passage of time, the strength of force $f_{x,g}$ increases and that of the conflicting forces in X decreases. Two consequences of this assumption are: (a) the greater the strength of the opposed forces in X, the longer the time required for their reduction to any particular lesser value, and (b) the greater the increase in the strength of $f_{x,g}$ required to resolve a conflict, the longer the time until the conflict is resolved.

It may also be that region X has a negative valence, i.e., that the situation of indecision has in itself a negative component and that this increases with the duration of indecision.

2. *Changes in the relative strengths of conflicting forces continually occur, and small changes are more frequent than large changes.* This means that, on the average, a longer time will elapse before a large change in the resultant of opposed forces will occur than before a small change will occur.

This assumption, like assumption 1, has to do with the general instability of psychological situations and with the speed with which change occurs. These are not the only instances of the unstable nature of psychological situations. The terms *learning, adaptation, satiation, fatigue,* for example, refer to processes by which psychological situations change. Another instance of this instability is the fluctuation character of needs and consequently of the forces that determine behavior. If this were not the case, conflicts between equal forces could never be resolved, and Buridan's ass would not be a fable.

3. *The strength of a force corresponding to a region of positive valence varies with its distance from the region in a way described by the schematic curve of Fig.* 10; *the amount of the variation is proportional to the strength of the force at the greatest distance.* There are considerable data [Hull (4), Wright (8)] which indicate that, despite a positive speed gradient as an animal or child approaches a region of positive valence, there is a great reduction in speed of locomotion when the goal is approached closely but is still out of "reach." This phenomenon has been variously interpreted. One suggestion by Wright (8) is that the strength of the force increases until the region

immediately preceding the actual goal region is reached. This region has the meaning "the goal is almost as good as attained" and possesses in some degree the dynamic properties of the goal itself. One property of a region of positive valence is that the force corresponding to it is reduced to zero when the region is entered. To the extent that the neighboring region possesses the dynamic properties of the goal region, a reduction in the strength of the force in the direction of the goal will occur when the neighboring region is entered. In accordance with this assumption, one would find the following constellations of forces in different positions in the present case. If forces $f_{x,y}$ and $f_{x,z}$ are opposed and derive from positive

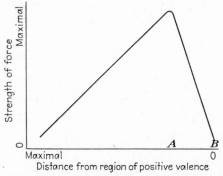

FIG. 10.—Assumed relation between distance from region of positive valence and strength of force. A = boundary of region preceding region of positive valence. B = boundary of region of positive valence.

valences in X and Y, (Fig. 7), and if $f_{x,y}$ is greater than $f_{x,z}$, locomotion will be made in the direction of Y, i.e., the lever will be moved in the direction of Y. However, when the region of activity immediately preceding that of the goal activity is entered—in this case, just before the sounding of the buzzer (region X_Y)—$f_{x,y}$ will be reduced by an amount proportional to its original strength, and it may become smaller than $f_{x,z}$. In the latter case, locomotion in the opposite direction will take place, and an instance of VTE behavior will have occurred.

Three consequences of this assumption follow: (a) VTE behavior will continue until the conflict is resolved by one of the means mentioned; (b) the more nearly equal the opposed forces, the greater the increase in the strength of one of them, or of force $f_{x,a}$, that is required to secure resolution of the conflict; (c) the greater the strength of the forces in conflict, the greater the increase in the strength of one of them, or of force $f_{x,a}$, required to secure resolution of the conflict.

4. *The strength of a force corresponding to a region of negative valence varies with its distance from the region in a way described by the schematic curves of Fig.* 11; *the amount of the variation is proportional to the strength of the force at the greatest distance.* This is similar to assumption 3; it leads to the following constellations of forces in different positions: if $f_{x,-y}$ and $f_{x,-z}$ are opposed forces deriving from negative valences (Fig. 8), and if $f_{x,-y}$ is greater than $f_{x,-z}$, locomotion will be made in the direction $d_{x,-y}$, which, in this case, is iden-

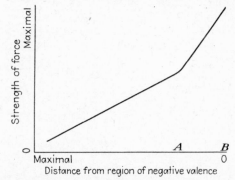

FIG. 11.—Assumed relation between distance from region of negative valence and strength of force. A = boundary of region preceding region of negative valence. B = boundary of region of negative valence.

tical with direction $d_{x,z}$. However, when the region of activity immediately preceding region Z is entered (region X_z), $f_{x,-z}$ will increase and may become greater than $f_{x,-y}$. In the latter case, locomotion away from region Z will occur, and an instance of VTE behavior will have taken place.

In terms of assumptions 3 and 4, the resolution of conflict requires not simply that one of the forces be greater than the other in region X, the region of decision; they require that in subregions X_Y or X_Z the force in the direction of Y or Z, respectively, be the larger. These assumptions account for VTE behavior in conflict situations where no discriminative difficulties are present.

On the basis of assumptions 3 and 4, an important difference in conflicts deriving from negative and from positive alternatives is apparent: when one of the alternatives is approached closely, the force *opposing* this resolution of the conflict *decreases* in strength *if the alternatives are positive,* whereas it *increases* in strength *if the alternatives are negative.*   If the forces involved in conflicts between negative and between positive alternatives are of equal strengths in region X, the forces in regions X_Y and X_Z resisting resolution will be greater in the case of the negative alternatives than in the case of the positive alternatives, and, hence, the strength of the force required to resolve the conflict will be greater for the negative than for the positive alternative.

5. *Speed of locomotion is positively related to strength of resultant force.*

6. *The forces involved in "real" conflicts are greater than those involved in "hypothetical" conflicts.*

In terms of these assumptions as to the structure and dynamics of the psychological situations occurring in the experiments, the following obtained results can be accounted for:

1. *There is an inverse relationship between the time required to resolve a conflict and the "distance" between the alternatives in the preference series.*   In the case of the one-, two-, and three-step "distances" (the first three points of the curves, Figs. 1 and 2), it may safely be assumed that the forces in X are opposed, deriving from positive valences in Y and Z.   It is clear also that the resultant of the opposed forces is least in case of the one-step distance and greatest in the case of the three-step distance.   These points of the obtained curve are accounted for, therefore, by assumption 3 and assumption 1 and/or 2.

In the case of the five- and six-step "distances" the forces in region X will not be opposed in most cases, the situation being as represented in Fig. 9.   The resultant force will be greater for the six-step distance.   The four-step distance will frequently be a transition case where conflict occurs in region X but where the resultant force in region X_Y or X_Z is great enough to secure immediate resolution.   The relationship between "distance" and time in these cases is covered by assumption 5.

2. *There is an inverse relation between amount of VTE behavior and "distance" between the alternatives in the preference series.*   According to assumption 3, VTE behavior will continue in cases of conflict until resolution occurs, and the curves for time and VTE scores should be parallel.

3. *Conflicts between negative alternatives require a longer time for their resolution than conflicts between positive alternatives.*   This is accounted for by assumptions 3 and 4 and assumptions 1 and/or 2.

The following results are demanded by the assumptions. The obtained data are in accord with expectations in general, but in no case are the relationships reliable by the available tests of significance.

4. *More VTE behavior should occur during the resolution of conflicts between negative alternatives than during the resolution of conflicts between positive alternatives.* This is in accordance with assumptions 3 and 4 and assumption 1 and/or 2.

5 and 6. *Conflicts between positive alternatives should require a longer time for their resolution and give rise to more VTE behavior than conflicts between neutral alternatives.* Assumption 3 and assumption 1 and/or 2 apply here.

7 and 8. *"Real" conflicts should require more time for their resolution and produce more VTE behavior than "hypothetical" conflicts.* This follows from assumptions 3 and 6.

References

1. BARKER, R. G., DEMBO, T., & LEWIN, K. Frustration and regression: a study of young children. *Univ. Ia Stud. Child Welf.*, 1941, **18**, No. 1.
2. DASHIELL, J. F. Affective value-distances as a determinant of esthetic judgment-times. *Amer. J. Psychol.*, 1937, **50**, 57–67.
3. FISHER, R. A. Statistical methods for research workers. Edinburgh: Oliver and Boyd, 1930.
4. HULL, C. L. The rat's speed-of-locomotion gradient in the approach to food. *J. comp. Psychol.*, 1934, **17**, 393–422.
5. LEWIN, K. The conceptual representation and measurement of psychological forces. *Contr. psychol. Theor.*, 1938, **1**, No. 4.
6. MUENZINGER, K. F. Vicarious trial and error at a point of choice: I. A general survey of its relation to learning efficiency. *J. genet. Psychol.*, 1938, **53**, 75–86.
7. WELLS, H. M. The phenomenology of acts of choice; an analysis of volitional consciousness. *Brit. J. Psychol. Monogr. Suppl.*, 1927, **4**, No. 11.
8. WRIGHT, H. F. Influence of goal distance and route security upon speed of locomotion. *Univ. Ia Stud. Child Welf.* (In preparation.)

CHAPTER III

A STUDY OF IDENTICAL TWINS REARED APART UNDER DIFFERING TYPES OF FAMILY RELATIONSHIPS[1]

By

BARBARA S. BURKS

Columbia University

The study of monozygotic twins reared apart is by wide consent the most sensitive of available methods for appraising the degree of stability and plasticity of developing human organisms. The method seems to offer promise, moreover, of shedding some light upon the nature of traits themselves: their focal character, their variable modes of expression, and their developmental transformations.

The writer has had an opportunity of studying a pair of girl twins, Adelaide and Beatrice, who were separated at the age of 9 days and placed at once in two families residing in a suburban city on the Eastern seaboard. The adoptive families were well known to one another and did not differ greatly in socioeconomic status, which was somewhat above average. Up to the age of $2\frac{1}{2}$, the twins saw each other frequently, and the two families compared notes on their development. At this point, the family of Adelaide moved to a distant city. The children were unaware of each other's existence until the age of $8\frac{1}{2}$, at which time they were brought together for 3 months: 1 month in the home of Beatrice and 2 in a girls' camp. For three summers thereafter, they spent a season together in the same camp. The following summer, when they were $12\frac{1}{2}$, Adelaide

[1] The writer wishes to express appreciation to Harold E. Jones, Lois Barclay Murphy, Gardner Murphy, and Mary Fite, as well as to the twins, their foster parents, teachers, and camp director. Professor Jones stimulated the writer to undertake the study while she was associated with the Institute of Child Welfare, University of California. He was instrumental in putting her in touch with the family of one of the twins and made available the resources of the Institute. Lois and Gardner Murphy collaborated in a day of testing and observation when the twins were brought together at age 12 for study, and Miss Fite furnished some carefully recorded observations.

35

spent at camp, and Beatrice stayed with her family, not far away. It was at this time that a psychological study of the twins was first undertaken. Following a brief visit together in the autumn (or winter), near their thirteenth birthday, the twins were again separated by the relocation of Adelaide's family. They had not seen each other again at the time of follow-up (age 18), although they had exchanged letters about twice a month.

FIG. 1.—Beatrice and Adelaide at 12 years 6 months.

In the account that follows, the names used are fictitious. Data that seemed likely to lead to the identification of the twins have been excluded, and hence the account is less elaborated than it may be 10 or more years hence, when contemporary data of interest and value have become historical and less likely to result in embarassing recognition.

EVIDENCE FOR MONOZYGOTIC ORIGIN OF THE TWINS

A variety of comparisons were made on physical traits used as criteria for one-egg origin by some of the leading investigators of twins. The results, briefly summarized in Table I, lead to the conclusion that Adelaide and Beatrice are monozygotic, though not falling at the most similar end of such a distribution as Newman and his associates report.

The several differences between the twins merit discussion. At 18, the differences in stature and in head length are a little greater

TABLE I
PHYSICAL CRITERIA OF ZYGOTIC ORIGIN

Age 12 years 6 months	Twin A	Twin B
Height (stocking feet).............	164.5 cm.	165.0 cm.
Weight (in light summer clothing)...	121 lb.	123 lb.
Head breadth....................	15.6 cm.	15.6 cm.
Head length.....................	19.4 cm.	19.3 cm.
Cephalic index...................	80.4	80.7
Head circumference..............	58.5 cm.	58.2 cm.
Interpupillary distance...........	67 mm.	66 mm.
Eye color (Martin chart)..........	16	15
Iris proper...................	Light blue	Slightly darker blue
Outer rim.....................	Green-gray	Same
Refraction......................	When 9 or 10, wore glasses for myopia	Never glasses; probably myopic
Hair:		
Color (Shur-on chart)..........	14 Light gold-brown	15 Light gold-brown
Thickness of growth............	Thick	Same
Form.........................	Straight	Same
Texture......................	Medium	Medium, slightly finer

Cross section (microns):*					
Area (square microns/100) M...	37.0	P.E. .7	33.8	P.E. .6
S.D...	8.8	P.E. .5	7.0	P.E. .4
Maximum diameter M...	82.5	P.E. .9	81.3	P.E. .8
S.D...	11.2	P.E. .6	10.5	P.E. .6
Minimum diameter .M...	55.7	P.E. .6	50.3	P.E. .5
S.D...	7.1	P.E. .4	6.4	P.E. .4
Index M...	67.8	P.E. .7	62.9	P.E. .8
S.D...	8.5	P.E. .5	10.5	P.E. .6

Age 12 years 6 months	Twin A	Twin B
Skin pigmentation................	Light	Slightly lighter
Freckles........................		A few on nose and forehead, similar distribution
Distribution of color..............		Pink cheeks, similar in both
Oral cavity:		
Teeth shade...................		Same
Occlusion.....................		Similar, excellent
Condition of gums.............	Healthy	Slightly inflamed
Number of fillings.............	5	9
Form of ear.....................		Convolutions and lobes similar
Feet, size of shoe................	7	7
Hands:		
Size and shape.................		Similar
Mid-digital hair................	None	None
Downy hair.....................		Similar distribution near ears and on arms

* Sample of 70 hairs.

TABLE I.—(*Continued*)

Age 12 years 6 months	Twin *A*	Twin *B*
Tastes P.T.C.	Bitter	Bitter
Dextr.-sinistr.:		
Writes from copy	Right	Right
Tosses ball	RRR	LLL
Kicks ball	RRR	LLL
V scope (eye dominance)	LLL	RLL
Hair whorl	Clockwise	Clockwise
Finger ridges	1 2 3 4 5	1 2 3 4 5
Pattern:		
Left	UL Wh Wh UL UL	Wh Wh Wh Wh UL
Right	UL RL Wh Wh UL	Wh Wh Wh Wh UL
Ridge count:		
Left	6 25 34 20 12	20 35 34 29 14
Right	19 24 37 33 12	26 35 36 25 13
Total	222 (L 97, R 125)	267 (L 132, R 135)

Age 18 yr.	18 yr. 8 mo.	18 yr. 10 mo.
Height (stocking feet)	171.6 cm.	169.4 cm.
Weight (stripped, reported by subjects)	143 lb.	142 lb.
Head breadth	15.8 cm.	15.9 cm.
Head length	20.4 cm.	19.5 cm.
Cephalic index	77.4	81.5
Hair:		
Color (Shur-on chart)	18 Light brown	18 Light brown
Cross section (microns):*		
Area (square microns/100) M...	37.4 P.E. .8	31.4 P.E. .6
S.D...	10.1 P.E. .6	7.2 P.E. .4
Maximum diameter M...	84.4 P.E. 1.2	74.8 P.E. .9
S.D...	14.5 P.E. .8	11.3 P.E. .6
Minimum diameter M...	53.4 P.E. .5	52.4 P.E. .6
S.D...	6.6 P.E. .4	7.7 P.E. .4
Index M...	63.9 P.E. .8	71.0 P.E. 1.0
S.D...	9.5 P.E. .5	11.8 P.E. .7

* Sample of 70 hairs.

than at 12 (at which time they were inappreciable). Adelaide's slight advantage in size may perhaps be referable to her residence for over 5 years in a Western "outdoor" climate.

Eye color, intense blue, appeared almost identical at first glance, but careful inspection against the standard Martin samples showed

(a)   (b)

(c)   (d)

FIG. 2.—Adelaide at 9 months (a) and 3 years 3 months (c). Beatrice at 7
months (b) and 3 years 4 months (d).

Beatrice's iris to be slightly darker blue.   Aside from this, iris structure and pattern seemed to be entirely similar.   The question may
be raised whether the slight difference was related to Adelaide's
residence for several years in the tropics, her trachoma at age 8, and
her wearing of glasses for a few months following trachoma.

Refraction reports have not been obtained for the twins.   Though
A has worn glasses for myopia for a short time and B has not, the
twins at both 12 and 18 read and wrote with eyes brought very close
to paper.

Hair color was very similar at 12 and indistinguishable at 18
(matched from specimens clipped at the rear, close to the scalp).
Nevertheless, at age 12, B's hair appeared slightly lighter and
slightly finer (by tactual inspection).   At 12, she was wearing her
hair long and had a permanent wave, whereas A's hair was worn
straight and short.   These facts (and possibly slight differences in
developmental rate of change in pigmentation) may have affected
the difference in hair shade at 12, which was fully assimilated by
18.   The perceptible difference in texture, however, was later
checked by microscopic cross-sectional examination of hair specimens
obtained from the twins at ages 12 and 18.   A method developed in
Steggerda's laboratory (6) was employed for measuring cross-sectional area and maximum and minimum diameters, the technical
work being done for us by Steggerda's assistant, Henri Seibert.
This appraisal showed B's hair to be of finer texture at both ages, but
we do not yet have standards to show the limits of disparity to be
anticipated in identical twins.   Preliminary data that Steggerda
has exhibited on twins tend to show that twins extremely similar by
the usual criteria of zygocity may differ appreciably in hair section.

Complexion appeared quite similar in the twins, including the
distribution of freckles and the moderately rosy cheeks.   The
slightly lighter cast of B's skin at 12 may have been due to the fact
that A was summering at camp whereas B was living with her
parents in a summer cottage.

The larger incidence of dental caries in B may conceivably be
accounted for by the accident in infancy that knocked out her two
lower median incisors, killing the roots and resulting in several defective permanent teeth.

It is interesting to note that both twins showed early left-handed
tendencies but that A was changed to the right hand for all uni-
manual activities, whereas B's parents, on physician's advice,

permitted her to use the left hand, the change to the right hand for writing being made voluntarily.

Finger-ridge patterns (which are all ulnar and radial loops or whorls) show six correspondences by either direct or cross comparison. This is not a high degree of similarity for identical twins (5, 7, 8) but represents a middle ground, in which appear both identicals and fraternals. In the present case, not much weight one way or the other can be attached to the circumstance, because a comparison between A's two hands shows no more symmetry than does a comparison between the hands of A and B. These comments are relevant to the ridge counts as well as to the pattern classifications.

Since the twins are similar with respect to a large number of criterion traits and do not differ in any of them by an amount suggestive of dizygotic origin, their classification as monozygotic seems well established. Some rather unusual developmental similarities to be reported on lend weight to the zygotic diagnosis. Although it is inadmissible to consider such items in the selection of twins when a study is undertaken to evaluate the influence of nature and nurture on the items, their emergence during the study supports the correctness of the diagnosis.

ENVIRONMENTAL SURROUNDINGS AND EXPERIENCES

Community. Adelaide has lived in a number of cities and towns in various parts of the world, usually not more than a year or two in any until the age of 13. From the age of 13 up to the time of follow-up (age 18) she has lived in a moderate-sized Western city of predominantly residential character.

Beatrice lived in an Eastern suburban town until nearly 9; since then she has lived in a small Eastern city in a farming region. At the time of follow-up, she had been in residence for 2 academic years at a professional school located in a suburban town.

Schooling. Adelaide's elementary-school experience was constantly interrupted because of the frequent moves of her family. She attended kindergarten in three cities, first grade in two, studied second- and third-grade work under her mother's instruction, attended fourth grade for 2 years, because the fifth-grade room was overcrowded, skipped fifth grade, and missed "all of decimals" at the same time, attended a different school in each of grades six to eight. At high school, she remained in one school for 3 years, transferring for the fourth year (which she completed at 17) to another school in the same city at the behest of her mother. She then remained out of school for a year, working most of this time at jobs that her mother found for her, until she could gain admission to a professional school.

Beatrice, in contrast, remained in one school from kindergarten through the fourth grade. She attended a different school (but in the same school system) in each of grades four to six, then went through junior high school and high school without further transfers, graduating at 16. She then entered a 3-year professional school.

During her junior and senior years in high school, *B* had an experience that may well be significant for her later development. Holding out membership on the girls' varsity basketball team as incentive, the teacher of physical education impressed on *B* the necessity of being "straightforward," of "looking people in the eye," of taking criticism "with a smile rather than being hurt about it." According to the teacher, the improvement and results were highly satisfactory both to *B* and the team, on which she was an outstanding forward during her senior year.

There is no indication that *A* had this kind of motivation while in high school. She was excused from physical education during her second and third years because of a chronic bronchial condition and did not play on teams. She was well known to the dean of girls, who attempted to get her to see at times of difficulty (which were fairly frequent) that *A* "was her own worst enemy."

Home and training. *A*'s family were possibly in somewhat more comfortable financial circumstances than *B*'s, but because of frequent moving during *A*'s childhood they accumulated very few possessions such as books, musical instruments, etc. Nevertheless, by the age of 12, *A* had had a year of piano lessons (discontinued by her mother because of the "struggle to get her to practice"), about 9 months of ballet dancing in her fifth year, and a year of athletic dancing in her eleventh year. She had also had opportunities to ride horseback. For five consecutive summers she had been sent to a private girls' camp. She had attended Sunday school, though not always regularly. She attended occasional movies but was not permitted to go regularly. She had not been taken to concerts or plays when she was seen at either 12 or 18. When she was 8 or 9, her father read her the *Five Little Peppers* books, and since that time she had been fond of reading independently but was not encouraged by the mother to do this during the school term lest it interfere with her study.   According to the mother, she did not care to read or be read to until she was 8 or 9, and showed little interest in *Child Life*, subscribed to when she was 9.

There was little emphasis on social training.   *A* was given a birthday party at 5 and up to age 12 had had three or four parties altogether.   When seen at 12, she was not permitted to remain with her parents in the evening after dinner but was sent upstairs at 7:30 and was supposedly in bed by 8:30.   She was up at 7 in the morning.   While in high school, she did little entertaining at home, since she and the mother disagreed about asking friends to help clear up dishes, etc.   The mother's friends had helped when she was a girl, and she felt that *A*'s friends should likewise help.

Occasionally the mother would try to get *A* interested in knitting or sewing with her, but without success.

Discipline was strict, administered by the mother, and usually took the form of spankings or deprivation in early childhood.   *A* was scolded or spanked for failures during bladder training.   Later, when having nocturnal enuresis, she was also scolded and punished.

There did not seem to have been systematic efforts to train *A* to assume responsibility, the mother stating that *A* (at 12) did not want to assume any tasks or responsibility and had to be told to do things.   She had the regular task of putting up her lunch for school and usually remembered to do so.   She received help, however, in such matters as mending and picking up clothes, washing hair, shopping.   She was given an allowance of two dollars a month to cover lunch extras and Sunday-school contributions.   At 18, the situation seemed not to have changed greatly.   She was expected to take care of her own room and was occasionally asked to assume household responsibilities but was said to do this poorly.   She received an allowance for incidentals (not for clothing) and was said to run through it quickly on "foolish things."

B's childhood was spent in homes of modest comfort.   She was given piano lessons from the age of 6 through high school, and, in contrast to *A*, practiced regularly.   She also learned drumming in a scout troop.   She took dancing lessons between ages 6 and 9 and ballroom dancing at the "Y" while in high school.   For four summers (ages 8 to 11), she was sent to camp with *A*.   She attended Sunday school regularly.   When seen at 12, she was permitted to go to Saturday-afternoon movies with other girls but had not been taken to theaters and only occasionally (about twice a year) to concerts. Her parents had bought her several "series" books and had recently subscribed to the *Girl Scout* magazine for her.

During the 6 months spent in bed between ages 4 and 5, she was read to a good deal and received attention from parents, grandmother, and nursemaid, though the parents report that she did not become dependent and was well able to amuse herself while ill. The grandmother played and sang to her during this period, and she often listened to the radio.

She was encouraged to have children come to see her after recovering from the 6 months' illness. The mother reported that they "make a lot of family birthdays—she'll grow up so fast." Ordinarily *B* invited two or three girls for dinner on her birthday. When seen at 12, she often had girls for luncheon on Saturday. Later the mother reported that the house was full of young people while *B* attended high school. She often invited girls who lived at a distance to stay overnight to attend evening events at school, and these guests would always "help with the dishes." While getting technical training after high-school graduation, *B* often brought her roommate home for week ends; the father would call for them and drive them back to school and would take them to movies and sports during the visit.

With respect to discipline, *B*'s mother reported "All you can do is talk to her" (age 12). The parents would talk over discipline, would "try to do the same things," and, if the father did not "think it's the way, we try something else." Bladder training was undertaken by timing, without scolding or punishment. Later, during the period of nocturnal enuresis, the mother consulted a doctor and tried the standard treatments. Punishment was not administered.

When seen at 12, *B* had certain regular tasks in the summer (making beds, washing dishes). The family had a maid during the winter. *B* was sometimes asked to do ordering from her mother's list. For the first time, she was now expected to help care for her own clothes, but she received help on mending and picking up clothes and on shopping. She received an allowance of 35 cents a week for Sunday school and incidentals. Seen again at 18, she was entrusted with managing her personal affairs, buying her own clothes, planning parties at home, etc. She participated in planning for the education of her younger foster sister. Her mother sent her, while in school, two dollars a week, saved out of her own summer earnings, to handle current expenses.

Family structure. Adelaide's foster family is composed of the father, mother, and an "own" daughter, born when *A* was nearly 5. Both parents come from families with business background, although the mothers of each had artistic interests. The father has followed several occupations in which he has had administrative responsibility. The mother had hoped to be a musician and had disliked the business course in which she had been trained. The interests of the family have tended to be more in activity—drives, picnics, sports, garden, and, with the mother, knitting and sewing—than in reading or personal hobbies. *A* has seen little of the parents' relatives.

A complete discussion of the intrafamily relationship is inexpedient at this time, but it may be observed that the relationship between *A* and the mother, particularly since the birth of the younger child, has frequently been one of cross-purposes. The father has been less critical of *A*. When seen at 12, *A* was reported to be domineering toward the younger sister, who, in turn, was resistant toward *A*. The relationship was reported as improved at the time of follow-up, when *A* was 18 and the sister 13, "no longer the little sister in the way."

Beatrice's foster family is composed of the father, mother, and a girl about a year younger than *B*, who has been a member of the family since the age of 6 but has not been legally adopted because she has living relatives. The parents each completed secondary school; the father holds a business job, and the mother had business-school training and an office job before her marriage. The father was himself a foster child and grew up on a farm; the mother grew up with four siblings in a family of business background. Both parents are fond of reading, and the father has frequently read to the mother—fiction, travel, and history—while she knits. The mother was active in church and women's-club work when first seen but was participating less at the time of follow-up. The parents have given *B* considerable companionship; when she was 12, *B*'s father would take her fishing and skating, and her mother would play croquet or cards and go for walks with her. When seen at 18, *B*'s interests continued to be shared by her parents, and she was encouraged to bring her own friends into the family group. When she returned from parties, she would waken her parents to tell them

about her fun. The maternal grandparents lived next door during
B's first 8 years, and she received affection and attention from them
as well as from uncles and aunts. At 12, B had a tendency to dominate her foster sister and to feel patronizing toward her. At 18, her
attitude had become more protective; she was anxious to see the
younger girl make educational plans that would lead to a vocation
and had volunteered to help with expenses if further training should
be sought after high-school graduation.

DEVELOPMENTAL HISTORY

From this point, it will be possible to summarize a considerable
mass of material in a series of tables and charts that need not be
repeated verbally, although certain points of particular interest will
be emphasized.

Table II shows similarity, though not exact coincidence, in the
development of weight, walking, handedness, two nervous problems
(enuresis and nail biting), and the onset of puberty. The twins
differed in that A crept before walking, whereas B never crept.
Table III shows specific differences in illness and accident histories,
the one having chief significance being B's pulmonary condition
between ages 4 and 5. In both children, however, there is a question
of predisposition to chronic infection: skin eruptions, bronchitis,
appendicitis in A; pulmonary tuberculosis, appendicitis, and ear
infection in B.

An inquiry was made of the parents as to early development of
interests, social adjustment, temperament, and "problem" behavior. "No special interests" were reported for A in early childhood;
her lack of concentration was reported in kindergarten. In early
contacts with other children, she was aggressive and "very bossy."
As a baby of only a few months, she would yell for attention; the
doctor "never saw such persistence in a child so young." She had
"always" demanded attention and had "always" been irritable
when crossed. She had truanted from school as early as the first
grade. Nervous habits have already been discussed. The mother
read books and listened to radio talks on child care and took A on
several occasions to a habit clinic but felt that none of these measures
had done any good.

B's early interests centered around dolls and sand box. (At
12, she was still fond of dolls and paper dolls.) She invented two
imaginary playmates at age 3, and her interest in them became very

strong while she was confined to bed between age 4 and 5.   She had few playmates until the age of 5 (because of long illness) and at first was aggressive and wanted to be "boss and leader."   She was a happy, good-natured baby but "very excitable."   While ill, though receiving considerable attention, she was able to amuse herself.   Her early behavior problems involved the same nervous habits noted in *A*.

TABLE II

DEVELOPMENTAL ITEMS REPORTED BY PARENTS*

	Twin *A*	Twin *B*
Birth weight......	Over 5 lb.	5½ lb. (R)
Weight at 1 yr....	24 lb. 3 oz. (R)	24 lb. 4 oz.(?) (interpolating between recorded weights at 6, 7, 10, 15, 18 mo.)
First creeping.....	13 mo. (R)	Never crept (R)
First steps........	14 mo.—holding on (R); mother reports slower than *B*	15 mo. (R)
Handedness.......	Left tendency as baby. Mother tied left hand; did not punish. *A* uses right hand	Left tendency as baby. Mother tied left hand but stopped on doctor's order. Later *B* learned to write with right hand of own accord; uses left otherwise
Bladder training...	Onset of enuresis 2 or 3 nights a week at age 4; continued up to 9 (mother). Occasionally (less than once a week) at camp at 8 and 9 (camp director)	"Broken at 2." Enuresis following whooping cough, 3½ until "at least 6" (mother); similar to *A* at camp at 8 and 9 (camp director)
Nail biting........	Almost continuous, 2 to 12. Stopped 1 mo. at 12 to earn reward. 12 to 18, periods of remission; relapsed when tense (mother). When seen at 18, *A* was biting at cuticles instead of nails	Onset not ascertained; bit nails while at camp (camp director); habit broken by 16, when offered manicure set as reward (mother)
Menarche.........	At 10 yr. 4 mo.; then not till *ca.* 11 yr. 6 mo.; then not till 12 yr. 5 mo.; dismenorrhea unsuccessfully treated at 12; largely outgrown by 18	At 11 yr. 6 mo. Irregularity, dismenorrhea, outgrown by 18

* With items marked (R), a written record was available in baby books kept by the foster parents.

Psychological Study at Age 12

When the twins were 12 years 7 months old, a series of tests, ratings, interviews, and observations was obtained. The twins were brought by *B*'s mother to be guests for a day at the summer home of Gardner and Lois Murphy, who participated in the testing and observation schedule. The similarity of the twins in appearance and superficial behavior (*e.g.*, gait) was impressive at the outset.

TABLE III
HEALTH HISTORY

Year of life	Twin *A*	Twin *B*
First.............	Many colds; boils lanced on nine occasions	General health good
Second............	Tonsillectomy	Two lower median incisors knocked out in fall downstairs
Third		
Fourth............	....	Whooping cough
Fifth.............	....	Pulmonary tuberculosis; in bed 4½ to 5
Sixth.............	Mumps; tonsils and adenoids operation	Chicken pox
Seventh..........	....	Tonsillectomy (or tonsils and adenoids)
Eighth...........		
Ninth............	Sties and boils; trachoma (cured with silver nitrate)	
Tenth............	Broken arm (fell off horse)	
Eleventh..........	Scarlet fever; "gland trouble," menarche	
Twelfth...........	....	Menarche; chronic appendicitis (according to camp director)
Thirteenth........	Measles; broken ankle (horseback accident)	
Fourteenth........		
Fifteenth.........	Chronic bronchitis; threatened bronchial pneumonia	
Sixteenth.........		
Seventeenth.......	Appendectomy	
Eighteenth........		
Nineteenth........	....	"Ear trouble" following cold; anemia

The writer extended a handshake to each twin, saying, "How do you do, Adelaide. How do you do, Beatrice." Each child shook hands without perceptible pressure, smiled fleetingly, and turned her head away.

Subsequently, several hours were spent with *A* and with the camp director at the camp where *A* was spending the summer, and visits were made at the homes of both *A* and *B*.

Tests. The results of the formal testing program are shown in Tables IV to VI and Figs. 3 to 6, some of which present comparative

TABLE IV

MENTAL TESTS ADMINISTERED TO TWINS *A* AND *B*

Test	Twin *A*			Twin *B*		
	Age	M.A.	I.Q.	Age	M.A.	I.Q.
Stanford-Binet..................	12-7	12-11	103	12-7	12-10	102
Terman Group Test B..........	12-7	13-2	105	12-7	15-6	123
Goodenough (nonverbal).........	12-7	11-0	...	12-7	10-6	
Otis (school report).............	14	.....	109	16	.....	111
Stanford-Binet..................	18-8	16-3	108	18-4	16-8	111

TABLE V

BERNREUTER INVENTORY ADMINISTERED TO TWINS *A* AND *B* AT AGE 12-7

Trait	Twin *A*		Twin *B*	
	Score	Percentile rank	Score	Percentile rank
Neurotic tendency....................	−97	18	−39	44
Self-sufficiency.....................	11	60	9	60
Dominance.........................	46	71	74	84

data for the later follow-up as well. The points of chief interest at age 12 are the following:

1. Similar performance level on Stanford-Binet and Goodenough nonverbal test[1] (intellectual factors in drawing); higher score of *B* (who had had the more regular schooling) on the Terman Group Test B (Table IV, Fig. 3).

[1] I.Q.'s were not computed for this test, because it had insufficient "top" for the twins' level of development.

TABLE VI
SPEED OF HANDWRITING

	Twin *A*			Twin *B*		
	Age 12	Age 18		Age 12	Age 18	
		1	2		1	2
Time to copy passage of 30 words..	2'34''	1'25''	1'23''	2'26''	1'25''	1'18''
Words per minute................	11.7	21.2	21.7	12.3	21.2	23.1

2. Similarity on the reading, spelling, language, literature and physiology and hygiene tests of the New Stanford Achievement

(a)   (b)

FIG. 3.—Goodenough test of drawing a man. (Reduction approximately one-half original size.) (a) Adelaide, age 12 years 7 months, score 32; mental age 11 years 0 months. (b) Beatrice, age 12 years 7 months, score 30; mental age 10 years 6 months.

Test, Form W, but dissimilarity on history and civics, arithmetic reasoning, and, above all, on arithmetic computation (Fig. 4). The differences (favoring *B*) are pronounced in those subjects most

dependent on formal school content and least in those more dependent on incidental learning or self-initiated activity (*e.g.*, reading,

TWIN A ————   ADMINISTERED AT AGE 12 YEARS 7 MONTHS
TWIN B -----
EDUCATIONAL PROFILE CHART: NEW STANFORD ACHIEVEMENT TEST, ADVANCED EXAMINATION

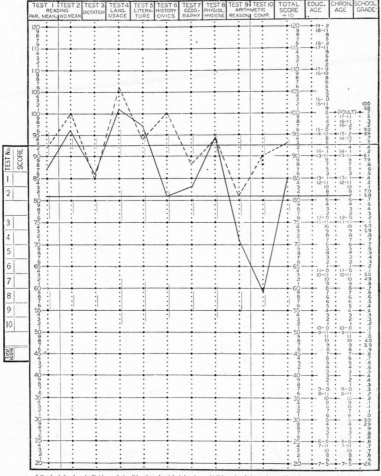

* Grade defined as in Table 1 of the *Directions for Administering*.   ** Educational Ages above this point are extrapolated values.
See *Guide for Interpreting* for explanation of vertical lines.
☞ *This Profile Chart is the table of norms for the Advanced Examination.*

FIG. 4.—Achievement profiles of Adelaide (*A*) and Beatrice (*B*).

literature). It will be recalled not only that *A*'s schooling was
irregular, but that she "missed all of decimals" at school.

3. Relatively little concordance between *A* and *B* in the occupations on which they score high in the Strong Vocational Interest schedule, though apparently more than chance parallelism in scores within the C range (Fig. 5). Carter (2) has reported separate correlations on 23 occupations for identical twins attending junior and senior high school to average .55 in boys and .45 in girls.

4. Similarity in Bernreuter "self-sufficiency" and "dominance" scores but not in "neurotic tendency" (Table V). *A*, the twin

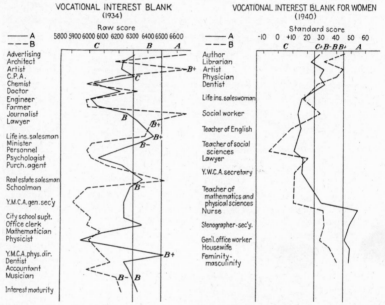

FIG. 5.—Vocational-interest patterns of Adelaide (*a*) and Beatrice (*b*) at ages 12 and 18.

whose developmental background presented more problems, was actually the one who tested least "neurotic," with a low percentile score. In scanning individual items, however, the writer found various points of discrepancy between *A*'s self-ratings and observations furnished by associates; so it may be questioned whether the inventory technique was presenting a valid picture of the subject. Carter (3) has reported correlations of .59 to .75 between identical twins scored on the several parts of the Bernreuter test.

5. Similarities in handwriting that were recognized at once by graphologists who were shown the specimens without being told that the subjects were related (Fig. 6). The specimens also present

differences that would permit an interesting study in themselves. Quite striking is the similarity in writing tempo, though no instructions had been given regarding rate of writing (Table VI).

Ratings. A rating schedule was prepared on which the foster parents and the camp director were asked to express their judgments on a number of traits or aspects of behavior. A number of the traits were those which had been earlier used in a twin survey at the California Institute of Child Welfare (4). For the present study, each "trait" was set up in five descriptive steps; the concept of "average" was not used. With behavior (*e.g.*, talkativeness, self-assertion) that, on the basis of clinical experience, the writer believed to be situational (*i.e.*, to represent adaptations in defined social groups) and with behavior or capacities that experimental work in psychology has shown to be mainly specific (*e.g.*, memory), the trait descriptions were narrowed down. With behavior believed on clinical grounds to be "focal" in Allport's sense (1), the "steps" were carefully defined but were not limited in a situational sense. Examples from the schedule:

Physical energy: S D 1. Abounding vitality, seldom tires.   2. Large amount but sometimes "overdoes."   3. Good endurance for routine activity but soon fatigued by strenuous activity.   4. Unable to carry on any strenuous activities. 5. Tires at slight exertion; exhausted at end of day.

Competitiveness: S D 1. Extremely eager to win games, unhappy when he loses.   2. Very eager to win but not discouraged by losing.   3. Fairly eager to win but enjoys the success of others.   4. Indifferent to winning; cares only for fun of game.   5. Prefers to play with and learn from players better than himself.

The symbols S D provided an opportunity for the raters who knew both of the twins well (*B*'s parents and the camp director when the twins were 12) to indicate whether the expression of the trait was similar or different.

The father and mother of each twin collaborated in making the ratings. The judgments of the two parents were seldom divergent, but if this happened or if they felt that two points on the scale described the subject equally well, both points were recorded. P designates ratings by parents, C ratings by camp director; "12" entries are the earlier ratings, and "18" entries are the follow-up ratings; "1" is high, and "5" is low.

There is seen to be considerable agreement (Table VII) between:

1. Parents' ratings and camp director's ratings for *A*; also for *B*.

2. *A*'s parents' ratings of *A*, and *B*'s parents' ratings of *B* at 12; also at 18.

3. *A*'s parents' ratings of *A* at 12 and at 18.

4. *B*'s parents' ratings of *B* at 12 and at 18.

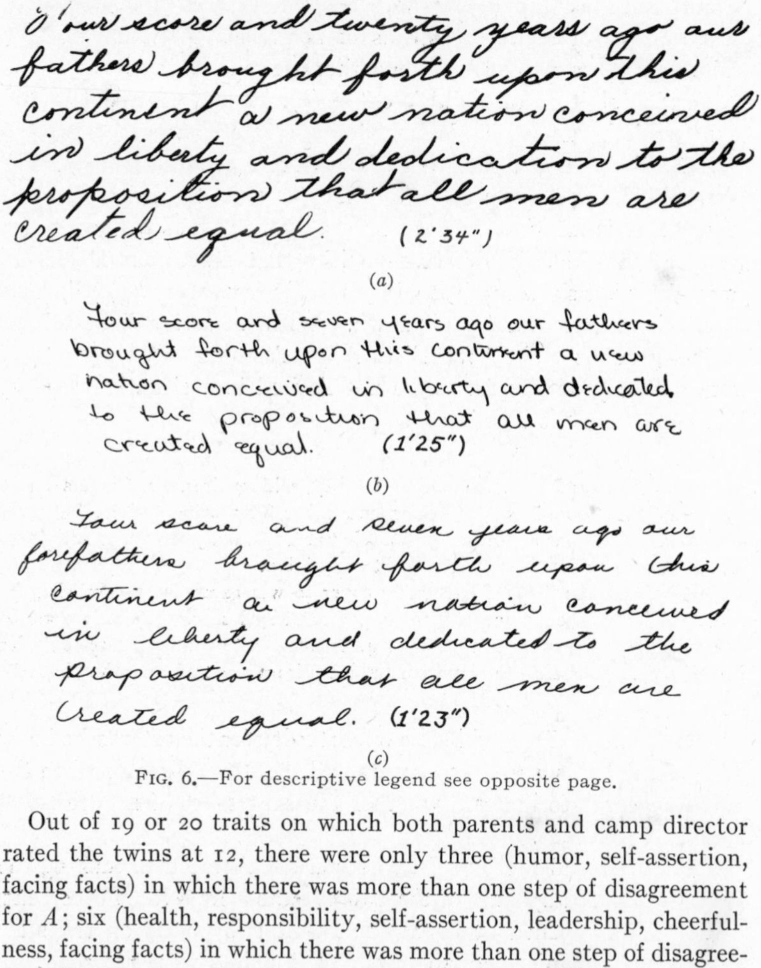

Four score and twenty years ago our fathers brought forth upon this continent a new nation conceived in liberty and dedication to the proposition that all men are created equal.   (2'34")

(a)

Four score and seven years ago our fathers brought forth upon this continent a new nation conceived in liberty and dedicated to the proposition that all men are created equal.   (1'25")

(b)

Four score and seven years ago our forefathers brought forth upon this continent a new nation conceived in liberty and dedicated to the proposition that all men are created equal. (1'23")

(c)

Fig. 6.—For descriptive legend see opposite page.

Out of 19 or 20 traits on which both parents and camp director rated the twins at 12, there were only three (humor, self-assertion, facing facts) in which there was more than one step of disagreement for *A*; six (health, responsibility, self-assertion, leadership, cheerfulness, facing facts) in which there was more than one step of disagreement for *B*. It must be remembered, however, that *B* had not been in residence at the camp since the previous year, so that certain changes may have intervened—responsibility? (*cf.* mother's statement that this summer was the first that *B* helped in care of clothes); facing facts? The disparity on *B*'s health rating may be explained by the camp director's statement that *B* had chronic appendicitis, a condition not mentioned by the parents when health history was obtained. Self-assertion was differently defined for the camp and home ratings; it is interesting to note that the parents' ratings of *A* and *B* on this trait agreed both for ages 12 and 18. Leadership

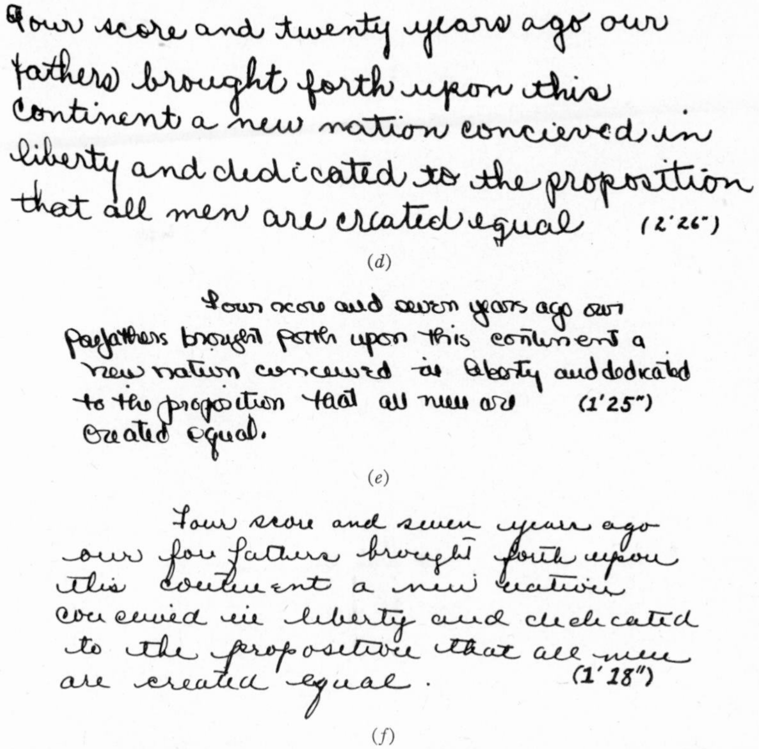

Four score and twenty years ago our fathers brought forth upon this Continent a new nation concieved in liberty and dedicated to the proposition that all men are created equal (2'26")

(d)

Four score and seven years ago our forefathers brought forth upon this continent a new nation conceived in liberty and dedicated to the proposition that all men are created equal. (1'25")

(e)

Four score and seven years ago our for fathers brought forth upon this continent a new nation conceived in liberty and dedicated to the proposition that all men are created equal. (1'18")

(f)

FIG. 6.—Handwriting specimens. (Reduction approximately one-half original size.) Adelaide at 12 years 7 months (a), 18 years 8 months (b), 18 years 8 months (c). Beatrice at 12 years 7 months (d), 18 years 4 months (e), 18 years 10 months (f).

was not defined situationally but probably should have been. *A*'s parents found it impossible to rate her at age 12 on leadership, as defined, but remarked that "she gets mad if she can't have her own way." In the case of cheerfulness in *B*, it seems at least possible that the strong rivalry behavior that was evident in the twins from the time they came to camp, as well as *B*'s irritability, influenced the director's estimate of her prevailing mood. *B*'s parents supported their rating of *B* as "cheerful and optimistic," in contrast to *A*, by

TABLE VII
Trait Ratings by Parents and Camp Director

	S	D*	1	2	3	4	5†
General health:							
A: P			18	12			
C			12				
B: P	12		12	18			
C		12			12		
Physical energy:							
A: P			12	18			
C			12				
B: P	12		12				
			18				
C	12		12				
Activity (restless):							
A: P				12			
				18			
C							
B: P	12						18
C							
Appetite:							
A: P				12	18		
C			12				
B: P	12		12	18			
C	12		12				
Depth of sleep:							
A: P				12			
				18			
C							
B: P	12		12	18			
C							
Stands pain:							
A: P					18	12	
C							
B: P				18			
C							
Outdoor sports (fondness):							
A: P			12		18		
C			12				
B: P	12			12			
				18			
C	12		12				
Perseverance (tasks):							
A: P						18	12
							18

	S	D	1	2	3	4	5
Perseverance (tasks) (continued)							
C							12
B: P			18				12
C	12						12
Promptness							
A: P					18	12	
C							
B: P					18	12	
C							
Speed of decision (impulse)							
A: P			12				
			18				
C			12				
B: P	12		12	18			
C	12		12				
Memory (events):							
A: P			12				
			18				
C							
B: P			18				
C							
Responsibility:							
A: P						12	
					18	18	18
C							12
B: P						12	
					18		
C	12						12
Imaginative play:							
A: P			12	12			
C							
B: P			12				
			18				
C	12		18				
Sense of humor:							
A: P					18	12	
C			12				
B: P	12		12				
			18				
C	12		12				

TABLE VII.—(Continued)

	S	D	1	2	3	4	5
Self-assertion:							
A : P				12	18		
C					12		
B : P	12			12	18		
C	12				12		
Talkativeness:							
A : P				12	18		
C					12		
B : P	12			12	18		
C	12			12			
Generosity (possessions):							
A : P						12	
C							
B : P	12			12	18		
C							
Self-conscious (strangers):							
A : P						12	
						18	
C						12	
B : P				18	12		
C	12					12	
Competitiveness (games):							
A : P				12			
				18			
C				12			
B : P	12			12			
				18			
C	12			12			
Sympathy (persons):							
A : P					18	12	
C							
B : P				12			
				18			
C							
Freedom from jealousy (parents):							
A : P						12	
C							
Freedom from jealousy (parents) (continued):							
B : P	12					12	
						18	
C							
Trustfulness:							
A : P							12
C						12	12
B : P			18				
C	12					12	12
Sociability (avoids solitude):							
A : P			12				
			18				
C			12				
B : P			12				
			18				
C	12		12				
Popularity (same sex):							
A : P				18		12	
C				12	12		
B : P				12	18		
C				12	12		
Leadership:							
A : P						18	
C						12	
B : P				12	18		
C						12	
Independence of parents (emotional):							
A : P				12			
				18			
C							
B : P				18			12
C							
Irritability:							
A : P			12				
			18				
C			12				

TABLE VII.—(*Continued*)

	S	D	1	2	3	4	5		S	D	1	2	3	4	5
B: P	12		12	18				Courage (moral):							
C	12		12					A: P			12		18		
Cheerfulness:								C							
A: P						18	12	B: P				18			
C						12		C							
B: P		12		12	18			Facing facts:							
C	12					12		A: P						18	12
Courage								C					12		
(physical):								B: P			12		18		
A: P					12			C		12			12		
					18										
C					12										
B: P	12			12	18										
C		12		12											

* S = similar.
D = different.
† 1 = high; 5 = low.

behavior incidents. In justification of the high rating on "facing facts," *B*'s mother admitted that she would lose her temper but would then accept a situation and say no more about it. The director gave the twins the same numerical rating on "facing facts" but remarked that *A* was more likely to fuss, whereas *B* was more likely to weep when disappointed. In the case of *A*'s ratings on humor and facing facts, in both of which the director's ratings were higher than those of *A*'s parents, it seems probable that in the group situation, temporarily released from a sense of failure to live up to her mother's standards for her, *A* was functioning more freely in both respects. *B*'s parents agreed with the director in giving both twins the highest rating on "humor."

Among 26 traits on which the parents of each twin made independent ratings at the age of 12, there were 8 traits in which the intertwin ratings differed by more than one step: generosity, humor, cheerfulness, sympathy, popularity, leadership, emotional independence (of parents), facing facts. In all but emotional independence, *B* had the higher rating, and, as the trait was defined (indifference or dependence on sympathy, encouragement, advice), *B*'s rating on the trait was distinctly the more "social" rating. On the whole, the ratings were documented during parent interviews by incidents that gave valid support. These traits all bear in one way or another on quality of social feeling. It is proposed that one fruitful way of studying "trait organization" or "focus" within the individual is through twin comparisons such as the foregoing, which might even be made with twins reared together (though with less likelihood of sharp results). Here it appears that B had reached a higher level of socialization—warmth coupled with developing skill.

There were also certain traits on which the twins at 12 received extreme and similar ratings from parents and camp director: physical energy, appetite, fondness for sports, impulsiveness, humor, talkativeness, competitiveness, irritability, lack of perseverance. The hypothesis may be offered that these traits find common ground in a physical vitality that colors a quick but nonadaptive reaction to immediate environmental stimuli. Through twin coincidence on extreme behavior patterns, as through twin differences, we may possibly find a tool for identifying the bases of personality. The results here obtained from the ratings have analogues in the developmental data on social adjustment and nervous habits already reported. We may also consider the interview and observational data to be forthwith reported for possible congruence. The suggestion may be contemplated that the primitive organic basis of the similarities in these twins lies in a high degree of tissue irritability.

Interviews and observations. A's mother reported B to have "a little happier disposition" and to be "a little less nervous" than A. B's mother mentioned a "tendency to be dissatisfied in both," which she believed to spring from natural temperament, but which appeared to be "much more severe in A." A's father reported that she was "more resentful than the average"; that she was "affectionate but doesn't show her affection much." B's mother commented that "neither has any perseverance; they never finish things." A's mother mentioned as supporting evidence for the low rating on perseverance the fact that A would not practice when given music lessons (*cf.* the mother's disappointment in not becoming a professional musician herself). B's mother reported both as fond of reading, B liking boys' adventure books and A liking "more grown-up books," *e.g., Helen's Babies;* both fond of arithmetic at school; both fond of baseball, swimming, and bicycle riding, A being a more expert swimmer and diver and caring more for bicycle riding than B.

The camp director who had them both in camp in the summer between ages 8 and 11 (and A at 12) reported that in 10 years of camp experience she had never heard such quarreling. "Each one of them carries a chip around on her shoulder." Each was unhappy unless she could pile up as many athletic points as her sister " . . . yet underneath it I think they are really fond of each other."

In interview, *A* indicated her favorite activities as swimming, diving, riding horseback, reading, knitting; favorite books, *Little Women, Tom Sawyer, Penrod and Sam.* She belonged to a scout troop, reported that she was patrol leader and secretary of class at school; also attended a Sunday-school club and a library club for discussing books. Her best friend was a girl of "14, but little," with whom *A* played tennis and jacks, rode bikes, and discussed books. Vocational ambition was to teach English, music, literature, manual training, and sports. Future mate was to be tall with brown eyes, owner of a bank, fond of children, and "just like my father." . . . "If I do entertaining there's going to be nothing to drink." There was to be just one child: "I'm going to spoil her, but I don't care," never send her to boarding school, and dress her in yellow, not be easygoing with her but "not a crab," teach her to love flowers and the outdoors. House was to have a garden and fish pool, a barn full of horses, and a garage. "Three wishes": "a good husband; the kind of house I ordered; a child just like I said." Fears or worries: snakes, that her mother might die (disguised antagonism?), that she might get tough and hard-boiled.

B indicated her favorite activities as riding a bicycle, reading, paper dolls, movies; favorite books, *X-Bar-X* books, *The Bat, Little Women.* She played with paper dolls only in the summer, because she would be "kidded" at home about it. Most of her best friends were members of her scout troop. She belonged to a dramatic club, a debating club, and a glee club at school; was president of dramatic club in the sixth and seventh grades and captain of math club in the eighth grade. Vocational ambition was to do something connected with music or dancing. Future mate was to be hard-working, good and clean and wholesome. She would like to have two children, since one would be spoiled, and would prefer to have identical twin girls. She would like to have lots of parties but would not want many servants, just one to do the dishes; would like to have a vegetable garden and a living-room set, not odds and ends. "Three wishes": "talent to be a great orchestra leader or great musician; would like to be able to dance an awful lot; I wish I could take a vacation or a trip to Siberia or Syria." Fears or worries: not telling father about a beau; growing up in a country town.

There follow a few excerpts from observations.

Situation: Taking Terman Group Test, individually. A "time-sample" record of accessory movements was made by Burks. *B* had many more movements and a wider range of movement. Most frequent in *B* were lip movements (almost continuous), putting finger to nose or mouth (more frequent than in *A*), putting pencil to mouth (not noted in *A*). Grimaces, however, were less frequent than in *A*.

Situation: Luncheon with six adults. Observations recorded by Fite. "Both children at beginning of meal seemed tense and ill at ease, but *A* more so than *B*. . . . Both seemed afraid of making some mistake in passing plates, etc., watched themselves carefully but were quite nervous about it. After a few minutes . . . they both gradually opened up until they were talking freely and pretty much dominating the conversation with tales of camp pranks. *A* poured forth glibly one tale after another, while *B* kept trying to match her tales but never quite succeeding. *B*, however, seemed to have more of a gift at turning the quick, short, amusing phrase than did *A*."

Three raters seeing the twins in this and other situations reported *A* as more talkative than *B* but having less physical poise; one reported them equal. Two raters reported *A* as being more easily embarrassed and more tense; two reported them as equal.

Situation: Table game, "Up, Jenkins," with about six adults. Each was given an opportunity to lead a side; *B* hesitated to lead but did so after *A* had. *A* was very much excited, screamed shrilly, gave orders sharply. *B* did less screaming, was more deliberate in giving orders, and less dominating. (Synthesis from notes of several observers.)

Situation: Anthropometric measurement of *A*. Observations by Fite. During fingerprinting of *A*, "B watching, laughing, giggling. *A* thought *B* was laughing at her, and in spite of *B*'s denial took on a look of injured innocence and refused to smile or be friendly for as long as I was watching, *ca.* 15 minutes. *B* kept twitting her about it, which made *A* still more upset and brought forth angry retorts. . . ."

Situation: Swimming in the lake; several adults on shore, one in water. *B* walked in steadily; *A* uttered cries and exclamations as she gradually became wet. *A* shrieked loudly when an adult splashed her slightly. *B* remarked, "It feels gucky"; when *A* splashed her twice, *B* said plaintively, "Please don't" each time. Both used diving board, which they were told was "private property" and not for the public. (Synthesis from the notes of several observers.)

Situation: Croquet game with Gardner Murphy, not in presence of each other. *B* was winning, *A* was losing, which prevented situation from being strictly comparable. *A* played carelessly (before or after she found herself outclassed?) but made impatient remarks: "Oh, for heaven's sake; Oh, *dear;* Don't hit me." Part way through the game, her interest appeared to shift to kittens; finally, she held a kitten in one hand while playing. (Question of "leaving the field" in which she was failing?) When *B*'s turn came, she asked if *A* had won; then settled down to play carefully; exclaimed, "Oh, how awful; Ooh," over her poor shots or attacks of opponent, but more plaintively and also with more laughter than *A*. "*A* was passionately interested in the kittens; *B* somewhat, but very much less so." (Synthesis from notes of Fite and Gardner Murphy.)

Situation: Attractive 4-year-old boy comes into room. *B* said rather slowly and softly, "Isn't he an adorable child." *A* said briskly, "He's a cute little boy."

Both the similarities and dissimilarities revealed in personality ratings came to light in the behavior observations: impulsiveness, quarreling, competition in both twins but less tension, less social domination, and more warmth of response in *B*—except for *A*'s strong positive response to kittens, which may not be so inconsistent with "total personality" as it appears at first glance.

Though impressing some observers as having more physical poise than *A*, *B* showed many more accessory body movements than *A* during paper-and-pencil tests, which permits speculation (*a*) as to whether *B*'s apparent advantage may have represented merely greater voluntary control when on the social alert, with compensation when off guard or (*b*) as to whether *B*'s actual expenditure of effort and *resulting* body tension during tests was greater than *A*'s.

Further light on personality was given by interviews with the twins themselves, in which the wishes expressed by *A* were connected with imago family and home, those of *B* (who had less need of compensatory fantasy in that domain) with personal achievement and expanding horizons.

Psychological Study at Age 18

It was possible to make follow-up visits to see *A* and her parents when *A* was 18 years 8 months; *B* and her parents when *B* was 18 years 4 months and 18 years 10 months. The twins had not seen each other since shortly after the 12-year study but had corresponded with one another regularly.

Data obtained at the follow-up consisted of: Stanford-Binet, Otis scores (obtained from schools), Rorschach Test, Strong Vocational Interest Blank for Women, handwriting specimens, transcripts of school grades, ratings by parents, observations, a few items on physical development, interviews with twins, their parents, and several of their teachers.

The writer made notes on the greeting and handshaking of the twins (as at the time of the previous study). *A* shook hands without pressure, smiled slightly, and turned her face away, as previously; *B* shook hands without pressure, smiled, and looked steadily at the observer. (*Cf.* note in background data regarding the teacher who encouraged *B* to look her "in the eye.")

The physical items have been discussed in connection with diagnosing the twins' zygotic type and in "developmental history." The other data will be discussed more briefly than those reported for the study made when the twins were 12 years old, since it is felt that the closer the study comes to being contemporary the fewer should be the identifying details in a published account.

The mental tests (the old form of the Stanford-Binet, scored according to new scoring standards, and the Otis, obtained from schools) show mental development that is consistent with previous Stanford-Binet records. *B*'s former advantage on a group test no longer appears (Table IV). Transcripts of high-school grades show *A* to have been graduated at 17½ in the "upper half" of a large high-school class. Grades were chiefly B's and C's; school subjects were both college preparatory (English, mathematics, history, Spanish, chemistry) and "practical" (shorthand and typing, nutrition). *B* was graduated at 16½ in the third quarter of a class of 220. Grades were numerically recorded, and all were in the 70's and low 80's; school subjects were all college preparatory (English, Latin, French, mathematics, history, chemistry, physics). In a transcript of grades during the first 2 years of professional school, the grades were nearly all A's and B's.

The Strong Vocational Interest Blank, in contrast to that filled out at age 12, shows striking parallelism (Fig. 5). The data, if confirmed in comparable studies, might mean that interest patterns, as maturity is approached, not only become stabilized but actually have a closer relation to native potentialities than do interests in early adolescence. The individual has had a wider array of experiences from which to select and is also freer to respond selectively. On the other hand, the changes may be partly developmental in a normative sense. The writer corresponded with Strong regarding this point. Strong kindly sent interest profiles prepared by an assistant for the "first five 18-year-old girls that she ran across in the file." These profiles, superimposed, showed some of the features of the profiles of *A* and *B*, although the latter—by inspection—were more similar than either was to the composite. Further study would be necessary for clear evaluation of the data.

Handwriting specimens continued to show both similarities and differences (Fig. 6). *B* had developed a stylized "manuscript" writing but on the second visit repeated the task in ordinary script at the writer's request. *A* was using script for writing letters and "manuscript" for addressing them. It is not known whether *A*'s style has been influenced by *B*'s; she herself is of the opinion that it has not been. It would be highly interesting to get a "blind" graphological analysis for these specimens.

Ratings by the parents on the same scale as used in the earlier study showed remarkable consistency over the 6-year period. The parents did not have access to their earlier ratings when making the 18-year ratings. Out of 26 traits that the parents rated on each occasion, there were only 6 in which *A* or *B* changed by more than one step. These were, for *A*: promptness, humor, popularity (increase), fondness for sports, self-assertion, moral courage (decrease); for *B*: perseverance (large increase), promptness (increase), self-assertion, talkativeness, generosity, emotional dependence (decrease). If we seek (as in the earlier discussion of traits) a common denominator as a clue to personality "focus," it would seem as if *A* were moving in the direction of greater social conformity; *B*, in the direction of capacity to form and work independently toward goals.

Interesting confirmatory data are found in the histories obtained in the follow-up interviews. *A*'s mother reported that despite the fact she had shown little perseverance in jobs found for her between high-school graduation and entrance to professional school, or in opportunities to take diving lessons, sing solos in church choir, etc., she had "blossomed out" in recent months, was getting along well with her foster sister, and regaling them all with humorous accounts of her new experiences away at school.

B, who at 12 had proceeded further toward socialization than *A*, and who, as far as one can evaluate interviews with teachers and parents, had built up a more stable and satisfying social environment at high school than had *A* and who (shortly after the parent ratings were made) was elected president of a social group at her school, now seemed to be genuinely interested in planning for her future and in helping her foster sister plan. The parents' rating on responsibility (defined only in terms of tasks) does not adequately picture her level of development in this respect. She had held summer jobs in which she had worked 12 hours a day without complaint, had managed her personal expenses well, and had saved money. She was planning to send an allowance to her foster sister, if she had a job the following year. With social adjustment somewhat consolidated, on a level of conformity, she was now free to extend out to another aspect of development. She was not entirely sure of her ground, however, as revealed in an interview in which she admitted that she "hates to think of finishing school" and "sometimes worries about disappointing the girls."

The "first memories" of the twins have interest with respect to the entire developmental picture. *A* remembered the birth of the young sister when she was nearly 5; letting off the brake and allowing the car to roll against a tree; the baby's having a fall for which the doctor was called while she waited outside in a swing; wetting her father while sitting in his lap. *B* remembered trips at the age of 3 to visit her great-grandmother, who had a bank containing pennies that she saved and gave to *B*. She also remembered singing and playing in sand boxes at the first kindergarten she attended and having a fight with her boy cousin. Motifs in these memories appear to be, in the first instance, deprivation and aggression against authority and, in the second instance, a bountiful world, with aggression against one's contemporaries.

The Rorschach Test, administered by the writer and interpreted "blind" by Anna Hartoch, who did not know of the relationship or histories of the subjects at the time, gave not only some illuminating data in terms of the life histories but a framework for prognosis as well. The Rorschach material will be presented at some length in a subsequent joint paper, and only brief and partial notations appear in the present study.

B's Rorschach Test came not long after a protracted and somewhat disturbing emotional experience. An "inquiry" on the Rorschach material was made 6 months later. Thus two appraisals of *B* were furnished by Miss Hartoch, but that based on the "inquiry" was not entirely "blind."

The mental approach in both cases was toward wholes ("wholes-details" in *B* at the time of later inquiry). Erlebnistype in *A*'s test, in *B*'s test, and in *B*'s subsequent inquiry was "coarted" (no color or movement responses in the original tests; three movement *tendencies* in *B*'s inquiry); succession was "loose."

From interpretation of *A*'s test:

"The double function of her intellect is (1) to do well and prove she is somebody; (2) to ward off threatening emotional influences. Her intellectual approach, though superficial and flighty, has proved safer. Easily feels lost in a situation where she has no direction and strict line to follow. She represses and deadens her emotions . . . succeeds in controlling them, but thereby becomes narrow and restricted. . . . There is a hidden repressed defiant quality. Unconsciously perhaps reproaches others . . . that now she has only one choice, to do right and well with her controlling intellect. This is like an agreement she has found to deal with demands. . . . This 'card house' may collapse if confronted with strong emotional experiences. The other possibility is continuing or increasing rigidity of the defensive constricted quality of her personality."

From interpretation of *B*'s test:

"Approaches a task as though there were a ready-made solution. She tries to get this to avoid failure. . . . As long as she has a line to follow, is not lost. . . . Confronted with emotional problems her 'puzzle-solving' technique doesn't work. . . . Lives under pressure . . . fear of not living up to demands of others, of disappointing them. . . . Has probably faced dangerous situations. . . . To protect herself against similar experiences and against pressure from authority, tries to make self invulnerable by (1) accepting the task, to 'solve the puzzle,' given by stronger authoritative persons, (2) not reacting at all in emotionally dangerous situations. . . . This is self-protective, and a hidden aggressive rebellion. Her approach is one of defense and extreme rigidity."

From interpretation of *B*'s inquiry (interval 6 months):

"*B* seems to work better, less laboriously now, though with the same student attitude of solving the tasks in the right way. She feels apparently more sure of herself . . . she can face relationships with less fear. . . . This attitude makes her . . . somewhat more cheerful and warmer. Underneath is to be found still much defense and rigidity. . . . She still lives under pressure and fear as to whether she can meet the demands of the authoritative persons, and whether she can live up to her standards. . . . But she seems to emerge and to reach out for a life of her own."

The mental approach and Erlebnistype (derived from quantitative scoring), as well as the qualitative inferences regarding emotional structure, show a higher degree of correspondence in the twins than would have been anticipated on the basis of studies by Verschuer (9) and others on Rorschach results from identical twins reared together. That resemblance was maintained despite marked environmental differences may possibly be a correlate of the "rigidity" shown in the Rorschach responses of both *A* and *B*.

SUMMARY

A pair of twin girls, diagnosed as monozygotic, were separated when under 2 weeks old and reared in different adoptive families. The main environmental differences may be briefly characterized as follows: in Adelaide (twin A), wide travel up to teen age, irregular early schooling, strict discipline, birth of an "own" daughter to foster parents when subject was about 5; in Beatrice (twin B), few changes in residence or school, illness of 6 months in fifth year, mild discipline, constant companionship from both foster parents, effective guidance from one of her high-school teachers, presence of a foster (nonadopted) sister a year younger, taken into family when subject was about 7.   The socioeconomic status of the two families was not widely different and was moderately above average.

A combination of tests, ratings, interviews, and observations was obtained in the areas of intelligence, school achievement, interests, temperament, and social behavior.   At 12, Adelaide and Beatrice were very similar and not far from average on individual intelligence tests, but Beatrice, the twin who had had the more regular schooling, scored higher on a group intelligence test and on the Stanford Achievement Test, especially on the subtests most closely related to specific school content (*e.g.*, arithmetic computation).   The twins were rather similar in play interests, both enjoying outdoor sports, scout activities, and reading, but B, unlike A, was interested in dolls and paper dolls.   Interest patterns as revealed by the Strong Vocational Interest Blank appeared to be only slightly similar.

In certain aspects of temperament and social behavior, the twins showed some striking parallels in behavior sufficiently unusual to suggest congenital predispositions, especially since the environments of the twins were quite dissimilar in many variables clinically related to personality development.   They had similar histories with respect to nail biting, enuresis, and early puberty; they were similar in observed expressive movements—gait, handshaking, writing tempo, and, to some degree, graphic form, and in a group of traits (ratings) that appeared to rest on an underlying physical vitality and non-adaptive irritability.   Decided differences were noted, however, in a group of social-emotional traits, B, whose home situation was more free from pressure having a more cheerful mood level resulting in, or at least accompanied by, greater warmth and skill in the handling of social relationships. A "tendency to be dissatisfied," however, had been noted in both twins.

By the time the twins had been in high school 2 or 3 years, their earlier differences in group-intelligence-test scores had been assimilated. There was no marked difference in level of high-school marks, although A's high-school career had been complicated by a succession of minor disciplinary infractions. A result of special note concerning tests administered to the twins at time of follow-up was the markedly greater similarity in their vocational-interest schedules at age 18 than at age 12. This at least suggests than an individual is more free to develop interests that are congruent with his native potentialities in late adolescence than in earlier years, when his option of choice and range of experience have been more restricted.

The trait ratings showed considerable consistency over the 6-year interval, speed of decision (impulsiveness), irritability, competitiveness appearing in marked degree at the two ages in both twins. There was a cluster of traits in each twin, however, that showed considerable change, the direction of change finding confirmation in the twins' vocational and social adjustments up to the time of follow-up. A appeared to be moving in the direction of greater social conformity; B, who had attained conformity earlier, was now developing the capacity to form and work toward distant goals. The subsequent development of the twins may furnish for at least one set of conditions some light on the question of whether relinquishment of individual patterns of behavior necessarily means sacrifice of the imaginative use of personal capacities. The twins may also contribute eventually some data on the clinical problem of whether symptomatic behavior deviations at times of environmental stress are laying the pattern for a permanent life-style or whether they represent secular aberrations from a developmental path, with final destination largely determined by the genes.

The answer to such problems may vary according to the rigidity or plasticity of the individual case, $i.e.$, the less plastic the organism, the more likely the fulfillment of individual potentialities, regardless of environment. Criteria for "plasticity" and "rigidity," however, are far from standardized in psychological terms, although irritability and competitiveness, both of which the twins had in marked degree, would appear to be related to rigidity. In the Rorschach Test, we have in at least one standardized situation a possibility of appraising rigidity as shown through the perceptual processes. In Rorschach interpretations, Miss Hartoch finds a defensive constricted quality associated with rigidity in both twins.

The Rorschach Test also provides dynamic interpretations of the "conformity" tendency found in the follow-up trait ratings and behavior reports: each subject is lost without a "line" to follow, A striving "to do well and prove she is somebody and to ward off threatening emotional influences"; B, to accept "the task given by stronger authoritative persons" and "not to react at all in emotionally dangerous situations."

The Rorschach analogue of the new goal-oriented tendencies seen in B's record of objective activity is found in Miss Hartoch's observation: "She seems to emerge and to start to reach out for a life of her own."

REFERENCES

1. ALLPORT, G. W. Personality: a psychological interpretation. New York: Holt, 1937.
2. CARTER, H. D. Twin similarities in occupational interests. J. educ. Psychol., 1932, 23, 641–655.
3. CARTER, H. D. Twin similarities in personality traits. J. genet. Psychol., 1933, 43, 312–321.
4. JONES, H. E., & WILSON, P. T. Reputation differences in like-sex twins. J. exper. Educ., 1932–1933, 1, 86–91.
5. NEWMAN, H. H., FREEMAN, F. N. & HOLZINGER, K. J. Twins: a study of heredity and environment. Chicago: Univ. Chicago Press, 1937.
6. STEGGERDA, M. Cross sections of human hair from four racial groups. J. Hered., 1940, 31, 475–476.
7. STOCKS, P. A biometric investigation of twins and their brothers and sisters. Ann. Eugen., Camb., 1930, 4, 49–108.
8. STOCKS, P., & KARN, M. N. A biometric investigation of twins and their brothers and sisters. Ann. Eugen. Camb., 1933, 5, 1–55.
9. VERSCHUER, O. V. Intellektuele Entwickelung und Vererbung. In Vererbung u. Erziehung. Just G. (Ed.). Berlin: Springer, 1930.

CHAPTER IV

THE APPRAISAL INTERVIEW: A Critical Consideration of Its Theory and Practice with Particular Reference to the Selection of Public Personnel[1]

By

FRANKLIN FEARING

University of California

(*Los Angeles*)

The interview is probably one of the oldest human social techniques. It is also the least studied, the most constantly used, and the most frequently challenged method of securing social data. Studies of the interview, although as divergent in method and type of data selected for analysis as those of Rice (19), Symonds (22), Hollingworth (9), Magson (13), Bingham and Moore (3), and Scott (20), agree, at least, in characterizing the interview as an instrument of doubtful validity and reliability. This unanimity of disapproval, however, has not noticeably reduced the frequency with which this instrument is used. Those whose professional activities include the collection of certain types of information or the appraisal of human personality still appear to find the interview an indispensable instrument. Medical diagnoses, legal findings, journalistic statements, judgments of occupational fitness, personality appraisals, and many other types of social data are obtained through the interview and possibly may be obtained in no other way.

[1] The writer desires to acknowledge his indebtedness to Burton L. Hunter, general manager of the Los Angeles City Civil Service Commission, for permission to use the material that forms the basis of a part of this paper. Members of the technical staff of the commission who cooperated in various ways were Dr. Joseph Hawthorne, then director of examinations, and Harry Rosenberg, principal personnel technician. The commission or the staff are in no way responsible for any interpretations or conclusions presented in this paper. The following students rendered clerical and statistical assistance: Marvin Goodwin, Shirley Maron, Sally Cunningham, Mary McDuff, Lawrence Ravitz, and Eugene Jacobson.

The dilemma is solved for some by various proposals, the general intent of which is to standardize the interview in some manner. Viteles (26) and, more recently, Hovland and Wonderlic (10) discuss the "inadequacy of the traditional interview" and suggest improvements in two directions: the development of standardized interviews and of more precise rating scales to make possible evaluations of personal traits "which are not otherwise amenable to measurement." Other proposals have included attempts to increase the "objectivity" of the interview by the elimination of "bias," "halo effects," and the like from the appraisal process. It is the purpose of the present discussion (a) to consider the interview as a social situation in which appraisals of human personality and aptitudes are made, (b) to consider some of the factors that condition the appraisal process with particular reference to "bias" and "objectivity," and (c) to analyze certain results of appraisal interviews held in connection with the Civil Service examinations of police officers.

DEFINITION OF THE INTERVIEW

Symonds has recently noted (21) that interviewing is an "elusive process," poorly defined and applied to a wide variety of verbal communications between persons. Formal definitions are of little value except to set the frame of reference within which a concept may be considered. In the case of the interview, the social-psychological context is wide. *Interviewing involves the social interaction in a face-to-face situation between two or more persons organized for the purpose of obtaining information from, or making appraisals of, or modifying the behavior of one of their number.* Psychologically, it has much in common with many types of group situations—particularly teaching situations.

As a group situation, the interview involves social interactions between the interviewer and the interviewee, and, in cases where there is more than one interviewer, there are social interactions between the interviewers. Certain conceptual formulations regarding group behavior, as developed by Lewin (11), Lippitt (12), and others of the field-theoretical school, may be used to characterize certain significant aspects of the interview; e.g., (a) those participating in the interview situation may be said to exhibit a certain degree of *interdependence* and (b) their behavior or any results of the interview may be considered as functionally related to the *goal* or goals for which it is held; (c) in addition, the interview may be said to have a certain *atmosphere* (*e.g.*, friendliness, formality, etc.) and to possess a certain degree of *stratification*. This latter characteristic indicates the existence of barriers such as differences in education, background, class, or in interests to be served, which may psychologically separate the interviewer and interviewee. The results of the interview expressed in any form of appraisal (*e.g.*, trait ratings) may not be considered apart from these factors. *The appraisal process is functionally determined by them.*

THE NATURE OF THE APPRAISAL PROCESS

"No person can understand any other person completely, for it is impossible for one human being to share directly the motives, thoughts, and feelings of another," according to Allport (1), and hence the problem of understanding people is always a problem of "partial understanding." The interview is a situation in which appraisals are made. These appraisals are made with respect to something called *personality*. Whatever this term may mean for the psychologist or layman, it cannot be conceived as something that exists; it can be conceived only as functionally dependent on an act of appraisal. Hence, it must be related to interview situations.

In considering the processes by which individuals make appraisals or judgments of other individuals, we may distinguish two contrasting explanations. Allport (1) terms these the theories of *inference* and *intuition*. We may quarrel with this particular use of terms, but the distinction is valid.

On the one hand, there are those—and they apparently are represented by most of the writers of texts and other treatises on personality, rating scales, and statistics—who conceive the appraisal of human personality, ability, aptitude, or talent in terms of a part-whole relationship. That is to say, they approach the problem in terms of a set of assumptions regarding the "traits" or other fundamental elements which, taken together, form the totality that they are endeavoring to assess. The principle of connection is additive, or associational, and the resultant is a mosaic, the parts of which may be separately identified and numerically expressed. The success of testing methods in psychology, particularly in the field of intelligence, has supported this view. The ease with which results of this type of analysis may be treated statistically, together with the enormous prestige that statistical procedures command in many circles—a prestige that amounts occasionally to the conclusion that there is no truth except statistical truth!—has led to the view that, if scientific respectability is to be achieved, the results of appraisal must be expressed in terms of "traits."

The opposing type of theory is termed by Allport *intuition*. Alternative terms are *insight* and *organismic*, of which the latter is preferred by the present writer. The essential characteristic of the judging process is that it is *immediate and direct;* is not separable into parts or component units. The judgment or appraisal, when made, is a unitary, structured whole.

Appraisals of this type made in the interview situation involve judgments regarding underlying, dynamic relationships as indicated by the behavior of the person under observation. The behavior of both the appraiser and the appraised is determined by the total constellation of forces that constitutes the interview situation.

This approach to the problem at once brings into question the feasibility of applying precise quantitative methods to interview procedures. In the field of personality "measurement," Terman (23) has voiced this skepticism trenchantly. He points out that the application of quantitative methods does not guarantee psychological insight, and he emphasizes the absurdity, even in the field of intelligence measurement, of undertaking, as Thorndike has done, to measure mental ability in the same sense as a physicist measures distance and mass. In the field of personality appraisal, the "clinical approach is absolutely necessary for the interpretation of personality as a whole, for a true picture of a personality cannot be pieced together from any number of test scores. The total is an organismic, not an additive, total. Personality traits are not merely intercorrelated, but are *functionally interactive in infinitely complex ways* now little understood."[1] With reference to the use of factor-analysis methods in personality study, Terman notes that these methods have been useful in reducing the "vast array of alleged personality traits" to four or five distinguishable components. He continues, however:

"It is well to know this, but it is another thing to conclude that the total personality can be accounted for so simply. There must be, certainly are, many factors of personality that have not been and can never be embodied in our tests. These unknowns are always entering to upset our interpretations of test scores and to limit their usefulness when we apply them in our attempts at personality diagnosis and adjustment. There are no statistical short cuts to the understanding of human nature."

[1] Italics are the author's.

Tryon (24) is equally dubious regarding the possibility that such methods will reveal "the underlying factors" or determiners of behavior; it appears to be his opinion that, at best, correlational and factorial methods will reveal only certain "operational unities" in the data.

The two theories (inference and organismic) regarding the nature of the process by which one individual appraises the status, value, or fitness of another individual proceed from such different assumptions and make use of such unlike methodologies that it is somewhat difficult to agree with Allport (1) that the process of understanding personality requires both. It is possible that by imposing certain artificial constraints on the interview situation, the process may be so disarticulated as to yield data in the form the inference theory demands. Examples of such constraint are found in the proposals to standardize procedures by the use of such devices as a schedule of questions prepared in advance and the precise definition of traits, which are then treated as discrete entities. For certain purposes, these proposals may have certain advantages, but that they define the nature of the appraisal process is doubtful.

In the appraisal type of interview, there is, first, the individual to be interviewed. He possesses a more or less unified personality, the underlying genotypic relationships of which are not immediately accessible. In the interview situation, he presents a pattern of behavior, the course of which is determined by his previous history and by the exigencies of the interview situation itself. There is, secondly, the interviewer or interviewers who are also structured personalities. Under the influence of the specific task set by the situation, they interpret the pattern presented to them by the interviewee. *These appraisals are not objective* in the sense in which this term is ordinarily used. Rather, they reflect the unifying activity of persons who are cognitively structuring the field under the demands of the total situation. Interviewing is essentially a perceptual activity. The correspondence between the evaluation that emerges in the form of an appraisal and the totality that is the individual evaluated may be very slight or very great, but it is always less than perfect. Nevertheless, it is extremely important for many social purposes to have it.

THE OPERATION OF BIAS AND THE "HALO" EFFECT

One of the earliest findings in regard to the interview and trait-rating methods was the discovery that sets of ratings on different traits show high intercorrelations. This is found to be true when there is no a priori reason for assuming a connection between the traits correlated. This "halo" effect is generally attributed to a generalized attitude on the part of the rater regarding the individual rated which modifies all the judgments about him. In most of the earlier discussions, the presence of this effect was deplored, and various safeguards were set up against it. It was regarded as a very serious source of error in ratings and an indication of their lack of "objectivity."

Closely related to the discussions of the "halo" effect were the discussions of the operation of bias. In his well-known studies Rice (18, 19) calls attention to the fact that stereotypes afford a necessary "economy of effort" in the process of cataloguing our environment, thus suggesting that the process is more or less inescapable. Allport (1), however, refers to the stereotype as an example of the "paralyzing effect of simplification upon the process of judgment." This, together with another type of bias, the so-called central tendency of judgments, in which judges avoid the extreme ratings, he regards as a serious source of error.

An experiment leading to a different type of conclusion is that of Harvey (8) who studied the effect of a bias introduced into instructions given to an interviewer on his attitude toward the person interviewed as reflected in character judgments. He found that the bias affected the judgments in 40 per cent of the cases. He notes that the "general impression" of the candidate is very important and may resist the bias or, in some cases, enhance it. He points out that this is similar to the "halo" effect and that it must be a fundamental condition of the process of judgment. Bingham (5) has been more emphatic in pointing out that "bias" in the form of "halo" is not to be regarded as a troublesome constant but a desirable characteristic of raters. He thinks that hasty and vague judgments should be eliminated. "But there is a halo that need not be looked at askance. Rather, it signifies that the rater has not abstracted the trait from its setting within the personality pattern; and that the person, moreover, has been seen against his proper background, namely, the position to be filled."

Similar conclusions were expressed by Estes (6), who found that those interviewers who used an analytical method of appraisal were "reliably inferior" to those who used an over-all type of appraisal. This is due to the fact that the over-all method "provides a greater opportunity for the judges to form totalized impressions which more adequately represent the 'realities of organized vital process' [cf. Allport and Cantril (2)] in the subject judged than is afforded by the type of perceptual-judging process which occurs under the set to rate discrete aspects of personality." Vernon (25), in a similar experiment, found that "personality can be more accurately and consistently judged as a structured whole."

This is not to say, of course, that ratings should not be made on traits. Even though the results of such ratings are probably highly artificial and psychologically meaningless, it is important in the interview situation to allow the rater to consider the candidate in a number of aspects as related to the purposes for which the appraisal is made, provided, always, that he does not come to regard these parts as real entities. But the over-all judgment, expressed in terms for which the interview is held, expresses the social and psychological meaning of the situation.

The Interview in Public-personnel Procedure

In the selection of public personnel under the merit system, the interview occupies a very important place in the examination procedure. As in other situations in which the interview is used for purposes of appraisal, the purpose of the oral examination is to elicit judgments about persons that cannot be obtained from other types of examination. Meriam (15) notes that the oral examination of candidates is, in spite of its difficulties, essential, since certain kinds of qualities cannot be tested in written examinations. In this connection, Bingham (4) believes that oral examinations are necessary to assess the personal qualities for positions that will require the candidates "to deal with the public, to train subordinates or to cooperate intimately with fellow-workers in a group."

However, the problems that face all interviewers in public personnel procedures have received comparatively little attention in personnel literature. The papers of Bingham (4, 5), O'Rourke (17), and Ordway and O'Brien (16) are important exceptions. The latter study is concerned primarily with the problem of objectivity. It is the conception of these two investigators that, insofar as possible, all "subjective" factors should be excluded from the interview, because they are legally contestable and psychologically unreliable. After pointing out that such traits as "neatness," "appearance," etc., are unreliably rated, because the judges may disagree or because the candidates, aware of the requirements, deliberately adapt themselves to the exigencies of the situation, Ordway and O'Brien take the position that no attempt should be made to rate such factors: the interview is to be concerned with the accumulation of evidence regarding what the candidate has done that demonstrates possession of the capacity or qualification at issue. Hence, the examiners must be versed in the "fundamental principles of the meaning of evidence and the method of its adduction in the oral process." The interview is regarded as a trial in which the examiners are like a judge who hears the issues of fact and law without a jury. At least one experienced trial attorney should be a member of the interview board. The candidates should be carefully cross-examined on all points.

Mandell (14) has criticized these proposals sharply. Of the various proposals for the improvement of the "objectivity" and reliability of the interview that have been presented from time to time, those of Ordway are the most drastic and, in many ways, psychologically the most naïve. It is difficult to understand the purpose of an interview under the proposed plan. The *facts* regarding a candidate's education, past performance, etc., could be established by other types of investigation with greater ease and greater accuracy. The only purpose for the presentation of these or any other "facts" in the interview is to have them *interpreted* from the point of view of the persons who conduct the interview. This interpretation is an appraisal process and can be understood only as a function of a constellation of factors that condition the total interview. This interpretative aspect of the situation is recognized by Ordway in the latter part of his paper, in which he discusses the standards to be applied to the "factual" evidence obtained. However, these ratings would seem to be contaminated with the same sources of error as the "factors of personality," which were excluded from consideration, *i.e.*, such ratings would be "subjective." To label these processes "subjective," with the implication that they are untrustworthy, is to fail to understand the nature of objectivity in science. The objective-subjective dichotomy is a dubious one at best. Its use harks back to prescientific notions regarding psychology and behavior.

A STUDY OF CERTAIN ASPECTS OF THE APPRAISAL INTERVIEW IN A CIVIL SERVICE EXAMINATION OF POLICE OFFICERS

The data that are here presented were obtained in connection with the oral examinations of 100 police officers who were candidates for promotion to the rank of captain of police. These oral examinations were part of a promotional examination conducted by the Civil Service Commission of Los Angeles, which was open to candidates from the ranks of sergeant and lieutenant of police.

A complete analysis of these data is not presented in this place but only a consideration of those data that are related to the operation of bias and "halo" in a particular interview situation. The fact that one member of the interview board was a psychologist who was aware of some of the problems involved and who had the opportunity to observe the phenomena presented by the internal dynamics of the situation may differentiate this analysis from similar analyses.

Each interview lasted approximately 40 minutes, and the interviews were held on 14 successive days. The interview board consisted of the following persons: D, a social worker and former Y.M.C.A. secretary, C, a chief of police in a city of approximately 60,000, N, a captain of police in a large city, and R, a psychologist and college professor. The interviews were informal, and the appraisals were expressed in the form of ratings on a five-point scale, on 10 traits. These traits were (1) physical appearance, (2) neatness and dress, (3) manner and bearing, (4) alertness, (5) tact, (6) ability to present ideas, (7) maturity of judgment, (8) quantity-quality of education, (9) quantity-quality of experience, (10) summary evaluation. The interviewers were told that the last item, summary evaluation, would be more heavily weighted in the final score and that it was to be considered independently of the other items. In making appraisals, the interviewers had, in addition to the behavior of the candidate, the information on the original application form. This included age of candidate, education, and description of his previous assignments in the police department. Although the interviewers sat as a board, the ratings on each candidate were made independently and privately.

The following generalizations regarding those factors that might be expected to structure the interview situation with respect to the appraisals may be made:

1. All the interviewers had had considerable experience in interviewing: N and C in connection with police personnel, D in previous Civil Service examinations, particularly in the field of social-work personnel, and R in connection with advisory work with college students and in a psychological clinic. Attitudes and biases appropriate to these activities were well established.

2. A stratification of a mild type might be expected to exist between the police officers and the laymen who were members of the board.

3. With respect to the candidates, N and C, the police officers, might be expected to have "in-group" attitudes. D and R might be less sympathetic; R, less so than D.

4. N and C had quite definite attitudes regarding two factors that characterized the candidates as a group: (a) A hesitancy to endorse the candidacy of any applicant who had not passed through all the ranks below the one for which the examination was held—that of captain. Under the announced terms, the examination was open to sergeants, who, if they qualified, would thereby skip the rank of lieutenant. N was more opposed to the omission of a rank than C. (b) Both N and C were dubious regarding candidates whose police experience was largely or wholly limited to the detective branch of the service or who had not served a considerable apprenticeship in the "uniform" rank, i.e., patrolled a beat. N's views on this point were more definite than those of C. Closely associated with these attitudes was the tendency on the part of N and C to regard length of service or seniority as in itself a worthy characteristic.

5. With respect to the attitudes described in the foregoing, D was probably neutral, although somewhat disposed to follow the lead of N and C. R, on the other hand, had little respect for seniority as such or for the disciplinary value of certain kinds of experience, although he probably had a slightly unfavorable attitude regarding the detective as compared with the "uniform" branch of the service.

Analysis of Ratings with Respect to Certain "Biasing" Factors

It has been the intent of the previous discussion to show that, psychologically, bias refers to the fact that human judgments are structured processes. On the basis of our knowledge of certain attitudes of the examiners, it is possible tentatively to determine the extent to which these attitudes affected their appraisals in those cases in which there exists some other criterion to which the supposed attitude may be related. These known attitudes are related to (a) the rank and length of service, (b) the type of service ("uniform" or detective), and (c) the education of the candidate.

Among the candidates examined, 43 held the rank of sergeant and 55 the rank of acting lieutenant, lieutenant, or acting captain. There were no reliable differences between the two groups with respect to age, educational level, or seniority. The differences between the means for the total oral grade and for the totals for each of the examiners are also not reliable, although they are all in the same direction, *i.e.*, they favor the lieutenants. However, when the data are analyzed with reference to the percentage of high ratings (a score of 5) given the two groups of candidates, certain significant differences appear. There is evidence that the lieutenants were favored as compared with the sergeants by examiners *D*, *N*, and *C* with respect to ratings on one or more of traits 7, 8, 9, and 10. By this is meant that the difference between the two groups in the percentage receiving the highest rating is a reliable difference. Expressed in percentages, for example, *D* gave a rating of 5 on trait 10 to 23 per cent of the lieutenant group and 9 per cent of the sergeant group; *N* gave 29 per cent of the lieutenants and 4 per cent of the sergeants a grade of 5 on trait 9, and 23 per cent of the lieutenants and 7 per cent of the sergeants on trait 10; *C* gave a grade of 5 to 18 per cent of the lieutenants and none to the sergeants on trait 9 and 29 per cent and 11 per cent on trait 10. These findings are interesting in view of the fact that *objectively*, so far as our data go, there is little difference between the two groups. Obviously, in the case of *D*, *N*, and *C*, some factors were involved in the appraisals of persons accorded the highest scores which were not present in the objective data. It is important to note also that these significant differences are found in the case of traits that, statistically, were the most reliable, as well as those with reference to which the raters have been most discriminating, *i.e.*, traits 8, 9, and 10.

Of the candidates examined, 64 were in the "uniform" service and 36 in the detective service. So far as the non-oral criteria are concerned, as in the case of the lieutenants and sergeants, there are no reliable differences between the central tendencies. The total oral grade favors the "uniform" group, but the difference is not reliable. The individual raters, if they favor either group, appear to favor the "uniform" group. When the differences between the percentages of those receiving the highest grade (5) on selected traits is determined, many are found to be reliable. The most significant differences are those on trait 4 for *R*; on traits 8, 9, and 10 for *N*; and on traits 4 and 9 for *C*. All these differences are in favor of the "uniform" service as compared with the detective service. In the case of trait 9, N assigned 28 per cent of the candidates from the "uniform" service a grade of 5, as compared with none in the detective service; and on trait 10, 23 per cent of the "uniform" as compared with 2 per cent of the detective group. Apparently the judgments of R (with the single exception of those on trait 4) were influenced only slightly, and those of D not at all, by the service to which the candidate belonged. N and C, on the other hand, were so influenced.

Two of the traits on which the examiners made ratings were quantity-quality of education (trait 8) and quantity-quality of experience (trait 9). To determine what relationship, if any, existed between the ratings on these traits and educational level and length of service (seniority), as reported by the candidates on the application form, the correlations were computed for each of the interviewers. In considering these correlations, it should be remembered that the interviewers had the application form containing this information before them at the time the candidate was interviewed. R's correlation between rating on education and education as reported is .67($\pm$.037) as compared with .39, .35, and .30 for the other interviewers. On the other hand, N and C show low, though apparently reliable, correlations between the ratings on experience and length of service, and the correlations for R and D are nonsignificant.

The examiners were informed that trait 10 (summary evaluation) was to be weighted in the final oral score. They were instructed to rate it independently of the other traits. Correlations were computed between it and the other traits in order to determine to what extent a "halo" effect existed. All the r's are positive and reliable and range from .27 to .80. Judged by the mean r for the four interviewers, traits 6 (ability to present ideas), 7 (maturity of judgment), and 9 (experience) are the least clearly differentiated from the factor or factors that resulted in the rating on summary evaluation. The mean r for C is .57; for N, .68; for D, .53; and for R, .61.

SUMMARY

The following statements summarize the more important findings:

1. With respect to "bias," interviewers D, the social worker N, the police captain, and C, the police chief, favored the candidates with the rank of lieutenant or acting captain as compared with the

sergeants. N and C showed a preference for the men whose primary service was in the "uniform" division. These preferences are shown in the tendency to give a larger proportion of the highest grade (5) to the favored group. These operate especially in the cases of traits 8 (education), 9 (experience), and 10 (summary evaluation), which were, statistically, the most reliably rated traits. It is important to note that the education and experience (insofar as the latter is indicated by length of service) of the two groups (sergeants-lieutenants and "uniform"-detective) *as actually attested by the candidates* do not differ significantly. This neatly illustrates the function of an appraisal; *i.e.*, the interviewer *makes a judgment* on certain information. This judgment is not a simple reflection of reality; in that sense, it is not *objective*, and therein lies its value. R, the psychologist, showed the highest correlation between the total oral grade and educational level, as reported by the candidate.

2. The traits most closely correlated with the summary evaluation ("halo") are 6 (ability to express ideas), 7 (maturity of judgment), and 9 (experience). All ratings show positive and reliable correlations with the summary evaluation. Interviewer C shows a particularly low correlation between trait 8 and the summary evaluation.

Interpretations

The purpose of the foregoing theoretical discussion and empirical analyses has been to present the interview as a social situation involving the interaction of persons organized with respect to an explicitly expressed goal—usually the appraisal of fitness for a specified task. Many of the previous attempts to rationalize the interview have stressed the units or devices that expressed the appraisals made in the interview. The result has been that the person who is the subject of the appraisal is conceived as the sum of the discrete units in which the appraisal was expressed. The evaluation of the results of this process by the conventional statistical criteria has forced the conclusion that, on the whole, the interview is an unsatisfactory device for the appraisal of persons. Yet its use has not notably diminished. The explanation of this appears to lie in the fact that *certain kinds of appraisal can be made in no other manner except in a situation involving continuous social interaction.*

It is here suggested that this dilemma reflects the situation in which, methodologically, psychology finds itself at present. The units of description and the units of measurement appropriate to certain orders of behavior phenomena are not appropriate to the type of phenomena that may be termed, somewhat loosely, social. The appraisal of human personality belongs in this category. If the interview is to be retained—and it must not be forgotten that there are other methods of evaluation—it will be necessary to develop a methodology that will make possible the investigation of the instrument itself as well as the results of its use.

Among the problems that confront those who use the interview as a social technique, perhaps the most discussed has been the problem of "objectivity" or "bias." It is the thesis of this discussion that "bias" is another word for the integrating factor that makes the judgment a structured whole. Its elimination is neither possible nor desirable, although it is possible that certain types of "bias" are, for certain social purposes, dangerous.

The empirical study presented falls far short of the type of study of the interview and interview-results that must be ultimately undertaken but supports the view that appraisals made in an interview situation, despite certain artificial constraints, are unitary evaluations and reflect the personality organization of the individuals who make the appraisals.

REFERENCES

1. ALLPORT, G. W. Personality, a psychological interpretation. New York: Holt, 1937.
2. ALLPORT, G. W., & CANTRIL, H. Judging personality from voice. *J. soc. Psychol.*, 1934, **5**, 37–55.
3. BINGHAM, W. V., & MOORE, B. V. How to interview. New York: Harper, 1934.
4. BINGHAM, W. V. Oral examinations in Civil Service recruitment with special reference to experiences in Pennsylvania. Chicago: *Pamphlet* 13, Civil Service Assembly, January, 1939.
5. BINGHAM, W. V. Halo, invalid and valid. *J. appl. Psychol.*, 1939, **23**, 221–228.
6. ESTES, S. G. Judging personality from expressive behavior. *J. abnorm. (soc.) Psychol.*, 1938, **38**, 217–237.
7. HARTOG, P., & RHODES, E. C. An examination of examinations. London: Macmillan, 1935.
8. HARVEY, S. M. A preliminary investigation of the interview. *Brit. J. Psychol.*, 1938, **28**, 263–287.
9. HOLLINGWORTH, H. L. Vocational psychology and character analysis. New York: Appleton, 1929.
10. HOVLAND, C. I., & WONDERLIC, E. F. Prediction of industrial success from a standardized interview. *J. appl. Psychol.*, 1939, **23**, 537–546.

11. LEWIN, K.   Field theory and experiment in social psychology: concepts and methods.   *Amer. J. Sociol.*, 1939, **44,** 868–896.
12. LIPPITT, R.   Field theory and experiment in social psychology: autocratic and democratic group atmospheres.   *Amer. J. Sociol.*, 1939, **45,** 26–49.
13. MAGSON, E. H.   How we judge intelligence.   *Brit. J. Psychol. Monogr. Suppl.*, 1926, No. 9.
14. MANDELL, M.   Civil Service oral interviews.   *Person. J.*, 1940, **18,** 373–382.
15. MERIAM, LEWIS: Public personnel problems.   Washington, D. C.: Brookings Institution, 1938.
16. ORDWAY, S. H., & O'BRIEN, J. C.   An approach to more objective oral tests.   Society for Personnel Administration, *Pamphlet* 2, 1939.
17. O'ROURKE, L. J.   Measuring judgment and resourcefulness as interview techniques.   *Person. J.*, 1929, **7,** 427–440.
18. RICE, S. A.   "Stereotypes": a source of error in judging human character.   *J. person. Res.*, 1926, **5,** 267–276.
19. RICE, S. A.   Contagious bias in the interview.   *Amer. J. Sociol.*, 1929, **35,** 420–423.
20. SCOTT, W. D.   Selection of employees by means of quantitative determinations.   *Ann. Amer. Acad. Pol. Soc. Sci.*, 1916, **65,** 182–193.
21. SYMONDS, P. M.   Research on the interviewing process.   *J. educ. Psychol.*, 1939, **30,** 346–353.
22. SYMONDS, P. M.   Diagnosing personality and conduct.   New York: Century, 1931.
23. TERMAN, L. M.   The measurement of personality.   *Science*, 1934, **80,** 605–608.
24. TRYON, R. C.   Cluster analysis.   Ann Arbor: Edwards, 1939.
25. VERNON, P. E.   Some characteristics of the good judge of personality.   *J. soc. Psychol.*, 1933, **4,** 42–57.
26. VITELES, M. S.   Industrial psychology.   New York: Norton, 1932.

CHAPTER V

THE USE OF FREE ASSOCIATION IN THE OBJECTIVE MEASUREMENT OF PERSONALITY

By

FLORENCE L. GOODENOUGH

University of Minnesota

"PROJECTIVE" VS. "OBJECTIVE" METHODS

One of the major difficulties that has beset the investigator of nonintellectual components of the personality patterns by which individuals are distinguished from each other is that of devising techniques that permit full play for the expression of such differences and at the same time yield results that can be expressed in quantitative terms by means of a system of scoring that is reasonably objective and can be readily learned by clerical assistants of moderate competence. According to the relative emphasis on one or the other of these desiderata, two rather widely separated schools of thought have developed in the field of personality measurement. On the one hand, we have the advocates of the so-called projective methods defined by L. K. Frank (1) as follows:

"A projection method for the study of personality involves the presentation of a stimulus-situation designed or chosen because it will mean to the subject, not what the experimenter has arbitrarily decided it should mean (as in most psychological experiments using standardized stimuli in order to be 'objective') but rather whatever it must mean to the personality who gives it, or imposes upon it, his private, idiosyncratic meaning and organization."

Elsewhere in the same article, Frank notes that

" . . . the dynamic conception of personality as a process of organizing experience and structuralizing life space in a field, leads to the problem of how we can reveal the way an individual personality organizes experience, in order to disclose or at least gain insight into that individual's *private world* of meanings, significances, patterns and feelings."

87

He suggests that one way of accomplishing this is

" . . . by giving him a field (objects, materials, experiences) with relatively little structure and cultural patterning so that the personality can project upon that plastic field his way of seeing life, his meanings, significances, patterns, and especially his feelings. Thus we elicit a projection of the individual personality's *private world* because he has to organize the field, interpret the material and react affectively to it."

As suitable devices for the projective study of personality differences, Frank mentions finger painting, modeling in clay, interpretative responses to pictures, play with toys, as well as "partially structured" materials such as the Rorschach ink blots.

Obviously, a major handicap to the use of these methods is the difficulty of interpreting the responses or "structures" so obtained. If experimenter A finds one meaning in X's completed model of clay, whereas experimenter B interprets it in a fashion diametrically opposed to this, both cannot be right. In a sense, perhaps, the occurrence of such contradictions is the best possible proof of the intrinsic validity of the method, for it means that, just as the original subject X "projected" some aspect of his own personality into his structuralizing of the amorphous lump of clay, so also experimenter A and experimenter B can regard this structure only through the refracting lenses of their own personalities. If the lenses differ, the images that they yield will also differ. Such conflicting results provide interesting examples of human nature at work, but they do not tell us very much about the individual X that we originally set out to study.

Recognition of this difficulty has led scientific workers to a constant search for more objective methods of studying the individual. Because the devices used for the measurement of various aspects of ability, such as tests of school achievement, of general intelligence, and the like, not only have met the requirement of objectivity in an almost complete degree but also have demonstrated their validity as measures of the characteristics that they were designed to measure, it is not surprising that, in the search for measures of nonintellectual aspects of personality, an attempt should be made to utilize similar procedures. This approach, however, is beset by many difficulties, not the least of which is the fact that direct motivation of the subjects is commonly not feasible, for disclosure of the true purpose of the test usually vitiates the results. On the other hand, the concealed approaches that are usually depended on are likely to be unequally effective for the different members of a group. Furthermore, there is the ever-present likelihood that the more intelligent subjects may "see through" a test in which some degree of social desirability or undesirability is attached to the various possible answers and thus select the former when strict truthfulness would call for the latter. And, finally, the presentation of a series of formal alternatives from which all responses must be selected often leaves insufficient play for the expression of attitudinal differences. Thus the sharp outlines of the individual personality tend to become blurred through the constant necessity of choosing responses of which the best that can be said is that they are the least inappropriate of those available. The finding by Rundquist and Sletto (3) that the rejection of a statement is a more significant indication of a personality tendency than is the acceptance of the contrary statement has some bearing on this point.

We are thus faced with a dilemma. Is it better to encourage free expression on the part of our subjects in spite of the fact that we may have only very imperfect ability to comprehend the language that they use, or shall we insist that they limit themselves to the commonplaces of the international phrase book? For a first adventure into foreign territory, the latter may be desirable, but I doubt that it will yield more than a superficial acquaintance with the personal idiosyncracies of the inhabitants. Arduous as the task may seem, if we wish to understand people, we must learn to comprehend their language.

The Free-association Method

The idea that free associations to common words provide one means of access to the "private world" of an individual is by no means new to psychology. The free-association technique has for many years been regarded as one of the most valuable tools of the psychiatrist and the clinical psychologist. As commonly used by them, however, the procedure does not lend itself well to objective research because of the large amount of subjective judgment involved in interpreting the responses. In spite of such objective features as careful timing, comparison with standardized lists of common responses, and the like, the free-association test, as ordinarily used, is of little value except in the hands of a thoroughly trained clinician.

Moreover, because of the necessity for individual administration, it cannot readily be used in large-scale investigations.

A number of attempts have been made to overcome the second of these two objections, of which the most notable is that by Wyman (5), who developed a method of scoring the associations given to a list of stimulus words in such a way as to yield indexes of intellectual, social, and activity interests. The idea was promising, and the coefficients of self-correlation obtained by Wyman from her own scoring were encouragingly high. However, there were a number of technical problems connected with the administration and scoring of the test that were never satisfactorily worked out; hence the procedure was not made available for general use.

In common with most previous investigations, Wyman's system of scoring involved comparison with a standard list that included all response words given by the standardization group. Separate weights were assigned to each of these words according to the relative frequency with which each response was given by the children rated "high" or "low" in each of the three interest categories considered. Inasmuch as the number of cases in the standardization group was only of moderate size, the experimental error of the weight assigned to an individual word was evidently high, though Wyman does not report exact figures on this head. As is usual in all association-frequency lists, a large proportion of the responses had been given but once. Weights assigned to such rare events are obviously highly unreliable. A further complication arises from the fact that no guide is provided for the scoring of new responses not listed in the key. The scoring of these comparatively rare responses has always been a major problem in the objective treatment of free associations. Even the utilization of the number of rare or "individual" responses as an index to mental abnormality is not free from difficulties, for who shall say what significance shall be assigned to the (possibly) accidental occurrence of a single-frequency response in the standard list? Variations in geographical location, educational background, sex, and similar factors also affect the number of new or "individual" responses likely to be made by any individual case.

In spite of all these difficulties, it has seemed to the writer that some form of the free-association method offers one of the most promising approaches yet available for the study of personality differences. The difficulty of using this procedure lies chiefly in the scoring of the wide variety of different words that are commonly given in response to each stimulus word. An objective principle of grouping is needed in order to simplify the task of the scorer and to increase the reliability of scoring by making it possible to base weights on a larger number of recorded instances.[1] Such a principle is provided by the use of homonyms as stimulus words and classifying the responses, not on the basis of the precise word given but in terms of the specialized meaning that is unconsciously selected by the subject as the basis for his response. An example of such a homonymic word is *light*, which has reference either to weight or to brightness, along with a number of other less common meanings. Another example is *wind*, which in its written form may refer to an atmospheric disturbance or to a rotary movement, as to *wind* a clock. Inasmuch as all stimulus words used in the present experiment were presented in written form, the difference in pronunciation in this and other instances is of no consequence, but oral homonyms having similar pronunciation but dissimilar spelling (such as *wood*, *would*) could not be used.

That the advantages of this procedure have been dimly seen by most students of free association is apparent from the fact that their lists commonly include a greater percentage of homonymic words than would be expected by chance, but, as far as the writer is aware, the present study is the first to make intentional and consistent use of the idea in the development of an objective device for the measurement of a given personality trend. Inasmuch as the study in question is not yet completed, this paper should be looked on as a contribution to methodology rather than as a finished report. However, enough has been done to demonstrate the feasibility of the method and to warrant the presentation of preliminary findings.

THE MEASUREMENT OF SEX DIFFERENCE

The choice of mental masculinity or femininity as an area wherein the procedure might be tried out was dictated both by personal

---

[1] From a standardization group of 1000 fairly homogeneous cases, from 50 to 200 different responses to each stimulus word may be expected. A very small number of these words account for the great bulk of the cases, with the result that from 50 to 75 per cent of the responses will be given but once or twice. Any method of deriving scores for these words, taken individually, is obviously subject to a large experimental error, yet in the aggregate they comprise so large a proportion of the responses of any individual that to ignore them means throwing away a large share of the data.

interest and by the felt need for beginning with a trait that would
permit the easy and objective classification of subjects into contrasted groups. The highly significant study by Terman and Miles
(4), which showed rather conclusively that individual differences in
interests and attitudes follow a pattern that is definitely discriminative as to sex and is sufficiently well integrated within the individual
to yield a self-correlation for their test of approximately $+.78$ for
single-sex groups, affords sufficient evidence that the trait in question
is both real and measurable. A further point of interest lies in the
possibility thus afforded of making certain direct comparisons
between the wholly objective procedure used by Terman and Miles
and the comparatively wide latitude of individual expression allowed
by the free-associational technique.

The first step was the choice of stimulus words. The criterion
of selection was as follows: Each word must have at least two well-
contrasted meanings that are in common use. The Thorndike word
list was used as a guide but could not be completely relied on, inasmuch as the placement of a word in that list might be determined
almost wholly by a single meaning, the second usage being much
more rare. The criterion of difficulty was, therefore, not merely the
occurrence of the word within the first 2000 of the Thorndike list
but also the judgment of the writer that both the homonymic meanings would fall within that level of difficulty. A preliminary list
of 223 words was tried out with 100 elementary-school children in
fifth and sixth grades and with a second group of 100 college freshmen. Both groups were equally divided as to sex. Responses
were tabulated by age and sex groups separately, and from this
preliminary list, all words meeting the following criteria were
selected: (a) not more than 5 per cent of all responses should be
ambiguous, i.e., the scorer should rarely be in doubt as to which of
the two or more contrasted meanings a given response had reference;
(b) the responses should lend themselves to grouping into a relatively
small number of objectively distinguishable categories; (c) of these
categories, at least one must yield a reliably greater frequency for
boys than for girls, and at least one must show the opposite tendency; (d) the sex-discriminative categories must conjointly make up
at least 50 per cent of all the responses given. Of the 223 words, 136
met at least two of these criteria completely and the third one
approximately. These were retained for further trial. An additional list of 104 words, selected on the same principles as the first,

was then added, thus making 240 words to be tried out in the final standardization.

It is a well-recognized principle of the free-association technique that the subject must be urged to give the first associated word that comes to his mind. "Considered" responses are of less significance, because, in the process of taking thought, ideas of social acceptability or intellectual value rather than basic attitudes, emotions, and interest patterns are likely to determine the response. In order to increase the likelihood of securing primary rather than secondary responses, the experiment was disguised as a speed test. The title at the top of the mimeographed list of words was SPEED-OF-ASSOCIA-TION TEST, and the printed instructions were as follows:

"This is a test to see how quickly you can think. In the space after each word, write the first word or phrase that this word makes you think of, no matter what it is. There are no right or wrong answers; this is just a test of speed. Work straight down the list as fast as you can. Give only one response for each word, but *do not omit any and be sure to write legibly, since words that cannot be read will not count toward your score.* Ask no questions after the test has begun."

These instructions were read aloud by the teachers while the children read them silently. Instructions for timing were then given, and after making sure that each subject understood what he was to do, the signal to start was given. Although it is impossible to be sure that the stress placed on speed invariably served its purpose of preventing undesirable deliberation, it was evident from the behavior of the subjects that they at least took the instructions very literally and made every effort to get through in the shortest possible time.

The key for scoring the revised list of words is based on the responses of 800 subjects, 400 of each sex, as follows:

50 children of each sex, ages 11 and 12, grades V, VI, Minneapolis Public Schools
100 children of each sex, ages 13 and 14, Stillwater[1] Junior High School
100 children of each sex, ages 15 and 16, Stillwater[1] Senior High School
100 children of each sex, ages 17 and 18, Stillwater[1] Senior High School
50 students of each sex, ages 18 to 22, University of Minnesota freshmen and sophomores

[1] Stillwater is a city of approximately 7500 inhabitants located about 25 miles from Minneapolis.

The responses of these subjects to each of the 240 stimulus words were tabulated by age and sex separately, and the same criteria for retention or rejection of a given word as had been employed for the preliminary list were again applied. A total of 40 were rejected, leaving a final list of 200 words, which forms the basis of the present report.

The original hope was that a masculinity-femininity score could be determined on the relatively simple basis of the major homonymic divisions, but it was found that better results could often be obtained by taking advantage of subdivisions within these main classes that were very apparent when the distribution of responses was examined. For example, responses to the word *ring* can be grouped into four main classes. The first class consists of references to sound, such as *bell* or *telephone*. The second includes references to an article of jewelry, such as *finger* or *wear*. The third is made up of references to shape, such as *circle;* the fourth of references to sports, as *boxing*. Responses in the first category are at all ages more often given by boys than by girls and so are classed as masculine; those in the fourth category are almost exclusively of masculine origin; and the third category shows no consistent sex trend. In these instances, the classification is in terms of main groupings only. Within the second category, however, three subclasses of response may be distinguished. The most exclusively feminine association has to do with the ring of personal and emotional significance. Such responses as *wedding, engagement, class ring*, etc., make up an appreciable percentage of the responses of the girls at all ages considered but are rarely given by the boys. The second subdivision includes all references to materials of which rings are made (as *gold, silver*, and, more rarely, *iron, copper*, etc.) or to settings (*diamond, ruby*, etc.). These responses are given about as often by one sex as by the other. The third subdivision embraces all other clear references to finger rings or earrings. *Finger, hand, wear, jewelry*, as well as descriptive adjectives clearly referring to finger rings (*pretty, beautiful*, etc.) belong in this group. Such responses are predominantly feminine but do not carry so great a feminine weight as those of the first subclass because of the greater overlapping of the sexes.

Over and above the classification of responses in terms of their overt reference to one or another of the various homonymic meanings of the stimulus word, it was found that, in a number of instances, significant differences between the sexes appeared to be based on

TABLE I
EXAMPLES OF DIFFERENTIAL SEX OVERLAP IN RESPONSE*
A. Stimulus word *bow*

Age group	Hair or hair ribbon		All clear references to archery		All references to persons		References to knots or tying	
	M	F	M	F	M	F	M	F
18-22	0	20	42	6	4	10	30	24
17-18	0	13	64	32	1	5	10	10
15-16	0	27	63	20	2	7	5	5
13-14	0	22	65	22	4	6	1	1
11-12	0	10	32	12	2	2	6	2

B. Stimulus word *file*

	All references to wood or metals		All references to fingernails or manicuring		References to tools or mechanical operations		References to offices or to office work	
	M	F	M	F	M	F	M	F
18-22	6	0	16	32	24	2	26	46
17-18	15	0	16	29	36	10	21	30
15-16	14	2	16	36	42	16	16	25
13-14	24	5	12	39	44	18	6	23
11-12	4	0	12	18	14	4	14	18

C. Stimulus word *ram*

	All references to ramrods or guns		Goat or buck		Sheep or lamb		Animal (nonspecific)	
	M	F	M	F	M	F	M	F
18-22	4	0	30	12	24	36	4	10
17-18	17	9	22	14	24	25	4	12
15-16	10	5	23	18	28	32	8	10
13-14	10	5	29	16	25	28	5	18
11-12	6	0	10	6	12	12	0	14

D. Stimulus word *trip*

	All references to falling, stumbling, etc.		References to trains or railroads		References to automobiles or driving		Names of specific places	
	M	F	M	F	M	F	M	F
18-22	28	8	2	18	10	2	12	16
17-18	24	9	1	9	12	9	13	15
15-16	17	14	2	6	10	4	4	11
13-14	35	22	5	12	17	9	4	14
11-12	20	14	0	14	10	6	12	12

* Partial list only. All figures are percentages. For number of cases at each age, see p. 93.

such small distinctions that in the interests of objectivity it seemed desirable to define them in terms of the specific words to be included within a given class, all others being excluded in spite of apparent similarity. Thus, in response to the word *firm*, the words *solid, hard, stiff*, and *tight* are "masculine," whereas *strong* and *strength* are "feminine." For the word *box*, the response *wood* is highly masculine, whereas the names of other materials, such as *paper* or *cardboard*, are as likely to be given by one sex as by the other. At all ages, boys more often than girls respond to the word *ace*, either with the nonspecific word *card* or by naming cards of low denomination, such as *deuce, five-spot*, etc., whereas girls more optimistically give the response *trumps* or specify a picture card as *king, queen*.

The question of differential *vs.* equal weighting of responses has been a point of controversy among test constructors almost from the beginning of group testing. The correlation between weighted and unweighted scores is usually high enough to lead many people to the conclusion that the relatively small increase in self-correlations and in agreement with other criteria that is generally accomplished by means of differential weighting is not great enough to compensate for the greater time requirement and the increased likelihood of errors in scoring. However, the enormous variation in the amount of the sex overlap for different responses to the same word (examples of which are seen in Table I) led us to feel that some sort of weighted scoring should at least be tried out. The problem is not a simple one, because of the many instances in which a given type of response is comparatively infrequent, yet when it does occur it not only is confined to a single sex (within the limits of the sample of 800 cases used in standardization) but conforms so closely to the general pattern of response of that sex as to leave little doubt that it should be included among the sex-discriminative responses. Nevertheless, any method of weighting that takes account of "statistical significance" will give a relatively low weight to these responses; others, in which the sex overlap is far greater, will nevertheless receive high weights if they are of sufficiently frequent occurrence.

The system of weighting responses used thus far is almost certainly not the best that can be devised, because of the spurious influences of the factor just mentioned. Weights from 1 to 5 were assigned according to the probability of recurrence of a difference in the same direction as calculated by the χ^2 method. Weights were assigned arbitrarily as follows:

Level of Significance	Weight
.10	1
.05	2
.02	3
.01	4
.001	5

A further requirement was that the direction of the difference must be the same in each of the five age groups, except that a weight of 1 might be given in cases in which, at one age level only, the frequency for the sexes was equal or showed a very slight inversion, provided that this was counterbalanced by a sufficiently marked difference in the other four groups to render the probability of nonrecurrence not greater than .05 and that the character of response conformed to the general pattern of sex difference appearing in the test as a whole.

This method promised to yield highly satisfactory results, but, as further data have accumulated, it has become increasingly evident that optimal weighting should be based chiefly upon the discriminative value of an item as indicated by small sex overlap and high internal consistency within single-sex groups. A further modification that now seems desirable is somewhat greater leniency, from the standpoint of probable recurrence, in the classification of a response as "masculine" or "feminine." Obviously, there is a difference in the amount of risk that one is willing to take in respect to a single one of 200 items and that which it is prudent to assume in respect to a final score. The present plan, which classes any response as ambivalent unless the probability of error in classification is not greater than 1 chance in 10, actually means that on the average paper about 30 per cent of the responses receive zero credit. A 3 to 1 risk is perhaps not too great, particularly for those responses in which the low level of significance is determined chiefly by comparative infrequency of responses of that type, whereas those that do occur show small overlap between the sexes and high conformity with the general pattern of sex difference on the test as a whole. Preliminary work with a method of weighting that takes account of the factors just mentioned indicates that an appreciable improvement in reliability and in correlation with other indications of masculine-feminine trends in behavior may be brought about through improved weighting of items, but this work is not far enough advanced to justify reporting at this time. The data presented herein are accordingly based on the method of weighting hitherto used. As will be seen, even this admittedly somewhat faulty procedure yields results of distinct significance.

Within the space limitations of this paper, it is impossible to present the scoring key in detail, but the following example of the scoring of a single word will perhaps serve as a sufficient example.[1] It will be noted that the principle followed is to list first, in capital letters, those responses that must be given verbatim, other words of the same apparent class not being credited. Following, in ordinary type, are descriptions of classes of response in which any word or phrase conforming to the described pattern is given the same score. Examples are given of each type of response. The most common of the ambivalent responses (which receive no score) are also listed.

SCORING KEY FOR STIMULUS-WORD "OPERATION"

Score

M............... DOCTOR, SURGEON

MMMM........ All references to *cutting* or to *surgical instruments*, as *incision, knife, surgery, cut*, etc.

MMM.......... All clear references to *nonsurgical operations*, as *machine, act, work*, etc.

FF.............. All references to *special kinds of surgical operation* or to *part of body operated on*, as *appendicitis, tonsils, eye*, etc.

FF.............. All references to *general bodily conditions*, nurses*, or *medication*, as *sick, medicine*, etc.

F.............. References to *place where operation is performed*, as *hospital, bed, table*, etc.

F.............. All references to *persons other than doctors or nurses*, as *mother, man*. Include *personal pronouns*, as *mine*.

Common ambivalent responses include all specific references to *pain, soreness*, or *discomfort*, to *degree of seriousness*, as bad, fatal, etc., or to *outcome*, as *success*, failure, recovery, death.

* Compare with ambivalent responses.

Points where confusion is most likely to occur are marked with an asterisk, calling the scorer's attention to the need for holding the distinction in question clearly in mind.

Objectivity of scoring was tested by having two clerical assistants, neither of whom had had any previous experience in the scoring of any kind of test, score 25 papers of each sex independently and compare the results. Before beginning the experiment, two other

[1] In addition to the specific instructions for each word, the key includes a set of general rules in which special attention is given to such matters as the handling of ambiguous responses, "klang" associations, different forms of the same word, etc.

papers of each sex had been scored in collaboration with the writer
in order to make sure that the procedure was understood. A correlation of slightly over $+.98$ was secured between the two scorings for
each of the two sex groups taken separately. This figure is the more
significant, because, in order to make the test of objectivity as rigid
as possible, the papers selected for scoring were from a small Southern
college for Negroes and contained a goodly sprinkling of colloquial-
isms as well as a greater number of errors in spelling than those from
a typical sixth-grade class in a Northern city. The average number
of responses out of the total of 200 on which the scoring differed was
3.3; this reduces to 2.6 if purely careless errors are omitted from the
total.

Self-correlations (odd *vs.* even items corrected for total length
by the Spearman-Brown formula) for single-sex groups are fairly
high, although, as was pointed out, the system of weighting now in
process of development promises to bring about considerable
improvement in this respect. For various single-sex groups,[1] the
corrected coefficients run from $+.64$ to $+.94$, with the median at
$+.79$. Preliminary results indicate that by the improved method of
scoring the self-correlations for typical single-sex groups may be
brought close to $+.90$.

The question of the validity of the test as a generalized measure
of masculine-feminine differences, as Terman and Miles have pointed
out for their more formalized procedure, is not so easy to answer as
it might seem. The mere fact that there is very small overlap
between the sexes[2] indicates that it measures at least a limited
area of the interests and attitudes that characterize the sexes,
whereas the comparatively spontaneous nature of the responses,
occurring as they do without specific suggestion, except for the
stimulus word which is the same for all, is evidence that they are
based on fairly well-integrated aspects of the personality. If the
responses were largely or wholly circumstantial, they could hardly
show the clear-cut differentiation of pattern that is evidenced both
by individuals and by sex groups.

[1] Needless to say, none of these cases had been used in the derivation of the
original scores, since the inclusion of such papers would bring about a spurious
increase in the apparent reliability.

[2] The total raw score is the sum of the M responses minus the sum of the F
responses, thus placing the indifference point at zero. Among our subjects,
about 5 per cent earn scores with sign opposite to that usual for their sex.

The correlation with the Terman-Miles M-F test (Form A), although positive, is, however, not high for single-sex groups. Both tests were administered to 45 boys and 60 girls, all students at Minnesota University High School. These students constitute a highly selected group, from the standpoint of both intellectual level and cultural background. Nearly all the fathers of these children belong to the learned professions or occupy important industrial positions; a large number of them are members of the university faculty. For these cases, the correlation between the association total and the Terman-Miles score was +.54 for the boys and +.33 for the girls. Because of the distinctly bimodal character of the combined distributions for both tests, the computation of a Pearsonian correlation for sexes combined is unwarranted, but, inasmuch as the scores of all except 7 of the 105 cases had the same sign in both tests (plus or minus, indicating, respectively, a masculine or feminine predominance in type of response) and in 3 of the 7 cases the disagreement in sign was of little significance, since both scores were close to the zero point, the relationship within the total distribution is fairly high.

On both tests, the girls showed slightly more than the usual number of minor sex inversions. Internal evidence suggests that this is mainly a cultural phenomenon. For 4 of the 5 girls who made plus scores on the Terman-Miles test, this score is determined wholly or in large part by Exercise 4 alone. This exercise has to do with claimed affective reactions—fear, anger, disgust, pity, and moral condemnation—toward a large number of specified situations. As a rule, the claim of a marked affective response is a feminine characteristic; that of a moderate or low response is masculine. Of the 60 girls in this group, 37 made a "masculine" score on this exercise. This tendency is especially noticeable in the case of the girl for whom the discrepancy between the association test and the Terman-Miles test is greatest. Her score on the association test was −148, which ranks her within the top 25 per cent of the girls of her age in "femininity." On Exercise 4 of the Terman-Miles test, her score was +58, which is exceeded by only 5 of the boys in our group. As a result, her score on the test as a whole was +25, in spite of the fact that on each of the other six exercises her score was slightly feminine. Terman and Miles have shown that highly educated women commonly tend toward the masculine norm on Exercise 4. It is therefore probable that the high educational and cultural level of the homes from which these girls come has something to do with their departure from the typical feminine norm on this exercise.

Cultural influence of a somewhat different kind appears to be responsible for the greater than usual number of "masculine" scores made by these girls on the association test. Of the four girls earning plus scores, examination of the responses suggests that more than the usual feminine interest in athletics is the main factor at work in the single case in which a masculine score on the association test is accompanied by a definitely feminine score on the Terman-Miles test. Her score on the former test was $+39$; on the latter, -57, which, according to the published tables, is equivalent to about a 35th percentile rank in terms of femininity. This girl has a twin brother who is an excellent athlete. As far as possible, the sister shares in his interests and strives to imitate his athletic accomplishments. Her association test is notable for its large number of athletic terms, which seem to crop out whenever such an association is in any way reasonable. In spite of this, there are enough counterbalancing feminine responses to keep her total score of $+39$ decidedly below the median of $+90$ earned by boys of her age. Her twin brother's score of $+85$ is perhaps less strongly "masculine" than might be expected in view of his marked athletic interests. It is possible that this score may likewise have been modified by the close association with his twin sister.

For the three remaining girls who made plus scores on the association test, the findings are as follows:

	Association score	Percentile rank	Terman-Miles score	Percentile rank
a	$+1$	3	-36	22
b	$+23$	1	$+26$	2
c	$+12$	2	-7	12

For the second of these cases, the agreement between percentile ranks on the two measures is very close. Although the correspondence is less marked in the other two cases, both scores nevertheless fall within the lowest 25 per cent. It appears, therefore, that, in spite of the very different methods of appraisal, the two measures agree rather closely in their selection of cases that deviate from the personality patterns that are usual for their sex. This conclusion is

verified by the results for the boys.   Only one boy makes a feminine
score on the association test; his score on the Terman-Miles is also
feminine.   One additional boy makes a feminine score of −12 on the
Terman-Miles; his score on the association test is +23, which corresponds to a percentile rank of approximately 15.

In the case of the boys, there is also fair agreement between the
scores at the most masculine extreme, but for the girls there are many
discrepancies at all levels except the lowest.   The two boys making
the most masculine scores on the association test also rank at the top
of the list on the Terman-Miles test.

DISCUSSION

The two main respects in which the free-association technique, as
herein described, differs from that used by previous workers are,
first, the use of homonyms as stimulus words, a practice that has the
effect of increasing the spread of responses, because, in effect, different subjects are actually responding to different words, the selection
of which depends on their own idiosyncratic pattern of interests and
attitudes.   The second feature consists in the categorizing of
responses into groups on the basis of some common characteristic of
meaning that has empirically been found to have unequal appeal for
individuals differing in respect to the trait that it is desired to
measure.

The device of disguising the test as a simple speed test is merely
an adaptation to group use of the usual procedure in the clinical testing of individuals.   It is nevertheless an important factor in lessening
the probability that the subjects may shift from the immediate and
spontaneous response that it is desired to secure to a more deliberate
and "intellectualized" choice among the various alternatives that,
given sufficient time, are likely to suggest themselves.

It should be emphasized that this study has thus far been largely
exploratory.   Nevertheless, the results obtained appear to justify
certain conclusions.

It has been demonstrated that the free-association technique can
be effectively utilized in large-scale investigations.   After a very
small amount of preliminary training, the responses can be scored by
clerical workers of moderate competence with a degree of accuracy
that is only slightly less than is ordinarily found for "wholly objective" tests.   This makes it possible to retain the advantages of free
expression without loss of objectivity in scoring and interpretation.

Further utilization of this type of approach lies in the possibility of the development of multiple scoring keys for the appraisal of various aspects of personality from a single administration of the test.   A comparison, for example, of the responses of delinquents and nondelinquents of similar age and sex or the responses of highly popular children with those of children who are shunned and avoided, as well as those of many other contrasted groups, might all be worked out by the preparation of multiple scoring keys for the same list of stimulus words.   Vocational interests, particularly in those areas where personality characteristics are of prime importance for success, might also be approached in this way.   It is very possible that, by comparing the responses of successful and unsuccessful members of such professional groups as elementary-school teachers or social workers, a valuable aid to the selection of candidates for training in these fields could be developed.

References

1. FRANK, L. K.   Projective methods for the study of personality.   *J. Psychol.*, 1939, **8**, 389–413.
2. MILES, C. C., & TERMAN, L. M.   Sex differences in the association of ideas. *Amer. J. Psychol.*, 1929, **41**, 165–206.
3. RUNDQUIST, E., & SLETTO, R.   Personality in the depression; a study in the measurement of attitudes.   Minneapolis: University of Minnesota Press, 1936.
4. TERMAN, L. M., & MILES, C. C., *et al.*   Sex and personality.   New York: McGraw-Hill, 1936.
5. WYMAN, J. B.   Tests of intellectual, social and activity interests.   *In* Terman, L. M., *Genetic Studies of Genius*.   Stanford University, California: Stanford Univ. Press, 1925.   Vol. I, 455–483.

CHAPTER VI

RESPONSES BY RHESUS MONKEYS TO STIMULI HAVING MULTIPLE SIGN-VALUES[1]

By

H. F. HARLOW

University of Wisconsin

INTRODUCTION

The study of human personality is by definition the study of man, and direct investigations within the field of human personality must be made with human beings as subjects. Indirect contributions to this field have, however, been made by comparative psychology in the investigation of problems relating to intelligence, drives, emotions, and even abnormal phenomena. One shortcoming of the comparative studies has been the simplicity of the problems studied. Intelligence has been measured by the performances of albino rats in running mazes; drives, by the aimless wanderings of rats in revolving cages; emotions, by the reflex responses of decorticate kittens; and abnormal phenomena, by the cataleptic stupors of severely puffed-at rats and shocked pigs.

The only escape of the comparative psychologist from the criticism of oversimplicity lies in the demonstration that more complex phenomena can be tested in subhuman animals than has previously been attempted. The closer the tests on such subjects can be made to approach the level of tests applicable to the human being, the greater their generality as they relate to the interpretation of both normal and pathological human behavior.

The following investigation is a demonstration of the ability of a subhuman animal to respond to complex learning situations. It is not an attempt to investigate the "limits" of the learning ability of the monkey but is merely a demonstration that complex learning

[1] This research was supported by graduate research funds of the University of Wisconsin 1940–1941 and by assistance from WPA official project 10957. Special credit is due to Anton Bollig, who tested subjects 52 and 53 through test V.

problems can be solved with relative ease by a subhuman primate. The general methods described have wide applicability, and by their use it is possible to simulate many test situations previously attempted on man alone. It is in the development of these procedures and their use in both normal and pathological subjects that a contribution can be made by the comparative psychologist to the field of human personality.

Many of the countless thousands of stimuli to which human beings react have multiple and diverse meanings dependent on the context imposed by the situation or on qualifications imposed by related signs. These secondary factors are of great importance, because they may not only influence but actually reverse the response to the primary stimulus. The formation of relationships of such a nature that appropriate differential responses are evoked not only by individual stimuli but also by changes of the total situation in which these individual stimuli operate makes possible a variability of behavior that would not otherwise be obtained.

A private garage may be a stimulus either to drive-a-car-in or to drive-a-car-out, depending on the context supplied by the position of the car—the whether-or-not-ness that the car is in the garage or is out of the garage. Related signs are the presence and position of the garage door. If the car is out of the garage and the garage door is open, the garage is a stimulus-to-drive-a-car-in, but it is usual for the meaning of the situation to be altered when the garage door is closed. In such situations, failure to obtain the appropriate meaning from the related signs or from the patterning and arrangement of the stimuli in the total situation is unfortunate.

PROBLEM

The purpose of the following investigation was to study the performance of the rhesus monkey in the solution of problems in which a single stimulus acquired multiple sign-values. Thus, a single stimulus evoked varying and even antagonistic responses, depending on the particular patterning of the total situation. The following problems are designed to produce increasing complexity of factors determining the response to the primary stimulus. In the final test, the animal can respond correctly only by relating appropriately four variables: (*a*) the nature of the primary stimulus, the sample-object, (*b*) the nature of the food-sign, the presence or absence of food beneath the sample-object, (*c*) the positions of the

choice-objects, and (*d*) the identity or nonidentity of sample-object
with either or both choice-objects.

SUBJECTS

Four rhesus monkeys were used as subjects.   These animals had
undergone an intensive taming procedure before any testing was

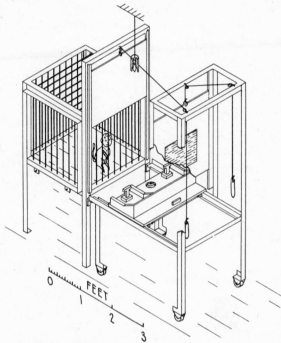

FIG. 1.—General test apparatus illustrating sliding tray and form of stimulus
objects.

carried out and had been tested on a series of discrimination and
discrimination-reversal problems.

APPARATUS

The apparatus used in these experiments is an adaptation of the
apparatus illustrated in Fig. 1 and consists of an experimental cage,
in which the subject is confined, and a framework in front of the cage,
so arranged that a sliding tray may be presented to the animal.   The
sliding tray fits on a wheeled base that runs along metal tracks.
Dimensions are indicated in Fig. 1, and materials used in the cage
are illustrated in Fig. 2.   Two screens are shown in the drawing.

The forward screen is made of presswood and hides the tray from the monkey when the stimulus-objects are being arranged and loaded. The back screen holds a one-way vision screen that makes it possible for the experimenter to observe the subject without danger of giving secondary cues. The one-way screen was used only in the control tests.

A narrow strip of wood separated the sliding tray into two divisions, a sample-object-area and a choice-objects-area. The tray was equipped with three food wells, one in the sample-object-area and two in the choice-objects-area.

Two sets of stimulus-objects were used throughout the experiment, and these objects are drawn on the tray in Fig. 1. One was a set of green crosses, 3 inches high, with a 2-inch crossarm and a 2-inch square presswood base. The other was a set of electric push buttons approximately $1\frac{3}{4}$ inches in diameter and $\frac{3}{4}$ inch high. Later in this chapter, the cross is indicated by the symbol x and the push button by the symbol o.

PROCEDURE

Preliminary procedures. Before the beginning of the present experiment, all four subjects had been trained to solve matching-from-sample, nonmatching-from-sample and alternation of matching-from-sample and nonmatching-from-sample when the same stimulus-objects were presented on different colored boards. The matching-from-sample tests were carried out on a black board and the nonmatching-from-sample tests on a yellow board. The procedures used in attaining these results were similar to those described by Weinstein (1) in his original investigation, which showed that monkeys could solve matching-from-sample problems.

General test procedures. In the following experiment, all testing was carried out with the use of a single sliding tray, painted green. Each test trial was initiated by lowering the forward screen and placing food under the appropriate stimulus-object or stimulus-objects. The sliding tray was then pushed forward just within reach of the subject, the screen raised, and the animal allowed to respond. In case of error, the tray was withdrawn, the unattained reward exposed, and the trial rerun.

With the use of the method described, a series of tests was given. The specific procedures used for each of these are individually described.

At the conclusion of the last experimental test, control trials were run, with the experimenter entirely hidden from the subject by the one-way screen.

Test I: Alternation of matching-from-sample and nonmatching-from-sample. In the matching-from-sample tests, the subject

(a) Food under sample.
Right-position object correct.

(b) Food under sample.
Left-position object correct.

(c) No food under sample.
Right-position object correct.

(d) No food under sample.
Left-position object correct.

FIG. 2.—Matching-from-sample (a and b), and nonmatching-from-sample (c and d).

first displaces the sample-object and then chooses the *identical* choice-object. A piece of apple lies beneath the sample-object, a piece of orange under the correct choice-object. As illustrated in Figs. 2a and 2b, either cross or push button may serve as the sample-object. Two of the four matching-from-sample configurations are shown in this figure.

To solve the nonmatching-from-sample tests, the animal must displace the sample-object and then choose the *nonidentical* choice-

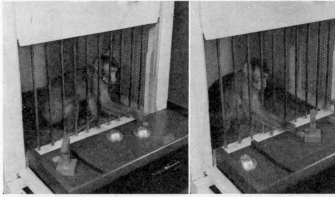

(e) Food under sample.   (f) No food under sample.
    Right-position object correct.   Left-position object correct.

(g) Food under sample.   (h) No food under sample.
    Left-position object correct.   Right-position object correct.

FIG. 2 (*continued*).—Sign-discriminated-antagonistic-position-habits (*e* and *f*), and reversed-sign-discriminated-antagonistic-position habits (*g* and *h*).

object. Since the four configurations used in the nonmatching problem are the same as those used in the matching problem, the sole cue for correct solution lies in the fact that there is no food under the sample-object in ·these tests, whereas there was food under the sample-object in the matching test. *Solution of the two antagonistic problems is made on the basis of differences in the food-sign.* In the nonmatching test, a piece of orange was placed within the food-well under the nonmatching choice-object.   Two of the four nonmatching-from-sample configurations are shown in Figs. 2c and 2d, and a comparison of these with Figs. 2a and 2b clearly illustrates the nature of the antagonistic responses.   Thus, in Fig. 2a (matching), response to an x sample-object evokes a *right-position x choice-object choice*, whereas in Fig. 2d (nonmatching), response to an x sample-object evokes a *left-position o choice-object choice*.

Each day's run consisted of 25 matching and 25 nonmatching trials, and these were run in an irregular but predetermined order. No more than three matching or three nonmatching trials ever followed each other.   No single choice-object, cross or push button, and no single position, right or left, was ever correct more than three times in succession.   The grouping of trials was so arranged that the problem shifted from matching to nonmatching or from nonmatching to matching 25 times in each day's run.

The three criteria for solution of test I were 23 correct out of 25 each of matching, nonmatching, and shift trials in a single day's run. A shift trial is a trial in which the problem reverses from matching to nonmatching or from nonmatching to matching; thus, the total number of trials is only 50 per day.

Test II: Sign-differentiated-antagonistic-position-habits. The procedure used in running the sign-differentiated-antagonistic-position-habits (designated as SDAPH) was the same during the training trials as that used in the alternation of matching-from-sample and nonmatching-from-sample, save for the configuration of the three stimulus-objects presented and the relationships existing between the sample-object and the correct choice-object.   In the SDAPH trials, the stimulus-objects were so arranged on the sliding tray that the *two choice-objects were identical*, and the sample-object did not match either choice-object.   When the cross served as the sample-object, the choice-objects were two push buttons; when a push button was placed in the sample-object area, two crosses were placed in the choice-objects area.

In half the trials, food (a piece of apple) was placed beneath the sample-object, and correct solution of the problem depended on the subject's choosing the choice-object most distant from the sample, the choice-object lying in the *right-position* (right and left always given in terms of the direction in which the experimenter faces). When no food was placed beneath the sample-object, the nearest choice-object (the *left-position* object) was correct. A piece of orange always served as a reward for selection of the correct choice-object.

Twenty-five right-position choices and 25 left-position choices made up each day's run, and these were always presented in an irregular but predetermined order. No more than three right-position or three left-position trials ever followed each other, and a single stimulus-object, cross or push button, was never correct more than three times in succession. It should be noted in this test that either stimulus-object, cross or push button, could stand for either the correctness of the right-position or the left-position choice-object. The differentiating sign was the presence or absence of food under the sample-object.

The three criteria for solution of test II were 23 correct out of 25 right-position, left-position, and shift trials in a single day's run.

Two of the four SDAPH configurations are illustrated in Figs. *2e* and *2f*.

Test III: Alternation of matching-from-sample, nonmatching-from-sample, and sign-differentiated-antagonistic-position-habits. As soon as the monkeys attained the criteria for learning the SDAPH, these two antagonistic-position principles (depending on the presence or absence of food under either of two different sample-objects) were combined in random sequence with the matching-from-sample and nonmatching-from-sample problems. The trial order was so arranged that matching, nonmatching, right-position SDAPH and left-position SDAPH were never presented more than twice in succession. Care was also taken to ensure that neither the right nor left position was ever correct more than three times in succession, regardless of the principle involved.

Each day, 40 trials were run (10 trials of each test) for a minimum of 5 days. The criteria for solution of the problem were made in terms of a block of 100 trials (25 trials each of matching, nonmatching, right-position SDAPH and left-position SDAPH). Forty-five out of 50 correct responses on each of the paired problems of matching and nonmatching and right- and left-position choices of the SDAPH was demanded, with the added provision that 22 correct out of 25 choices be made on each of the four principles involved.

Test IV: Reversed-sign-differentiated-antagonistic-position-habits. The reversed-sign-differentiated-antagonistic-position-habits (designated as RSDAPH) differed from the SDAPH both in configuration of objects presented and in the fact that the *sign-value*

of the presence or absence of food under the sample-object was reversed.
In the RSDAPH, three identical stimulus-objects—three crosses or
three push buttons—were always placed on the sliding tray, one in
the sample-object-area and two in the choice-objects-area.

In half the trials, food (a piece of apple) was placed under the
sample-object, and in these trials correct solution of the problem
depended on the subject's choosing the nearest choice-object, the
left-position object.   When no food was under the sample-object
the choice-object in the *right-position* was correct.   Two of the four
RSDAPH are illustrated in Figs. 2g and 2h, and comparison of these
figures with Figs. 2e and 2f shows the nature of the antagonistic-position responses demanded by the food-sign of presence or absence of
food under the sample-object.   Even when the sample-object is the
same in the two problems (RSDAPH and SDAPH), the food-sign
elicits antagonistic spatial responses, the sole cue for correct response
being the configuration of the stimulus-objects.

The number of trials run daily, the order of presentation, and the
criteria for correct solution for the RSDAPH was, in all cases, similar
to those of the SDAPH.

**Test V: Alternation every five trials of sign-discriminated-
antagonistic-position-habits and reversed-sign-discriminated-
antagonistic-position-habits.**   Combination of the SDAPH and
RSDAPH was first accomplished by running groups of 5 trials of
each test alternately until a total of 50 trials was completed each day.
A particular stimulus-object and a particular choice-object-position
was never correct more than three times in succession.   The test was
considered solved as soon as a subject made not less than 23 correct
out of 25 trials on each of the problems in a single day's run and made
not more than one error on the 10 shift trials, *i.e.*, trials in which the
problem changed from SDAPH to RSDAPH or from RSDAPH to
SDAPH.   The first trial in each day's run was counted as a shift trial.

**Test VI: Random alternation of sign-discriminated-antagonis-
tic-position-habits with reversed-sign-discriminated-antagonistic-position-habits.**   The final step in the combination of the
SDAPH and the RSDAPH consisted in running these problems in a
random but predetermined order.   A total of 50 trials, 25 on each
problem, constituted a day's run.   No more than three SDAPH or
three RSDAPH trials ever followed each other.   No single choice-
object, cross or push button, and no single position, right or left, was
ever correct more than three times in succession.

The three criteria for final solution of test VI were not less than 23 correct out of each of 25 SDAPH, RSDAPH, and shift trials.

Test VII: Alternation of matching-from-sample, nonmatching-from-sample, sign-differentiated-antagonistic-position-habits, and reversed-sign-differentiated-antagonistic-position-habits. In the final stage of testing the responses of the monkeys to stimuli having multiple sign-values, the four situations previously described were all combined. The general procedure used was the same as that employed in test III, save for the fact that equal numbers of matching, nonmatching, SDAPH, and RSDAPH trials were run. Criteria for the solution of the problem were set up in terms of blocks of 100 trials (first hundred, second hundred, third hundred, etc.). The subjects were required to make 90 out of 100 correct responses and to make not less than 22 correct out of 25 responses on each of the four problems.

After the subjects had solved this problem, 100 additional trials were run, with the experimenter concealed from the animals by means of a one-way vision screen.

RESULTS

Preliminary tests. The results obtained in the preliminary tests are briefly presented in the following table and indicate the previous experience of the monkeys on tests of the matching-from-sample type.

NUMBER OF TRAINING TRIALS TO ATTAIN A CRITERION OF 90 PER CENT CORRECT IN 50 TRIALS FOR MATCHING-FROM-SAMPLE, NONMATCHING-FROM-SAMPLE, AND ALTERNATION OF THE TWO PROBLEMS*

Subject number	Matching-from-sample	Nonmatching-from-sample	Alternation of matching and nonmatching
50	500	325	250
51	600	300	300
52	1150	325	400
53	900	425	350

* These preliminary tests were all run with the use of a black sliding tray for all matching trials and a yellow sliding tray for all nonmatching trials.

Regular test series.

Test I: Alternation of matching-from-sample and nonmatching-from-sample. The results for test I, in which matching and nonmatching trials were run in a random order on a single green tray, with no differentiating sign other than the presence or absence of food under the sample-object, are presented in Table I.

TABLE I

NUMBER OF TRAINING TRIALS AND NUMBER OF CORRECT RESPONSES IN THE LAST 25 MATCHING, NONMATCHING, AND SHIFT TRIALS FOR SOLUTION OF TEST I

Subject number	Training trials	Number correct responses in last day's run		
		Matching trials	Nonmatching trials	Shift trials
50	150	23	25	24
51	350	24	24	24
52	1050	24	24	23
53	300	23	24	23

Test II: Sign-differentiated-antagonistic-position-habits. In Table II are presented the data on the SDAPH. As these data indicate, little difficulty was encountered by any of the subjects in the formation of these antagonistic *spatial* habit systems.

TABLE II

NUMBER OF TRAINING TRIALS AND NUMBER OF CORRECT RESPONSES IN THE LAST 25 LEFT-POSITION, RIGHT-POSITION, AND SHIFT TRIALS FOR SOLUTION OF TEST II

Subject number	Training trials	Number of correct responses in last day's run		
		Left-position trials	Right-position trials	Shift trials
50	100	24	24	24
51	150	25	23	23
52	150	23	23	23
53	250	24	24	24

Test III: Alternation of matching-from-sample, non-matching-from-sample, and sign differentiated-antagonistic-position-habits. Combining the SDAPH with the previously learned matching-from-sample and nonmatching-from-sample tests also occasioned little difficulty. Subject 51 solved these problems in random alternation in the first 100 trials. Subjects 52 and 53 failed only because they made five and four errors, respectively, on the matching tests. Subject 50 failed to meet the criteria of success in the first 100 trials on both matching and SDAPH. All subjects, however, would have met success in the first 100 trials had the criterion been 20 correct out of 25 trials, which would still have been statistically above chance. The data for test III are presented in Table III.

TABLE III

NUMBER OF TRAINING TRIALS AND NUMBER OF CORRECT RESPONSES IN THE LAST 25 MATCHING, NONMATCHING, AND RIGHT- AND LEFT-POSITION SDAPH TRIALS FOR SOLUTION OF TEST III

Subject number	Training trials	Number of correct responses in last 100 trials			
		Matching trials	Nonmatching trials	Left-position trials	Right-position trials
50	400	23	24	24	23
51	100	25	23	24	25
52	300	24	23	23	23
53	200	23	23	24	24

Test IV: Reversed-sign-differentiated-antagonistic-position-habits. The results obtained on the RSDAPH showed considerable individual differences on the part of the monkeys. *Subject 51 made an error on trial 1 and then proceeded to solve the problem without another error.* Subject 52 made 12 errors in the first group of 50 trials but attained the criteria for success in the next day's run. Subjects 50 and 53 encountered great difficulty, as indicated both by the trials to learn and by disturbed behavior. The difficulty appeared to result from interference between the SDAPH and the RSDAPH. The data are presented in summary form in Table IV.

Test V: Alternation every five trials of sign-discriminated-antagonistic-position-habits and reversed-sign-discriminated-antagonistic-position-habits. The same subjects that did well in the formation of the RSDAPH (51, 52) also did well in the combination of the RSDAPH and the SDAPH. Subjects 50 and 53 encountered difficulty in this test as well as in the previous test. The salient data for all four subjects are given in Table V.

Test VI: Random alternation of sign-discriminated-antagonistic-position-habits with reversed-sign-discriminated-antagonistic-position-habits. As is indicated by the data of Table VI, no serious difficulty was encountered by any of the subjects, except 50, in transferring the alternation of the SDAPH and the RSDAPH from the trial order sequence used in test V to the trial order sequence used in test VI.

TABLE IV

NUMBER OF TRAINING TRIALS AND NUMBER OF CORRECT RESPONSES IN THE LAST 25 LEFT- AND RIGHT-POSITION RSDAPH TRIALS FOR SOLUTION OF TEST IV

Subject number	Training trials	Number of correct responses in last day's run	
		Left-position trials	Right-position trials
50	400	23	23
51	50	24	25
52	100	24	23
53	350	24	23

TABLE V

NUMBER OF TRAINING TRIALS AND NUMBER OF CORRECT RESPONSES IN THE LAST 25 SDAPH AND RSDAPH TRIALS AND THE LAST 10 SHIFT TRIALS FOR SOLUTION OF TEST V

Subject number	Training trials	Number of correct responses in last day's run		
		SDAPH trials	RSDAPH trials	Shift trials
50	400	23	23	9
51	100	25	23	10
52	150	24	23	10
53	350	23	23	9

Test VII : Alternation of matching-from-sample, nonmatching-from-sample, sign-differentiated-antagonistic-position-habits, and reversed-sign-differentiated-antagonistic-position-habits. The data for the final test, in which all four of the foregoing problems were combined in random but predetermined sequence, are given in Table VII. These data show that it is possible for the rhesus monkey to learn to respond appropriately to signs having multiple and antagonistic meanings and to obtain these meanings from the food-sign of presence or absence of food beneath the sample-object and from the patterning of the three stimulus-objects.

The data of Table VII show that, with the exception of subject 50, the final combination of all four problems was solved without undue difficulty. Subject 52 met all criteria for the solution of the problem in the first 100 trials. Subject 51 made only nine errors in the first 100 trials, but five of these were on the 25 RSDAPH trials. Similarly, subject 53 failed to attain all the criteria for success in the first 100 trials only because he made five errors on the first 25 SDAPH trials.

TABLE VI

NUMBER OF TRAINING TRIALS AND NUMBER OF CORRECT RESPONSES IN THE LAST 25 SDAPH, RSDAPH AND SHIFT TRIALS FOR SOLUTION OF TEST VI

Subject number	Training trials	Number of correct responses in last day's run		
		SDAPH trials	RSDAPH trials	Shift trials
50	350	23	24	23
51	150	25	23	24
52	50	25	25	25
53	150	24	24	23

TABLE VII

NUMBER OF TRAINING TRIALS AND NUMBER OF CORRECT RESPONSES IN THE LAST 25 MATCHING, NONMATCHING, SDAPH AND RSDAPH TRIALS FOR SOLUTION OF TEST VII

Subject number	Training trials	Number of correct responses in last 100 trials			
		Matching trials	Nonmatching trials	SDAPH trials	RSDAPH trials
50	600	24	23	23	22
51	200	25	24	25	25
52	100	22	23	25	23
53	200	24	24	25	23

On the control trials for test VII, with the experimenter hidden behind a one-way screen, subject 52 made 100 successive correct responses, 51 made four errors, 53 made five errors, and 50 made nine errors. Subject 50 was the only animal to fail to attain the regular criteria for solution of test VII during the control trials, and his scores were reliably beyond chance. These data show that monkeys can solve the above problem when all possibility of the use of secondary cues by the animals has been eliminated.

DISCUSSION

The discussion will be limited to the data of problem VII. The previous tests are considered as steps leading to the solution of the final test, in which the four antagonistic problems are combined in a random sequence.

The nature of the problem presented by test VII may be envisaged by consideration of the differential characteristics of the 16 situations that comprise the problem. These are listed in Table VIII. The symbols x and o stand for the stimulus-objects, cross and push button, respectively. A bar beneath a symbol indicates the presence of food. The fact that the situations are listed in systematic, regularly alternating order in this table has no connection with the order in the actual tests.

TABLE VIII
TEST SITUATIONS

Matching		Nonmatching	
Sample-object	Choice-objects	Sample-object	Choice-objects
(1) $\underline{x}$	$\underline{x}\ o$	(5) x	$\underline{o}\ x$
(2) $\underline{x}$	$o\ \underline{x}$	(6) x	$x\ \underline{o}$
(3) $\underline{o}$	$\underline{o}\ x$	(7) o	$\underline{x}\ o$
(4) $\underline{o}$	$x\ \underline{o}$	(8) o	$o\ \underline{x}$

SDAPH		RSDAPH	
Sample-object	Choice-objects	Sample-object	Choice-objects
(9) x	$\underline{o}\ o$	(13) $\underline{x}$	$x\ \underline{x}$
(10) $\underline{x}$	$o\ \underline{o}$	(14) x	$\underline{x}\ x$
(11) o	$\underline{x}\ x$	(15) $\underline{o}$	$o\ \underline{o}$
(12) $\underline{o}$	$x\ \underline{x}$	(16) o	$\underline{o}\ o$

Each combination of sample-object and associated food-sign calls for a variety of responses. The responses to sample-object

x may be considered in situations 1, 2, 10, and 13 in Table VIII. In only two of these situations, 1 and 13, is the correct choice-object an x object in the left position. In situation 2, the *position* of the correct choice-object differs from that of situations 1 and 13, and in situation 10, both object and position correct are the opposite of *object and position* correct in situations 1 and 13. Sample-object x may have four different sign-values: (*a*) choose a right-position x choice-object, and avoid the o choice-object, (*b*) choose a left-position x choice-object, and avoid the other o choice-object, (*c*) choose a left-position x choice-object, and avoid the other x choice-object, and (*d*) choose a right-position o choice-object, and avoid the other o choice-object.

There are four different relationships between the sample-objects and the food-signs: $\underline{x}$, x, $\underline{o}$, o. Each of these sample-object and food-sign combinations initiates a complexity of possible responses equal to that described above.

If consideration is given to the relationships that any particular choice-object pattern has to the varying sample-object patterns instead of considering the relationships that any particular sample-object has to the various choice-object patterns, a similar complexity appears.

Thus, each of the four choice-object configurations (*xo, ox, xx,* and *oo*) is associated with each of the four sample-object and food-sign relationships ($\underline{x}$, x, $\underline{o}$, and o). Again, each of the four choice-object configurations may be further differentiated on the basis of the location of the food reward, which may be under either the right or the left choice-object. Thus, the *xo* configuration, *e.g.*, may be broken down into an $\underline{xo}$ or an $x\underline{o}$ pattern. Each of the two *xo* patterns is combined once with an x and once with an o sample-object. For the $\underline{xo}$ pattern, the combined sample-objects are an (*unrewarded*) o and a (*rewarded*) $\underline{x}$. The $x\underline{o}$ pattern appears in combination with an (*unrewarded*) x and also a (*rewarded*) $\underline{o}$. These relationships between sample-object and choice-object patterns hold consistently for all four choice-object configurations. One of the two patterns that comprise each choice-object configuration will appear in combination with an $\underline{x}$ and an o sample-object and the other pattern in combination with an $\underline{o}$ and an x sample-object.

These facts make it obvious that problem VII can be solved only if the subjects respond appropriately to the particular *complex of factors presented in each situation*. This complex of factors consists of four variables: (*a*) the nature of the sample-object, (*b*) the nature of the food-sign, the presence or absence of food beneath the sample-object, (*c*) the positions of the choice-objects, and (*d*) the identity or nonidentity of the sample-objects with either or both choice-objects.

The interaction of these four variables may be demonstrated by holding one variable constant and observing the permutations that appear in the others.

Nature of the sample-object as a constant.   In situations 1, 2, 5, 6, 9, 10, 13, and 14, the *nature of the sample-object is a constant*, since it is always an *x*. In four of these situations, 1, 2, 10, and 13, the *food-sign is positive;* and in four of the situations, 5, 6, 9, and 14, the *food-sign is negative.* A *right-position* choice-object is correct in situations 2, 6, 10, and 14, and a *left-position* choice-object is correct in situations 1, 5, 9, and 13.   The sample and the correct-choice-object are *identical* in situations 1, 2, 13, and 15 and *nonidentical* in situations 5, 6, 9, and 10.

If, instead of considering the eight situations in which an *x* is the sample-object, the eight *o* sample-object situations had been chosen, the same relationships would have obtained.

The food-sign as a constant.   The *food-sign* is positive and *is a constant* in situations 1, 2, 3, 4, 10, 12, 13, and 15.   The sample-object is an *x* in situations 1, 2, 10, and 13 and is an *o* in the other four situations.   The left-position choice-object is correct in situations 1, 3, 13, and 15, and the right-position choice-object is correct in situations 2, 4, 12, and 15.   In situations 1, 2, 13, and 15, the sample-object and correct choice-object are identical.   In the remaining four situations, they are nonidentical.

A similar set of relationships is found in the eight situations in which the food-sign is negative.

Choice-object position as a constant.   In situations 1, 3, 5, 7, 9, 11, 13, and 15, the correct choice-object is always in the left position. An *x* sample-object is correct in situations 1, 5, 9, and 13 and an *o* sample-object in the other four situations.   The food-sign is positive in situations 1, 3, 13, and 15 and is negative in situations 5, 7, 9, and 11.   In situations 1, 3, 13, and 15 the sample-object and the correct choice-object are identical, and in the remaining four situations they are nonidentical.

The correct choice-object is always in the right position in all even-numbered situations, but the basic relationships between the variables are the same as described in the foregoing paragraph.

Identity or nonidentity of the sample and correct-choice-object as a constant. Sample-object and correct choice-object are identical in situations 1, 2, 3, 4, 13, 14, 15, and 16. In four of these situations, 1, 2, 13, and 14, the sample-object is an x, and in the remainder, the sample-object is an o. The food-sign is positive in *six* situations, 1, 2, 3, 4, 13, and 15, and is negative in only two, 14 and 16. The left choice-object is correct in situations 1, 3, 13, and 15, and the right choice-object is correct in situations 2, 4, 14, and 16.

A similar set of relationships is found in the eight situations in which sample-object and correct choice-object are not identical.

The difficulty of the problem is further enhanced by the fact that it cannot be solved by immediate observation of the total situation. The monkey must displace the sample-object before the nature of the food-sign is revealed, and only then can he respond appropriately to the other two variables, the positions of the choice-objects and the identity or nonidentity of sample-object with either or both choice-objects.

After the monkey responds to the sample-object and the food-sign, the cues furnished by the choice-objects further delimit the problem. If the two choice-objects are identical, selection of the appropriate choice-object must be made on the basis of position, an SDAPH or an RSDAPH trial. The differential-position sign is furnished by the identity or nonidentity of the sample-object with the choice-objects and by the nature of the food-sign. The nature of the sample-object has meaning only in relation to the nature of the choice-objects and is a sign of *where* not *what* the correct choice-object is.

If the two choice-objects differ, selection of the appropriate choice-object must be made on the basis of the nature of the object, a matching or nonmatching trial. The differential signs that indicate the nature of the correct choice-object are the nature of the sample-object and the food-sign. These signs designate *what* not *where* the correct choice-object is. The identity or nonidentity of sample-object and choice-object has no sign-value, since the sample-object is always identical with one choice-object and nonidentical with the other.

These data show that the rhesus monkey is capable, after a careful taming period and a consistent, regular series of training trials, of solving problems of greater complexity than has heretofore been demonstrated. A single stimulus acquires differential sign-values for each of four different situations, the nature of these sign-values being determined by the operation of three variables other than that of the nature of the stimulus, the sample-object itself.

SUMMARY AND CONCLUSIONS

Four rhesus monkeys were trained to solve problems of matching-from-sample, nonmatching-from-sample, sign-discriminated-antago-nistic-position-habits, and reversed-sign-discriminated-antagonistic-position-habits. In the final stage of the problem, the four separate tasks were presented in random sequence. This final problem was solved by all four monkeys.

Solution of the last problem is possible only if the final response set of the monkeys is governed by four variables, the nature of the sample-object, the nature of the food-sign, the positions of the choice-objects, and the identity or nonidentity of the sample-object with either or both choice-objects.

REFERENCE

1. WEINSTEIN, B.   Matching-from-sample by rhesus monkeys and by children. *J. comp. Psychol.*, 1941, **31**, 195–213.

CHAPTER VII

THE RELATION OF PHYSIOLOGICAL AND SOCIAL INDICES OF ACTIVITY LEVEL

By

L. P. HERRINGTON

Yale University

THE PROBLEM

Pressure of activity is a very important characteristic of the individual. We sense it in the tempo of motion, in posture, in expressive movements, in speech, in flow of ideas, and in a dozen other functional attributes. In one person, a high degree of activity pressure will seem to have largely a nervous or emotional background; in another, it will appear to be more closely related to the ready stimulability of a well-integrated organism. In either case, we can speak of the "activity" level of an individual and, with surprising economy in adjectives, convey to others a well-understood impression that is promptly interpreted in relation to a rough subjective calibration of factors for age, profession, sex, and the interest areas peculiar to these terms. Much quibbling can be done about the disturbing breadth of meaning possible in the term *activity level*, yet it has a long and useful history in the practical art of personality description that recommends it to our attention. As is a rather usual case in the personality field, the present status of the activity trait as a defined and measurable variable is such that the wise investigator lets the general public bear the onus of definition and measurement.

The present study is an informal report of a project begun some years ago which has attempted to attack this problem in one of its simpler and restricted areas, namely, to investigate the relation, if any exists, between certain indexes of physiological activity and activity level in individuals as it is appreciated by social observers.

We live in a social environment in which human activity is neither random nor individually organized, but in which it is directed into patterns and toward important ends that are typical and general for the social environment. Because of this factor of social pressure and direction, a really competent knowledge of the mode of energy disposal in the individual might well deserve a psychological importance that is not apparent when mechanisms of personality formation are minutely studied or when the total personality is approached from a subjective and qualitative angle. A similar problem is raised if we attempt to give certain types of personality reaction a psychological status independent of direct factors of physical energy and activity. Aggression conceived of as a purely psychological mode of reaction is a case in point. Aggressive behavior (1), either physical or social, stands in what often appears to be a simple relation to psychological frustrations. But aggressive behavior is a very real species variable in animals. Obviously, it is not necessary to conclude that the lion is frustrated and that the lamb is not. Among humans there are likewise individual differences in proneness to aggression or submission that are more closely related to physically and physiologically conditioned modes of action than to psychological reaction formations. Indeed, may it not be that such physical or physiological differences are, through cumulative interactions with the social environment, a fundamental condition of the mature psychological trait?

A similar argument might be made with reference to introversion. At the mature level, this trait, either as appraised clinically or as appraised by test methods, stands in close association with attitudes and situations in the individual's life that have a predominating reference to the psychological level of integration. Only a limited experience with children is required, however, to convince one that physiological stability and the physical capacity required for success in group activities are certainly important factors. Again, at the mature level we find significant alterations in the degree of introvertive inclination as a result of illness, accidents, and even moderate reductions in physical capacity.

Many considerations of this general nature suggest that level of intensity in physiological function and reaction threshold define an "activity" characteristic that infiltrates generally into the qualitative organization of personality. Certain special features of social organization, however, tend to give a practical importance to this "activity" factor that is often overlooked in detached evaluations of the relative dignity and importance of exceptional degrees of physical as opposed to intellectual traits.   It seems rather certain that social groupings which represent the cooperative mechanics of specific activities tend to induct their membership by processes that reduce rather than increase the range of variability in mental capacity. Many qualifications should be made, especially with regard to the type of motive operative in the grouping process.   In the important occupational field, however, it seems necessary to assume that college professors, shoemakers, and ditchdiggers represent individual ranges in mental ability that are contained well within the general range. Under such circumstances, factors other than differences in mental ability become of vastly greater importance in the social value of the individual within the group than might otherwise be the case.   This is a commonplace observation in educational circles, and it is the obvious explanation of the frequent lack of relationship between capacity and performance.   This situation encourages the placement of a high value on the "activity" trait, whether we choose to think of it as a general motivational factor or to identify it directly with intensity of function and stimulability on a physiological plane.

Although a great deal of research has been done with psychopathic material with the aim of relating measurements of available energy and reactivity to psychiatric classifications, the results have been suggestive rather than conclusive.   Many of the difficulties are clear. Hospitalization itself has a definite influence on findings.   Patients are usually in a state of change that makes the experimentally convenient cross-section type of study of far less value than longitudinal studies.   The most reliable evidence has shown that alterations in basal metabolic rate—in particular, a reduction of the rate—is frequent in psychotic individuals who are not excited.   Total metabolism is obviously increased in excited patients and in a periodic manner in certain types of depression, but it is doubtful whether we can properly speak of basal rates in such cases.   Similarly vague findings have been made with reference to blood sugar, respiratory regulation, and vasomotor function.

The most frequent criticism of the meaning of these results rests on the unquestioned occurrence of similar conditions in individuals who show no perceptible personality disturbance and, conversely, the occurrence of similar personality disturbances in the absence of a physiological syndrome.   Although this is an admitted fact, such criticism puts too much stress on a simple explanation and fails to emphasize the probability that a satisfactory analysis of personality must recognize many qualitatively different signs or symptoms that have an "equivalent" status in relation to some socially valued criterion of behavior.

In retrospect, the initial important successes in intelligence testing appear to have rested largely on the relation of an adequately conceived test program to an available criterion, school performance, on which a socially clear evaluation had been placed years before intelligence testing as such had been developed. The importance of this item should not be discounted in view of later developments which have extended the theoretical and qualitative study of intelligence under circumstances that have been independent of the initial social validation.

A similar movement closer to social value criteria has been obvious in personality testing for some time. In the 1920's, tests of introversion-extroversion were probably more widely exploited than any others, and it was usual to find these conceived of as measures of fundamental styles of psychological operation, with insistence that neither one nor the other extreme was necessarily desirable as an individual trait. In succeeding years, various investigators became increasingly active in rounding up the items of such "pure variable" tests and incorporating them in omnibus scales, in which increasing significance was attached to validation of the scale in terms of criteria whose extremes had definitely opposed social value connotations. The neurotic inventory, emotional maturity, and delinquency scales all moved closer to social values, and these have been supplemented by a host of similar scales of "social values" covering smaller ranges of human behavior.

Many of these test instruments have real merit. It is difficult to avoid the conclusion, however, that they represent a case in which derivative and restricted measures have been discovered prior to some primary measure of wider usefulness. Studies of achievement or of special ability with numbers stand in a rather understandable and derivative relationship to tests of general intelligence, in which the latter represents the primary trait of most general social significance. But where is a similar basic reference for tests in the non-intellectual field? In view of the great interest in the field of personality measurement, it does not seem unreasonable to suppose that the failure to hit on a primary reference has been due to a very understandable stereotyping of professional views as to the type of information that is relevant. Existing tests have been of such variety and wide range at the psychological level that one wonders if the reference is to be found at this level, as it is ordinarily conceived.

The burden of this argument has been to suggest that activity as descriptive of the level of available physiological energy in the individual may occupy a relationship to more highly differentiated personality concepts in some degree analogous to the relation between general intellectual ability and variously qualified special aspects of intelligence. In fact, the author has been greatly impressed by the frequency with which psychologists speak of intelligence as a general trait, as though it were an intensity factor. In contrast, the operation of this factor in restricted areas such as language or number relations is apt to invite a qualitative description which is not unlike the special views of personality given us by trait tests.

The question must arise in the reader's mind as to the nature of this "activity intensity" that has been set up with a generous logic as a useful analogy in considering the personality. The author should in all fairness admit immediately that he is in no position to define it accurately, or perhaps even usefully. It is believed, however, that the concept is used intelligently by psychologists and others with a considerable degree of operational definiteness. If any reader will examine his files on personal recommendations, he will find continued emphasis on two aspects of personality. The first is the matter of general intelligence, only moderately qualified by estimates of special abilities. The second is a vague "activity-intensity" evaluation that is found lurking behind innumerable adjectives and sticking its head out in plain English here and there. Without going into literary details concerning this trait, it is certain that considerable effort should be made to establish some type of correlation between possible relevant factors and a rather decided social consensus as to the existence of such a general trait.

The present study has approached the problem at the level that is most definitely suggested by the term *action*, namely, the physiological and physical plane. This does not reveal any special prejudices as to the relative importance of psychogenic or physiogenic factors. It is simply an obvious approach aimed at the first level of possible significance.

In a much earlier unpublished study (2), we have reported on the results of basal metabolism tests, simple circulatory measures such as blood and pulse pressure, pulse rate, and on total acidity and

creatinine excretion indexes for two groups of individuals falling at
the extremes of the Conklin and Laird tests of introversion-extroversion. Perhaps the most striking differences associated with the
extroversion-introversion (E-I) variable involved basal metabolic
rate and score on a test of general athletic ability. A higher metabolic rate was found for the introvert group, somewhat to the
surprise of the investigator, and rather understandably a much
poorer introvert-group performance on the athletic tests. The
results were not published, because in immediately succeeding
years the author had the opportunity for extensive experience in
calorimetric work at the strictly physiological level (3, 7, and 8) and
became convinced that the E-I difference in basal metabolism, as
experienced with this type of group selection, did not represent a
fundamental attribute but measured, instead, the greater suscepti-
bility of the test "introvert" to tension and excitement. This
effect requires a considerable time to adapt and is not usefully
evaluated by one or two repeated observations. More unfortunately, the tension effect is not very suggestive as to fundamental
physiological substrates peculiar to the E-I axis, since it is also characteristic of younger-older, naïve-sophisticated, male-female, under-
weight-overweight, and instructed-uninstructed groupings. What
the true distinction between these particular varieties of test E's and
I's in basal rate may be, still remains an item of conjecture. The
problem was not pursued further than a qualification of the early
results, principally because of a loss of confidence in the ultimate
value of the tests used for the psychological groupings. These later
experiences did indicate, however, that intensive studies of small
groups at the physiological level, with later extensions to the possibility of correlation at the psychological level, were needed. The
present paper details a number of informal excursions into this field.

THE EXPERIMENTAL MATERIAL

The initial plan of this investigation provided for the study of
two characteristics of physiological measurements, mean level and
individual variability, in relation to one another and to simple
indexes of physical activity. Basal metabolic rate, total metabolism,
pulse, respiration, and blood pressure were the principal physiological
measures. These measurements were secured under basal circumstances with strict observance of dietary and bed-rest requirements
in an environment at a standard temperature of 70°F. Metabolic

rates were measured with a Benedict-Roth closed-circuit apparatus and results referred to the DuBois standards. A Tycos recording sphygmomanometer was used for blood-pressure reading. The program was a long one, covering some 90 days, and the interest of these relatively commonplace measurements was expected to derive from the extremely accurate determination of individual mean level and variability possible from 45 repeated measures. Such a program would ordinarily be a rather tedious approach to the problem, but in this instance it was profitable to undertake it, since the physiological measures desired were being routinely obtained as control procedures on a small group of paid subjects. During the course of these control procedures and later in the year, pedometer records, catalogues of daily social, physical, and erotic activity were obtained when possible. Ratings of activity and drive, as judged by three raters well acquainted with the subjects, were obtained in all cases.

The subject group consisted initially of 14 members, and records are substantially complete for 11 of these. Subjects were all young men (19 to 24 years) in good physical condition, of unexceptional height and weight, who at the time of the study were medical students—for the most part, in the first or second year of study. Criteria of selection were absence of cardiovascular defects, any chronic disease, and willingness to serve as paid subjects for an extended period. The intensity of the program precluded a large population, and it was necessary to sacrifice the advantages of a large and representative sample in the interest of high individual reliability of results. There was, therefore, no intention of securing a sample representative of anything other than young and healthy medical students of a rather standard educational background. Inspection of the data, however, do show that, even with so small a sample, a very considerable part of the *normal* physiological range in the functions measured is represented. As an example, we expect about 90 per cent of the general population to fall within ± 10 per cent of the norm for basal metabolic rate. In the present data, approximately 75 per cent of this range is covered.

INTENSITY AND VARIABILITY IN BASAL METABOLIC RATE, SYSTOLIC BLOOD PRESSURE, PULSE RATE, AND RESPIRATORY RATE

In Table I are given the means and standard deviations for four physiological functions, as obtained on 11 young men under strictly basal conditions, over a period of 90 days.

The shifting of the population mean on basal metabolic rate (B.M.R.) from 100 per cent of the normal DuBois standards to about 96 per cent is immediately conspicuous. This result is always to be

TABLE I

MEANS AND STANDARD DEVIATIONS OF FOUR PHYSIOLOGICAL FUNCTIONS UNDER BASAL CONDITIONS

Subject*	Basal calories, per hour	Basal rate, per cent DuBois	Systolic blood pressure, millimeters of mercury	Respiration, per minute	Pulse, per minute
Populations of 45 daily observations for each individual					
Ga	75.8 ± 4.15	104.1 ± 5.70	110.4 ± 6.93	17.6 ± 2.82	70.1 ± 5.53
R	72.5 ± 3.95	100.2 ± 5.45	113.4 ± 5.06	10.8 ± 1.50	64.7 ± 2.57
J	61.5 ± 3.28	94.2 ± 5.05	99.5 ± 4.28	15.6 ± .93	68.8 ± 4.30
O	62.4 ± 3.84	89.4 ± 5.50	103.6 ± 6.78	7.2 ± 1.33	53.8 ± 4.31
Vi	74.9 ± 3.56	94.5 ± 4.50	104.8 ± 4.77	9.2 ± 1.68	65.2 ± 3.43
Lc	73.7 ± 4.45	97.4 ± 5.80	108.9 ± 3.57	10.1 ± 2.69	65.3 ± 4.95
Ki	69.0 ± 3.59	102.6 ± 5.35	103.2 ± 4.34	14.5 ± 2.23	64.1 ± 4.64
L	61.0 ± 4.49	96.3 ± 7.10	96.8 ± 6.07	10.0 ± 1.40	58.2 ± 2.80
V	64.0 ± 5.46	90.8 ± 7.75	96.2 ± 3.74	8.7 ± 1.84	52.8 ± 3.39
Rm	70.2 ± 3.16	96.6 ± 4.35	116.4 ± 5.31	12.1 ± 1.03	53.3 ± 4.44
M	61.9 ± 3.35	90.5 ± 4.90	102.8 ± 3.83	10.1 ± .91	50.7 ± 2.94
Populations of 15 daily observations for each individual					
Ga	77.1 ± 3.08	....	110.5 ± 8.10	16.3 ± 2.38	69.0 ± 5.44
R	73.1 ± 3.12	....	111.0 ± 5.38	11.6 ± 1.13	63.2 ± 1.92
J	60.8 ± 2.66	....	100.3 ± 5.30	15.8 ± .75	70.1 ± 5.23
O	62.7 ± 3.46	....	108.1 ± 9.40	6.7 ± 1.08	55.7 ± 3.85
Vi	75.5 ± 2.92	....	108.0 ± 4.56	10.0 ± 1.40	66.5 ± 2.09
Lc	72.7 ± 3.94	....	110.0 ± 4.11	7.8 ± 1.47	62.7 ± 3.60
Ki	69.6 ± 2.53	....	104.7 ± 3.59	15.3 ± 2.18	62.6 ± 4.62
L	61.6 ± 3.84	....	95.1 ± 5.88	9.5 ± .72	57.7 ± 2.15
V	63.9 ± 3.90	....	97.5 ± 4.70	7.9 ± 1.86	54.3 ± 3.25
Rm	68.3 ± 2.02	....	116.8 ± 4.88	12.6 ± 1.02	53.5 ± 3.41
M	60.9 ± 3.24	....	104.4 ± 3.27	10.9 ± .57	50.3 ± 3.74

* Subjects are arranged in order of descending rank on pooled "activity level" ratings.

expected with practiced subjects under the best conditions, as opposed to a few tests under the usual clinical or laboratory conditions. This effect is of importance in the use of metabolic tests for nonclinical purposes, and if it does not appear the conditions are almost certainly less than ideal.   It is also of interest to see that a population of 15 tests on separate days fixes the mean value for the individual within from 2 to 3 per cent of the larger series, with occasional variation as high as 5 per cent.   This is also approximately true of systolic blood pressure and pulse rate.   Respiratory rate shows a definitely larger variation (extreme value 20 per cent). Perhaps, for our purposes, the most definitive item is the relation of the average standard error of the mean of 45 measurements to the range of the individual means.   In these data, the observed range is about 25 times the typical standard error of the individual means for basal metabolic rate and systolic blood pressure.   The factor is about 33 for pulse rate and over 100 for respiratory rate.   It is clear from this item that, with standard conditions and frequent sampling, values for the individual levels which are characteristic in these four physiological variables may be fixed.   The especial distinctiveness of the individual respiratory rate is an interesting finding in view of the very high order of psychosomatic integration represented by this very immediately observable variable and the increasing attention (6, 9) that respiratory regulation is receiving in connection with a number of functional disturbances.   This is an appropriate point at which to suggest that the probability of a relationship between "physiological" and "social" aspects of behavior is more nearly determined by the level of integration of the respective variables than by the fact of their first-order classification as either "physiological" or "psychological."

There is good reason to believe that the data in Table I represent the most reliable individual determinations of the level of these particular functions in any group, a fact that should give them greater significance than may be attached to studies in which they have been only casually reported in relation to psychological interests.

INTENSITY AND VARIABILITY IN METABOLIC AND CIRCULATORY FUNCTIONS AS SEPARATE CHARACTERS

There are two elements of variation in the data under discussion. One is in part technical and in part the result of unknown and uncontrollable factors that are peculiar to a given measurement; the second is, we believe, basically biological and is a reflection of the delicacy with which a given function is regulated.   Experience clearly shows that it is possible to reach by repeated measurements a very characteristic value for the mean level with no substantial reduction in variation around this mean even when observations are extended greatly beyond the 45 reported here. It then becomes of importance to know what relation there is between intensity of function, as judged by the mean value, and variability as indicated by a stable standard deviation that we suspect may be heavily weighted with intraorganic factors of homeostatic significance.

In order to answer this question, we have computed the correlation between the mean (M) and standard deviation (S.D.) for each of the four variables, using the 11 paired means and standard deviations.

INTERCORRELATIONS BETWEEN M_{45} AND $S.D._{45}$

	r	σ_r
B.M.R.	.10 ±	.30
Systolic blood pressure	.13 ±	.30
Respiration rate	.30 ±	.27
Pulse rate	.42 ±	.25

Although the standard errors are large with so small a population, the conclusion seems warranted that the relation between mean value for these functions and their variability is not impressive. It is not surprising to find that the pulse rate, which is certainly the most labile of these functions, shows a somewhat higher relation than is typical of the remaining variables. We believe there are good grounds for supposing that the level of intensity in these functions and their typical variability are, under such observational conditions as have been described, relatively independent indices of physiological adjustment.

Such a conclusion immediately suggests that the standard deviation of a set of measurements of a single variable may be an estimate of some general factor of intraorganic control. Since there are four functions measured, the individual standard deviations may be thought of as four estimates of a general factor of variability, and it would be interesting to combine these estimates into a single index for purposes of investigating a possible relation to other factors. In order to do this, the distribution of standard deviations must be made comparable, since we have no a priori basis for concluding that the variability in one factor is more important than in another. The populations are small and the procedure open to a number of criticisms from the standpoint of the physiological interrelatedness of these factors. We believe, however, that in an empirical approach it is proper to transmute the observed distributions of standard deviations into new distributions with comparable means and standard deviations. This was done according to the method of Hull (5). The transmuted scores on four variables for each individual were then summated to give a combined index of variability (Table II) for correlation purposes.

TABLE II

COMPARISON OF ACTIVITY RATINGS AND VARIABILITY IN FOUR PHYSIOLOGICAL FUNCTIONS

Subject	Activity ratings							Comparable indexes of variability for physiological means†				
	1	2	3	Σ	Linear score	Rank	Rank	Σ	Systolic blood pressure	Respiration	Pulse	B.M.R.
Ga	9*	10	7	26	83	1	1	453	117.2	117.1	117.3	101.1
Lc	3	6	6	15	50	6	2	416	87.7	115.2	111.0	102.1
O	7	9	4	20	59	4	3	414	115.9	94.9	104.0	99.1
L	3	3	5	11	41	8	4	409	109.7	96.0	87.6	115.4
Ki	6	4	4	14	45	7	6	408	94.5	108.4	107.6	97.6
V	2	5	3	10	35	9	6	408	89.2	102.5	94.0	122.0
Vi	6	6	7	19	55	5	6	408	98.3	100.2	94.5	88.9
Rm	3	1	2	6	28	10	8	386	103.0	90.5	105.4	87.4
R	6	8	8	22	72	2	9	382	100.8	97.5	85.1	98.6
J	9	3	9	21	65	3	10	381	94.0	89.0	103.9	94.5
M	1	0	0	1	17	11	11	361	90.0	88.7	89.1	93.0

* Rated more active in 9 out of 10 comparisons by rater 1.
† Transmuted scores derived from distributions of standard deviations on 45 measures of each variable on each subject.

The question as to what type of behavior criterion should be compared with such indexes had been previously considered, and in Table II activity ratings secured in the following manner are available for comparison with individual and combined indexes of physiological variability. Since all subjects were medical students, the possibilities of securing good social observers were better than usual. Three raters were chosen, one a junior member of the laboratory staff, who had been specifically charged with receiving subjects in the evening, arranging sleeping accommodations, and payment for services. This included contact with every subject during the hours prior to retiring as well as group contact in schoolwork. A second rater of faculty status had class and laboratory contact with all subjects and was personally acquainted with each man. The third rater was a member of the same medical class and generally known

for his wide acquaintance and leadership in class affairs.   Each rater
was provided with the following instructions:

"In the course of the next 90 days please observe the following 11 men
for the purpose of rating them individually on general activity and drive.
We cannot define this trait precisely but you are asked to consider (1)
physical vigor as suggested by athletic pursuits, speed of movement, and
typical postures at work or when idle, (2) excitable speech and pressure
for expression in group situations, (3) energy and enthusiasm in meeting
class work requirements.   At the end of the period each man will be compared with every other member of the group, in turn, and judged as *more*
or *less* active in terms *of the general* impression you gain from considering
at frequent intervals the criteria listed above.   Since the period of observation will be relatively long, it is probable that you will often see all or
several of these men together, in class, gymnasium, laboratory, lunch
room, or at social gatherings.   We believe the final judgment will be
improved if you make trial ratings in these face-to-face situations without
preserving the results."

This approach to the rating problem probably gives a fair index of
drive or activity as it is evaluated in the common-sense social world
by persons who have long experience and contact with a given individual.   In Table II, the individual activity ratings are given in
conjunction with indexes of variability for four physiological
measures.

The author was well acquainted with raters as well as subjects, and
in many instances it was quite easy to see that substantial disparities
in rating are probably related to different samples of behavior rather
than to radically different concepts of activity.   In any event, it
would probably be difficult to secure an observationally better
grounded estimate of general activity than is given by the summed
ratings of these three judges.   The numerical rating is the number of times each subject was judged "more active" in 10 paired
comparisons.

In Table III, correlations between linear scores (5) for activity
rating and the variability index for four combined physiological
factors are shown, as well as the intercorrelations involving the
separate indexes of variability for each function.   Since populations
are 11 in every case, the standard errors of the coefficients are large.

The results are encouraging in that they definitely show that the
rated activity and objective measures of physiological variability are
related to some degree.   It is apparent that the method of equal
weights does not give the best combination of the separate physi-

ological indexes of variability—in fact, blood pressure variability alone is apparently equally useful in predicting rated activity. The possibility of improving the prediction by a best weighting of the dependent variables is quite limited. Several combinations have been used in a multiple correlation analysis, the simplest and most efficient gives a multiple of about .60 with rated activity when blood pressure and pulse variability are the dependent factors.

TABLE III

a. Intercorrelations of Activity Ratings and Indexes of Physiological
Variability

	Activity	Pulse	Respiration	Systolic blood pressure
Pulse...................	.33 ± .27			
Respiration.............	.39 ± .26	.57 ± .22		
Systolic blood pressure....	.56 ± .22	.23 ± .29	.05 ± .31	
B.M.R.................	−.08 ± .30	−.19 ± .30	.26 ± .28	−.02 ± .31
Combined index of physiological variability.......	.51 ± .23			

b. Intercorrelations of Activity Ratings and Means on Four Physiological Variables

	Activity	Pulse	Respiration	Systolic blood pressure
Pulse...................	.81 ± .10			
Respiration.............	.44 ± .26	.66 ± .17		
Systolic blood pressure....	.24 ± .29	.23 ± .29	.20 ± .29	
B.M.R.................	.45 ± .26	.73 ± .14	.75 ± .13	.49 ± .23

The data suggest that two characteristics of circulatory adjustment, pulse rate and systolic blood pressure, have a *variability* component that is substantially related to activity ratings when the variability estimate is based on as many as 45 measurements taken under strictly basal conditions.

Interrelations of Activity Ratings and Mean Values for
B.M.R., Systolic Blood Pressure, Respiratory and
Pulse Rates

A similar analysis of the relations of mean levels in the four physiological measurements to activity rating was made for the 11 subjects. These intercorrelations are given in the lower section of Table III. All physiological values are based on the levels established by 45 daily measurements. It is immediately apparent that the mean values not only tend to be more highly associated with activity ratings than do variability indexes but that the interrelations of the means are high in expected spots. The coefficient for activity and pulse rate is particularly high, with respiration and B.M.R. of moderate order. In view of the relatively high correlation of respiration with pulse and with B.M.R. and the low relation of systolic blood pressure to activity, we have eliminated systolic pressure and B.M.R. for the moment and computed a multiple between activity as an independent variable and pulse and B.M.R. as dependent factors. As in the case of the variability data, interrelations between these physiological factors are such that relatively little improvement over the predictive value of the best single factor is possible. The value of .81 for mean pulse level and activity may be increased by 2 or 3 points by taking basal level into consideration. It does appear, however, that mean pulse level, carefully determined, is a variable of considerable statistical importance in relation to rated activity. In view of the interrelations of the mean values of the physiological variables, there seems to be little point in computing a general intensity index, a finding quite similar to the experience with the combined index of physiological variability.

An over-all study of these relationships suggests that, as a measure of physiological variability in relation to rated activity, the standard deviation of 45 repeated measures of systolic pressure is of value. The most representative intensity factor in relation to rated activity is the mean pulse level in 45 repeated measures. The correlation between pressure variability and mean pulse level is low, of the order of .10; hence it is not surprising that a combination of mean pulse and pressure variability yields a multiple coefficient in the prediction of activity rating of the order of .90.

We have naturally regarded this estimate conservatively. If taken at face value, it means that the popular impression of activity in the individual is very closely related to the balance of autonomic influences acting through the vagus and cardiac accelerator nerves upon resting cardiac rates and to the lability of blood pressure control, which, in turn, not only is affected by the above-mentioned factors but also reflects the general action of the vasomotor centers on the circulation.

It is of more than ordinary interest that this analysis should have directed attention to these two factors. In recent years the reaction of systolic blood pressure to the cold-pressor test has been widely used in studies of hypertensive individuals and their relatives in rather successful attempts (4) to demonstrate a genetic and familial basis for hypertensive phenomena. The activity and emotional characteristics of the hypertensive are well known, but it is probably not so well appreciated that the prehypertensive is characterized, not by an elevated pressure, but by a surprising sensitivity of the systolic level to pressor stimuli. Insofar as cardiac rate factors are concerned, one should note that practically all the current tests of cardiovascular function in use clinically or for such special purposes as high-altitude fitness are based on rate and pressure phenomena. In general, a relative brachycardia is found in physically active individuals, but it is recognized that moderate degrees of tachycardia are compatible with competent function in individuals of apparently constitutional circulatory hypertonus.

The intensive study, both on the side of rated activity and physiological measurement, needed to establish reliable data have necessarily limited these investigations to a few subjects, and for that reason it is scarcely permissible to generalize on the basis of the relations here reported. The implications of these relations, however, have encouraged us to continue these studies in an individual and clinical sense with a view toward obtaining a clearer insight into the detailed life of our subjects.

One of the many questions that occur to one in connection with a rated activity index is the extent to which behavior influencing such a rating is actually reflected in total energy cost to the individual. We have seen in this small group that the basal rate of energy turnover bears a moderate relation to rated activity in the expected direction. Within very wide limits, however, there is no necessarily fixed relation between basal rate and the total energy expenditure of the individual, and it is quite conceivable that any relation between basal rate and rated activity is an indirect one involving the level of nervous activity rather than an amount of physical action. In Table IV, data on this point are presented. All our subjects were familiar with the general procedures required to estimate the calorie equivalent of the diet. They were provided with record forms and uniform schedules of the calorie equivalent of standard measures of various foods. On 5 successive days, records were made of the kind and amounts of food ingested and calorie equivalents computed. Considerable reliance must necessarily be placed on cooperation under such circumstances, but we believe that the medical interests of the group warrant accepting the records as substantially accurate. We have not computed standard deviations but have indicated the range of daily calorie intake.   In column 1 are the total basal calories for 24 hours as very reliably estimated from 45 basal measurements. Standard deviations proportionate to those for this item on an hourly basis (Table I) apply here.   Subjects have been arranged in descending order of rated activity.   In column 2 the total calorie intake (or energy output) is given.   This has been reduced to an hourly basis in column 4, and in column 5 has been expressed as a percentage of the individual's basal calorie level.

TABLE IV

RELATION OF BASAL TO TOTAL ENERGY OUTPUT

Sub-ject*	Total basal calories per 24 hr.	Total calories per 24 hr.	Range of estimates for total calories	Total calories per hour as 24-hr. aver-age	Total calories as percentage of basal calories
Ga	1655	3365	410	140	195
R	1740	2802	346	117	160
J	1470	2970	210	124	219
O	1498	3147	283	131	188
Vi	1790	2919	364	122	153
Lc	1770	3060	297	128	168
Ki	1667	2865	407	119	176
L	1465	2438	285	102	164
V	1559	2620	268	108	168
Rm	1684	2863	437	119	163
M	1478	2798	395	116	171

* Subjects arranged in descending order of rank on rated activity level.

The last column is the most informative.   The relation of total energy to rated activity in this group is conspicuous only in the subjects rated most active.   This may not be unreasonable in view of the fact that the total energy output has a definite minimum value in homogeneous groups engaged in similar pursuits, and we might well expect the highly motivated individual to increase energy expenditure well above the sufficient level and find less active persons content to meet the just necessary requirement.

It is of some interest to estimate the energy equivalent of the difference between our highest and lowest estimated total energy output (subjects *Ga* and *L*). If we assume a theoretical basal of 1600 calories per 24 hours, the energy equivalent of the observed percentage difference is about 900 calories in the extreme case. This is the equivalent of about $2\frac{1}{2}$ hours of hard work, as in sawing wood, or about $3\frac{1}{2}$ hours of walking at a brisk clip. Naturally, we hardly expected the extra energy to be expended in this manner. In investigations of the daily habits of the two cases under consideration, it appeared that from 200 to 300 calories could be charged off to a distinct difference in habits of exercise, approximately 150 more to a constitutionally lower basal rate. Our limited data here suggest that within the normal range basal rates are not very substantially related to total energy expenditure, although the highest levels of total energy tend to be associated with high rated activity.

Individual Case Histories

In the year following the major part of this work, a considerable amount of time was devoted to case history studies, and in the several years that have elapsed since that time all members of the group have completed or been forced to terminate their professional training, so that a limited amount of career information is available. The group is too small to lend much statistical dignity to the results, yet it is apparent that the activity factor, considered either as a rated or a physiological trait, has a suggestive association with later career developments. For example, if we arrange our subjects in order of rated activity into high-, medium-, and low-activity groups containing, respectively, four, three, and four individuals, certain interesting differences appear. Of the entire group, three men did medical work with honors. Two of these were in the high-activity group, the third in the mid-group. Either transfer or withdrawal is usually associated with unfavorable scholastic progress. Two withdrawals and two transfers associated with scholastic difficulties occurred in the group as a whole. One withdrawal and one transfer of this type occurred in both the medium- and low-activity groups. These data are summarized in Table V. Probably none of the differences noted is individually very reliable, but the trend of results on all comparisons is impressive. It is rather amusing to find that the "active" group scored higher on the written and oral examinations of the National Board of Medical Examiners than their less "active" classmates, in spite of an apparent slight handicap in intelligence.

One of the most interesting comparisons is the matter of present employment. The contrast of military activity and welfare work at the two extremes of the list is perhaps a happy accident but will bear thought. Government or institutional service, which demands only moderate initiative, tends to concentrate in the lower ranks on activity.

In this study, three items have come to final consideration in relation to activity pressure in the individual, namely, rated activity and its two principal physiological correlates, mean pulse level and an index of systolic-pressure variability. Two subjects, *Ga* and *M*, were, respectively, high and low in conspicuous fashion on each of the three variables. A short review of their case histories is in order.

Subject M. This young man was born in a small town in upper New York State, the son of a Methodist minister of restricted means. He was the intermediate child in a family of three boys. His childhood was unmarked by serious illness or by any psychological developments that might be considered out of the ordinary. In high school, he did well scholastically, experiencing some minor difficulties with mathematics. He took a moderate degree of interest in social activities and devoted some time to tennis and track with special success in the former.

Undergraduate college work was passed with better than average performance, and his social participation was greatly increased. In a phase of reaction to the religious atmosphere of his early life, he indulged rather conspicuously in alcohol and encountered his initial sexual experience. His alcoholic excesses were, on several occasions, sufficient to bring him to the attention of the college authorities. He rather enjoyed his reputation at the time and feels that the motivation for his drinking was "display and self-proving" rather than any great enjoyment of the effects of alcohol per se.

His entry into medical school was made possible through the financial assistance of a relative who took a considerable interest in him and whom he was extremely careful to please in every way. In medical school, his progress was decidedly unsatisfactory, and he felt depressed and unequal to the work. Socially he was well received, and in the confines of his student club he found in gambling and drinking solace for his insufficient scholastic performance. After several conspicuous scholastic failures, he was asked to withdraw,

TABLE V

Tabulation of Available Career Information in Relation to Activity Rating

Subject	National Board Medical Examination	Mean	Oral examination, pre-clinical	Mean	Intelligence*	Mean	Record	Present activity†	Rated activity
Ga	....		....		..		Honors first year;‡ withdrew	Foreign military service	High-activity rating
R	82.8, 78.8	84.3	80.8, 76.1	78.9	54	54	M.D.	Private practice	
J	85.4, 86.2		80.8, 68.3		51		M.D.	Institutional practice	
O	89.5, 83.2		88.0, 80.2		57		M.D. *cum laude*	Foreign medical service	
Vi	90.0, 86.2		82.0, 77.5		81		M.D. *cum laude*	University appointment	Medium-activity rating
Lc	76.3	84.9	52.8, 61.6	66.2	50	62	Withdrew	Business	
Ki	87.0		63.3		64		Transfer;§ M.D.	Institutional practice	
L	....		....		..		Withdrew‡	Civil service	Low-activity rating
V	82.2, 80.6	78.3	75.0, 66.6	67.6	57	61	M.D.	Institutional practice	
Rm	74.0, 69.0		..		..		Transfer;§ M.D.	Institutional practice	
M	67.4		59.6, 69.1		64		Withdrew	Social worker	

* Scores on Chapman, Anderson, Burr Medical Classification test. 70+, A; 55–70, B; 35–55, C; 20–35, D; 20–, E.

† Institutional practice means second or third year of hospital residence except in case of *Rm*, whose appointment is permanent.

‡ These withdrawals not forced by scholarship.

§ Transfers were, in both cases, to institutions of lower standing.

although it was the general opinion among his instructors that he was mentally well equipped to handle his assignments. He feels that his impending failure in schoolwork was apparent before his general deportment took a turn for the worse. Following his withdrawal, he worked at odd jobs for a time until certain events made it possible for him to continue school if he so desired. He decided to train for social work and, following a year's study, was admitted to a welfare group, in which profession he has remained as a social case worker. He finds himself well able to meet the demands of this situation. He has married a somewhat older woman who is engaged in the same work and he is now, in most respects, quite well adjusted.

Subject Ga. Subject *Ga* was the older of two brothers, the sons of a relatively young couple. The father was active as a sales manager and had enjoyed many periods of relative affluence. Subject *Ga* was active physically as a child and usually average or slightly superior in athletic pursuits. His school progress was entirely satisfactory until he went to high school, when a severe infectious episode seriously disrupted his schoolwork. He feels, however, that his intellectual interests date definitely from the period of confinement and long convalescence incident to this illness. He recovered completely from this illness and completed his schoolwork with moderate success. He was very much intrigued by the opposite sex, and his adolescence was marked by many escapades. He describes himself as the sort of individual who was generally thought of when some prank or disturbance occurred at school. After high school, he worked at a number of jobs and was generally successful in supplying himself with money. He qualified for college entrance, earned his way without assistance from home, and was graduated in the upper 10 per cent of his class. He voluntarily withdrew from medical school at the end of his first year, although all prospects were exceedingly favorable. The immediate incident provoking this was the death of his father under circumstances that left his mother financially embarrassed. He had always been eager for travel and soon found that the most attractive solution of his problem was foreign service with the armed forces. By reason of R.O.T.C. training and the obvious fitness of his personality for the profession, he was quickly accepted in an officer's grade and is at present abroad in an active military capacity.

The two histories are clear contrasts in many respects. It is unfortunate that the possibilities of identification are such that it would not be professionally proper to expand these histories with a large amount of available detailed history that would considerably increase the impression to be gained from these relatively superficial facts. The contrasts of selling and ministerial activities in the fathers, of dependent and independent financial attitudes, of failure and success under similar scholastic situations, and the final respective selections of military and altruistic occupations as solutions to immediate, pressing problems are indeed interesting. With the exception of the first of these items, the foregoing facts deal with the course of personality since the collection of the physiological data and activity ratings. We believe these two extreme cases do much to emphasize the trends to be seen in the group as a whole in such comparisons as those in Table V.

The majority of this group cooperated in a study of the relation between erotic activity and time devoted to social, scholastic, and physical activity as indicated by specially arranged diary records. This material has a substantial interest in its own right. Relations to the present problem are, however, suggestive in only one respect. Level of erotic activity, as judged by frequency of experience, was not reliably related to our measures of activity, but there was a definite indication that the number of individuals with whom physical relations had been established was greater among subjects falling in the upper as opposed to the lower group in rated activity.

SUMMARY

Pressure of activity, in a broad psychosomatic sense, is an important aspect of personality. In groups in which variations in intelligence and educational background are controlled, it is possible to evaluate the trait by rating methods in a manner that yields considerable objective evidence of validity. A partial physiological background for the trait is strongly suggested by the association between it and several characteristics of circulatory regulation. There is no reason to believe that this association is a direct one. It appears more probable that the physiological signs appearing as correlates are superficial indicators of much more general properties of the autonomic nervous system.

REFERENCES

1. DOLLARD, J., DOOB, L., MILLER, N., SEARS, R. R., & SOLLENBERGER, R. Aggression and frustration. New Haven: Yale Univ. Press, 1939.
2. HERRINGTON, L. P. The psychophysiological profile of introverts and extroverts. Unpublished Ph. D. thesis, Stanford Univ., 1930.
3. HERRINGTON, L. P., WINSLOW, C.-E. A., & GAGGE, A. P. The relative influence of radiation and convection on vasomotor temperature regulation. *Amer. J. Physiol.*, 1937, **120**, 133–143.
4. HINES, E. A. The heredity factor in essential hypertension. *Ann. Int. Med.*, 1937, **11**, 593–601.
5. HULL, C. L. Aptitude testing. New York: World Book, 1928.
6. MCFARLAND, R. A., GRAYBIEL, A., LILJENCRANTZ, E., & TUTTLE, A. D. An analysis of the physiological and psychological characteristics of 200 civil air line pilots. *J. Aviation Med.*, 1939, **10**, 2.
7. WINSLOW, C.-E. A., HERRINGTON, L. P., & GAGGE, A. P. A new method of partitional calorimetry. *Amer. J. Physiol.*, 1936, **116**, 641–655.
8. WINSLOW, C.-E. A., HERRINGTON, L. P., & GAGGE, A. P. Physiological reactions of the human body to varying environmental temperatures. *Amer. J. Physiol.*, 1937, **120**, 1–22.
9. ZIEGLER, L. H., & ELLIOTT, D. C. The effects of emotion on certain cases of asthma. *Amer. J. Med. Sci.*, 1926, **172**, 860.

CHAPTER VIII

PERSONALITY AS RELATED TO SOURCE AND ADEQUACY OF SEX INSTRUCTION[1]

By

E. LOWELL KELLY

Purdue University

PROBLEM

During the last quarter century, sex education has been receiving an ever-increasing amount of attention from both professional educators and lay writers. This emphasis on sex instruction by its proponents assumes the prime importance of satisfactory sex instruction for later personal and social adjustment. This assumption, in turn, seems to be largely the outgrowth of clinical studies of individual cases in which unhealthy sex attitudes or a lack of specific sex information seem to have been a primary causal factor in the maladjustment of the individuals concerned.

There seem to have been no studies made, however, with the avowed purpose of evaluating the results of varied types of sex education or the allegedly untoward effects of the lack of suitable sex education. Davis (1), in her extensive investigation of sex factors in the lives of 2200 women, found what appeared to be a slight value in early sex instruction as indicated by the fact that 57 per cent of her group of happily married women had received some sex instruction in early life, whereas only 44 per cent of the unhappy wives had had such instruction. Hamilton's research (2) did not entirely corroborate these results, but for his group of married women, it seemed that the best source of early sex instruction was the mother.

Terman (9) reports a very low relationship between both source and rated adequacy of sex instruction and the marital happiness of

[1] This study is one of a number resulting from preliminary analyses of data collected for a major investigation on personality factors underlying marital compatibility, financial support for which was provided by the Committee for Research on Problems of Sex, the National Research Council.

his subjects.   On the basis of these findings, Terman writes, "that the sex instruction given has apparently had such meager results as far as the marital happiness of these couples is concerned, does not, of course, prove that this phase of the child's education is unimportant" (9, page 239).   But after pointing out certain limitations of his data, Terman continues, " We believe that they justify a certain amount of skepticism as to the alleged benefits of sex education.   It is quite possible, as Davis and many others have pointed out, that the good effects of sex instruction may in individual cases be largely offset by the unintended effects causing the child's mind to become unwholesomely preoccupied with sex" (9, page 240).

Thus, it would seem that even for adjustment in marriage, where sex instruction might be presumed to be maximally important, present available evidence in support of this contention is very meager indeed.   In an unpublished study made available to the writer, Wilkening (10) has shown a similar low relationship between source and adequacy of sex instruction and the attitudes of engaged persons, both men and women, toward marriage and divorce, attitudes that one might reasonably assume to have been at least partially a function of the type of sex instruction received.

In the present study, we have raised the question as to possible relationships between source and adequacy of sex instruction and personality in general.   Do persons who have had adequate sex instruction from "approved" sources differ as human personalities from those whose sex education was badly neglected or of the "wrong" kind?   Even though no marked relationships have been found between source and adequacy of sex instruction and marital compatibility, nevertheless certain specific personality traits may be related to if not determined by the particular variety of sex education experienced.

SOURCE OF DATA

In the spring of 1934, the writer began collecting data for a long-time genetic study of psychological factors underlying marital compatibility.   During the next 3 years, a large body of sociological, psychological, and anthropometric data was collected from 300 engaged couples who at that time lived in the New England area. Each couple was interviewed personally, given a battery of psychological tests, and asked to fill out a rather elaborate personal data sheet covering each person's background, childhood experiences, etc. (4). These couples represented a small proportion (about 10 per cent) of a much larger group that had been invited to participate in this long-time study of marital compatibility. Since participation involved the contribution of several hours of time and also a willingness to participate in a study, the results of which would not be available for a number of years, the investigation naturally appealed to persons of superior intelligence and educational background. The subjects certainly represent a selected group of the general population. Ideally, we should have preferred to secure a random sample of the population, but to do so is practically impossible in investigations of this sort. It is simply necessary to remember that any conclusions growing out of the data will apply only to the sort of population of which our group is representative.

The disadvantage of this lack of randomness in the sample is perhaps more than offset by the fact that those persons who did participate in the study had an intense and intelligent interest in the project, which leads us to believe that the information obtained from our subjects is highly reliable and little subject to intentional falsification.

The 300 men and women studied ranged in age from 18 to 50, although most of them were between 21 and 30. The mean age of the men at the time of the interview was 26.6 years and that of the women 24.6 years, and the standard deviation of each group was about $3\frac{1}{2}$ years. All but 5 per cent of the group had at least a high-school education, and one third of the men and one fourth of the women were college graduates. Roughly, one fifth of the men and nearly one seventh of the women had some graduate training beyond 4 years of college. As regards church membership, nearly 70 per cent of the group were Protestants, 10 per cent Roman Catholics, 7 per cent Jewish, and 13 per cent were unaffiliated with any religious group.

Among the questions appearing on the personal-data sheet, which was filled out by both members of the couple, under the supervision of the interviewer, were:

"The sex instruction which you received from *responsible adults* before you were 18 years old was: (check) entirely adequate ＿＿＿; reasonably adequate ——; rather inadequate ＿＿＿; very inadequate ＿＿＿; none whatever ——."

and

"Your sex information before you were 18 years old was received chiefly from: (check one or more) parents ____; physician ____; teachers ____; other adults ____; other children ____."

Because this information was requested after a high degree of rapport had been established with the subjects and since the questions appeared in a booklet with many other questions concerning parental background, childhood experiences, etc., it is believed that the resulting responses were honest, even though the questions did

TABLE I

SOURCE AND RATED ADEQUACY OF SEX INSTRUCTION OF 282 MEN AND 280 WOMEN

Source	Adequacy	Men		Women		Total	
		N	%	N	%	N	%
I. Parents	Extremely adequate	28	64	67	73	95	70
	Reasonably adequate	16	36	24	26	40	29
	Very inadequate	0	0	1	1	1	1
	Total	44	16*	92	33	136	24
II. Other adults	Extremely adequate	15	30	7	32	22	31
	Reasonably adequate	21	43	13	59	34	48
	Very inadequate	13	27	2	9	15	21
	Total	49	17	22	8	71	13
III. Other children	Extremely adequate	11	11	8	10	19	10
	Reasonably adequate	46	46	43	57	89	51
	Very inadequate	43	43	25	33	68	39
	Total	100	35	76	27	176	31
IV. Miscellaneous (physicians, teachers, combinations)	Extremely adequate	42	47	53	59	95	53
	Reasonably adequate	37	42	31	34	68	38
	Very inadequate	10	11	6	7	16	9
	Total	89	32	90	32	179	32
V. All sources	Extremely adequate	96	34	135	48	231	41
	Reasonably adequate	120	43	111	40	231	41
	Very inadequate	66	23	34	12	100	18
	Total	282	100	280	100	562	100

* Read: The 44 men receiving their sex instruction from "parents" constitute 16 per cent of the 282 men studied.

concern sex.   Table I presents a summary of the answers to these
two questions regarding the source and rated adequacy of the sex
instruction of these young people.   (One or both questions were
unanswered by 18 men and 20 women; so this table and all subsequent computations are based on 282 men and 280 women for whom
complete information was available.)   In this table and throughout
the remainder of this discussion, it is of no particular import that the
men and women were engaged to each other.   Rather, it seems
advisable to regard them as fairly large samples of young men
and women representative of the better educated segment of our
population.

Among the many interesting facts appearing in Table I, we may
note the marked sex difference with respect to source of sex information.   Sixteen per cent of the men report receiving their sex instruction from their parents, whereas 33 per cent of the women were so
instructed.   Males, it appears, are more likely to have received their
sex instruction from other adults or from other children.   It is of
considerable interest that approximately one third of both men and
women report receiving this type of education from physicians and
teachers (or a combination of these professional persons).

Looking next at the bottom part of the table, at the tabulation for
rated adequacy irrespective of the source of sex information, we find
that 34 per cent of the men and 48 per cent of the women regard the
information that they received as extremely adequate; further, that
43 per cent of the men and 40 per cent of the women regard it as
reasonably adequate.   Only 18 per cent of the group, 23 per cent of
the men and 12 per cent of the women, regard their sex instruction as
very inadequate.[1]   Irrespective of source, women are more likely
than men to consider their sex instruction adequate.   Whether this
indicates a real superiority of the sex instruction provided women in
our population or only a tendency for women to be more readily
satisfied with that which is available is, of course, not known.

On the basis of rated adequacy, sex instruction received from the
parents is more frequently rated adequate than that received from
any other source.   Next in order of rated adequacy of instruction is
that received from physicians, teachers, or a combination of these
individuals.   On the other hand, both men and women agree

[1] These findings are in sharp contrast to those of Landis, who reports that only
12 per cent of his 295 women subjects considered their early sex instruction even
"fairly sufficient" (6, page 30).

regarding the inadequacy of sex instruction received in childhood from other children.   Only 10 per cent of the persons receiving their information from this source regard it as extremely adequate, and 43 per cent of the men and 33 per cent of the women consider it very inadequate.

The 282 men and the 280 women for whom this information is available represent rather wide individual differences with respect to both the source and the rated adequacy of their sex instruction.   We now raise the question as to whether these differences in educational experience are significantly related to the personalities of the individuals concerned.

During the personal interview with the subjects, the members of each pair were asked to rate each other and themselves on a 36-item personality rating scale.   Immediately thereafter, they were asked to address 5 envelopes to acquaintances who knew them well enough to rate them on the 36 traits concerned and to give the name of 2 or 3 alternate acquaintances who might be used as judges in case any of the original 5 failed to return the rating scales.   In this manner, 5 ratings on 36 personality traits were obtained for each of the individuals.   The rating scale was one especially devised for the purpose and has been described in some detail elsewhere (5).   In this connection, we may note only that it was of the graphic type, that each of the items was introduced by a question such as "How jealous or how religious is he?" and that the ratings have been shown to have reliabilities of from .39 to .86 for the pooled judgment of five acquaintances.   Although these reliabilities are not high enough for accurate individual measurement, they are satisfactory for evaluating differences in group means such as we are investigating in this problem.

The 36 traits covered by the rating scale were as follows:

1. Is he physically energetic and "peppy"?
2. How intelligent is he?
3. How does he meet new social situations?
4. How sociable and friendly is he?
5. Is he physically attractive?
6. Is he nervous, and does he "fly off the handle" easily?
7. Is he popular with other people?
8. What is his attitude about religion?
9. How does he meet his appointments?
10. How much initiative does he have; is he a "self-starter"?
11. How courteous is he?
12. How jealous is he?

13. What sort of voice does he have?
14. How cooperative is he?
15. How cultured is he?
16. Is he awkward or graceful in his movements?
17. How well does he stick to a task?
18. How is he with regard to money?
19. How honest and fair is he?
20. How does he dress?
21. Is he patient?
22. Does he possess common sense?
23. Are his interests wide or narrow?
24. What is his usual disposition?
25. How conventional is he?
26. Is he a good sport or a poor one?
27. Is he generally quiet or boisterous?
28. How sincere is he?
29. What kind of temper does he have?
30. Is he boring or entertaining?
31. How vain is he?
32. Is he tactful and diplomatic?
33. Does he have definite ideas which he is sure are right?
34. How good is his sense of humor?
35. Can you count on him to do a thing?
36. How selfish and self-centered is he?

The returned rating scales were scored on a scale ranging from 0 to 9 for each trait, and an average of the 5 judges' ratings was made for each trait. In this manner were obtained personality measures on each of the 36 traits for the 282 men and 280 women studied. In spite of their many limitations, ratings by associates are among the best personality measures available, and certainly they have considerable social significance. On all 36 traits, these persons differed widely in the impressions that they had made on their associates who rated them. We therefore turn to the question of whether any significant relationship exists between a person's personality as evaluated by his associates and either the source of his sex instruction or his rated adequacy of such instruction.

ANALYTICAL PROCEDURE

Because of the relatively small number of cases falling in certain categories, it was originally planned to use the small-sample statistical technique known as the *analysis of variance* in the study of these relationships. With this plan in mind, tables were prepared showing the distributions of personality ratings for each trait according to the source and rated adequacy of sex instruction. In all, 72 such tables were constructed, one for men and one for women for each of the 36 traits. A sample of such a summary for trait 1, for women, is shown in Table II. Each of the 12 columns of the table, it will be noted, represents a subgroup of the 280 women grouped according to a combination of the source and adequacy of instruction. Thus, the one woman who considered the sex instruction received from her parents as entirely inadequate was rated by her associates as 4 on the trait "pep." The 24 women who considered the information received by parents as reasonably adequate received "pep" ratings ranging from 0 to 8, etc.

TABLE II

SAMPLE TABULATION FOR COMPUTATION OF η AND ϵ

(Trait 1: "Pep"—Women)

SOURCE

Personality Rating	I. Parents			II. Other adults			III. Other children			Miscellaneous			f
	Adequacy			Adequacy			Adequacy			Adequacy			
	a	b	c	a	b	c	a	b	c	a	b	c	
9			1					1			1	1	4
8		2	4		1		3	1	1	1	4	1	18
7		5	9		4	3	3	8	1		5	12	50
6		4	16	1		1	4	8	1	1	4	11	51
5		7	14		3	2	4	10			8	13	61
4	1	3	11	1	3	1	5	8		3	4	7	47
3			5		1		5	5	3		2	5	26
2		1	7		1			1	2	1	1	2	16
1		1					1	1			2	1	6
0		1											1
Nc	1	24	67	2	13	7	25	43	8	6	31	53	280
Mc	4.0	5.2	5.1	5.0	5.2	5.9	5.0	5.1	4.3	4.7	5.4	5.3	

Adequacy ratings: a = very inadequate.
                    b = reasonably adequate.
                    c = extremely adequate.

Our next task was that of examining these tables to determine whether the personality ratings for the various groups differed according to the source and adequacy of sex instruction. Obviously, one approach to this problem would be that of determining the mean rating of each column and then computing the statistical significance of the differences of each of the 66 combinations of means in each table. Fortunately, however, this tedious process is not necessary, since the F test of the analysis of variance enables us at one operation to determine the presence or absence of any significant differences among any combination of means in an entire table of this sort. If this test reveals the existence of significant differences, we can then proceed to examine the means of the various columns and to determine by the t test just which of the means differ significantly from each other (7, pages 87–100).

Just as we were about to proceed with the F test for each of the 72 tables, we discovered T. L. Kelley's recently developed formula for an unbiased correlation ratio, which he has designated as ϵ, epsilon (3). Thanks to the recently published tables of Peters and Van Voorhis (8, pages 494ff.), showing the distribution of ϵ^2 when the true correlation is zero, it is possible to use the ϵ technique in the analysis of variance, not only to discover the presence of significant differences among the means of the columns, but also to obtain a standardized coefficient indicative of the degree of relationship existing between the variables. Accordingly, therefore, we have computed first the conventional correlation ratio η, eta, for each of these tables, then corrected it for bias, thus obtaining the new coefficient ϵ.

According to the above-mentioned table prepared by Peters and Van Voorhis, an ϵ^2 as large as .032 could arise by chance in a correlation table of 12 columns containing 280 cases as often as 5 times in 100, and an ϵ^2 as large as .049 could arise by chance as often as 1 time in 100. Calculation of the 72 ϵ^2 coefficients (36 for the men and 36 for the women) revealed that only one of them was higher than .032, and it was less than .049. Hence, we must conclude that there are no statistically significant differences among the means of the columns for any of the tables. In other words, the variations in the means of the columns of the various distributions of personality-trait ratings are no greater than might have occurred had we made purely chance distributions in each column instead of sorting the data according to source and adequacy of sex education. We are forced to conclude, therefore, that, as far as these 36 aspects of human personality are concerned, they do not seem to be related to either the source or the rated adequacy of sex instruction received before the age of 18.

Significance of Findings

What is the meaning of these results? Do they prove that sex education is unimportant and that, no matter what type or how much or how little sex instruction an individual receives, his personality will be uninfluenced as a result of it? Certainly this is not a justifiable conclusion. Our data simply show that for persons in general to have received their sex instruction from a particular source does not mean that they will, as a group, impress their associates as being more or less peppy, more or less well adjusted socially, more or less religious, etc., than those who have received their sex instruction from other sources. In other words, variations in source, or even adequacy of sex instruction, as we have known them in the past, seem to be of little import as a determinant of personality as here rated. Just as being an only child does not necessarily mean that a youngster grows up in a poor social and psychological environment, provided his parents are intelligent enough to realize the potential hazard of this condition of "only-ness," so, in the case of sex information, we are forced to conclude that the mere securing of such information from any particular individual or group of individuals is not in and of itself a particularly significant fact in the psychological history of the individual.

Negative findings such as these are always difficult to interpret. We have not proved that source and adequacy of sex information have no effect on the personality of the developing individual but only that no relationship exists for the particular group of personality traits studied. However, in view of the rather extensive sampling of both social and personal behavior covered by the rating scale, it seems rather unlikely that a more elaborate investigation of this type would reveal any significant relationships between type of sex education and personality traits. It must be remembered that education of all sorts, including sex education, is given to individuals who at the time of receiving the information already differ widely with respect to immediate background, experiences, and attitudes. Then, too, it must be remembered that we have grouped together all individuals who received their sex education from any one source, such as "parents." Certainly it is not fair to assume that all parents did an equally good job in handling this difficult educational task. These parents certainly differed in their competence as educators in the degree to which they were sensitive to the amount of information that the child was ready to assimilate at the time and in many other respects.   Also, it must be remembered that we had no objective measure of the adequacy of sex instruction but only the subjects' rating of its adequacy.

The statistical analysis employed made no assumptions regarding the possible presence or absence of a causal relationship but asked only whether or not any relationship was present.   For such a trait as rated intelligence (which correlates about .50 with scores on the Otis Self-administering Test of Intelligence) we might have expected to find a correlation with type of sex instruction because the more intelligent children were more likely to have come from intelligent parents, who might be assumed to have handled the problem of sex instruction somewhat differently than average parents.   Even for this trait, however, ϵ^2 was not high enough for the relationship to be considered other than as resulting from chance.

A possible explanation of our failure to find any relationships between type of sex instruction and later personality traits would be that the adult personality, to a very large extent, is already well determined before the child receives any sex education in our culture. In this respect, these findings might be used to support either a hereditary theory of personality or the psychoanalytical theory that personality is largely the result of the psychosexual development occurring before the child reaches the age of 6.   Although these findings do not prove either theory, it should be pointed out that they are not inconsistent with either view.

Before concluding that sex education is unimportant as a personality determinant, we might well pose the question as to whether any of the subjects in this study had a really adequate sex education. To be sure, they differ widely in the reported source and rated adequacy, but perhaps they simply experienced different varieties of inadequate instruction.   In all probability, good vs. poor instruction in geometry, ancient history, or Latin would also be found to be unrelated to adult personality adjustment!

A greater significance of these results seem to lie in their implications concerning the inadequacy of simple correlational studies of human traits and experiences and the tacit assumption of such studies concerning the simplicity of personality structure.   Experience A is not the same for individuals X and Y, nor is it the same for either X or Y if it occurs before or after experience B.   This statement is not to be interpreted as an argument for forsaking statistical studies in favor of the clinical approach (a case study is simply a statistical study where $N = 1$) but rather as a plea for the development and use of more penetrating statistical techniques for the analysis of the complex dynamic patterns and constellations of traits and experiences that seem to characterize human personality.

REFERENCES

1. DAVIS, K. B.   Sex factors in the lives of twenty-two hundred women. New York: Harper, 1929.
2. HAMILTON, G. V.   A research in marriage.   New York: A. & C. Boni, 1929.
3. KELLEY, T. L.   An unbiased correlation measure.   *Proc. nat. Acad. Sci., Wash.*, 1935, **21**, 554–559.
4. KELLY, E. L.   A preliminary report on psychological factors in assortative mating.   *Psychol. Bull.*, 1937, **34**, 749.
5. KELLY, E. L.   A 36 trait personality rating scale.   *J. Psychol.*, 1940, **9**, 97–102.
6. LANDIS, C., *et al.*   Sex in development.   New York: Hoeber, 1940.
7. LINDQUIST, E. F.   Statistical analysis in educational research.   New York: Houghton Mifflin, 1940.
8. PETERS, C. C., & VAN VOORHIS, W. R.   Statistical procedures and their mathematical bases.   New York: McGraw-Hill, 1940.
9. TERMAN, L. M., *et al.*   Psychological factors in marital happiness.   New York: McGraw-Hill, 1938.
10. WILKENING, H. E.   A study of relationships between certain selected variables and expressed attitudes toward marriage and divorce.   Ph.D. Thesis, department of educational sociology.   N. Y. Univ., 1941.

CHAPTER IX

PSYCHICAL BELIEF[1]

By

JOHN L. KENNEDY

Tufts College

I. GENERAL INTRODUCTION AND ORIENTATION

The aspect of human personality to be discussed here has to do with the individual's evaluation of evidence for and against supernormal or "occult" phenomena. The scientific side of this study has been called *psychical research*. To the writer, at least four general problems are of interest in the field of psychical research. They are (*a*) the proof of the objectivity or subjectivity of certain "supernormal" phenomena such as telepathy, clairvoyance, precognition, and survival after death, (*b*) the extent of belief in these phenomena, (*c*) the causation of belief in these phenomena, and (*d*) the possible "energizing" effect of such belief on action and observation when evidence either in support or against the beliefs is collected. This chapter deals primarily with the second and third problems, namely, with the extent of psychical belief in a sample population and with some suggestions as to possible "causative" factors. A few observations on the fourth problem will also be presented.

In 1927, under the editorship of Carl Murchison (5), a volume entitled *The Case for and against Psychical Belief* appeared. This work consisted of chapters written by a physicist, the physician husband of a medium, several novelists, a philosopher, several psychologists, and a famous magician. The several varieties of psychical belief were represented by the grouping of these contributions as "Part I: Convinced of the Multiplicity of Psychical Phenomena," "Part II: Convinced of the Rarity of Genuine Psychical

[1] The study here reported was made possible by a grant from the Social Science Research Committee of Stanford University. The writer wishes to acknowledge the assistance of Howard F. Uphoff in collecting and analyzing the data.

Phenomena," "Part III: Unconvinced as Yet," and "Part IV: Antagonistic to the Claims That Such Phenomena Occur." A plethora of conflicting opinions are presented. Some quotations from these authorities will make clear the state of opinion in this field.

"The evidence is already strong and is growing in bulk and cogency, that we are in communication with minds which are discarnate, that is, minds which have been deprived of their normal bodily material mechanism."

—Sir Oliver Lodge (5, p. 13)

"The ultimate aim of the whole movement [spiritualism] is to afford earnest minds in this age of doubt and stress some method of gaining a knowledge of our duties and our destiny which shall be dissociated from outward observances and conflicting faiths, so that by actual contact with intelligences which are above our own we may pick our path more easily amid the morass of Religion. The ultimate result will be the union of Science with Religion, and such an increase of inspired knowledge as will lift humanity on to a higher plane and send it reassured and comforted upon its further journey into the unknown."

—A. Conan Doyle (5, pp. 22–23)

"Science is bankrupt at the edge of the grave. Religion only offers a sleepy comfort. Psychic research will not only kill Materialism which is already dying, but knock out Agnosticism which is the prevalent condition of our college graduate. It will prove that man is a spirit, that the whole universe is spiritual, that matter is spirit attuned to vibrations which our bodily senses can perceive in our present state of development. . . . "

—L. R. G. Crandon (5, p. 105)

"In my view the evidence for telepathy is very strong; and I foretell with considerable confidence that it will become stronger and stronger, the more we investigate and gather and sift the evidence. In my opinion there has been gathered a very weighty mass of evidence indicating that the human personality does not always at death cease to be a source of influence upon the living. I am inclined to regard as part of this evidence the occurrence of ghostly apparitions, for it seems to me that, in many of these experiences, there is something involved that we do not at all understand, some causal factor or influence other than disorder within the mental processes of the percipient. I hold that a case has been made out for clairvoyance of such strength that further investigation is imperatively needed; and I would say the same of many of the supernormal physical phenomena of mediumship. I am not convinced of the supernormality of any of these in any instance. But I do feel very strongly that the evidence for them is such that the scientific world is not justified in merely pooh-poohing it, but rather is called upon to seek out and investigate alleged cases with the utmost care and impartiality."

—William McDougall (5, pp. 161–162)

"The main thing for Psychical Research, in my opinion, is to get more direct control with regard to conditions of experiment. . . . We must try to make the medium our object, and not be his. As soon as we shall have reached the new standard of conditions and controls just mentioned scepticism will become quite impossible. For it would be ridiculous, as a good deal of it is now."

—Hans Driesch (5, p. 178)

"The readiness of metapsychists to rely upon observations of seance phenomena, their insistence that illusions can be avoided, and their quick condemnation of the competence of an observer who is tricked, clearly indicate that they do not understand that error is inevitable. Consequently, the psychologist remains incredulous in the face of all the accumulating 'evidence.'" (5, p. 261)

"The incredulity of the psychologist does not spring from an *a priori* judgment that metapsychic phenomena are not possible; it comes from his knowledge of psychological causes of error, and the resulting conviction that reliance upon the scientific method alone is the price of admissible evidence."

—John E. Coover (5, p. 264)

"The task before the investigator today is not a polemic one. It is simply the task of steadily improving the quality and quantity of experimental work, the task of controlling more and more the elusive variables involved, and of working towards a thorough understanding of the physiological and psychological factors which underlie the phenomena."

—Gardner Murphy (5, pp. 277–278)

"What cannot be avoided is the charge of a common weakness in logical armament, a prejudiced interpretation, a hospitality to extreme, unscientific hypotheses, an overlooking or too complacent dismissal of the sources of error, which gave rise to the Psychical Research counterpart of what was and remains the ancient error of occultism. Such errors, fallacies, intellectual misemployments, congenial convictions have, then, a folklore, a pseudoscientific, and a modernly fallacious status and origin with enough in common running through them all to justify their inclusion in one evolutionary picture. They contribute covertly or overtly to the animus of Psychical Research."

—Joseph Jastrow (5, p. 291)

"It has been my desire in this book to convey to the reader my views regarding Spiritualism which are the result of study and investigation, the startling feature of which has been the utter inabilty of the average human being to describe accurately what he or she has witnessed. Many sitters, devoid of the sense of acute observation, prefer to garnish and embellish their stories with the fruits of their fertile imaginations, adding a choice bit every time the incident is reported, and eventually, by a trick of the brain, really believing what they say. It is evident, therefore, that by clever misguidance and apt misdirection of attention, a medium can accomplish seeming wonders. The sitter becomes positively self-deluded and actually thinks he has seen weird phantoms or has heard the voice of a beloved one.

"To my knowledge I have never been baffled in the least by what I have seen at seances. . . . "

—Harry Houdini (5, p. 362)

Coover (1) and Rhine, *et. al.* (7) have listed other conflicting beliefs, both ancient and modern, concerning the evidence for psychic phenomena.

To the psychologist, the problem of the genesis and extent of belief or conviction when the data are open to several interpretations is at least as interesting as the eventual proof or disproof of the evidence by scientific means. Not only is belief per se a legitimate object of inquiry but its possible "energizing" function in perception, as Coover points out in the foregoing, is also worthy of experimental analysis. Three examples of this energizing effect will be presented as an introduction to the experimental work on belief to be reported subsequently.

During the writer's tenure as the Fellow in Psychical Research at Stanford University (1937–1939), several opportunities arose to observe the influence of belief on perception. The simplest case was one in which a normal sensory phenomenon, *i.e.,* the increase in sensitivity of the retina after prolonged dark adaptation, was erroneously called an unusual "supernormal" phenomenon. An invitation to view these events as part of a seance group was received and accepted. On the appointed evening, a group met at the home of the medium. One of the rooms of the house was made light-tight by covering the windows with heavy sheets of roofing paper and by stuffing the cracks with newspapers. The group assembled in a circle and sat in complete darkness for approximately half an hour, at which time it was usual for one of the sitters to say, "I see a light over there in the corner." Soon other members of the group would claim to observe lights. The medium was credited with producing these "abnormal" manifestations as evidence of her supernormal power. Now, the phenomenon of increase in sensitivity of the retina after dark adaptation and the projection of occasional metabolic changes in the retina into the environment as "seen light" have been described for many years in the literature of visual sensitivity. Anyone who has a dark room available may repeat the experiment and obtain cases of such "projection" without the presence of a medium. To illustrate the point, a very sensitive photoelectric cell, amplifier, and recording system was used to record any "objective" light present in the situation. The photoelectric system was so sensitive that it would discharge a condenser and activate the recording system, even though the eye could not discern any light in the room. In order to test the objectivity of the seance report of light in the room, the members of the group who saw lights were required to press a button and record this response on the record of the photoelectric cell. No correspondence between the subject's report and the behavior of the cell was obtained.

At another seance in a different city, the medium claimed to be able to demonstrate "spontaneous generation" or the supernormal increase in the number of counted objects. The members of the seance group sat around a large table, on which two earthenware bowls were placed. In one bowl, 20 or 30 raisins were counted out. After suitable invocation, the exact number of raisins was determined by counting them one by one into the other bowl with a spoon. When the preliminary counting had been carried out, the lights were extinguished, and the group sat in the dark, concentrating on an increase in the number of raisins. At the end of the period of concentration, the lights were turned on, and the raisins were counted one by one back into the first bowl. Sometimes, at the second counting, more raisins would be present than at the first counting. Rarely, however, according to the report of the medium, fewer raisins would be present. Most often, the same number would be counted, indicating that the conditions were not quite right for generation or degeneration to take place. An entire evening was spent in this counting procedure. The writer carried out the count several times, taking extreme care. Nothing happened. He observed closely while others counted out raisins before and after periods of darkness. The phenomenon did not occur. Finally, with the writer in another room, success was reported from the group.

When the writer rejoined the group and observed the counting, no increase or decrease was obtained.

This incident is a striking example of the subtle influence of belief on perception. How easy it would be to make a mistake at the original or final count, how easy to count two raisins stuck together slightly as one at the original counting, in which case a "spontaneous generation" of one raisin would be observed at the final count. How easy to count two stuck-together raisins as one in the final count and come out with a "spontaneous degeneration" of one raisin. There is no question of the integrity or honesty of the persons involved in the counting procedure. Rather, the "energizing" effect of extreme belief that would allow such a method to be used must be censured.

H. F. Uphoff and the writer (3) have reported an interesting case of the effect of extreme belief on the simple act of recording, with the use of one of the methods proposed by Rhine (6) for studying extrasensory perception. The subject was a woman who believed in the existence of thought currents, was favorably impressed with seance phenomena, and reported successful personal experiences in telepathy and clairvoyance. She was allowed to act as "sender" and recorder in a test for telepathy. Her job was to take a card from the top of a shuffled deck, look at the symbol, concentrate on the symbol, indicate to the "guesser," who was in an adjoining room, that she was concentrating by pressing a key, and then, when the guess was made, record the guessed symbol in a prepared column, drop the card, and go on to the next. At the end of a run through 25 cards, the sender also recorded, next to the guessed symbol, the actual symbol she was concentrating on at the time the guess was made. The sender was allowed to record the results of 1000 guesses. In order to check on the objectivity of the recording, a separate record of the card symbols in the decks she used was prepared beforehand. To check on the recording of the subject's guesses, an independent observer, stationed in the room with the guesser, made a record of the guesses without knowing what the card symbol was. The application of these two checks, then, to the recording of the believer revealed the presence or absence of recording errors. Under conditions of excitement, the "believer" recorded 46 spurious successes, *i.e.*, where her record showed a correspondence between symbol concentrated on and guessed symbol and our record did not show such a correspondence. When she was told that her recording was being checked by an independent observer, her errors ceased. The writer does not believe that the errors committed were "voluntary," *i.e.*, due to a desire to mislead. Rather, it would seem that extreme belief and the nature of the complicated task produced automatisms that allowed the subject to record wrongly without realizing the error.

A similar experiment (3) with college students as recorders did not yield comparable results in quantity of errors. The subjects did not have such "extreme" belief as the individuals cited in the previous three cases. A tendency was discovered, however, for recorders to make errors that were in line with their previously determined belief concerning telepathy, *i.e.*, those who believed in telepathy tended to make errors that spuriously increased the telepathy score; those who disbelieved tended to make errors that decreased the score.

These instances and many others illustrate the importance of psychical belief in determining the kinds of evidence and experimental techniques used in obtaining evidence of supernormal phenomena. The remainder of this paper will be devoted to a study of the incidence of such belief in several populations of Stanford University students.

II. Psychical Belief in Stanford Students

A. Method.

In 1913–1917, the late Professor John E. Coover gave a 10-item questionnaire on psychical belief to over 1000 undergraduate students in psychology courses. These questionnaires were kept on file in the Psychical Research Library and form the basis of the present study. In 1938 and 1939, the writer attempted to contact by mail[1] as many of these individuals as possible. They were asked to fill out and return the same questionnaire and to answer Form A of the Attitude toward Telepathy Scale constructed by Uphoff (3). About 240 of the original group returned the data in a form that could be used for statistical analysis. A number of other questions related to psychical belief were also asked. Also, during the years 1938 and 1939, a large number of Stanford students in the elementary psychology classes answered the questionnaire and filled out the attitude scale. Reference to Table I will indicate the groups on which the present study is based.

[1] The assistance of the Stanford Alumni Office in providing present addresses of the subjects in group II is gratefully acknowledged.

236 of the original 1095 returned the questionnaire. A few more (242) answered the attitude scale but did not complete the questionnaire. Of the 1938–1939 group of students, 310 filled out the attitude scale.

TABLE I
GROUPS OF SUBJECTS

Group	Number	Members	When tested
I	1095	Stanford students in psychology classes	1913–1917
II	236	A sample of the members of group I	1939
III	544	Stanford students in psychology classes	1938–1939

The questions from the Coover questionnaire[1] here used for comparative purposes are the following:

1. Do you ever feel that you are being stared at, with the conviction that your feeling can be relied upon?

2. Do you have premonitions of events; such as important news, journeys, visits, accidents, etc.?

3. Have you ever seen pictures (visions) in water glasses, ink, crystals, etc.?

4. Have you had experiences in telepathy and clairvoyance?

The percentages of "yes" responses to these questions were tabulated and compared in the three groups defined in the foregoing. The questions will be referred to as staring, premonitions, visions, and telepathic and clairvoyant experiences. In cases in which experience in telepathy without clairvoyance or vice versa was reported, the answer was counted as a "yes" response.

The attitude scale used has already been reported (3). A set of 19 statements indicating belief, neutrality, or disbelief in telepathy were prepared in such a way that the subject could indicate on a 5-point scale his degree of acceptance of the statement. The points were: strongly approve, approve, neutral, disapprove, and strongly disapprove. With the use of the scoring method devised by Likert (4), these opinions were given numerical scores. The range of the attitude scale is from 19 to 95, 19 indicating extreme disbelief and 95 indicating extreme belief. Exact neutrality is indicated on this scale by a score of 57.

---

[1] The Coover questionnaire contained 10 questions. The four selected for analysis bear most directly on "psychical belief."

B. Results of Questionnaire.

1. *Comparison of groups I and III.* The differences between percentages of "yes" response to the questions between Stanford students tested in 1913–1917 and Stanford students tested in 1938–1939 are shown in Table II. If the two samples may be looked on as typical of the student populations at their respective times of testing, it is evident that large and significant changes have occurred. The size of the percentages of "yes" response on the "staring" question is startling, *i.e.*, over three fourths of the students in 1913–1917

TABLE II

DIFFERENCES IN PSYCHICAL BELIEF BETWEEN GROUPS I AND III IN TERMS OF PERCENTAGE OF "YES" RESPONSE

Question	Group I	Group III	D	CR*
Staring..........................	83	59	24	10.00
Premonitions.....................	46	28	18	7.28
Visions..........................	13	20	− 7	3.48
Telepathic and clairvoyant experiences...	17	12	5	2.76

* The CR's in this table and in Tables III, IV, V, and VI are obtained by dividing the difference between the percentages by the standard error of the difference. Values of CR over 3.00 are considered statistically significant. For a similar problem, see Holzinger (2, p. 249).

TABLE III

DIFFERENCES IN PSYCHICAL BELIEF IN GROUPS I AND II IN TERMS OF PERCENTAGE OF "YES" RESPONSE

Question	Group I	Group II	D	CR
Staring..........................	83	37	46	15.33
Premonitions.....................	46	26	20	6.66
Visions..........................	13	6	7	3.50
Telepathic and clairvoyant experiences...	17	33	−16	5.33

stated that they could tell when stared at, and over half of the students in 1938–1939 claimed the same ability. Coover (1) discusses the reasons why this belief is so prevalent. For premonitions, a decided drop in frequency is noted in the 1938–1939 group. Apparently the frequency of visions is increasing in our student population. Few people in 1913–1917 reported actual experiences with telepathy and clairvoyance and fewer still in 1938–

1939. In general, a significant shift of opinion with regard to belief in psychic ability has taken place.

2. *Comparison of groups I and II.* The second comparison is between individuals tested in 1913–1917 and a sample of these same persons tested in 1939. Table III presents the data. The results shown in Table III indicate that significant changes have taken place in psychical beliefs in the "older" generation of Stanford students. Significant decreases in psychical belief are observed both in the present-day student group and in the 1939 sample of those tested in 1913–1917 when they are compared with the 1913–1917 group. The increase in telepathic and clairvoyant experiences is probably due to the effect of 25 years of additional opportunity for incidents attributable to telepathy and clairvoyance to occur.

3. *Comparison of groups II and III.* Table IV shows the way in which the sample of the "older" generation compares with the present group of Stanford students with regard to psychical belief.

TABLE IV

DIFFERENCES IN PSYCHICAL BELIEF IN GROUPS II AND III IN TERMS OF PERCENTAGE OF "YES" RESPONSE

Question	Group II	Group III	D	CR
Staring..............................	37	59	−22	5.82
Premonitions.........................	26	28	− 2	.58
Visions..............................	6	20	−14	6.06
Telepathic and clairvoyant experiences...	33	12	21	6.25

The significant difference in favor of the young group on the "staring" question seems to indicate that age is an important factor in determining the response to this question. The frequency of premonitions remains at about the same level for both groups, and the frequency of visions is significantly greater in the "young" group. Again, the greater opportunity for incidents of a telepathic and clairvoyant nature to occur in the older group shows up in the significant difference on the telepathic and clairvoyant experiences question.

In summary, Tables II, III, and IV show that a general change in attitude toward these beliefs has taken place in the last 25 years, since groups II and III are more alike in belief than groups I and III or groups I and II. A hypothesis concerning the causation of these changes will be presented later. The young group, however, still shows a greater frequency of individuals who state that they know when they are stared at and that they have visions.

4. *Educational differences.* Data are available as to the educational status of the members of group II in relation to psychical belief. Table V shows the percentage of "yes" answers to the questions in 1939 for two classifications of education: (*a*) those who had 4 years or less of college and (*b*) those who did graduate work.

TABLE V

PERCENTAGES OF "YES" RESPONSE IN TWO EDUCATIONAL CLASSES IN GROUP II

Question	4 years of college or less ($N = 122$)	Graduate work ($N = 114$)	D	CR
Staring..............................	42	30	12	2.00
Premonitions........................	29	23	6	1.05
Visions.............................	8	5	3	.95
Telepathic and clairvoyant experiences.	37	29	8	1.33

Although the differences between these two classes are not significant, a trend toward less psychical belief in the more highly trained group is evident. Further results on the relation between attitude and education will be presented in a following section.

5. *Sex differences.* When the results of the questionnaire are distributed according to the sex of the subjects, interesting and significant differences in incidence of psychical belief are found. Table VI shows sex differences in the frequency of "yes" response to the four questions in groups I, II, and III. In all but one of these comparisons, women have higher percentages of belief than men. Significant differences are found, particularly in the "staring" question and the "premonitions" question. Although the differences in group II are not statistically significant because of the small number of cases, the general trend of the differences indicates a greater frequency of belief among the women.

C. Attitude-scale Results.

Scores on Form A of the Attitude toward Telepathy Scale are available for members of groups II and III. The mean scores for the two groups are almost identical. Table VII presents other data for

comparing the groups. It is evident that, although the mean scores
of the groups are almost equal, group II represents a greater range

TABLE VI
SEX DIFFERENCES IN GROUPS I, II, AND III IN TERMS OF PERCENTAGE OF "YES"
RESPONSE
Group I

Question	Men ($N = 616$)	Women ($N = 479$)	D	CR
Staring..........................	78	90	12	4.62
Premonitions......................	40	54	14	4.67
Visions..........................	14	11	− 3	1.50
Telepathic and clairvoyant experiences.	15	20	5	1.79

Group II

Question	($N = 151$)	($N = 85$)	D	CR
Staring..........................	32	44	12	1.83
Premonitions......................	22	32	10	1.58
Visions..........................	3	12	9	2.37
Telepathic and clairvoyant experiences.	27	44	17	2.80

Group III

Question	($N = 334$)	($N = 210$)	D	CR
Staring..........................	49	76	27	6.75
Premonitions......................	23	35	12	3.00
Visions..........................	18	22	4	1.13
Telepathic and clairvoyant experiences.	10	15	5	1.69

TABLE VII
MEAN SCORES ON ATTITUDE TOWARD TELEPATHY SCALE FOR GROUPS II AND III

Group	Mean score	Standard deviation	Standard error of the mean	Range
II ($N = 242$)....................	58.04	15.80	1.02	92–19
III ($N = 310$)..................	58.26	11.17	.63	86–23

of opinion with opinions held more strongly than in group III.
Both the "older" and the "younger" generations of Stanford

students, then, have about the same group opinion toward telepathy. The score of 58 represents almost exact neutrality of belief.

1. *Sex differences in attitude.* Both groups have been analyzed with regard to possible sex differences in attitude scores. Table VIII shows these differences and their significance for both groups.

TABLE VIII

SEX DIFFERENCES IN MEAN-ATTITUDE SCORE FOR GROUPS II AND III

Group II

	Mean	σ	σ_M	CR*
Men ($N = 164$).....................	55.45	15.22	1.19	3.11
Women ($N = 78$)...................	62.11	15.71	1.78	

Group III

Men ($N = 169$).....................	56.17	10.70	.82	.97
Women ($N = 141$)................	57.42	11.76	.99	

* The critical ratios here are obtained by dividing the difference in scale scores by the standard error of the difference. Values of 3 or over are significant.

The group of 1913–1917 Stanford students tested in 1939 shows a significant sex difference in mean score on the Attitude toward Telepathy Scale, with the women significantly more inclined to belief in this psychical phenomenon. With present Stanford students, however, the sex difference is not significant, even though it is in the direction of greater belief on the part of the women. In group II, the mean score of 62.11 indicates a tendency to score on the "believer" side of the scale, and the score of 55.45 shows a tendency to score on the "disbeliever" side.

2. *Educational differences in attitude.* The members of group II have been tabulated with regard to the amount of education they received in college and in graduate work. Three categories of education have been set up: (*a*) 4 years and less, (*b*) 5 and 6 years, and (*c*) 7 years and over. Table IX presents the means for these three categories. The difference of 9.86 between the mean scores of the class with 4 years of college or less and the mean score of the 7-years-and-over class is statistically significant. The data appear to show a progressive trend toward less belief among the more highly educated.

3. *Occupational differences in attitude.* The men of group II have been distributed according to the occupation in which they were engaged when tested. Here the data are of doubtful significance, since the number of cases in any one category is small. The placing of the subjects into occupational categories was also somewhat arbitrary. Table X shows a progressive trend in belief with regard to specialization, part of which is the result of more education for the highly skilled professions.

TABLE IX

MEAN ATTITUDE SCORES OF THREE EDUCATIONAL CLASSES OF GROUP II

	4 years and less ($N = 126$)	5 and 6 years ($N = 73$)	7 years and over ($N = 40$)
Mean score...................	59.96	57.74	50.20

TABLE X

MEAN SCORES OF THE MEN OF GROUP II IN CERTAIN OCCUPATIONS

Occupation	College professor ($N = 10$)	Doctor ($N = 24$)	Salesman ($N = 6$)	Business (owners and executives) ($N = 22$)
Mean-scale score.......	49.10	51.36	55.33	56.16

Occupation	Lawyer ($N = 34$)	Banking, insurance ($N = 30$)	Farmer ($N = 7$)	High-school teacher ($N = 5$)
Mean-scale score.......	56.82	57.04	59.71	61.80

III. SUMMARY AND CONCLUSIONS

The data presented here are meager, yet they show significant trends. To recapitulate, the results may be stated in the following way:

1. Significantly smaller percentages of belief in the feeling of being stared at and in premonitions were obtained when a group of present Stanford students was compared with one tested in 1913–1917.

2. A significant difference between those members of the "older generation" who had had 4 years or less of college education and those who had had more than 4 years was obtained on the feeling of being stared at. Those with the greater amount of education showed less belief in this ability.

3. Significant sex differences with regard to the feeling of being stared at and premonitions were found in the group tested in 1913–1917 and in the group tested in 1939. No significant sex differences were found in the sample of the 1913–1917 group tested in 1939. The women were more prone to psychical belief in all the comparisons except one (visions).

4. A comparison of mean attitude toward telepathy scores for the "older generation" and the "younger generation" showed no difference.

5. A significant sex difference was found when men and women of the "older generation" were compared on mean telepathy scores. The women were more prone to believe in telepathy than the men.

6. The mean scores of the "younger generation" of Stanford students did not show a significant sex difference, although women had a slightly higher average score than men.

7. Attitude toward telepathy was related inversely to amount of education (i.e., the greater amount of education, the less belief in telepathy) in the members of the "older generation" tested in 1939.

Although the two types of test (questionnaire and attitude scale) have yielded disparate results in some cases, the results as a whole suggest a hypothesis that the increase in scientific knowledge and attitude in the last 25 years, particularly with regard to communication, is related to the decrease in amount of belief in psychical means of communication. In 1913–1917, modern means of communication were not in common use; hence, a large percentage of belief in telepathic ability in both men and women tested at that time. With the increase and extension in scientific knowledge of "normal" ways of communication, the percentages of belief in telepathy decrease markedly in the 1939 tests. The significant sex difference in attitude toward telepathy (not present in questionnaire results) may be taken to indicate that the impact of modern scientific attitudes has been less in women educated in 1913–1917 than it has been in men educated at that time. Men and women now being educated show no significant difference in attitude toward telepathy (except in regard to the "staring" question), probably because women are now taking more scientific courses than they did 25 years ago. A more comprehensive study of the causes of psychical belief should be carried out in order to provide additional evidence on the foregoing hypothesis.

REFERENCES

1. COOVER, J. E. Experiments in psychical research. Stanford University: Stanford Univ. Press, 1917.
2. HOLZINGER, K. J. Statistical methods for students in education. New York: Ginn, 1928.
3. KENNEDY, J. L. & UPHOFF, H. F. Experiments on the nature of extra-sensory perception. III. The recording error criticism of extra-chance scores. J. Parapsychol., 1939, 3, 226–245.
4. LIKERT, R. A technique for the measurement of attitude. Arch. Psychol., N. Y., 1932, 22, No. 140.
5. MURCHISON, C., ed. The case for and against psychical belief. Worcester, Mass.: Clark Univ. Press, 1927.
6. RHINE, J. B. Extra-sensory perception. Boston: Boston Society for Psychical Research, 1934.
7. RHINE, J. B., et al. Extra-sensory perception after sixty years. New York: Holt, 1940.

CHAPTER X

MECHANISMS OF HALLUCINATIONS[1]

By

HEINRICH KLÜVER

Otho S. A. Sprague Memorial Institute, University of Chicago

The theories that have been evolved for an understanding of hallucinatory phenomena have frequently stressed one set of factors to the exclusion of others. They have stressed either psychological or physiological factors, "peripheral" or "central" factors, sensory or motor factors, cortical or subcortical mechanisms. In recent years, however, it has been generally recognized that all these factors are of importance. Since all of them are involved in any complex behavioral reaction, it is to be expected that they are involved in hallucinations. An investigator may insist, for instance, that pathological changes in the lens of the eye in conjunction with certain psychological factors are primarily responsible for the appearance of a given hallucinatory phenomenon or that the combined effects of vestibular dysfunction and a lesion of the occipital cortex determine another hallucinatory picture. The fact that certain agents can be found which banish or provoke hallucinations does not mean that the mechanisms involved in bringing about such a result are known. We know at present that hallucinations are influenced by a large number of widely different factors and that they exhibit a wide diversity of phenomenal characteristics. Confronted with these etiological and phenomenal differences, we may ask whether it is possible at all to identify something like a general "structure" in hallucinations or whether such a structure is dissolved by the operation of heterogeneous factors. In other words, are there any *hallucinatory constants?* This question will be briefly discussed by utilizing certain findings in the literature as well as the author's

[1] This research has been aided by a grant from the Committee for Research in Dementia Praecox founded by the Supreme Council, Thirty-third Degree, Scottish Rite, Northern Masonic Jurisdiction, U.S.A.

own studies in the field of eidetic phenomena and his studies of the
effects produced by mescaline.

HALLUCINATORY CONSTANTS

Mescaline (3, 4, 5-trimethoxyphenethyl amine) has been of unusual
interest because of its remarkable psychological and physiological
effects (4, 7, 22, 32, 33, 41, 42, 52, 56, 75, 87).   Particularly the visual
effects have been the subject of many studies.   Veit and Vogt
(81, 82) injected various alkaloids, including mescaline, into animals,
which were then killed to determine the concentration of the poison
in different parts of the central nervous system and in other tissues.
The amount of mescaline recovered from the occipital cortex of
monkeys and dogs did not differ significantly from that found in the
frontal cortex.   As regards the effects on the optical sensorium,
Maloney (46) claimed that injections of mescaline sulfate led to an
enormous enlargement of visual fields in "blind or nearly blind"
tabetics and to an improvement in visual acuity, as measured by
Snellen's test types.   Some of the patients were enabled to read who,
previous to the injection, could not; one of them went to a motion-
picture show.   Recently Zádor (88) reported that mescaline restored
perception of movement in the hemianopic field of one of his patients
(case 6).   In this connection, the appearance of the "reddish-blue
arcs" of the retina in the mescalinized state is of interest.   It is
generally agreed that these elliptical reddish-blue arcs, discovered by
Purkinje (64), correspond to fibers of the optic nerve, which become
entoptically visible (10, 40).   Normally, these arcs are very distinct
for only a moment, but after an injection of mescaline sulfate the
author noticed that they could be seen for a long time.

It is characteristic of the action of many drugs that visual effects
predominate.   Dominance of visual phenomena, a *traduzione visiva*
(Sante de Sanctis), seems to be also typical of deliriums, dreams, and
eidetic imagery.   As regards the hallucinatory phenomena produced
by mescaline, their chief character, according to Havelock Ellis, is
their "indescribableness."   More than a decade ago, the author
raised the question whether it was possible to find any constants in
the flow of these "indescribable" experiences and analyzed the
available data with reference to the *form* of the hallucinatory
material (33).   Investigators, such as Berze (5), emphasizing the
importance of motor, kinesthetic, or "myopsychic" components in
hallucinations, have called attention to the fact that most visual

hallucinations are *formed*. There is no doubt that most reports on hallucinations refer to forms of some kind and not to the appearance of visual "dust" or similar material.

The author's analysis of the hallucinatory phenomena appearing chiefly during the first stages of mescaline intoxication yielded the following *form constants:* (*a*) grating, lattice, fretwork, filigree, honeycomb, or chessboard; (*b*) cobweb; (*c*) tunnel, funnel, alley, cone, or vessel; (*d*) spiral. Many phenomena are, on close examination, nothing but modifications and transformations of these basic forms. The tendency towards "geometrization," as expressed in these form constants, is also apparent in the following two ways: (*a*) the forms are frequently repeated, combined, or elaborated into ornamental designs and mosaics of various kinds; (*b*) the elements constituting these forms, such as the squares in a chessboard design, often have boundaries consisting of geometric forms. At times, the boundaries are represented by lines so thin that it may be impossible to say whether they are black or white. Many observers have stressed the fineness of these lines, especially Ceroni (6) and Möller (54). As Möller has pointed out, the "absolute one-dimensional" appears to have become a reality.

For the sake of analysis in terms of "form," we have ignored aspects of color, brightness, and movement, but it is just these aspects which often deeply impress the subject and which he cannot adequately characterize when describing the kaleidoscopic play of forms and patterns. He may, for instance, claim that colors unknown in his previous experience appear; he may even be more impressed by the textures of colors—"fibrous, woven, polished, glowing, dull, veined, semi-transparent" (11); he may insist that the hallucinatory objects consist of materials that are never seen in nature and yet may strangely resemble certain kinds of wood, straw, hair, jewels, wool, silk, or marble. If we ignore the colors and movements as well as the "meaning" with which the phenomena are invested by the subject, the geometric-ornamental structure of the hallucinations becomes apparent. This appears even in the drawings made by artists during or after mescaline intoxication. Such drawings have been published by Szuman (77), Marinesco (48), and Maclay and Guttmann (44).

The fact that certain geometric forms and designs constantly recur has led us to assume certain hallucinatory form constants. Although further analysis may reveal additional form constants, it seems certain that the number of basic forms is limited. At certain stages of the poisoning, the geometric forms and designs may be seen with open as well as with closed eyes, e.g., on the face of a person or on the soup the subject is about to eat. It is significant that the tendency toward these forms may be so strong as to dominate the perception of external objects. One of Beringer's subjects looked at the small branch of a tree and reported: "The leaves . . . suddenly appeared in an ornamental pattern as if joined in a circular design having the form of approximately a cobweb. I looked at other branches, and, looking at them, all leaves assumed the same lattice-like arrangement" (4).

Some or all of the form constants found in mescaline hallucinations are also found in certain hypnagogic hallucinations, in entoptic phenomena, in the visual phenomena of insulin hypoglycemia, and in phenomena induced by simply looking at disks with black, white, or colored sectors rotating at certain speeds (9, 23, 49, 64, 84). Occasionally they seem even to occur in fever deliriums. One of the patients of Wolff and Curran (86), who happened to be a trained observer and physician, reported that he observed the same hallucinatory phenomenon during four illnesses precipitated by four different agents (measles, malaria, tonsillitis, influenza) at the ages of 8, 12, 30, and 41: he saw a cloud "with a spiral motion shape itself into a brilliant whorl." In two of these illnesses he saw that "brilliantly illuminated green, yellow and red angular crystalline masses shaped themselves into ever-changing patterns like those formed by bits of glass in a revolving kaleidoscope." It can be easily seen from the descriptions and drawings furnished by Purkinje (64) that all the geometric forms and designs characteristic of mescaline-induced phenomena can, under proper conditions, be entoptically observed.

Let us consider, for instance, the form constant for which "funnel," "tunnel," "cone," or similar descriptive terms are used. This form occurs again and again in mescaline hallucinations; it also appears in hypnagogic hallucinations, in entoptic phenomena, and in the phenomena arising when flickering fields are viewed under certain conditions. Or let us consider the "honeycomb" design consisting of hexagons. Purkinje and a number of other observers saw hexagonal patterns entoptically. After awakening in the morning, König (38) frequently noticed, with eyes closed, that his whole visual field was filled up with hexagons (as in a honeycomb).

The author saw after awakening, on two different occasions, a pattern almost identical with König's but saw it on the ceiling and not with closed eyes. One of Klien's (31) patients frequently saw, with eyes open, a hexagonal network during migraine attacks. Weil (84) reported that he saw König's design when observing visual phenomena in the hypoglycemic state. The subjects of Haack (23) saw hexagonal patterns when viewing flickering fields. It is clear, therefore, that the honeycomb design, with its hexagonal elements, appears not only in the hallucinatory phenomena produced by mescaline but also under many other conditions. The same is true with respect to the other form constants.

In an "enquiry into the causes of mescal visions," Marshall (50) has tried to show that the form constants proposed by the author can arise only from some peripheral stimulation that is common to different persons. He accounts for the different form constants by reference to various structures within the eye. It is of special interest that among these he includes retroretinal structures and the choriocapillary circulation. He concludes from anatomical, physiological, and observational data of various kinds that "the rods and foveal cones can look backwards" and that the retinal pigment and the choriocapillary circulation can, therefore, be seen under certain conditions. Similarly, physiologists have attempted to account for entoptic phenomena in general by connecting them with secretions on the cornea, moving particles in the vitreous humor, the network of retinal vessels, the properties and states of the cornea, lens, or other intraocular structures (10, 49).

Hoppe (26), one of the chief exponents of a peripheral theory of visual hallucinations, maintained as early as 1887 that "central (direct, immediate, psychic) hallucinations" arising somewhere in the brain do not exist and that "the entoptic content of the eye" always furnishes the "hallucinatory material." Morgenthaler (55) and others have emphasized peripheral factors even in the hallucinations of dementia praecox patients. Zucker (90) injected mescaline into patients who had hallucinations. As a result of these injections, the tapestry design and modifications of the chessboard design appeared, among other hallucinatory phenomena, in some of his schizophrenic patients. Zádor's patients with tract hemianopia (amaurosis of one eye, blindness in temporal region of other eye) saw, under the influence of mescaline, kaleidoscopic phenomena, squares, and other geometric figures in the whole visual field before both eyes (88). A totally blind patient (amaurosis due to tabes) frequently reported seeing a beautiful chessboard design in the mescalinized state, but he also saw a blue pattern with regularly distributed white points when he was not under the influence of the drug.   Mescaline did not induce any visual phenomena in a 23-year-old patient whose eyes had been enucleated during the second year of life.

It must be said that the experiments on patients with some pathology of the visual system leave so many points unsettled that no general conclusions are warranted. The visual effects, as well as the conditions under which they have been obtained, are often so incompletely described that even available data cannot be interpreted. As Guttmann (21) has pointed out, the crucial experiment with congenitally blind persons still remains to be done. It is a well-known fact that blind persons often report subjective visual phenomena, such as scintillation or photopsiae like "flames" or "sparks," but sometimes they also report definite forms and figures. Whether these figures ever show the patterning indicated in the various form constants described has not yet been systematically investigated. Clear-cut results as to the form constants present in the visual experiences of persons with loss of both eyes or totally blind for other reasons, examined at different intervals after the onset of blindness, are not available.

One of the author's blind subjects (enucleation of left eye, glaucoma of right eye) saw "balls with oval shape," either still or moving, appearing before him at a distance of about 5 feet. The balls were about as large as a dime and were only occasionally colored, chiefly red or violet. He also reported seeing "silver bars," "arabesques," "rings into which you can put your finger," and "shiny test tubes." He claimed that the phenomena were more prominent before his left eye, which had been removed 1½ years ago, and that they did not appear at all on certain days. It was impossible to elicit more definite information. Alternating current did not influence or banish these phenomena. The flicker phenomena that are seen by normal subjects under certain conditions of stimulation with alternating current (65) could not be electrically produced in this subject.

It should be mentioned that the form constants that we have discussed are apparently not typical for the visual phenomena produced by electrical stimulation of the occipital lobe in man.   Urban

(78) found that the photopsiae consisted mostly of glowing and colored "roundish forms, disks, or rings" when faradic current was used and of stars and ragged forms such as "pointed sparks" when galvanic current was used.

It should be obvious that the factors determining the appearance of certain form constants are so numerous that all theories stressing either "peripheral" or "central" factors are too simple. That there is an interaction of these factors may be true, but this remains in the present state of our knowledge a vague assertion. We wish to stress merely one point, namely, that under diverse conditions the visual system responds in terms of a limited number of form constants. Any general theory, however, will have to go beyond a consideration of visual mechanisms per se. The mescaline-produced phenomena demonstrate this point in a striking manner. Mescaline induces changes not only in the visual field but also in other sensory spheres, particularly in the somatosensory sphere. "Haptic hallucinations" and other somatosensory phenomena may dominate the symptomatology to the exclusion of phenomena in the visual sphere.

We shall not enter into a description of the somatosensory changes, but merely mention that Professor Forster (16), for example, felt a net similar to a "cobweb" on his tongue: "When I opened my mouth, a cold wind passed through and the net moved." Serko (72) frequently had the sensation that his legs or his feet consisted of "spirals." In his case, sometimes the haptic spiral of a leg blended with a luminous spiral that had been rotating in the visual field. "One has the sensation of somatic and optic unity." To dismiss such phenomena as synesthetic experiences merely emphasizes the present lack of knowledge concerning the processes involved in synesthesias and intersensory relations in general. A physician, a subject of Beringer (4), "saw" and "felt" the sounds of a concertina played by the experimenter, and the pain produced by it coagulated as luminous curves in the spiral turns of his body, the lower part of his body being a green varnished cone with spiral windings. Such experiences would probably be classified as instances of complex synesthesias. However, a form constant may involve so many spheres that even a synesthetic basis would be too narrow. In one of Beringer's subjects (also a physician), the "lattice" or "fretwork" constant became so dominant that it appeared to penetrate the whole personality.

The subject stated that he saw fretwork before his eyes, that his arms, hands, and fingers turned into fretwork and that he became identical with the fretwork. There was no difference between the fretwork and himself, between inside and outside. All objects in the room and the walls changed into fretwork and thus became identical with him. While writing, the words turned into fretwork and there was, therefore, an identity of fretwork and handwriting. "The fretwork is I." All ideas turned into glass fretwork, which he saw, thought, and felt. He also felt, saw, tasted, and smelled tones that became fretwork. He himself was the tone. On the day following the experiment, there was Nissl (whom he had known in 1914) sitting somewhere in the air, and Nissl was fretwork. "I saw him, I felt him; Nissl was I."

It seems necessary to assume some basic process operative in different sense modalities to cope with all varieties of synesthetic experiences. Even the fact that a sensory impression or a hallucination in one of the sense fields is followed by manifestations in other sense fields does not give us the right to speak of "primary" and "secondary" sensations (or hallucinations) except in the sense of a temporal succession. One event may be primary and another one secondary in this sense, and yet the intersensory relation may involve only one basic process. Similarly, we may doubt whether the preceding example of a "mescal psychosis" with "fretwork" or "lattice" as the central theme can be understood by considering the hallucinatory occurrence of the fretwork in the visual field as the "primary" event that determines "secondary" and "tertiary," etc., events, such as changes in other sense fields and in the mechanisms of thought and emotion.

In a further search for hallucinatory constants, we shall again start with a consideration of the form factor. We note that a single form (figure, object) may be duplicated or multiplied, that its size may change or that its shape may be altered or distorted; i.e., we may have monocular or binocular diplopia or polyopia; dysmegalopsia (micropsia or macropsia); metamorphopsia or dysmorphopsia.

If we analyze the visual phenomena produced by mescaline, we find diplopia, polyopia, dysmegalopsia, and dysmorphopsia not only of hallucinatory objects but also of real or imaginal objects. That is to say, the same mechanisms may be operative, no matter whether an object is perceived, imagined, or hallucinated. The mescaline experiments demonstrate, therefore, that we must go beyond the level of visual hallucinations to determine hallucinatory constants. In fact, we must even go beyond the visual mechanisms that cut across distinctions between perception, imagery, and hallucination and raise the question whether similar mechanisms are operative in nonvisual spheres. There is no doubt that polyopia, dysmegalopsia, and dysmorphopsia find their parallel in experiences in the somatosensory sphere. Subjects in the mescalinized state feel that their limbs shrink or grow, that they are shortened or elongated, or that they are distorted in many ways. The experience of changes in size and the sensation of distortions and alterations may involve the whole body. As regards polyopia, its counterpart is found, for example, in a "polymelia" of the fingers or of the arms. The subject may feel several arms growing out of his shoulder until he feels "like the Buddhas." At times, the alterations in the somatosensory sphere may be so profound that parts of the body feel separated from the rest. As Serko insisted, there may be, not a "sensation" but a "somatopsychic hallucination" of two bodily forms, e.g., of an amputated leg and of a foot entirely separate lying beside it.

The tendency toward reduplication appears not only in polyopia and "polymelia" but also in hallucinatory experiences involving the presence of one or many persons in the room. Although these persons are not seen, their reality is in some way experienced or "felt." In this connection, it is of interest that "splitting" of personality and various degrees of "depersonalization" have been frequently reported. It may be said, therefore, that polyopia, dysmegalopsia, and dysmorphopsia involve mechanisms that are characteristic of mescaline-induced phenomena not only in the visual sphere (hallucination, imagery, perception) but also in the somatosensory sphere.

Further analysis reveals the fact that mescaline is only one of many agents bringing about polyopia, dysmegalopsia, and dysmorphopsia. Thus, under certain conditions, the same effects can be observed in "psychogenic" and "nonpsychogenic" hallucinations, even in the *hallucinations autoscopiques*, in the perception of real objects, in visual imagery, in dreams, in eidetic imagery, in hypnagogic hallucinations, in the phenomena that arise when flickering fields are viewed (4, 12, 14, 15, 23–25, 29, 36, 51, 53, 58, 66, 69, 83, 84). In other words, reduplication or changes in size or shape of a given visual form may occur, no matter whether the object in question is real or has appeared as the result of looking for a considerable time at a flickering field; whether it is hallucinated, visually imagined, or seen as an eidetic or hypnagogic image. In fact, some spontaneous drawings seem to exhibit similar tendencies, so that Maclay, Guttmann, and Mayer-Gross speak of a "mescaline type" of drawing (45). By way of summary, it may be said that polyopia, dysmegalopsia, and dysmorphopsia occur not only in visual hallucinations but also in many other phenomena of the visual sphere (visual perception, eidetic imagery, dreams, etc.).

The fact that diverse visual phenomena commonly assigned to different functional levels of the visual system may show the same typical behavior becomes of still greater interest if we consider the various conditions and clinical states in which such typical behavior occurs. The "symptoms" of polyopia, dysmegalopsia, and dysmorphopsia have been observed in different psychoses, especially in toxic psychoses or at the beginning of certain psychoses, in deliriums, in insulin hypoglycemia, in hysteria, in patients with cerebral lesions, particularly with parieto-occipital or occipital lesions, in the basedoid constitution, in eidetic individuals, and in poisonings produced by certain drugs (hashish, cocaine, etc., chronically used). Beringer (4) has called attention to the existence of these symptoms in the acute phases of schizophrenia. The symptoms were especially striking in one of his hebephrenic patients. Gurewitsch (18, 19) has described an "interparietal syndrome" in which polyopia, dysmegalopsia, and dysmorphopsia are combined with alterations in the postural model of the body or in the bodily schema (Head). According to him, this syndrome is found in nosologically different diseases, such as *lues cerebri*, epilepsy, schizophrenia, hysteria, and cerebral trauma. Thus, the optical symptoms are paralleled in the somatopsychic sphere in other conditions as well as in mescaline intoxication.

In trying to account for polyopia, dysmegalopsia, and dysmorphopsia, ophthalmologists have stressed the importance of dioptric and retinal conditions. Such conditions, however, are not likely to explain the occurrence of similar visual changes in imaginal objects or the fact that the alterations selectively affect only specific objects in a room or only parts of certain objects. Since the optical symptoms occur under many different conditions and in diseases with different etiology, the relative importance of the various factors influencing the visual mechanisms may be expected to vary in different conditions or from one disease to the other. However, we should not necessarily expect entirely different factors to become operative if polyopia and related symptoms appear in a schizophrenic, a mescalinized or eidetic individual or in a patient with a parieto-occipital lesion. The search for some basic factor underlying the optical symptoms in etiologically different conditions is undoubtedly surrounded by the same difficulties as the search for so-called neurological syndromes in psychoses. The "interparietal syndrome" of Gurewitsch is present, for instance, not only in patients with cerebral lesions but also in schizophrenic patients in whom such lesions are absent. It would be rash to conclude that the same syndrome is produced by two different agents. Unfortunately, we are far from knowing the pathophysiological mechanisms that become operative as the result of a parieto-occipital lesion. Once the nature of these mechanisms is known, we shall perhaps understand why the same symptoms may appear, for instance, in schizophrenic patients.

The diversity of conditions in which polyopia, dysmegalopsia, and dysmorphopsia occur has not deterred investigators from looking for some fundamental mechanism. That such a mechanism must be assumed is strongly suggested by the fact that polyopia and related symptoms are characteristic not only of different functional levels in the visual sphere (perception, imagery, hallucination, etc.) but also of the somatosensory sphere. In recent years, the analysis of these symptoms has led most investigators to assign a fundamental role to vestibular factors. It is thought that reduplication of objects, micropsia, macropsia, and dysmorphopsia in hallucinations are indicative of a vestibular influence. The same conclusion is reached, for example, by Menninger-Lerchenthal (53) in his thoroughgoing analysis of autoscopic hallucinations. His view is that autoscopy is a hallucination of the bodily schema which has a visual and a tactile-kinesthetic component. He believes that it does not make any difference whether the study of autoscopic hallucinations is approached from the phenomenological angle or from facts of brain physiology, since the analysis always leads to vestibular factors. Skworzoff (74) has presented similar views. Other investigators have emphasized tonic, postural, and oculomotor factors. In this connection, it is of interest that Pötzl and Urban (63) have stressed the importance of the supravestibular system (in the sense of Muskens).

The experimental data on the influence of the vestibular apparatus on the visual sphere are rather meager. Most of the experiments have been concerned with determining the effects of various forms of labyrinthine stimulation (rotation, galvanic, or caloric stimulation) on different visual phenomena. There is no doubt, however, that the available anatomical, clinical, and experimental data are sufficient for supporting the view that any future research directed toward elucidating the role of the vestibular system is bound to yield extremely significant results not only for the study of hallucinations but also, as some neurologists and psychiatrists insist, for a deeper understanding of neurotic and psychotic behavior. It has even been maintained, particularly by French neurologists, that great strides will be made in psychiatry by obtaining data on vestibular chronaxy.

At this point, it is not possible to outline the various experimental problems that urgently require a solution. We shall be content with calling attention to a new technique that may be employed in analyzing different factors influencing hallucinations or other subjective visual phenomena. By applying alternating current of low intensity and frequency, it is possible to produce flicker that is visible with open or closed eyes under conditions of light as well as dark adaptation. During recent years, the author has obtained some data on the behavior of negative after-images, eidetic images, and hallucinations in the presence of electrically produced flicker. For evaluating the flicker phenomenon itself, it was necessary to examine patients with some pathology of the visual system (hemianopia, enucleation of one eye, etc.). In general, negative after-images disappear almost entirely or change radically in appearance the moment the stimulating current is turned on. Cessation of electrical stimulation immediately leads to a reappearance of the after-image and to a restoration of its normal properties. Eidetic images and certain types of hallucinations may vanish, change, or remain unaltered upon appearance of the electrically produced flicker.

To illustrate: one subject, a student, saw an eidetic image of the face of a person looking at him. When the current was turned on, he suddenly saw the profiles of five faces looking to the right. These faces rapidly changed into other faces; they were seen through the "muslin curtain" of the flicker, as the subject expressed it. More than three decades ago, Urbantschitsch (79, 80) used galvanic current for influencing eidetic images. He reports, e.g., that one of his subjects saw an eidetic image of a hepatica. Application of the galvanic current immediately led to the appearance of a large number of hepaticas. It should be realized, of course, that rotation of the subject or electrical and other forms of stimulation may merely accentuate tendencies inherent in eidetic imagery and other subjective phenomena, since polyopia and related visual changes frequently occur in the absence of any stimulation.

To sum up, in our search for hallucinatory constants we have found (*a*) that the reduplication of objects and the alterations in size and form occurring in hallucinations occur also in other visual phenomena and in phenomena of the somatosensory sphere; (*b*) that these symptoms appear under many different conditions and in diseases of different etiology. The involvement of different senses and the occurrence of these symptoms in etiologically different conditions suggest that we are dealing with some fundamental mechanisms involving various levels of the nervous system. To elucidate these mechanisms, we must rely on future research to provide the necessary anatomical, pathological, biochemical, and clinical data. Some investigators have advanced the view that tendencies toward reduplication of objects and toward seeing or feeling objects "enormously large" or "very small" or distorted in certain ways satisfy certain intellectual or emotional needs. Let us assume that there is a desire to reduce a dignified person to Lilliputian dimensions "because he will look so funny." The desire itself is likely to be ineffective in producing micropsia unless it is coupled with a basedoid constitution, some disease process, or some other condition that throws certain neural mechanisms into gear. In fact, emotional or intellectual needs of such a kind, if they should exist, may be merely another expression of the existence of such mechanisms. At any rate, there is an interdependence of many different factors.

A further point should be emphasized. We may say that under normal and pathological conditions certain mechanisms are available for producing a limited number of fundamental alterations in a visual object. Such alterations manifest themselves in polyopia, dysmegalopsia, and dysmorphopsia. But the fact that an alteration, *e.g.*, in shape, occurs as one of a limited number of fundamental alterations does not mean that there is any constancy in the sense that particular shapes or distortions are invariably produced. It seems as though there were no limit to the number of different shapes an object may assume in the visual experiences of different subjects. Every conceivable distortion has been reported. The situation is similar with regard to alterations in size or number of objects. A few fundamental alterations may, therefore, produce phenomenologically a very complex picture, especially since changes in number,

size, and shape of objects may combine in many ways. Furthermore, all these changes may occur within the framework of altered
spatio-temporal relations. For example, the perception of movement may be radically changed or even become impossible; all
objects may appear at the same distance, or they may recede into
space without changing size (porrhopsia).

In determining hallucinatory constants, we have so far been
primarily concerned with the properties or changes of single objects
and configurations. Our next step is to consider the behavior of
these objects in space and the relation of objects to each other. We
shall start from certain facts obtained in experimental investigations
of eidetic imagery (34–36, 68–70).

In studying the behavior of certain types of eidetic imagery, we
find an occurrence of the following changes: there is a translocation
of objects or parts of objects; parts or properties of one object are
transferred to another object; only fragments or certain parts of an
object appear; the appearance of one object is accompanied by the
disappearance of another; an object undergoes rotational displacements of various kinds (mirror reversals, etc.); there occurs a splitting up of objects into many fragments; objects appear that did not
constitute parts of the preceding stimulus situation; a given object
disappears and reappears periodically; objects or parts of objects
are entirely missing; objects that appeared in the stimulus situation
are missing but appear after relatively long periods of time, even
after hours, in the eidetic image of some other stimulus situation.
The changes just described are characteristic of eidetic images
produced by previous stimulation, e.g., by letting the subject view a
picture for a certain length of time. But it should be remarked that
changes occurring in spontaneous eidetic images are often similar in
nature.

It is perhaps safe to assume that these changes involve some
basic mechanisms, since similar changes in spatio-temporal relations
have been found to occur in visual agnosia. The fact that the visual
perception of patients with traumatic lesions of the occipital lobes
should exhibit the same type of spatio-temporal changes as certain
eidetic images is, as Schilder (68) puts it, "exceedingly surprising"
to anybody familiar with the facts of brain pathology. Pötzl
(62) has called attention to the fact that even the perceptions
of normal persons may show similar changes under conditions of
peripheral vision and in tachistoscopic experiments. It is of special

interest in this connection that Pötzl (61) was able to produce visual hallucinations by tachistoscopic exposures of pictures or objects in a patient with latent hemianopia and an alcoholic hallucinosis. The experimentally produced hallucinations were characterized by changes of the kind found in eidetic imagery. It is apparent that similar changes are characteristic of dreams. In brief, under certain conditions, the same structure of spatio-temporal transformations becomes apparent in eidetic imagery, hallucinations, dreams, and visual perception.

In an attempt to define hallucinatory constants, we have purposely taken visual forms and their interrelations as a point of departure. It is obvious that we have ignored many aspects of hallucinatory phenomena in order to arrive at these constants. *The hallucinatory constants that we have found may be tentatively assigned to three levels: (a) the level of "form constants"; (b) the level of alterations in number, size, and shape (polyopia, dysmegalopsia, dysmorphopsia); (c) the level of changes in spatio-temporal relations.* We have shown that the same constants appear in other visual, and even in nonvisual, phenomena. These constants are, therefore, not specific for hallucinations but represent general characteristics. The "structure" of hallucinations is a general structure that is typical of numerous phenomena in the visual sphere.

THE CONTENT OF HALLUCINATIONS

Since we have been interested in an analysis in terms of formal criteria, we have paid no attention to the *content* of the hallucination. If a childless woman hallucinates many babies, it is readily assumed that the hallucination represents a "projection" of affective needs. But if it should be found that the same woman, when looking at a pencil or a chair, suddenly sees a row of pencils or a row of chairs, it appears unlikely that emotional factors are responsible for the multiple seeing of objects. Of course, any object, no matter whether it is eidetically seen, hallucinated, imagined, or perceived as a real object, may be of emotional significance. It is one thing to admit that objects in multiple vision may have emotional significance; it is an entirely different thing to assert that polyopia itself is created by emotional factors. One of Schilder's (67) patients, an officer with a crippled arm, saw in a fever delirium all persons around him with crippled or missing arms and legs. A blind patient hallucinated heads with empty eye sockets. Following an ophthalmological examination, a schizophrenic woman stated that one of her eyes was red and inflamed; subsequently she saw all persons in the room with one red eye (53).

It may be said that in such cases of transitivism, to use Wernicke's expression, affective factors determine the content of the hallucination. However, to say that the "projection" of disturbances in the motor, vasomotor, and cenesthetic spheres, or of other disturbances, occurs on an affective basis is an empty statement and adds nothing to our knowledge of the workings of affective mechanisms. We want to know the exact nature of these mechanisms in a given case. That a particular object should appear in a hallucination under the stress of some affective need is not more surprising than the fact that the perception of objects, even of a black line, may be "modified" by affective factors.

Psychologically, objects per se have no existence; they exist only as nodal points in a network of perceptual, affective, or logical relations. It is the determination of these relations that is the task of psychology. A live bull snake, a boa constrictor in a motion picture, and a wavy black line of certain dimensions may lead to reactions of "fear" in a certain monkey, whereas a live garter snake and a boa constrictor in a film running at a higher speed may not. It is not a certain size, color, shape, or speed of movement that leads to the manifestation of "fear" in the monkey but a specific form of "togetherness" of these properties that constitutes the behaviorally effective stimulus, and this can be determined only experimentally. We cannot specify the psychological nature of the "fear" existing in the animal without specifying the effective stimulus properties existing outside the animal. Certain objects or events become emotionally equivalent because they share certain properties. By studying the properties of equivalent and nonequivalent situations, we may be able to learn something about the nature of the affective mechanism. Under the influence of *different* affective factors, objects and events become imbued with *different* properties, just as under one set of conditions a circle becomes perceptually "similar" to and, under another set of conditions, "different" from an ellipse. The affective mechanism in a crippled patient who hallucinates the absence of a leg not only in other persons but also in their photographs and mirror images, as well as in dogs and chairs, is undoubtedly not the same as the affective mechanism in Schilder's patient, who saw his defect only in other persons.

As far as dreams are concerned, a widely held theory explains their content by reference to affective factors. It is assumed that all dreams are wish fulfillments. According to this theory, the appearance of certain objects and events in a dream is determined by some egocentric wish. Certain considerations are pertinent here.

Objects and events, no matter whether they exist in the external world, in a hallucination, or in a dream, may be similar and dissimilar in many respects. To understand particular forms of similarity, we have recourse to mechanisms of sensory organization, to affective factors, to logical relations, etc. The author previously pointed out (37) that it is by virtue of certain similarities that heterogeneous objects and events lie in the same "dimension" or belong to the same "series" and that the problem of determining basic mechanisms in animal and human behavior often reduces itself, therefore, to determining and locating properties or factors in terms of which diverse objects and events may become similar.

It may be said that the behavioral reactions of animals as well as the perceptual and affective reactions or processes of "abstraction" in man proceed by constantly shifting "dimensions," *i.e.*, by constantly destroying similarities and constantly creating new ones. The existence of similarities presents, therefore, no problem; the only problem consists in determining just why particular similarities exist. The occurrence of similarities, *i.e.*, the fact that there exist certain characteristics, factors, or processes that bind objects together and relate them in many specific ways, seems to be of such fundamental nature that the physiologist, Kries, considered it simply an expression of some basic property in the functioning of the central nervous system. Freud, for instance, was forced to the conclusion that the factor of similarity is of paramount importance in the mechanism of dream formation. Since the fundamental role of similarity is apparent in any other group of psychological phenomena, it is not surprising that any superficial analysis of dreams leads to the same result.

However, we must demand that the analysis of the phenomena provide us with the *particular* factors that account for the specific ways in which objects and events are related. To account for particular similarities, factors ranging from physical *Gestalten* to castration complexes have been advanced. It is not the large range of such factors that presents a serious problem; the chief difficulty lies in determining which particular factor accounts adequately for certain relations between objects and events, whether it is, for instance, "visual asymmetry" or "fear of bodily injury."

We recall that in eidetic images and certain other phenomena we find translocation of objects or transfer of certain characteristics of these objects, fusions and composite formations, substitutions, the appearance of parts instead of wholes, the nonappearance or the belated appearance of objects or parts of objects, reversals of right and left, up and down, or of other directions. In other words, we find condensation, displacement, and other mechanisms that have been considered typical of dream formation. In eidetic individuals, similar changes may occasionally appear in the perception of real objects and thus become more easily amenable to an experimental approach. From various studies, it is evident that phenomenal properties of objects, visuo-spatial factors, and motor factors play a great role in effecting condensations, displacements, and similar changes in eidetic imagery. *This suggests the possibility that the changes in dreams, such as condensations and displacements, frequently result from an operation of the same (visuo-spatial, motor, etc.) factors.*

In eidetic images, some of these changes can be experimentally demonstrated by setting up certain conditions. The fact that colors, shapes, movements, etc., occur at all in eidetic images, dreams and related phenomena can be understood only by reference to some fundamental properties and processes in the visual system; it seems that the occurrence of certain condensations and displacements can be accounted for only on a similar basis. It should also be recalled that G. E. Müller went so far as to consider the behavior of the eidetic images studied by Urbantschitsch as an example of the influence of "apsychonomic" (anatomico-physiological or metabolic) factors. Urbantschitsch was able to produce a variety of changes in eidetic images by a compression of blood vessels or by the application of visual, auditory, thermal, and other stimuli. At any rate, if visuo-spatial factors lead, for instance, to the fusion of several houses or persons into one, the condensation itself is obviously not created by some affective reaction toward nudity or some similar factor, although, once created, it may still serve as a vehicle for affective needs.

To understand the occurrence of certain spatio-temporal changes in visual phenomena, we must have recourse not only to such factors as brightness, color, shape, and spatial organization but also to factors by virtue of which colors and geometric figures, colors and melodies, sounds and lines may become similar and belong to the same "dimension." Recently, it has even become necessary to resort to "physiognomic characters" to account, for instance, for the similarity between a handwriting, a painting, and the gait of a person. We merely wish to emphasize that the operation of visual factors alone may lead to reversals, displacements, condensations, etc. This does not mean that numerous other factors may not play a role. In an experimental study, Pötzl (62) found that the development of dreams was determined by visual, motor, and "symbolical" factors and that the first two factors were "relatively independent of psychoanalytical factors." He believes that "repressed psychic material," being itself *Gestalt*-less, may act like a catalyzer for optical and motor processes. Whether the psychic material is "repressed" or not does not concern us here, but it is obvious that any color, shape, movement, reversal, displacement, condensation, etc., once supplied by visual or motor processes, may become imbued with "meaning" and that "meaning," in turn, may guide visual and motor reactions.

There is no question that all these factors are also operative in the visual perception of the outer world, but the spatio-temporal stability of external objects is such that fusions, displacements, and the like do not occur in general. Dreams, it has been said, are similar to "eidetic images of the basedoid type." They seem at least similar in that the visual "stuff" they are made of is more open to an invasion of psychic factors than the "stuff" of other visual phenomena. The visual "stuff" provided by entoptic phenomena, flickering fields, ink blots, dreams, eidetic images of the basedoid type, pseudohallucinations, and certain types of hallucinations is apparently more easily invaded by psychic factors than the "stuff" furnished by the perception of real objects, after-images, eidetic images of the tetanoid type, mescaline hallucinations, and certain other types of hallucinations. It is for this reason that phenomena of the first type have frequently been utilized to learn something about the deeper layers of "personality." *If, for physiological reasons, sleep should suddenly provide us with phenomena of Sinnengedächtnis or belated after-images instead of dreams, even "repressed" wishes would not succeed in changing and distorting the visual material.*

At this point, attention should be called to certain facts that may prove to be of interest in connection with physiological or psychological studies of dreams. Since, in most dreams, visual elements are dominant and since striking alterations in the visual sphere are characteristic of mescaline effects, it seems reasonable to expect an enhancement of dream phenomena under the influence of mescaline. An analysis of available data, however, indicates that most subjects report an absence of dreams for the night following the intoxication, and others refer only to "ordinary dreams." Even though the night may have been dreamless, the next day often provides evidence that the visual system has not yet returned to its normal state. In the literature, the author found only one reference to "unusually plastic, colorful dreams," the nature of which was not described (4). It seems, therefore, that, contrary to our expectations, mescaline does not lead to an enhancement of dreams and that it may even suppress dream activity. This can be only a tentative conclusion, since the whole problem has not been systematically investigated. We know nothing about the effects in chronic mescalinism.

Ludlow (43), who has given the most detailed account of the effects of chronic hashish intoxication, points out that his rest was absolutely dreamless during the whole progress of his hashish life, whereas "he never slept without some dream, more or less vivid" before acquiring the habit. "The visions of the drug entirely supplanted those of nature." Further research should explore the mechanisms of drugs which, under certain conditions, produce striking visual effects in the waking state and at the same time do not increase or even suppress dreams, *i.e.*, phenomena that are primarily visual in nature. In contrast to mescaline and hashish, drugs such as alcohol may turn sleep into a *sommeil vigile* that is constantly interrupted and haunted by extremely vivid dreams ("200 dreams in a night"). According to Epstein (13), such effects are particularly characteristic of the prepsychotic phases of alcoholic psychoses. This author even speaks of a "hypnagogic form of alcoholic insanity," since the long-lasting and colorful hypnagogic images in such alcoholics become frequently the starting point for various delusions.

The self-observations of the writer confirm the impression gained from the literature that the night following the mescaline intoxication is either dreamless or practically devoid of visual dream elements.

In one of the author's experiments, he saw, on awakening in the morning after a dreamless night, that the kaleidoscopic play of mescaline patterns was still present. The patterns were pre-dominantly violet and could be seen with open or closed eyes. He fell asleep again. During this period of sleep he had a dream that may be properly called a "mescaline" dream.

I am lying in bed in a large hall. It seems to me that there are many similar beds in this hall which are also occupied. I turn over to my right side and see a large window which I subject to close inspection. I see clearly the following black letters R E 2 T A U R. It surprises me that I can even distinguish letters. To the right of the last R is a vertical pipe, and I am aware of the fact that it covers additional letters. In the window is a large bottle containing red liquid. There are three words on this bottle. These words are complete and meaningful; yet I am dissatisfied with the third word, because I feel that it is somehow too short. The words are surrounded by a reticulated pattern in delicate greenish colors giving the effect of a decorative label. The scene suddenly shifts, and I find myself looking at the gray wall of a house. Very delicate and fragile objects resembling unshelled peanuts are regularly distributed over the whole surface, thus forming a latticelike pattern. Each husk stands on end, forming an angle of approximately 45 degrees with the surface of the wall. Violet clouds pass across the surface. This makes me wonder whether the whole phenomenon is merely a hallucination. To determine whether such is the case I close my eyes; but I still see violet clouds. I conclude that the house and the peanut lattice have objective existence and that the violet clouds are of hallucinatory origin.

At this point, we cannot undertake an analysis of this dream with reference to mescaline phenomena in general and the phenomena experienced on the preceding day or consider it in the light of other psychological factors. We merely wish to state that the mescaline structure of this dream is fairly obvious and that its mescaline-determined elements range from *presque vu* experiences (33) to mescaline patterns on objects.

In studying hallucinatory and related phenomena in the visual field, we find that they are interrelated in many ways, not only in terms of certain "constants" but also in the sense that the *same* content is experienced on different levels or that a transformation in content is accompanied by a transition from one level to another. It is, of course, well known that the same content may again and again appear on the same visual level, *e.g.*, in an eidetic image, in a hallucination, or in a dream, etc. An eidetic subject may always see the same red cap or the same house when he closes his eyes. One of Ewald's patients (14) saw in three different deliriums the same

three huge brown dogs with blue eyes entering his room, except that
the third time they suddenly opened their mouths and said, "But
this time it's really we." In contrast, we have the appearance of
the same content on different visual levels, *e.g.*, when a visual scene
experienced in a fever delirium in childhood reappears several
decades later in a mescaline hallucination. Guttmann (20) describes
a mescaline hallucination that reappeared as a hypnagogic image 2
years later, when one evening he fell asleep after an exhausting day
during the First World War. He recognized the identity of the
content only when he studied old protocols 5 years afterward. It
has also been reported that the content of a hypnagogic image may
reappear in a dream. A mescaline hallucination may be the reproduction of a previously perceived visual object, such as a geographical
map. In the experience of the individual, a visual memory-image
may transform itself into an eidetic image; a positive or negative
after-image, into a mescaline hallucination; and a pseudohallucination, into a hallucination.

"Hallucinations" vs. "Syndromes with Hallucinatory Elements"

Although it may be true that the complexity of visual hallucinations and related phenomena is somewhat reduced by an analysis
which shows that the same constants or even the same contents
appear on different visual levels, it does not alter the fact that there
still remain many phenomenal characteristics and forms of behavior
in hallucinations, eidetic images, dreams, etc., which are refractory
to such an analysis. For example, if we consider the phenomenology
of mescaline-induced hallucinations, we find "primitive" as well as
"scenic" or "panoramic" hallucinations or, expressed differently,
"mescaline-specific" and "mescaline-nonspecific" hallucinations
(91). It should be remarked that our analysis has been largely
confined to "primitive" or "mescaline-specific" hallucinations.
Furthermore, it is clear that the total picture of "primitive" and
"scenic" mescaline hallucinations is related to changes in other
sense fields and ultimately can be understood only by also considering
alterations affecting the total personality. We are undoubtedly safe
in assuming that the hallucinatory phenomena in a mescalinized
person dictating a description of his visual experiences to an assistant
are in some way not the same as those of a person in a "mescal
psychosis." Kinnier Wilson (85), for instance, refers to an indi-

vidual who, under the influence of mescaline, was found "crawling about the floor with extreme care, but averred he was a fly walking on the ceiling upside down and that if he moved quickly he would fall and be injured."

In applying the term *hallucination* to phenomenologically and genetically different phenomena, most investigators have tacitly assumed that they are dealing with the "same" symptom and that criteria employed in studying, for instance, visual hallucinations are also applicable to hallucinations in other fields. However, a "hallucination" always appears as an element in a complex of other symptoms. Schröder (71) doubts, therefore, that there is such a thing as a "hallucination," *i.e.*, something which, as an elementary symptom, can be detached from other symptoms and independently studied by comparing it, for instance, with "hallucinations" in other sense fields. He insists that only the whole complex of symptoms, in which the hallucinations appear, can be profitably studied and describes four such "complexes with hallucinatory elements": (a) deliriums; (b) verbal hallucinosis; (c) sensory deceptions associated with affective states (anxiety, delusions of reference); (d) hallucinosis phantastica (paraphrenia). He questions the sensory basis of many so-called sensory deceptions.

It is apparent from a study of the literature that ever-renewed efforts have been made to evolve criteria suitable for describing and classifying the whole range of hallucinatory phenomena. The literature has grown to such proportions that Mourgue (57), for instance, found it necessary to consult more than 7000 titles. In an attempt to cope with the wealth of subjective phenomena arising under normal and pathological conditions, investigators have considered such factors as levels of reality, states of consciousness (degree of "clouding"), phenomenal appearance, the relation to "inner" and "outer" space, and the relation to "intentions" or "acts" of the subject. The employment of such criteria has led to a classification of the phenomena into hallucinations, pseudohallucinations, illusions, eidetic images, eidetic images with *Realitätscharakter*, hypnagogic images, reperceptions, *Sinnengedächtnis*, memory-after-images, pseudo-memory-images, and phantastic visual phenomena. This does not exhaust the number of distinctions drawn on various grounds. For example, hallucinations have been divided into "psychogenic" and "nonpsychogenic," *eigentliche* and *uneigentliche*, positive and negative hallucinations.

In view of the large number of distinctions available, we should expect that an investigator would have no difficulty in assigning the various sensory deceptions in his subjects or other forms of subjective experiences their proper place in a classification of hallucinatory and related phenomena. However, this is far from being the case. The *first* difficulty arises from the fact that in actual experience there are many transitions and transformations, so that, for example, an illusion or a hynagogic image may turn into an hallucination. A *second* difficulty is more serious. It frequently happens that the hallucinatory experience of the subject is such that it cannot be adequately described and classified in terms of available concepts. Klein (30), for instance, found that current definitions were of no use in characterizing the hemianopic hallucinations of his patients and that these could be described only as "special forms of pathological experience." Many other phenomena arising under normal and pathological conditions display the same resistance to being labeled and do not fit into any classificatory scheme. In the case of eidetic imagery, for instance, the question has been raised whether the experience of the subject should be classified as a projected memory-image, a pseudohallucination, or a hallucination (28, 60). A similar question arises with regard to "mescaline hallucinations."

We have used the term, "mescaline hallucinations," only to characterize the phenomena in a preliminary way. Even the self-observations of qualified observers have not settled the point whether the phenomena arising at certain stages of the poisoning should be designated as hallucinations or pseudohallucinations. Some observers hold that they are pseudohallucinations in the sense of Kandinsky; others believe that the phenomena can be described only by reference to a new concept of "pseudohallucination" different from that of Kandinsky. Instead of classifying the phenomena, some investigators have been content with references to the state of consciousness of the subject or the level of reality on which the phenomena appear. Claude and Ey (7) state that an "hallucinogenic substance" such as mescaline produces an *osmose du réel et de l'imaginaire*. Ewald (14) thinks that we are dealing with hallucinatory-dreamlike experiences occurring in "a kind of delirium without clouding of consciousness" and reports that a similarly "rich optically delirious picture" without clouding of consciousness is sometimes found in cases of chronic encephalitis and in patients with hypophysial tumors.

The fact that present concepts in the field of hallucinations cannot do justice to the wealth of normal and pathological experiences can be remedied in only two ways. It must be recognized, first, that most categories employed in describing psychic phenomena in general are neither clearly defined nor generally agreed upon. It follows that any improvement in the conceptual tools of psychology will benefit the study of hallucinations. In the second place, many normal and pathological experiences have either not been analyzed so far by using techniques already available or could not be analyzed because of the difficulties of an experimental approach. It follows that new approaches and more thorough analyses will help to define more clearly the varieties of hallucinatory experiences.

Psychiatrists have recognized that many hallucinations of dementia praecox patients are not really hallucinations but, to use the German expression, *uneigentliche Halluzinationen*. Although the patients refer to sensory experiences of all kinds, it remains frequently obscure in what sense field the hallucinations occur. In fact, it is questionable whether the hallucinations really represent visual, auditory, or cenesthetic experiences or have any sensory content. It is of interest that an investigation of synesthesias in normal individuals leads into similar difficulties (27). It is true that an auditory stimulus may give rise to a sensation of color in some subjects, but in others the color, *e.g.*, purple, is not actually *seen*. Instead, the subject experiences a "feeling like purple" or a feeling "as if purple." In these subjects it is a similarity in affective relations that is apparently responsible for the quasi-visual "as if" character of the synesthetic experience. In still another group of subjects, the auditory stimulus calls forth merely the visual image of a color.

There are also "complex synesthesias" that are characterized by the fact that the thinking of an abstract concept (infinity, peace, sin, negation, etc.) invariably leads to seeing or imagining certain colors, figures, or lines or to some "as if" experience of such colors, etc. The subject, for example, may have the experience of a "horizontal, sharp, thin, square plate of white metal" when thinking about "negation." We may say, therefore, that there are not only *eigentliche* and *uneigentliche* hallucinations but also *eigentliche* and *uneigentliche* forms of synesthesia. The results of a chemical approach to these problems, however, should warn us that we cannot entirely dismiss the possibility that certain or even all "cenesthetic hallucinations" of dementia praecox patients may have some sensory basis. The profound effects of mescaline on the sensorium are known, and yet, as Mayer-Gross (51) correctly observes, the descriptions of abnormal somatosensory experiences by mescalinized persons are often as fantastic and unintelligible as those of schizophrenics.

The *third* difficulty in arriving at clear concepts in the field of hallucinations arises from the complexity and inconstancy of "hallucination" as a symptom in a group of other symptoms. It is characteristic of drugs, disease processes, and other hallucinogenic factors and conditions that they produce more than one type of sensory deception. In fact, in some psychoses, there are apparently hallucinations of different types and of different sensory origin, "reflex hallucinations," pseudohallucinations, illusions, and almost every kind of sensory deception ever described. Bleuler has presented a truly impressive picture of the varieties of sensory deceptions in schizophrenia. Even in mescaline poisoning, we find different kinds of illusions, pseudohallucinations, and hallucinations. Furthermore, all these phenomena may be very inconstant in the sense that all or some of them may be present or absent under certain conditions or at certain stages of the disease or the poisoning. "Voices" not heard for many months may suddenly be heard again. At one time, the hallucinating may be interrupted by weak forms of external stimulation; at other times even strong stimuli are ineffective.

The fact that the same dose of mescaline may produce at different times different types of hallucinations in the same subject has led Franke (17) to suggest serial poisonings, with intervals of days instead of months. He believes that long intervals may introduce differences in the "actual biological condition" of the individual, a condition that is undoubtedly influenced by factors such as age, hunger, thirst, fatigue, weather, nutrition, emotional states, etc. The question may be raised, however, as to why certain psychic functions remain fairly constant and are only little affected by marked changes in the "actual biological condition," whereas hallucinatory phenomena and the hallucinatory process undergo marked fluctuations. It is of interest in this connection that similar fluctuations seem to be characteristic of the performances of patients with visual agnosia. For example, the patient may be able to recognize certain details or general relations on one day but not on the next, or only under certain conditions; he may be able to do it spontaneously but not at will, or vice versa. At any rate, the factors responsible for these fluctuations in hallucinatory symptoms cannot be clearly defined at present.

Mourgue (57) has advanced the view that they are due to a dys-regulation of the normal relations between the vegetative system (in the sense of Kraus) and the cortex. The hallucination, according to his view, represents an invasion of the world of "instincts" into the "sphere of orientation and causality"; it is not a "morpholog-ical" but a "secretory" disorder (in the sense of Mourgue and von Monakow) indicative of disturbances in the normal relations between the "vegetative" or "instinctive" sphere and the cortex. Mourgue is not surprised that fluctuations and oscillations in hallucinatory symptoms represent the normal state of affairs, since the hallucina-tion is essentially not a static phenomenon but a dynamic process, the instability of which merely reflects an instability in the conditions of its origin. Although the value of such concepts as "sphere of orientation and causality" and "sphere of instincts" for actual research may be questioned, there is no doubt about the importance of vegetative mechanisms for hunger, thirst, sex, sleep, and affective states. Furthermore, it appears that further information on factors influencing the excitability of the vegetative system (electrolytes and lipoids, hormones, colloidal balance, etc.) will be of far-reaching significance for the problem of hallucinations.

Research in the field of hallucinations has been dominated by two chief interests. Either the investigators have been interested in the structure of the various phenomena commonly classified as "hallucinations" or they have studied the hallucination as a "symptom" in an aggregate of other symptoms. For investigative work, it matters little whether we start from the phenomenology of hallucinatory experiences or from "syndromes with hallucinatory elements," since any thorough analysis will lead to a study of many related factors.

The hallucinatory constants that we have described are charac-teristic not only of certain aspects of hallucinations but also of a variety of other phenomena. The existence of these constants suggests some constancy in the underlying conditions. Other aspects of hallucinations and the hallucinatory process itself are often characterized by instability and fluctuations, and it is the task of future research to deduce the occurrence of these fluctuations from the nature of the underlying mechanisms. No one would have thought a short time ago, Mourgue points out, that there ever could be any connection between tetany and the subject of hallucinations. And, we may add, no one would have thought of electrolytes and hormones in connection with hallucinations. Ultimately we are not interested in hallucinatory constants per se but in the conditions producing them. There is no doubt that the study of these conditions will be significant for the analysis of certain disease processes and the exploration of fundamental reaction systems in normal individuals.

The phenomenological approach finally leads to the study of certain syndromes and general reaction systems in the organism; the study of "syndromes with hallucinatory elements" finally leads to an analysis of the hallucinatory phenomena. Only by studying the whole complex of symptoms in mescaline intoxication, including the hallucinatory symptoms, has it become possible to recognize mescaline as an agent for the production of "experimental psychoses," and only in such a way have psychiatrists recognized the symptomatological similarity between mescaline intoxication and the acute phases of schizophrenia (3, 4, 7, 8, 22, 47, 76). No matter what the symptomatological relations may be, the "mescal psychosis" is produced by a well-defined chemical substance and not by hypothetically assumed toxins, "metatoxic intermediaries," and the like. It seems that psychotic symptoms resembling those of mescaline intoxication appear not only in the course of the schizophrenic disease process but also under other conditions. Serko (73), for instance, described the "unusually interesting psychosis" of a patient whose symptoms were strikingly similar to those produced by mescaline. In view of these findings, it is unfortunate that at present so little is known about the biochemical processes involved in mescaline action.

To complete the picture of the total effects produced by mescaline, we should mention some facts that have a more particular bearing on the study of normal and abnormal personality. It was found, for example, that posthypnotic suggestions may influence mescaline-produced hallucinations and that, in turn, posthypnotic sensory deceptions may become altered under the influence of the drug (59). A patient with spontaneous hemianopic hallucinations declared herself *blind* for the duration of the mescalinized state (1). A patient who had not heard "voices" for half a year heard them again while under the influence of mescaline (89). Other investigators have used mescaline for more frontal attacks on problems of personality. They have been interested, for example, in the reactions of different personality types, different races, and mentally subnormal individuals and in the possibility of obtaining "confessions" during the intoxication (2, 4, 39, 47, 48, 59). The results suggest that mescaline investigations cannot be considered the royal road to "the hinterland of character" and that the chief value of this drug lies in its effectiveness as a research tool in the solution of some fundamental problems of biological psychology and psychiatry.

REFERENCES

1. ADLER, A., & PÖTZL, O. Über eine eigenartige Reaktion auf Meskalin bei einer Kranken mit doppelseitigen Herden in der Sehsphäre. *Jahrb. Psychiat. & Neurol.*, 1936, **53**, 13–34.

2. BENSHEIM, H. Typenunterschiede bei Meskalinversuchen. *Z. ges. Neurol. Psychiat.*, 1929, **121**, 531–543.

3. BERINGER, K. Experimentelle Psychosen durch Mescalin. *Z. ges. Neurol. Psychiat.*, 1923, **84**, 426–433.

4. BERINGER, K. Der Meskalinrausch. *Monogr. Gesamtgeb. Neurol. & Psychiat.*, 1927, **49**, 1–315.

5. BERZE, J. Eigenartige Gesichtshalluzinationen in einem Falle von akuter Trinkerpsychose. *Z. ges. Neurol. Psychiat.*, 1923, **84**, 487–521.

6. CERONI, L. L'intossicazione mescalinica. (Autoesperienze.) *Riv. sper. Freniat.*, 1932, **56**, 42–104.

7. CLAUDE, H., & EY, H. La mescaline, substance hallucinogène. *C. R. Soc. Biol., Paris*, 1934, **115**, 838–841.

8. DESCHAMPS, A. Éther, cocaïne, hachich, peyotl et démence précoce. Paris: Éditions Véga, 1932, pp. 210.

9. DYBOWSKI, M. Conditions for the appearance of hynagogic visions. *Kwart. psychol.*, 1939, **11**, 68–94.

10. EBBECKE, U. Receptorenapparat und entoptische Erscheinungen. *Handb. norm. u. pathol. Physiol.* Berlin: Springer, 1929. Vol. XII, Pt. 1, 233–265.

11. ELLIS, H. Mescal, a new artificial paradise. *Ann. rep. Smithsonian Instit.*, 1897, 537–548.

12. ENGERTH, G., HOFF, H., & PÖTZL, O. Zur Patho-Physiologie der hemianopischen Halluzinationen. *Z. ges. Neurol. Psychiat.*, 1935, **152**, 399–421.

13. EPSTEIN, A. L. Somatologische Studien zur Psychiatrie. *Z. ges. Neurol. Psychiat.*, 1933, **146**, 525–547.

14. EWALD, G. Psychosen bei akuten Infektionen, bei Allgemeinleiden und bei Erkrankung innerer Organe. *Handb. Geisteskr.*, Ergänzungsband. Berlin: Springer, 1939. Pt. 1, pp. 205–247.

15. FISCHER, O. Ein weiterer Beitrag zur Klinik und Pathogenese der hysterischen Dysmegalopsie. *Mschr. Psychiat. Neurol.*, 1907, **21**, 1–19.

16. FORSTER, E. Selbstversuch mit Meskalin. Z. ges. Neurol. Psychiat., 1930, 127, 1–14.

17. FRANKE, G. Variierte Serienversuche mit Meskalin. Z. ges. Neurol. Psychiat., 1934, 150, 427–433.

18. GUREWITSCH, M. Über das interparietale Syndrom bei Geisteskrankheiten. Z. ges. Neurol. Psychiat., 1932, 140, 593–603.

19. GUREWITSCH, M. Weitere Beiträge zur Lehre vom interparietalen Syndrom bei Geisteskrankheiten. Z. ges. Neurol. Psychiat., 1933, 146, 126–144.

20. GUTTMANN, A. Medikamentöse Spaltung der Persönlichkeit. Mschr. Psychiat. Neurol. 1924, 56, 161–187.

21. GUTTMANN, E. Artificial psychoses produced by mescaline. J. ment. Sci., 1936, 82, 203–221.

22. GUTTMANN, E., & MACLAY, W. S. Mescalin and depersonalization. J. Neurol. Psychopath., 1936, 16, 193–212.

23. HAACK, K. Experimental-deskriptive Psychologie der Bewegungen, Konfigurationen und Farben unter Verwendung des Flimmerphaenomens. Berlin: Karger, 1927, pp. 263.

24. HOFF, H., & PÖTZL, O. Über Störungen des Tiefensehens bei zerebraler Metamorphopsie. Mschr. Psychiat. Neurol., 1935, 90, 305–326.

25. HOFF, H., & PÖTZL, O. Zur diagnostischen Bedeutung der Polyopie bei Tumoren des Occipitalhirnes. Z. ges. Neurol. Psychiat., 1935, 152, 433–450.

26. HOPPE, I. Der entoptische Inhalt des Auges und das entoptische Sehfeld beim hallucinatorischen Sehen. Allg. Z. Psychiat., 1887, 43, 438–452.

27. JAENSCH, E. R., et al. Grundformen menschlichen Seins. Berlin: Elsner, 1929, pp. xv + 524.

28. JANKOWSKA, H. Eidetische Bilder und Halluzinationen. Kwart. psychol., 1939, 11, 189–230.

29. KANNER, L., & SCHILDER, P. Movements in optic images and the optic imagination of movements. J. nerv. ment. Dis., 1930, 72, 489–517.

30. KLEIN, R. Beitrag zur Frage der hemianopischen Halluzinationen. Mschr. Psychiat. Neurol., 1936, 92, 131–149.

31. KLIEN, H. Entoptische Wahrnehmung des retinalen Pigmentepithels im Migräneanfall? Z. ges. Neurol. Psychiat., 1917, 36, 323–334.

32. KLÜVER, H. Mescal visions and eidetic vision. Amer. J. Psychol., 1926, 37, 502–515.

33. KLÜVER, H. Mescal. London: Kegan Paul, 1928, pp. 111.

34. KLÜVER, H. Fragmentary eidetic imagery. Psychol. Rev., 1930, 37, 441–458.

35. KLÜVER, H. Eidetic phenomena. Psychol. Bull., 1932, 29, 181–203.

36. KLÜVER, H. The eidetic type. Proc. Ass. Res. nerv. & ment. Dis., 1933, 14, 150–168.

37. KLÜVER, H. The study of personality and the method of equivalent and non-equivalent stimuli. Character & Pers. 1936, 5, 91–112.

38. KÖNIG, A. Eine bisher noch nicht bekannte subjective Gesichtserscheinung. Arch. Ophthal., 1884, 30, 329–330.

39. LA BARRE, W. The peyote cult. New Haven: Yale Univ. Press, 1938, pp. 188.

40. LADD-FRANKLIN, C.   Visible radiation from excited nerve fiber: the reddish blue arcs and the reddish blue glow of the retina.   *Science*, 1927, **66**, 239–241.

41. LINDEMANN, E.   The neurophysiological effect of intoxicating drugs. *Amer. J. Psychiat.*, 1934, **13**, 1007–1037.

42. LINDEMANN, E., and MALAMUD, W.   Experimental analysis of the psychopathological effects of intoxicating drugs.   *Amer. J. Psychiat.*, 1934, **13**, 853–879.

43. LUDLOW, F.   The hasheesh eater.   New York: Rains, 1903, pp. 371.

44. MACLAY, W. S., & GUTTMANN, E.   Mescaline hallucinations in artists. *Arch. Neurol. Psychiat.*, Chicago, 1941, **45**, 130–137.

45. MACLAY, W. S., GUTTMANN, E., & MAYER-GROSS, W.   Spontaneous drawings as an approach to some problems of psychopathology.   *Proc. roy. Soc. Med.*, 1938, **31**, 1337–1350.

46. MALONEY, W. J. M. A.   Locomotor ataxia (tabes dorsalis).   New York, London: Appleton, 1918, pp. 299.

47. MARINESCO, G.   Recherches sur l'action de la mescaline.   *Presse méd.*, 1933, **41**, 1433–1437.

48. MARINESCO, M. G.   Visions colorées produites par la mescaline.   *Presse méd.*, 1933, **41**, 1864–1866.

49. MARSHALL, C. R.   Entoptic phenomena associated with the retina.   *Brit. J. Ophthal.*, 1935, **19**, 177–201.

50. MARSHALL, C. R.   An enquiry into the causes of mescal visions.   *J. Neurol. Psychopath.*, 1937, **17**, 289–304.

51. MAYER-GROSS, W.   Psychopathologie und Klinik der Trugwahrnehmungen. *Handb. Geisteskr.*, ed. by Bumke. Berlin: Springer, 1928.   Vol. I, Pt. 1, pp. 427–507.

52. MAYER-GROSS, W., & STEIN, H.   Über einige Abänderungen der Sinnestätigkeit im Meskalinrausch.   *Z. ges. Neurol. Psychiat.*, 1926, **101**, 354–386.

53. MENNINGER-LERCHENTHAL, E.   Das Truggebilde der eigenen Gestalt. *Abh. Neur., Psychiat., Psychol. u. ihren Grenzgeb.*, 1935, **74**, pp. iv + 196.

54. MÖLLER, A.   Einige Meskalinversuche.   *Acta psychiat. et neur.*, 1935, **10**, 405–442.

55. MORGENTHALER, W.   Über Zeichnungen von Gesichtshalluzinationen.   *Z. ges. Neurol. Psychiat.*, 1919, **45**, 19–29.

56. MORSELLI, G. E.   Contribution à la psychopathologie de l'intoxication par la mescaline.   *J. de Psychol.*, 1936, **33**, 368–392.

57. MOURGUE, R.   Neurobiologie de l'hallucination.   Bruxelles: Lamertin, 1932, pp. 416.

58. NEUHAUS, W.   Makropsie und Mikropsie bei Basedowoiden.   *Z. ges. Neurol. Psychiat.*, 1926, **105**, 257–313.

59. PAP, Z. v.   Einwirkung des Meskalinrausches auf die posthypnotischen Sinnestäuschungen.   *Z. ges. Neurol. Psychiat.*, 1936, **155**, 655–664.

60. PISK, G.   Zur Frage der Pseudohalluzinationen bei der Schizophrenie und ihrer Beziehungen zur eidetischen Anlage.   *Mschr. Psychiat. Neurol.*, 1936, **92**, 150–156.

61. PÖTZL, O.   Tachystoskopisch provozierte optische Halluzinationen bei einem Falle von Alkoholhalluzinose mit rückgebildeter zerebraler Hemianopsie.   *Jahrb. Psychiat. Neurol.*, 1915, **35**, 141–146.

62. Pötzl, O. Experimentell erregte Traumbilder in ihren Beziehungen zum indirekten Sehen. *Z. ges. Neurol. Psychiat.*, 1917, **37**, 278–349.

63. Pötzl, O., & Urban, H. Über die isoliert erhaltene temporale Sichel bei zerebraler Hemianopsie. *Mschr. Psychiat. Neurol.*, 1936, **92**, 67–106.

64. Purkinje, J. E. Opera omnia. Prague: Society of Czech Physicians, 1918. Vol. I, pp. 1–162.

65. Rohracher, H. Ueber subjektive Lichterscheinungen bei Reizung mit Wechselströmen. *Z. Sinnesphysiol.*, 1935–1936, **66**, 164–181.

66. Schilder, P. Über monokuläre Polyopie bei Hysterie. *Dtsch. Z. Nervenheilk*, 1920, **66**, 250–260.

67. Schilder, P. Über Halluzinationen. *Z. ges. Neurol. Psychiat.*, 1920, **53**, 169–198.

68. Schilder, P. Psychoanalyse und Eidetik. *Z. Sex.-Wiss.*, 1926, **13**, 56.

69. Schilder, P. Experiments on imagination, after-images and hallucinations. *Amer. J. Psychiat.*, 1933, **13**, 597–609.

70. Schilder, P. The vestibular apparatus in neurosis and psychosis. *J. nerv. ment. Dis.*, 1933, **78**, 1–23, 137–164.

71. Schröder, P. Das Halluzinieren. *Z. ges. Neurol. Psychiat.*, 1926, **101**, 599–614.

72. Serko, A. Im Mescalinrausch. *Jahrb. Psychiat. Neurol.*, 1913, **34**, 355–366.

73. Serko, A. Über einen eigenartigen Fall von Geistesstörung. *Z. ges. Neurol. Psychiat.*, 1919, **44**, 21–78.

74. Skworzoff, K. Doppelgänger-Halluzinationen bei Kranken mit Funktionsstörungen des Labyrinths. *Z. ges. Neurol. Psychiat.*, 1931, **133**, 762–766.

75. Stein, J. Über die Veränderung der Sinnesleistungen und die Entstehung von Trugwahrnehmungen. *Handb. Geisteskr.*, ed. by Bumke. Berlin: Springer, 1928. Vol. I, Pt. I, pp. 352–426.

76. Stockings, G. T. A clinical study of the mescaline psychosis, with special reference to the mechanism of the genesis of schizophrenic and other psychotic states. *J. ment. Sci.*, 1940, **86**, 29–47.

77. Szuman, S. Analiza formalna i psychologiczna widzeń meskalinowych. *Kwart. psychol.*, 1930, **1**, 156–212. *Cf.* summary in German, pp. 214–220.

78. Urban, H. Zur Physiologie der Okzipitalregion des Menschen. *Mschr. Psychiat. Neurol.*, 1935, **92**, 32–39.

79. Urbantschitsch, V. Über subjektive optische Anschauungsbilder. Leipzig, Wien: Deuticke, 1907, pp. vi + 211.

80. Urbantschitsch, V. Über subjektive Hörerscheinungen und subjektive optische Anschauungsbilder. Leipzig, Wien: Deuticke, 1908, pp. iv + 123.

81. Veit, F., & Vogt, M. Die Verteilung subcutan verabreichter Alkaloide auf verschiedene Regionen des Zentralnervensystems. *Naturwiss.*, 1934, **22**, 492–494.

82. Vogt, M. Die Verteilung von Arzneistoffen auf verschiedene Regionen des Zentralnervensystems, zugleich ein Beitrag zu ihrer quantitativen Mikrobestimmung im Gewebe. II. Mitteilung: Chinin und Mezkalin. *Arch. exp. Path. Pharmak.*, 1935, **178**, 560–576.

83. WALTON, R. P. Marihuana. Philadelphia: Lippincott, 1938, pp. ix + 223.
84. WEIL, A. Die optischen Wahrnehmungsphänomene in der Hypoglykaemie. *Mschr. Psychiat. Neurol.*, 1938, **100**, 98–128.
85. WILSON, S. A. K. Neurology. Baltimore: Williams & Wilkins, 1940. Vol. I, pp. xxxvi + 751.
86. WOLFF, H. F., & CURRAN, D. Nature of delirium and allied states. *Arch. Neurol. Psychiat.*, *Chicago*, 1935, **33**, 1175–1215.
87. ZÁDOR, J. Meskalinwirkung auf das Phantomglied. *Mschr. Psychiat. Neurol.*, 1930, **77**, 71–99.
88. ZÁDOR, J. Meskalinwirkung bei Störungen des optischen Systems. *Z. ges. Neurol. Psychiat.*, 1930, **127**, 30–107.
89. ZUCKER, K. Über die Zunahme spontaner Halluzinationen nach Meskalin. *Zentbl. ges. Neurol. Psychiat.*, 1930, **56**, 447–448.
90. ZUCKER, K. Versuche mit Meskalin an Halluzinanten. *Z. ges. Neurol. Psychiat.*, 1930, **127**, 108–161.
91. ZUCKER, K., & ZÁDOR, J. Zur Analyse der Meskalin-Wirkung am Normalen. *Z. ges. Neurol. Psychiat.*, 1930, **127**, 15–29.

CHAPTER XI

PSYCHOLOGICAL STUDY OF A YOUNG ADULT MALE PSEUDOHERMAPHRODITE REARED AS A FEMALE

By

CATHARINE COX MILES

Yale School of Medicine

When Martin Murgy[1] was born, abnormality in the external genitals was noted by the attending physician. As is customary in cases of this kind, when the sex is questioned, the infant was declared to be a female. The parents were informed that the child was not quite normal in structure, but nothing of this was known to him in his childhood. He was called "Martha," was regarded as a girl and brought up as one. When he was about 12 years of age, he first noticed that his genital organs were not like those of other girls, and at about this same time he became aware of the fact that his parents considered him "different" in physical structure. His father told him on one occasion that he was not made right and that he "could never be any good." Yet the classification as a girl was apparently not questioned at this time by either the parents or the child.

The parents, Hungarians by birth and Catholics by faith, were hard-working, self-respecting residents of a small New England town, in which "Martha" grew up with three normal siblings, a brother and two sisters. There was a close feeling of family solidarity and sympathy, especially between the mother and the children. The father was a strict, somewhat harsh parent who required of his children that they do right, work hard, and maintain the family status. The mother and sisters were kind and understanding with "Martha," who was the youngest child, although the father and, to some extent, the brother never quite accepted him.

[1] Names and other distinguishing items have been changed in this report for the sake of anonymity. No essential data have been altered. The author gratefully acknowledges the kindness of Dr. Clyde L. Deming, clinical professor of urology, Yale School of Medicine, in referring this patient for psychological study and permitting the inclusion here of a summary of the medical history.

In his early teens "Martha's" voice began to deepen and his musculature to develop strongly. However, he entered high school as a girl and associated with girls as one of them. During this period, he was quite puzzled, knowing that something was wrong but not knowing exactly what it might be. His recollections at a later date indicate that he felt attracted to girls and was beginning to be somewhat stimulated sexually by them. He never felt any sexual attraction toward males, although he preferred to associate with them. He was considered a "tomboy," since he definitely preferred talking sports, playing baseball, or participating in other athletic pursuits with boys to engaging in sewing or other girls' activities. He had no nocturnal emissions, nor did he menstruate.

At 17, still regarded as a girl, he was graduated from high school. At about this time, his mother died. The duties of keeping house fell to him, and these he found very irksome. His older sisters, employed in industry, were sympathetic and kind, but when he began to grow a beard life became truly embarrassing. He began to feel that he was looked on as a freak. His father seemed indifferent to his situation, but other relatives finally decided that something should be done for him. He was then seen by several physicians, who came to the conclusion that he was fundamentally a male. He was sent to a city hospital with a view to full study and possible treatment. A few days before admission to the hospital, he had his hair cut short, put on his first male clothing, and adopted the name of Martin.

At the hospital, he told his physician that he would be satisfied to belong to either sex, although he said also that he would rather have the independence and freedom of life that being a man would give him. He appeared intelligent and cooperative in a series of physical examinations. In these, he was described by the examining physicians as a well-developed, muscular young adult with a rather husky voice, a typically masculine face, a masculine trunk outline, arms, legs, thighs, and loins without the usual female curves, the breasts typically male, without any obvious glandular tissue. The systems, with the exception of the genitals, appeared normal to observation and medical examination. The patient's head hair was coarse and black, and there was a fairly well-developed mustache and a beard. Arms and legs were covered with a moderate amount of coarse, black hair. The hair outline above the forehead, however, followed the female pattern; and the distribution of the pubic hair was more female than male in type, although there were a few scattered coarse hairs between the pubis and the navel.

Examination of the external genitals showed a well-developed phallus, about 5 cm. long, with a ventral curvature, and a well-developed glans with a meatal fossa. The phallus lay behind the folds of the labia majora. The urethra was visible at the base of the phallus, and behind this was a vaginal orifice that admitted of exploration to a distance of 4 cm. Cystoscopic examination revealed apparently normal urethra and vagina, a small cervix, and a cervical os. Study of the patient up to this point indicated that the internal organs were female, although male secondary sex characteristics were present. Studies of the urine for male hormone, X ray of the sella turcica and of the long bones, and an abdominal exploration for a definite diagnosis as to sex were advised. It was thought at this time that the patient might be almost a true hermaphrodite. The X-ray studies revealed a normal sella turcica, a definitely masculine pelvis, and long bones masculine in character. The larynx was found to be prominent and definitely male. The question as to the presence or absence of a suprarenal tumor was not conclusively answered.

Two possible plans for treatment were outlined by the surgeon in charge, one designed to eliminate the male, the other the female factors, choice between the two to be determined by abdominal exploration. It was believed at this time that correction in the direction of femaleness would prove to be the more favorable of the two possibilities because if testicular function were only partial, reversion to the female sex after 10 or 12 years might occur. Use of sex hormones might aid in maintaining the sex balance after surgical treatment.

On November 20, 1939, an exploratory study of the abdominal organs was made and surgical treatment carried out. A rather infantile uterus was found, with complete fallopian tubes and near the usual position of the left ovary a small round gonad which appeared to be a testicle. Microscopic examinations of a frozen section of this gonad proved the presence of testicular tissue. No ovary and no epididymis or vas deferens were found, although some rudimentary tissue appeared to be present, possibly suggesting the latter organs. There was no adrenal tumor, but there was some accessory adrenal tissue in the vicinity of the right fallopian tube. Total hysterectomy and salpingectomy were performed as the first part of the treatment now seen to be desirable. It was still necessary to remove the vagina and repair the essential hypospadias in order to complete the procedure necessary for the comfort and convenience of a male person. The patient stood this first operation well and had an uneventful convalescence. He was discharged after 2 weeks with instructions to return in 1 month for plastic repair.

Two days before discharge from the hospital, Martin was first given psychological study. He had been somewhat antagonized a few days previously by intense questioning by a physician about his sexual life. This had resulted in his being irritated and offended. It was therefore necessary in the psychological examination to proceed with great caution and to limit the study to objective and impersonal questions. A Stanford-Binet (1916) intelligence test was given; also, the Ferguson Form Boards, the Otis Higher Intelligence Examination, Form A, as a 15-minute test (5), a short form of the New Stanford Achievement Dictation (Spelling) Test, the Freyd Occupational Interests Sheet for men, and the Terman-Miles Attitude-Interest Analysis Test, Form A (9). The surgeon in charge generously invited the psychological study and advised the patient to cooperate in the interest of vocational guidance.

The day following completion of this preliminary psychological study the patient was discharged to his home. He spent a quiet month there and returned late in December for further study and treatment. He then reported to his physician that he had been in good health, had gained 4 pounds, and had no complaints. He stated that his beard had increased in density, and his voice had become slightly deeper. He had not observed any other physical changes. He stated that his mental outlook had changed, that he felt unable to put the change into words, but it appeared that he now regarded himself as definitely masculine and through this orientation he had achieved considerable peace of mind. On January 3, 1940, a resection of the vagina was done; also, plastic construction of a penile urethra and meatus. The patient stood the procedure well and made good recovery. He was discharged from the hospital 2 weeks later. The day preceding discharge, he was again referred by his physician for psychological study. At this time, he was given Form B of the Otis Higher Intelligence Examination, without time limit (6), Strong's Vocational Interest Blank, and the Terman-Miles Attitude-Interest Analysis Test, Form B.

Three months later, in April, the patient was admitted for the third time to the hospital urological service. He reported that he had been in excellent health during the preceding weeks, with no unfavorable symptoms.   He stated that his feelings had now become entirely masculine, and he "couldn't understand how he once happened to be a girl."   He said that he had noted penile erections on several occasions.   He reported that he was "now interested in a girl friend." Physical examination showed satisfactory healing of the tissue involved in the previous surgical treatment.   Some breakdown had occurred, producing virtual hypospadias.   Again the bodily systems were found normal, with the exception of the genitals.   Again the well-developed phallus, about 6 cm. in length, was noted lying between the large labia majora; labia minora were also present.   At the base of the phallus was a small urethral opening.   Rectal examination showed no evidence of prostate.   The day following admission, a complete urethra was made surgically from skin flaps by Dr. Deming.   The wound healed satisfactorily, and the patient again returned home.   In June, the last stage of plastic repair was done by the creation of a new urethral meatus at the tip end of the penis to replace the hypospadias.   Healing of the tissue and general convalescence occurred satisfactorily; function was adequately established.   Recovery was complete and the patient in normal good health.   No later history is available.

The patient came to the psychological laboratory from the hospital ward in a wheel chair.   On the second occasion, as on the first, he was comfortably and cheerfully convalescent.   He gave the impression of being a quiet, rather shy, docile, amiable young man, mild rather than aggressive, willing to do what was asked of him but not accustomed to exerting himself beyond a suitably moderate level.   He worked quietly and continuously but without evidence of special drive or exceptional ambition.   He seemed simply to accept the routine that was given him.   One had the impression of an underlying sensitiveness and some protective obstinacy with reference to his personal affairs.   Superficially he was shyly agreeable.   He gave the impression of not having a great amount of physical energy, although this was no doubt in part due to his physical condition at the time.   He seemed, on the whole, to be one of those persons of average competence and average composure and balance who have practically no psychopathic difficulties and no serious personality conflicts.   In view of his peculiar physiological development and life experience, this seemed rather remarkable.   He was quite good-natured and tolerant of what was required of him in the psychological study. He showed ordinary practical efficiency and insight, was appropriately serious and reserved, was at no time silly or unduly embarrassed, although appropriately apologetic about his mathematical deficiency. He adjusted to the total situation in a normal, matter-of-fact manner.

Psychological study revealed an individual of average intelligence with high average facility in speech and high average ability to comprehend and formulate in verbal terms. Visual imagery and exact mathematical reasoning and mathematical memory were low average. The Stanford-Binet mental age was 15 years; I.Q. was 94 on a 16-year or 100 on a 15-year average adult basis. The basal mental age was 9; designs were failed at year 10; 5 digits backward at year 12; the clock problems at year 14; enclosed boxes, digits backward, and code at year 16; and all the tests except the vocabulary at year 18. In this one test, the performance rated as moderately superior. Verbal interpretations and generalizations showed common sense, good understanding, and thoughtful, straight-forward judgments. In the Otis Speed Test of Intelligence, Martin used the practical expedient of skipping the hard, especially the mathematical items and so earned a quotient of 110 (7) in what was thus an almost purely verbal test. On the Otis Higher Intelligence Examination, Form B, with unlimited time allowance and the instruction to "attempt every item and try hard to get a correct answer in every case," the patient rated at I.Q. 96. Failures on mathematical items had decreased the score. On the Terman-Miles Information test, Exercise III of the Attitude-Interest Analysis Test, standardized as a measure of (verbal) intelligence (9), Martin's scores on Forms A and B averaged at mental age 16 years, 8 months, I.Q. equivalent 111. The score of 47 on the Ferguson Form Board Series gave an age rating of 14 years, 10 months, quotient 99. A short version of the dictation (spelling) test of Form X of the New Stanford Achievement Series was well written, scoring 113, educational age 17 years, 6 months, a high average, adult performance.

On the Freyd Occupational Interests Sheet it was found that Martin gave almost twice as many dislikes or negative answers as he did positive ones (negative 32, positive 18). The very much liked occupations were aviator, explorer, foreign correspondent, forest ranger, magazine writer, newspaper reporter, and novelist. Other exciting masculine activities, further types of creative literary work, scientific, and outdoor pursuits were favored in the secondary choices. This is a rather typical male adolescent profile. The Strong Vocational Interest Blank, marked 2 months later, and the occupational items on the attitude-interest analysis tests conform, in general, to this same pattern. The Strong ratings are given in the order of the standard scores in Table I. They show Martin's trends of interest toward certain typically masculine occupations, especially in groups involving verbal, artistic, and scientific elements, but avoiding those most obviously mathematical, his taste for outdoor activities and for social-athletic pursuits. The occupations and professions that do not attract this youth are those obviously and primarily involving responsibility for leadership in social welfare, business management, bookkeeping and accounting pursuits, and accurate mechanical construction. The interest maturity shown in this profile rated a standard score of 44, at the 17th percentile on the 20-year-old norms. Martin's masculinity scored just above the male average on the Strong test.

Two attitude-interest analysis tests (Terman-Miles, M-F Test, Forms A and B) taken with an interval of 2 months between them, gave thoroughly masculine total scores. The exercise profiles and the total masculinity-femininity (M-F) scores for the two forms of the test and their averages are given in Table II. The male standard scores for each are as follows:

Martin Murgy M-F Test. Standard scores. Male norms	Exercises							
	I	2	3	4	5	6	7	Total
Form A...............	−.55	+.75	+.10	− .10	+ .95	−.45	+ .25	+ .45
Form B...............	−.70	−.85	−.90	0	+2.85	+.95	−1.10	+1.60
Average, A + B........	−.65	−.05	−.40	− .05	+1.95	+.25	− .40	+1.05

If the scores are rated in terms of the female norms instead of the male, the corresponding standard score values are:

Martin Murgy M-F Test. Standard scores. Female norms	Exercises							
	I	2	3	4	5	6	7	Total
Form A.............	+.70	+1.70	+1.25	+.75	+3.60	+ .20	+1.05	+3.40
Form B.............	+.60	0	+ .30	+.85	+5.90	+1.60	− .25	+4.90
Average, A + B......	+.65	+ .85	+ .75	+.80	+4.75	+ .90	+ .40	+4.20

TABLE I
STRONG VOCATIONAL INTEREST TEST (1938)

Martin Murgy

January, 1940

Age 20 years. Sex: Male

Education: High-school graduate

Occupation	Raw score	Standard score	Rating	Occupation	Raw score	Standard score	Rating
Printer............	+ 59	54	A	School man......	− 7	..	C*
Forest service....	+119	49	A	President manu-			
Boy Scout master.	+102	..	A*	facturing con-			
Group I........	+ 64	49	A	cern...........	− 17	24	C
Policeman........	+ 91	46	A	Sales manager....	− 25	23	C
Dentist..........	+ 70	45	A	Carpenter........	− 30	21	C
Musician........	+ 38	45	A	Mathematician...	− 67	18	C
Farmer..........	+ 37	45	A	Advertising......	−109	16	C
Group X.......	+ 10	43	B+	Real-estate sales-			
Chemist.........	+ 70	42	B+	man...........	−221	14	C
Group II.......	+ 47	41	B+	Office clerk.......	− 68	13	C
Physician........	+ 38	41	B+	Minister.........	− 67	12	C
Mathematics-sci-				Certified public			
ence teacher....	+ 42	40	B	accountant.....	− 53	7	C
Y.M.C.A. physi-				Life-insurance			
cal director....	+ 73	39	B	salesman.......	−198	3	C
Author-journalist.	+ 35	39	B	Purchasing agent.	−112	2	C
Group V.......	+ 6	38	B	Accountant......	− 84	− 2	C
Artist...........	+ 59	37	B	Y.M.C.A. general			
Lawyer..........	+ 27	36	B	secretary.......	−175	− 4	C
Architect........	+ 34	32	B−	City-school super-			
Production man-				intendent......	−163	−10	C
ager...........	+ 4	32	B−	Vacuum-cleaner			
Engineer........	+ 33	31	B−	salesman.......	−220	..	C*
Psychologist......	+ 44	30	B−				Per-
Group IX......	− 34	30	B−				cen-
Social-science							tile
teacher........	− 3	30	C+	Masculinity-femi-			
Personnel........	+ 4	27	C+	inity..........	+ 82	52	61
Group VIII....	− 22	26	C+	Studiousness.....	− 48	..	49
Banker..........	− 27	26	C+	Occupational level	+ 2	48	42
Physicist........	+ 90	..	C*	Interest maturity.	− 21	44	17

Occupations he has thought of entering: Army, navy, aviation, technical work in movies, exploring.

* From 1933 Strong.

The relative importance of the exercise scores is indicated by their percentage contribution to the total score variance in the general population as follows:

Exercises	1	2	3	4	5	6	7	Total
Percentage	9.5	1.3	10.2	27.2	40.5	9.0	2.3	100.0

The percentile scores from male and female high-school-junior norms for the five more significant exercises and the total are as follows:

M-F test	Test form	Exercises					Total
		1	3	4	5	6	
Male high-school-junior percentiles	A	15	25	45	55	20	45
	B	10	5	50	99	60	80
Female high-school-junior percentiles	A	75	99	85	99	50	99
	B	70	70	85	99	85	99

The authors of the test have strongly recommended (9) that, for clinical purposes, scores be used based on the administration of both test forms. The average of the two obviously offers a more generally dependable measure than can either one alone. In the case described here, the deviations from this average of the separate A and B scores in the more reliable parts of the test are interesting in connection with their reflection of the unusual life experience of this patient and the peculiar conditions of personality orientation under which the tests were taken.

Martin's scores are, of course, meaningful only as they resemble or deviate from trends shown in the averages of typical, unselected, and atypical, selected groups. With his profiles in Table II are entered the exercise and total scores of a number of male and female groups. The male groups are naturally included because Martin has proved to be structurally a male: his single gonad is a testicle. The female groups are included because until recently he was thought to be a female and was reared as one to the age of 20. To the extent that the test (a) registers male or female orientation or (b) reflects interests and attitudes culturally inculcated, he may be expected to resemble some òr other of these groups. The scores of male and female inverts have been added because of a certain hypothetical

TABLE II
M-F Scores of Individuals and Groups

Individual or group	Number	1	2	3	4	5	6	7	Total	Standard score
Martin Murgy:										
Form A....................	1	− 8.0	+1.0	+ 2.0	+14.0	+ 58.0	− 5.0	0	+ 62.0	+ .45
Average, A + B.............	1	− 8.5	0	− 2.5	+15.0	+ 90.0	+ .5	− 1.3	+ 93.4	+1.05
Form B....................	1	− 9.0	−1.0	− 7.0	+16.0	+122.0	+6.0	− 2.7	+124.7	+1.60
Adults, 20 years old, group average, high-school education:										
Matched group A..........	26	− 5.2	0	+ 6.6	+18.4	+ 41.1	+1.5	− .4	+ 62.0	+ .45
Matched group B..........	16	− .1	+ .6	+ 6.5	+35.3	+ 81.0	0	+ 1.1	+124.5	+1.60
Male-norm group averages:										
Adults, 20 years old (I)...	35	− 4.0	+ .2	+ 6.6	+24.9	+ 53.9	+1.2	0	+ 82.9	+ .85
High-school education (II)..	24	− 6.8	0	+ 5.8	+20.2	+ 39.5	+1.4	− .4	+ 59.6	+ .40
Adults, total population*..	1083	+ 2.8	0	+ 2.2	+21.5	+ 23.0	0	− .8	+ 43.3	+ .10
High-school boys*........	308	+ .8	0	+ 5.2	+14.4	+ 56.7	+ .8	+ .7	+ 77.1	+ .75
College men*										
Small stature............	43	− 8.2	0	+ 8.5	+27.8	+ 29.6	+4.3	− 1.3	+ 61.7	+ .45
Special male group averages:										
Inverts*.................	77	− 5.7	− .9	− .1	+21.3	− 36.2	−2.8	− 2.7	− 28.0	−1.20
Inverts†.................	26	− 8.1	− .6	− 3.1	+30.7	− 21.3	− .7	− 1.3	− 4.4	− .75
Effeminate men†..........	13	−10.5	− .7	− 7.7	+27.1	− 23.4	−3.4	− 2.4	− 21.2	−1.60
Female norm group averages:										
Adults, 20 years old*.....	604	−14.2	−1.0	− 8.5	+ 4.1	− 45.5	−5.6	− 2.7	− 74.2	+ .25
Adults, total population*..	1867	−14.2	−1.0	− 8.9	+ 1.3	− 48.0	−5.8	− 2.3	− 80.9	+ .10
High-school girls*........	245	−14.3	−1.1	−10.7	−12.9	− 32.3	−6.6	− 2.4	− 79.3	+ .10
Special female group averages:										
Inverts*.................	18	−18.2	+ .3	− 7.5	+11.5	− 18.0	−1.6	− 1.6	− 36.4	+1.15
Inverts†.................	21	−11.7	− .6	−11.0	+14.2	− 24.1	− .4	− .9	− 34.6	+1.15

* Data from Terman and Miles (9), Tables 96 and 97.

† The scores from Henry's (2) published data for Exercises 2, 5, and 7 are given here, recalculated to agree with the other figures in this table.

similarity between them and our subject.   The male inverts, supposedly males in gonadal structure, have in many cases been reared
under various feminizing influences.   The female inverts, although
presumed to be females in gonadal structure, have reacted aggres-
sively in a masculine direction, as Martin has done, to the feminizing
culture in which they were brought up.

The score profiles in Table II are drawn from three sources: (a)
data reported by Terman and Miles (9), (b) data reported by Henry
(2), and (c) data assembled by the writer for presentation in the
present report.   The latter include besides (a) Martin's two profiles
and their averages, (b) the profiles of combinations of scores of 35
young male adults of approximately the same age and level of education as our subject.   These 35 were individuals regarded by their
associates as of average normality in adjustment.   Their cooperation in marking Form A of the Terman-Miles test was solicited by
individuals in their own social groups who were known to the writer.
The conditions for securing these tests were similar to those under
which the general unselected populations were contacted whose
scores are reported by Terman and Miles (9).   From the 35 cases,
groups were built up to match Martin's two M-F total scores and a
third group of 24 was assembled that approximately equaled in
total score the 20-year-old high-school-graduate norm group of the
Terman-Miles study.

Martin's scores are entered in Table II with the averages of these
various selected and unselected male and female groups.   Many
interesting observations may be made from an examination of these
data.   A few may be mentioned.   The average of the two total
M-F scores of our subject is higher than any mean total M-F score
of any unselected group of his age and education.   Compared with
two matched groups of New England youths of equal age and
schooling, he rates more masculine on Exercise 5 but less so on the
other exercises.   On those parts of the test in which the results of
experience and habit seem to be especially registered, his ratings are
more feminine than the comparable male norms, but on no significant
part of the test does the average score ever reach the general female
mean.   Where the wish to be masculine can weight the score, he
rates on both test forms more masculine than other young men whose
total scores average at the same high point as his.

Martin's scores for the five more important and more reliable
exercises seem to reflect both his masculine orientation and his mixed

life history.   In word association (Exercise 1), a test known to measure cultural experience (8), his responses rate at a point intermediate between the male and female general population norms, and with the masculine-scoring women (athletes, professional women, Henry's inverts) and the feminine-scoring men (men of small stature,[1] cultured and artistic groups, Henry's inverts).   In information (Exercise 3) and in favorite characters and prejudices (Exercise 6), he rates once each in the intermediate zone and once each above the male norm.   In emotional attitudes (Exercise 4) he rates on both forms of the test near the mean for the general population of males. With respect to the occupational and varied interests that make up Exercise 5, he rates more masculine on both forms than does, on the average, any male group of which we have record.

Two questions are suggested by this brief summary and the exhibits in Table II.   The stability of Martin's scores is one of them; the question of his possible score faking is another.   In Table III are the values for $\sigma_{1\infty}$, the standard error of a single score, and the standard deviations of distributions of the scores of typical groups. Martin's exercise scores on all exercises except Exercise 5 deviate from their own mean to an extent that is less than the standard error of a single score and less also than the standard deviations of the distributions in typical groups.   Only on Exercise 5, where the alteration is in the direction of increasing masculinity (from the 55th to the 99th percentile of masculinity on the high-school-junior norms) is the deviation from his mean score greater (1.8) than the standard error of a single score.

With respect to faking, there is evidence in a comparison with experimentally faked scores.   These are the scores of a group reported by Kelly, Miles, and Terman (4).   As has been noted, Martin makes his most masculine scores in Exercise 5.   This is the part of the test in which the largest faked score is possible, yet he fails to take advantage of other opportunities for faked score gains

---

[1] Martin is 5 feet 3 inches in height and weighs 122 pounds.   His metabolism on first admission per square meter per hour was 37.7 calories; and the surface area, 1.56 square meters.   The result is −8 per cent on usual male standards or +2 per cent, if compared with female standards.   The pulse rate was 66 to 68. The average pulse rate for males weighing 122 pounds is 61; for females, 69 or 68, according to the norms of Harris and Benedict; but these results are based on distributions with large standard deviations, and the sex difference is not highly reliable.   It does seem, however, that in this case the pulse rate is nearer the expected for the female than for the male.

TABLE III

(I) STANDARD ERRORS OF INDIVIDUAL M-F SCORES AND S.D.'s OF GROUP M-F SCORES COMPARED WITH (II) FAKED TEST DEVIATIONS AND DEVIATIONS FROM THE MEAN OF REPEATED TESTS OF A SINGLE INDIVIDUAL (MARTIN MURGY)

Item, group, or individual	Number	Exercises							Total
		1	2	3	4	5	6	7	
$\sigma_{1\infty}$ M-F score............	...	7.48	1.26	6.18	11.38	17.47	6.23	1.63	23.35
Male adults, 20 years old (I)........	35	7.91	1.02	8.04	23.58	31.97	5.60	2.07	48.72
High-school education (II)......	24	7.14	.95	8.03	20.85	26.09	6.76	2.09	36.39
Male total population, adults........	1083	8.16	1.19	7.81	22.12	33.94	7.23	1.98	51.79
Female total population........	1873	7.96	1.16	9.22	23.45	28.43	7.48	1.99	43.32
Amount of change in M-F score with →M and →F orientation.*									
→M......................		+21.6	+.83	+3.10	+15.40	+83.0	+9.15	+1.90	+135.00
Males →F....................	19	-22.5	-.47	-.85	-48.10	-114.0	-3.30	-4.00	-191.00
Critical ratios $\left(\frac{\text{Diff.}}{\text{S.D.}_{\text{diff.}}}\right)$ →M ─ → F*.		(11.6)	(2.94)	(1.14)	(10.5)	(13.0)	(4.75)	(7.00)	(14.5)
M. Murgy, score diff. $(A-B)/2$......	- .5	-1.0	-4.5	+1.0	+32.	+5.5	-1.35	+31.15

* These are the changes in score and their critical ratios achieved by 19 males who were instructed to make their responses (1) as masculine (→M) and (2) as feminine (→F) as they possibly could (4). It may be noted that these changes are in most cases much larger, than the differences between Murgy's average scores and his A and B scores.

(Exercises 1 and 4). Martin's first score on Exercise 5 is highly masculine, and his second score on this same exercise is even higher. Interests, occupational and other, are primarily registered here. His scores reflecting verbal habits and emotional attitudes remain, in contrast, fairly stable in the intermediate zone between the male and the female general population means (Exercise 1) or near the more typically masculine region of the male averages (Exercise 4). Since both of these trends, although diverse from each other, are appropriate in terms of Martin's experience, it seems unlikely that he was trying consciously to register a masculine profile or, in fact, to do other than express his interests and attitudes as he evaluated them at the time.

TABLE IV

EXERCISE 3—MENTAL-AGE EQUIVALENTS AND RATIOS OF RIGHT ANSWERS:
M/F AND F/M

Males	Number	M.A.	M/F ratio	Females	Number	M.A.	F/M ratio
Low-scoring (M-F) college students..	30	17- 4	. 107	Prostitutes....... High-school jun-	12	14- 0	123
High-school juniors.	98	16- 0	106	iors.............	98	16- 3	116
Army recruits......	30	14-10	105	College students..	33	17- 3	115
Artists, high-school education........	20	18- 7	101	Inverts.......... College athletes...	8 26	18- 5 18- 7	114 106
Inverts (active)....	45	15- 3	101	Artists and musi-			
Inverts (passive)...	83	16-11	98	cians............	30	18- 5	106
Murgy A..........	1	16-10	93	Murgy A.........	1	16-10	107
Murgy B..........	1	16- 7	87	Murgy B.........	1	16- 7	115

In the information exercise (Exercise 3), in which his M-F scores were $+2$ and -7—one a slightly masculine, the other an intermediate rating—Martin's "right" answers on both forms were, in contrast, predominantly feminine and thus quite out of line as compared with the typical masculine ratios. In Table IV, the ratios for males of "right" masculine to "right" feminine answer scores are given. Males have commonly ratios M/F of over 100, the range of norm averages is from 100 to 110; the male inverts rate the only ratio below 100. Martin's M/F ratios are, in contrast, 93 and 87. Females have commonly ratios F/M ("right" female to "right" male answers) of over 100; the range of normal averages is in these groups from 100 to 120. Martin's F/M ratios are 107 and 115.

Here, in his factual knowledge, he seems to be registering without a doubt his definitely feminine upbringing.

Martin Murgy, although reared as a girl and regarding himself as one during childhood and adolescence, had thus, it appears, at 20, the interests and, to some extent, also the attitudes of a male. His word associations and his knowledge of common facts are, no doubt naturally enough, feminine, there is some instability in the present expression of his prejudices, and his emotional reactions and standards of censure, although predominantly masculine rather than feminine, are immature. His early life experience may be, in certain respects, compared to that of inverts of both sexes whom he appears to resemble in some trends revealed by the M-F test.

Not infrequently has a male invert been reared with a feminine orientation, protected by an affectionate mother, dominated and ill used in physical or in psychological terms by a tyrannical father (2, 9). The sexual inversion has sometimes been attributed to early conditioning of this kind. Female inverts have had, like Martin, to conform to feminine social customs while protesting inwardly. Is Martin, then, after all, something of an invert? His total average M-F score is about 2.0 S.D. more masculine than the score mean of the male inverts and exceeds the mean score of effeminate men and female inverts by somewhat more than this. But he does rate like the male inverts in word associations and like the female inverts in emotional attitudes. What, then, of his M-F test pattern as a whole? In Table V and Fig. 1, his M-F invert score (9) is compared with the M-F invert scores of several male groups. No female invert scale is available. The average score on the M-F invert scale of 82 male inverts is +644, with a standard deviation of their score distribution amounting to around 375. Within the noninvert score range of our 24 young adult males of high-school education and apparently adequate normal adjustment is the average invert score of 46 low-scoring males, M-F score +18.9 (9). Eleven young adult males of high masculinity, averaging total M-F scores of +134.7, have the excessively noninvert score of −498.8. Martin's invert rating is still further in the noninvert direction, with a score of −609.0. Within homogeneous groups, there is little correlation (9) between the M-F and the invert scores,[1] although both are measures of aspects of masculinity and femininity in males.

[1] In our group of 24, the correlation between inversion and feminity of score is +.15 ± .12.

TABLE V

INVERT SCORE MEANS AND S.D.'s (in parentheses)

Male	Number	Exercises							Total	M-F score average
		1	2	3	4	5	6	7		
Inverts*............	82	......	......	......	......	......	......	......	+644.0	− 28.0
Inverts,†............	16	− 17.6 (39.2)	+ 5.2 (17.0)	+134.0 (54.2)	+ 7.58 (104.1)	+193.1 (160.7)	+26.7 (60.1)	+ 55.7 (70.0)	+403.8 (341.6)	− 35.1
Males, low M-F scores*...	46	......	......	......	......	......	......	......	−187.0	+ 18.9
Adults, 20's.............. High-school education..	24	− 74.4 (46.2)	+ .67 (11.15)	+ 76.1 (53.5)	− 55.4 (65.6)	−111.0 (133.2)	−33.4 (34.7)	− 61.3 (59.7)	−258.7 (167.7)	+ 59.6
Adults, 20's, high-school education.............	11	−104.3	− 3.55	+ 56.3	− 8.2	−314.2	−27.6	− 97.4	−498.8	+134.7
Martin Murgy..........	1	−102.0	−14.0	+ 79.0	− 32.0	−315.0	−65.0	−160.0	−609.0	+ 62.0

* Reported by Terman and Miles (9).

† Results calculated from the scores reported by Terman and Miles (9, Chap. 13).

"Martha" was brought up as a female, dressed in girl's clothes, regarded as their younger sister by his siblings and as a daughter by his parents.   His family and community attempted, in ignorance of his true sex, to condition him in the feminine social culture.   But he was a tomboy while he was still in skirts, and, at 20, relieved of his anatomical anomalies and of the psychological restrictions of enforced femininity, he was quite ready to be a man in attitudes and

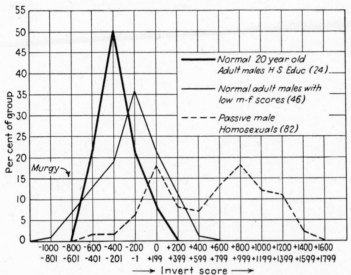

FIG. 1.—Invert score of Martin Murgy compared with the invert-score distributions of normal 20-year-old adult males of high-school education (urban New England group), normal adult males with low M-F scores (9), and passive male homosexuals (9).

functions. Feminine habits of thought and feminine knowledge were, however, still characteristic, and it would be hard to predict how soon they might give way before adult experience, masculine in orientation.

Inverts are generally recognized to have many psychopathic traits (2, 3).   Martin is, in contrast, apparently a normally stable, well-adjusted person.   On the emotionality items of the Woodworth-Cady scale included in Exercise 7 of the M-F test, only three of his answers are psychopathic indicators.   He therefore rates a high stability score (1).   He is emotionally immature, no doubt, but in terms of objective observation, supported by test results, he appears to be in no true sense a psychopath.

Young (10) estimates the incidence of pseudohermaphrodites as 1 in 1000. Histories of these unfortunates show no persistent or typical patterns of psychological development or psychosexual adjustment. The factors are far too complex for conclusions to be drawn until cross-sectional and longitudinal psychological studies are made of the personalities of considerable numbers of them.

The present study is, so far as we are aware, the first attempt at a psychological profile of a pseudohermaphrodite, or of a male thought to be a female and reared as one. The development and traits of an individual in this class may suggest some of the interrelationships of constitution and culture. There have been and may be again male pseudohermaphrodites so conditioned by social pressures and so influenced by these, plus prevailing feminine secondary sex characteristics, that they prefer, even when choice is offered, to continue in the feminine role (10). Martin Murgy had been taught from childhood to play the part of a girl and to believe that he was a girl. He said at 20 that he would be content to belong to either sex. But he had been a tomboy; male secondary traits had made him unhappy in his feminine part; he welcomed the suggestion of physicians that he was essentially a male; he took the initiative in having his hair cut and putting on male clothing before he appeared for final diagnosis and treatment. After he had been surgically treated and told his true gonadal status, he was ready to score by a standard test above the 80th percentile of psychological masculinity. How he might have scored at an earlier period is a matter for pure guessing.

The account given here is descriptive and clinical. Scores and ratings are reported with the more obvious interpretations. Any attempt at a deeper objective analysis of the masculinity-femininity traits of a single case, whose early development is no more completely reported than the present one, would be idle. Nor is this the place for critical evaluation of the techniques employed. The psychological study of this one pseudohermaphrodite suggests certain important footnotes in the psychophysiological study of masculinity and femininity and of inversion that only further similar data on other pseudohermaphrodites can support or contradict.

REFERENCES

1. Burks, B. S., Jensen, D. W., & Terman, L. M. Genetic studies of genius III. The promise of youth. Stanford University: Stanford Univ. Press, 1930.

2. HENRY, G. W.   Sex variants.   A study of homosexual patterns.   (2 vols.)
   New York: Hoeber, 1941.
3. KAHN, E.   Psychopathic personalities.   (Trans. by H. F. Dunbar.)   New
   Haven: Yale Univ. Press, 1931.
4. KELLY, E. L., MILES, C. C., & TERMAN, L. M.   Ability to influence one's
   score on a typical pencil-and-paper test of personality.   *Character & Pers.*,
   1936, **4**, 206–215.
5. MILES, C. C.   The Otis S-A as a fifteen minute intelligence test.   *Person. J.*,
   1931, **10**, 246–249.
6. MILES, C. C.   Influence of speed and age on intelligence scores of adults.
   J. gen. Psychol., 1934, **10**, 208–210.
7. MILES, C. C., & MILES, W. R.   The correlation of intelligence scores and
   chronological age from early to late maturity.   *Amer. J. Psychol.*, 1932,
   44, 44–78.
8. MILES, C. C., & TERMAN, L. M.   Sex differences in the association of ideas.
   Amer. J. Psychol., 1929, **41**, 165–206.
9. TERMAN, L. M., & MILES, C. C.   Sex and personality.   Studies in masculinity and femininity.   New York: McGraw-Hill, 1936.
10. YOUNG, H. H.   Genital abnormalities, hermaphroditism, and related adrenal
   diseases.   Baltimore: Williams & Wilkins, 1937.

CHAPTER XII

A TECHNIQUE FOR DETECTING ATTEMPTS TO FAKE PERFORMANCE ON THE SELF-INVENTORY TYPE OF PERSONALITY TEST

By

FLOYD L. RUCH

University of Southern California

From the beginning, psychologists have suspected that the ability of the subject to influence his score on the self-inventory blank would constitute a serious limitation of its use as a means of selecting employees, certifying a list of names for appointment, or as a means of deciding future promotions. It must be pointed out that the ability of the testee to influence his score in a given direction, if he so desired, would not be a serious limitation of the use of self-inventory tests in vocational guidance. In this situation, it is to be presumed that the subject has submitted of his own will and has little to gain by influencing his scores.

That self-inventories can be influenced in a desired direction has already been clearly shown by a wide variety of clinical and consulting experience and by at least two well-conceived and carefully conducted experiments.

Steinmetz (5) administered the Strong Vocational Interest Blank under standard conditions, and then with instructions to the subjects to attempt to qualify themselves for an occupation chosen at random. The results support the following conclusions: (*a*) College students can distort their scores sufficiently to make themselves appear qualified for an occupation selected at random. This apparent qualification can be achieved regardless of the individual's score for that vocation when the test is given under standard conditions. In fact, those whose actual scores were poor for the occupation selected were able to improve their scores more than did those whose honest scores were high. (*b*) The faking of a score for one occupation seriously distorts and invalidates the scores for at least half of the other occupations for which stencils were available at the time the study was conducted.

Kelly, Miles, and Terman (3) gave the M-F test three times to a group of college sophomores containing 33 women and 19 men. Three experimental conditions were employed: (a) At the time of the original administration of the test, the subjects were merely told that the investigator was making a study of interests and attitudes of college students. Later inquiry revealed that none of the subjects suspected the real purpose of the experiment. (b) A week later, the subjects were told that the test measures masculinity or femininity of interest and that the investigator now wished to find out how much they could influence their scores for masculinity-femininity. Half of the men were detailed to make themselves as masculine as they could; the other half, as feminine. Similar instructions were given to the girls. (c) A week later, 2 weeks from the first testing, those who influenced themselves toward masculinity were asked to try for feminine scores; those who had tried to get feminine scores before were to influence their score toward masculinity as much as they could.

The results are summarized in the following table.

	Males		Females	
	Mean	S.D.	Mean	S.D.
Naïve scores............................	+ 66.8	39.2	− 56.2	48.1
Masculinized scores..................	+208.8	68.9	+189.1	93.9
Feminized scores......................	−140.5	51.8	−147.6	62.6

Careful study of this table will show that the group of typical male college students were able to earn a mean score for femininity far more to the feminine side than the mean score of college women; the typical college female could make herself more masculine than the average male. Males could shift themselves more to the feminine side than to the masculine, whereas females could shift themselves more to the masculine than to the feminine. These findings are consistent with the observation of Steinmetz that students with the poorest interest scores for a particular occupation could improve their influenced score more than could those who stood high for the occupation when the test was given under standard conditions.   The explanation is probably simply that more room on the scale is available over which one's influenced score may shift.

Recently authors of pencil-and-paper personality tests of the self-inventory type have tried to guard against deliberate and unconscious faking on the part of the testee.   Various methods have been used.   Humm and Wadsworth (2) attempt to guard against faking and other invalid responses by rescoring blanks when the number of "no" responses falls outside an empirically determined range. Other authors have attempted to avoid the pitfall by careful wording of the questions to conceal their significance or to set up situations in which each response is "desirable" in some way.   A good example of this technique is to be seen in the Preference Record of Kuder (4). The subject is asked to express a preference for one of two carefully paired activities, both of which are approximately equal in prestige or social acceptability.   An example follows:

"Take a photograph of a champion swimmer.
            (or)
"Take a photograph of a table you would like to make."

As far as the present writer is aware, no author of a test has taken the trouble to investigate and publish figures describing the "influenceability quotient" of his test.

The present investigation was conducted with two objectives in mind.   In the first place, it seemed desirable to extend the researches on the influenceability of pencil-and-paper self-inventory tests to include the well-known and widely used Bernreuter Personality Inventory (1).   In the second place—and this was the main objective—it was desired to develop a scoring stencil that would reveal the extent to which scores on this test had been influenced by the subject, to detect cheating.

The whole investigation employed two different groups of college undergraduates.   The first or standardizing group was made up of 245 students in elementary psychology, all of whom were men.   On the day that the discussion of personality and its measurement was to start, the assembled students were given copies of the Bernreuter Personality Inventory and were requested to fill out the blanks under standard conditions.   The students were told: "This test does not count toward your grade, but if you follow the printed directions carefully this test will give you some interesting information concerning your personality."

After the tests had been filled out according to the standard directions, the subjects were given another blank, with the following instructions: "Imagine that you are applying for a position as salesman. Your showing in this test will decide whether or not you get the job. You know the characteristics of a good salesman. See if you can answer these questions as a good salesman would, whether you really feel that way or not."

The students entered into the spirit of the experiment with zest.

The standard and influenced blanks were both scored for introversion-extroversion (B3-I). A tabulation of the results showed the median of the group taking the test under standard conditions to fall right at the college median given in the author's Tentative Norms (1). The median of the distribution of influenced scores fell at the 98th percentile for extroversion (the 2d percentile for introversion). It was thus seen that the average college man could make himself more extroverted than 98 per cent of the college population by trying to answer questions as a good salesman would.

The Pearson coefficient of correlation between the raw scores for the two conditions of the test was −.17. This low magnitude was presumably due to the low variability of the scores obtained when the students attempted to fake the replies of salesmen.

It is quite possible that the reported correlations between pencil-and-paper tests of introversion-extroversion and actual performance as salesmen would rise if cases of faking had been detected and eliminated. On the other hand, it is quite possible that this type of dishonesty is just as valuable as real extroversion in the psychological make-up of a salesman.

The next phase of the investigation consisted in building a scoring stencil to reveal faking after the fact. The present investigator is unable to think of any way of preventing attempts to fake when self-inventory tests are used for hiring.

The argument is rather simple. If answers to items on a test like the Bernreuter can be faked at all, the chances are that some are easier to fake than others. Therefore, it should be possible to give each item a weight to represent the extent to which it can be faked by the average college student. This was done by tabulating the frequency of each answer to each question for the standard condition and for the influenced condition. These frequencies were converted into percentages, and an "honesty" weight was assigned to each reply according to the magnitude of the critical ratio of the difference between the frequency of the reply in the honest and in the influenced conditions.

The two sets of blanks of a fresh group of 100 college men who had taken the test under the two conditions were scored for honesty, with the use of the weights derived by the procedure just described. The blanks filled in under standard conditions were also scored for introversion, with the use of the Bernreuter key. The subjects were then cast into two subgroups as follows: an *introverted* group, made up of 39 subjects who were more introverted than the average college student, according to the Bernreuter norms; and an *extroverted* group of 61 men who were less introverted than the average. The honesty scores of both groups under both conditions are shown in Table I.

TABLE I

HONESTY SCORES OF INTROVERTS AND EXTROVERTS UNDER STANDARD AND INFLUENCED CONDITIONS

Honesty score	Introverted group		Extroverted group	
	Honest	Influenced	Honest	Influenced
60	1			
55	1			
50	5		1	
45	10		4	
40	16		11	
35	6		11	
30		2	10	
25			12	2
20		3	11	4
15		17	1	19
10		14		31
5		3		5

From a study of this table, it becomes clear that an introvert who attempts to make himself appear to be a good salesman is virtually certain to obtain an honesty score below 35; *i.e.*, if a critical score is set at 35, any introvert who is attempting to influence his score in the direction of salesmanlike qualities will be caught on the evidence of an honesty score of less than 36.

The device does not work so well in the case of the extroverted individual who attempts to make himself more like a salesman. The data show that 11 of the extroverted group who attempted to fake the salesman's replies equaled or exceeded an honesty score of 19, which was the lowest such score received by an extrovert under standard conditions. For practical purposes, however, this shortcoming is not serious, since the real problem is to eliminate introverts who have made themselves appear to be extroverted.

The fact that the lowest honesty score of the introverts was 36, whereas that of the extroverts was 19, when both were supposedly telling the truth about themselves, is of considerable interest.

This technique for the detection of influenced scores on the self-inventory type of test appears to have some promise. Its possibilities should be studied in relation to other of the numerous tests of the same type now in use. If further work with this technique bears out the findings of the present study, one of the shortcomings of the self-inventory type of test as an instrument in employment may well have been circumvented.

REFERENCES

1. BERNREUTER, R. G. The personality inventory. Stanford University: Stanford Univ. Press, 1935.
2. HUMM, D. G., & WADSWORTH, G. W., JR. The Humm-Wadsworth temperament scale. Los Angeles: Doncaster G. Humm, 1934.
3. KELLY, E. L., MILES, C. C., & TERMAN, L. M. Ability to influence one's score on a pencil-and-paper test of personality. *Character & Pers.*, 1936, **4**, 206–215.
4. KUDER, G. F. Preference record. Chicago: Science Research Associates, 1939.
5. STEINMETZ, H. L. Measuring ability to fake occupational interest. *J. appl. Psychol.*, 1932, **16**, 123–130.

CHAPTER XIII

SUCCESS AND FAILURE: A Study of Motility

By

ROBERT R. SEARS

Institute of Human Relations, Yale University

INTRODUCTION

Perhaps not the most compelling, but certainly the most pervasive, of all socially determined rewards and punishments are those leading to feelings of success or failure. In the home, the school, on the playground, in the church, competitive strivings for position and prestige vitalize the social organization. Change after change, event after event, is conditioned by someone's desire for achievement. A broken factory window proves that one lad can throw farther than another; a Phi Beta Kappa key testifies to another kind of struggle; a deadly explosive, a new melody, a two-column editorial may all point to rewarded ambition. And each of these rewards serves to reinforce the behavior that led to its existence. Each represents success.

From earliest childhood, good performances are greeted by praise and bad ones by reproof or disapproval. In any competition, the winner gets the prize; the loser has only fatigue for his efforts. The former is cheered, the latter jeered. These very expressions themselves eventually develop rewarding and punishing properties, and the older child or adult will work for the rewards of social approval alone. And if he is familiar with the pains of failure, he will struggle to avoid disapproval as much as to gain its opposite.

If this secondary drive remained oriented solely toward social situations, if the presence of other people were always necessary to evoke it, the problem of success and failure would have the same kind of stimulus relevancy to the human personality that bread and thunderstorms have. Man craves food and fears injury, but these factors are environmental and to them he responds manipulatively. The significant thing about the drive to gain social approval or to avoid disapproval is that the manipulative techniques themselves take on

235

value. They become not merely instruments for gaining rewards but are rewards themselves. They become goal responses. The worker is proud of his work, the painter of his painting, the runner of his speed. No one need be present. The good performance is itself the reward.

There are many names for this learned drive: pride, craving for superiority, ego impulse, self-esteem, self-approval, self-assertion, but these terms represent different emphases or different terminological systems, not fundamentally different concepts. Common to all is the notion that the feeling of success depends on the gratification of this drive, and failure results from its frustration.

Everyone has to fail occasionally; no one is good enough at everything so that he is never subordinated at anything. In our own social milieu, nearly every kind of goal-directed activity is tinged in some way with competition. With adolescence and adulthood come new sources of striving, love affairs, vocational activities, social position. Every face-to-face contact serves as a challenge or a threat. This rich variety of opportunities for winning and losing ensures that no person can lack the complexities of personality structure, the habits of attack and defense, that are dependent on success and failure.

Curiously enough, although considerable scientific attention has been given to the antecedent *competition* (15), these *consequences* of competition have been largely ignored. Educational psychologists have investigated the influence of praise and reproof on efficiency of performance, but only recently have students of personality begun a direct attack on the interaction of success and failure with motivation as reflected in substitution and the level of aspiration. A review of our hard-won knowledge on these matters is most desirable. Especially is it necessary here to provide a more meaningful setting for the present experiment than a mere statement of the immediate problem could. With this experiment, as with most other experiments in this field, the results obtained, no matter how laborious the process, seem pitifully small by themselves and gain significance only in relation to the rest of the literature.

Performance. According to the law of effect (20), those behaviors followed by a satisfying state of affairs are reinforced, stamped in. Since success is unquestionably satisfying, it might be predicted that instrumental acts preceding the final occurrence of gratification would be strengthened. Within limits, this has proved to be the case. The effects of failure should be equally predictable. Since it represents a painful or punishing experience, the antecedent instrumental acts should be reduced in strength. But this has not proved to be the case. Here again, as is so often true of experiments on punishment, nonreward, and frustration, there are a maximum of confusion and a minimum of consistency in the collated results. Superficially, at least, the unsatisfying events in experience appear to produce more sheer *variability* than any other predictable consequence.

Various techniques have been used for studying the effects of success and failure or praise and reproof. Thorndike's studies (20) of verbal learning, in which the rewarding and punishing agents were the words *right* and *wrong*, represent the simplest possible method, but the "effect" value of these agents is so low that the results have little direct relevance to the problems of self-esteem. In 1923, Gates and Rissland (7) compared the influence of a more dynamic form of encouragement and discouragement on college students. With appropriately matched groups, they found that on a coordination and a color-naming test both experimental groups had more subjects who increased and fewer who decreased their performances than had the control group. Praise proved more effective in raising performance than reproof. Hurlock (11, 12), in a much more elaborate investigation, secured similar results from school children of several different grades between the third and eighth. Two kinds of material were used, Otis Intelligence Test scales and Courtis Research Tests in arithmetic. All groups were carefully matched for chronological age, I.Q., race, school grade, and test score on the first trial of the performance material itself. Thereafter the children were praised, reproved, or given no comment. The performances on repetition showed praise somewhat superior to reproof, on the average, and both markedly superior to the control condition. Brenner (3), Briggs (4), Warden and Cohen (21), and Wood (22) have secured very similar results with a variety of tasks, and it appears that this facilitating effect of both kinds of stimulation is not only genuine but fairly easy of replication.

These comparisons, however, are all based on a single repetition of a given test. When repeated trials are given, the results are somewhat different. Hurlock (12) continued her praise and reproof for 4 days in the classroom situation, using the Courtis arithmetic tests, and found that although the two groups improved equally after the first stimulation, thereafter the reproved group became progressively less efficient, whereas the praised group continued its improvement. R. R. Sears (18), using university freshmen, obtained this same decrement on a card-sorting task continued over 3 days. In other words, failure or reproof may be a stimulant at first but it eventually becomes a depressant.

This general principle is not without contradictions, however, and the conditions under which performances are improved or disrupted by failure can be better understood if four aspects of the experimental situation are defined more adequately. First, a distinction must be made between presence and absence of motives. The so-called control groups described in connection with some of the foregoing experiments in reality represent *unmotivated* groups; both the praised and reproved groups by virtue of these kinds of stimulation are given signals that rewards and punishments are in prospect. The arithmetic test is something to be done not only because the teacher has given instructions for such a test but because the performance will be followed by rewards (social approval) or, if the performance is inadequate, by punishments (disapproval). The addition of hope of reward and fear of punishment to the total motivation increases the strength of instigation and hence should raise the level of performance.

That such additions can be effective was demonstrated by Chase (5), who combined praise with objective success and reproof with objective failure for comparison with mere repetition of objective success and failure. Although the differences were not large, they indicated a greater effect from the multi-incentive groups. Anderson and Smith (2) were able to trace about 40 per cent of these same youngsters 3 years later and repeated the experiment. Their results were virtually the same as Chase's.

Second, there is good reason to believe that social approval and disapproval operate as such only when they represent a *change* in stimulation. With a child used to constant praise, a mere cessation of approval can operate as active disapproval. This factor must be taken very seriously into account in interpreting any data on success and failure; especially is this true when the tasks involved sufficiently resemble school tasks to be so identified by children. The importance of this factor was clearly exemplified by Sullivan (19) in her study of the effect of praise and reproof on nonsense-syllable learning in Whittier State School boys. There were three main groups having average I.Q.'s, respectively, of 70, 79, and 100.   Each group was divided into success, failure, and control subgroups after having learned one eight-syllable list.   After appropriate stimulation, another list was learned.   Sullivan found that the brighter children were unaffected by success but were reduced in efficiency by failure, whereas the duller children were unaffected by failure but were definitely facilitated by success.   The intermediate group was influenced by both conditions, but more by success than by failure. All these relationships are explicable on the assumption that the mere continuation of stimulation to which a person is habituated cannot operate effectively as either facilitator or inhibitor.

Sullivan's results in this respect receive support from those of Gilchrist (8), who found that the better students in a reproof group did more poorly and the poorer students in a praise group did better on a retest with the Courtis English Test 4B; these results are also confirmed by the studies of Hurlock (10, 12).   The latter found reproof most effective on superior, average, and inferior children, in that order; and praise most effective on average, superior, and inferior, in that order.   It was found, too, that white children were more affected by reproof and Negro children by praise.   In view of the usual relative standing of these two groups in schoolwork, this finding probably belongs with the others.

Third, the induction of feelings of success may indicate to the subject either that the task is completed or that he has hit on a good way of getting praised.   Failure, too, may be either punishment for something all done or interruption at something being worked at— namely, the securing of success feelings.   H. H. Nowlis (16) has shown that both success and failure, as they are artificially induced in the laboratory, may have either effect, and resumption of an interrupted task may occur because the subject "likes it" or because "it is hard" and he wants "another chance to show I'm not so dumb."   The actual presentation of success or failure stimulation may reinforce, interrupt, consummate, or increase the strength of instigation to whatever task is being performed.

Finally, the performance that is being rewarded or punished must be indicated.   At least three aspects of every task *may* be influenced: starting the task, completing it, and doing well at it.   Doing well is a function of practice as well as of motivation and therefore may be less influenced by factors that change motivation than simply starting or completing the task, which are almost entirely a function of the strength of motivation. Nowlis (16) found that, in comparison with failure, success tended to facilitate the resumption and completion of· an incompleted task, whereas failure led more frequently than success to resumption without completion. As will be seen later, similar results were obtained in the present study under quite different experimental conditions.

It is difficult, and so far no one has attempted, to control success and failure with reference to these various aspects of the task. Indeed, none of the four main factors mentioned has been much considered. The consequence is that in each experimental situation

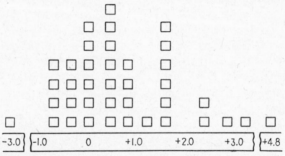

FIG. 1.—Comparative variability of behavior after success and failure. Plus values represent comparisons with greater variability in the failure group. Data from 2, 3, 5 to 8, 10 to 12, 18, 19, 21, 22.

some subjects respond to the praise and reproof or success and failure in each of the possible ways. The failure situation seems to be susceptible to more kinds of interpretation than the success, and there are more techniques of responding to frustration than to gratification; as a result, there is a tendency toward greater variability of behavior with failure.

This finding is far from universal, but Fig. 1 indicates its preponderance. There are plotted 38 critical ratios of the differences between the standard deviations of success and failure groups in the experiments listed, the only ones providing adequate data for such calculation. In the figure, the plus values represent experimental group comparisons in which the variability of the failure group was greater than that of the success.

Level of aspiration. Less confusion has arisen concerning the effects of success and failure on the level of aspiration. The increased variability consequent upon failure has been demonstrated by P. S. Sears (17) in an analysis of the effects of experimentally induced success and failure at tasks on which school children have high ego involvement. Some children increased the discrepancy between performance and level of aspiration during a series of failure trials and some decreased it. But these differences, striking as they were, were small compared to the initial differences in variability between groups composed of children who had been uniformly successful in their schoolwork for years and ones who had as uniformly failed. Sears found the difference in variability of the discrepancy scores on a reading test to be more than four times its standard error. Equally clear were various other comparisons of the same sort with different materials and different groups of children.

Sears suggests that in connection with the level of aspiration there may be two main techniques with which a child can react to failure: self-protection, *i.e.*, the ensuring of some modicum of success by placing the level of aspiration below previous performances (negative discrepancy), and the gaining of substitute gratification through attempts to get rewards for *effort* by placing the level of aspiration very high (high positive discrepancy). These two reactions, and perhaps others, each occurring in some members of a group, would account for the variability ensuing on failure. Sears points out, further, that the successful subjects continue to give the realistically oriented levels of aspiration because these have been rewarded and stamped in by operation of the law of effect.

There is evidence, too, from this investigation that the successful children are more responsive to failure stimulation than to success and that the unsuccessful children are more influenced by success. This corroborates findings trending in the same direction in the studies of performance.

Motility: the present problem. A third area of behavior in which success and failure can be of importance is *motility*. The experiments on performance and on level of aspiration limited the subjects' behavior to a circumscribed routine of formal tasks; the measurements were confined to relatively limited aspects of the behavior. Needless to say, much of a person's adjustment to his environment has little to do with goodness of performance *at the moment* or even with his aspirations for future performance. He must move about, make choices between objects and incentives that present themselves, respond to other people, make decisions about future goals to be attempted, and, in general, keep his environment from over-

whelming him.   In all this activity he inevitably prepares the way
for future gratifications in some directions and frustrations in others
—how much and in what ways will depend on how he behaves,
whether he is active or passive, hostile or kind, dominant or submis-
sive, manipulative or contemplative.   The goodness of his future
performance and the quality of his future levels of aspiration are
partly laid down by his behavior before a task is presented or a wish
exists.

Motility, defined by Warren as the "style and speed" that characterize a person's movement, undeniably governs to some extent these
relations between person and milieu.   The present experiment has
been designed to permit of a measure of this quality of behavior and
to find out what happens to it when the subject experiences success
or failure.

METHOD

This problem has been approached by artificially inducing feelings
of success and failure, respectively, in two groups of high-school
boys.   Various measures of motility were taken before and after the
task on which the success or failure was induced, the two groups
being matched on the basis of one of the measures.   The technique
was designed to permit as free an expression of spontaneous interests
as possible on the part of the subjects.   To this end, most of the
critical observations were made through a one-way transparent
mirror from an observation chamber next door.   The experimental
room was thus always under observation, but the occupants were not
influenced by the observer.   The character of the measurements and
the significance of *motility* can be made clear through a description
of the experimental situation and the procedure.

The experimental room, diagramed in Fig. 2, was a fairly bare and
unattractive officelike room made less formal by rugs and such
furniture as is indicated in the cut.   For purposes of this diagram,
the four walls have been pushed outward so that they may be seen
from above.   The room was 14 × 25 feet, with cement floors painted
brown, cement walls painted cream.   Light came from the one large
window and two 100-watt overhead fixtures.   The only entrance
to the room was by the door into the hall.   On the left wall beside
the desk at the far end of the room was a 12 × 18 inch mirror in a
frame screwed to the wall.   This mirror was transparent from the
observation chamber on the other side of this wall, and with the two

ceiling lights on in the experimental room an observer could see through clearly; there was no possibility that a subject could see

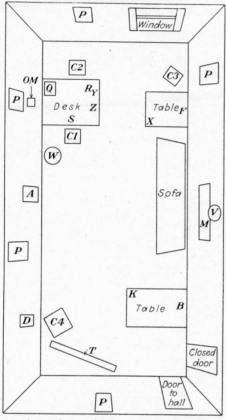

FIG. 2.—The experimental room from above, with walls flared out. *A*, chart of Ohio High School scores; *B*, table bowling game; *C1, 2, 3,* straight chairs; *C4*, overstuffed leather rocker; *D*, chart showing average scores on Dembo problem; *F*, Flipp game (a modified tiddly-winks); *K*, big rubber knife; *M*, wall mirror; *OM*, transparent observation mirror; *P*, pictorial railroad posters; *Q*, old radio with hidden microphone; *R*, mimeographed record sheet of card-sorting performance; *S*, cards; *T*, dart target board; *V*, wall clock; *W*, waste basket; *X*, folding ruler; *Y*, ash tray; *Z*, one dart.

into the observation chamber. The remainder of the furniture in the room is sufficiently indicated in the diagram and the legend.

The 24 subjects for the experiment were high-school seniors, whose services were secured by another student paid to hire them. Although all were acquaintances of this one boy, more than half proved not to know each other, and their residences were in no one part of town.   All were white, but they varied widely in nationality background: Irish, Polish, Italian, and Swedish.   None was from a family belonging to the professional class.

Each subject came to the laboratory twice.   The first session required about an hour and a quarter, the second a half hour less on the following day.   When the subject arrived at the main information desk in the Institute, he was instructed by the attendant to go to the experimental room and wait there, that Dr. Sears was a little late but would be down in a few minutes; he was told also that he would find some things there with which he could amuse himself while waiting.   On a few occasions, the experimenter himself saw the subject and asked him to wait because "I'm not quite ready yet."   In no case did any subject give evidence of being suspicious of this procedure.

Measurements of motility were taken by an observer[1] during the following 6-minute period while the subject waited alone in the experimental room.   These measurements were made with a short sample observation technique for which the basic observation unit was 5 seconds.   There were 70 of these 5-second units during this initial preexperimental period as well as in each of the other three observation periods that came later.

Behavior was recorded as to both degree and direction of activity. Three degrees of activity were discriminated: (1) apparently autistic thinking; standing or sitting without focus of attention on either the body or the environment; daydreaming; (2) orientation toward objects in the environment perceptually but without actual manipulation of anything; and (3) overt movement such as walking; manipulation of the environment; object-directed behavior.   These three classes of action lie descriptively on a continuum of amount of activity, with (1) being the least and (3) the most.   This is a phenotypic continuum, however, and for some purposes it may be desirable to treat the behavior as three discrete kinds of behavior.   The usefulness of either course can be determined only empirically.

The direction or kind of activity occurring during any given 5-second period was recorded by notation of the object toward which it was directed.   A symbol was available for each object in the

[1] The writer acknowledges with deepest gratitude the able assistance of Charles E. Osgood, who has served as observer, experimental "stooge," and intellectual goad throughout this work.

experimental room and for a few simple actions like walking and nervous gestures that involved no objects. Each symbol was followed by a number (1 to 3) to indicate the degree of activity.

The observer had a mimeographed sheet with 70 squares and wore earphones that clicked every 5 seconds. He recorded what the subject was doing at the time of each click. Thus, a sample record of 100 seconds might appear as follows: $+ + Z_2 +F\ F_2\ F_3\ F_3 +D\ D_2\ C_3 + O_2\ O_2\ O_1\ O_1\ O_1\ L_3\ O_1\ O_1\ O_1$. The behavior represented is as follows: subject walks into room, looks at dartboard, crosses over to Flipp game on table by window, examines game, plays with it or manipulates it for 10 seconds, crosses to desk by mirror, looks at desk, picks up cards and ruffles them in some way, walks over to couch and sits down, becomes abstracted (daydreaming), performs a nervous gesture, and continues just to sit until the end. This is characteristic exploratory behavior for a subject who has entered the room for the first time.

The reliability of measurement with this technique is a direct function of the amount of practice the observers have had. A statistical measure of consistency is, therefore, of no great importance, since its size will depend on the point in practice at which it is taken. Data for the present experiment were collected only after the observer and the experimenter, making simultaneous observations, had reached a point at which they consistently disagreed on no more than 3 of the 70 judgments per observation period.

The kinds of measures that can be secured from these data are, of course, quite varied, since the record is virtually a quantified statement of everything the subject does. The simplest measure of sheer activity is the frequency of "3" ratings. These can vary from 0 to a maximum of 70 for a single observation period.

The 24 subjects were divided into two equally matched groups of 12 each on the basis of this preexperimental measure of activity. By using falsified scores on a card-sorting test, together with either encouraging or discouraging comments and comparisons, one group was then given *success* and the other *failure* in the subsequent experimental procedures.

The procedure was designed to provide the appropriate feelings of success or failure for the subjects and to establish further situational measures of motility. A glance at Table I will enable the reader to see clearly the sequence of events in the rather complicated experimental procedure.

TABLE I

SEQUENCE OF EVENTS AT THE TWO EXPERIMENTAL SESSIONS

Day 1

1. Subject enters experimental room, expecting to have to wait a few minutes for experimenter.
2. Observation of motility for 350 seconds.
3. Experimenter enters room, apologizes for being late; explains card-sorting experiment and asks subject to be seated.
4. Card sorting, 15 trials; artificial induction of feelings of success or failure. Observer records all comments; experimenter records falsified time scores and subject's levels of aspiration.
5. Experimenter excuses himself to get mimeographed material for "the next experiment." Exits, leaving the record of subject's performance on table.
6. Observation of motility for 350 seconds.
7. Observer enters room for social motility measurement; duration is 180 seconds. Experimenter records duration of subject's social interaction.
8. Observer exits, and experimenter reenters room within 30 seconds.
9. Imitation test.
10. Subject fills out rating scale concerning imitations.
11. Subject released after verifying appointment for the morrow.

Day 2

1. Experimenter in room when subject enters; start card sorting immediately (success or failure as before).
2. Knock at door interrupts; experimenter leaves to answer telephone.
3. Observation of motility for 350 seconds.
4. Experimenter returns and instructs to proceed with another form of the imitations test.
5. All subjects complimented on imitations, and half of subjects in each group given from three to five trials on a different card-sorting technique; other half given a modified Dembo problem; all receive success.
6. Experimenter announces end of experiment and leaves to get money to pay subject.
7. Observation of motility for 350 seconds.
8. Experimenter reenters and asks subject to fill out a rating scale.
9. Subject released.

An important aim was to have every occurrence seem as natural and unforced as possible to the subject. For example, there were four observational periods during which the subject was left alone, and therefore various reasonable excuses were required for the experimenter's leaving the room. Otherwise he might have seemed a most erratic and curious person, and the carefully established feelings of success or failure might have been superseded by suspicion and annoyance.

After the *preexperimental* observation period, during which the subject's fate as to whether he should succeed or fail was decided on the basis of how much "3" activity he had performed, the experimenter entered the room and made a brief apology for being detained. The subject was then asked to sit in chair 1, the experimenter seated himself in chair 2, and then the technique of sorting cards to the suit of the previous card was explained (13). Either at this point or after the second trial of card sorting, the subject was told in a conversational way about the chart pinned to the wall behind him. This chart gave the distribution of card-sorting scores of 446 Ohio high-school students; the chart was a large colored bar diagram, clearly labeled and completely fictitious. The times given on it were designed to make almost any subject feel himself a failure if he compared his own true times with the chart. False times were given the success-group subjects, however, so that they would feel superior to at least 85 per cent of the "Ohio students." This chart was used to add a social frame of reference to the feelings of success and failure.

With the failure subjects, the experimenter adopted a dour expression during the sorting session and tried to give the impression of suppressed irritation and boredom. All comments implied invidious comparison, some by apparent sympathy and others by contempt not too well veiled. Considerable effort was devoted to making the subject feel that it was definitely *he* and not the task or the experimenter that was at fault. With the success subjects, the experimenter was congratulatory and enthusiastic about the subjects' skill. He tried to give an impression of being quite impressed. All comments and comparisons implied high praise for the subject. With both groups, the chart was referred to twice, and the experimenter walked over to it once during the card sorting to emphasize his comments.[1] The subjects were instructed to give a level of aspiration for each trial, the terminology used being, "What are you going to try for?"

At the end of the 15 trials of card sorting on day 1 the experimenter excused himself in order to get the materials for the "next experiment" from his office. The subjects were given to understand that the card sorting was over. The usual motility observations were made during the subsequent 6 minutes.

In order to measure social motility or responsiveness, the observer, whom the subject had never seen, then entered the room and stayed

[1] For a discussion of the comparisons that lead to feelings of success and failure and for a more complete description of the technique of artificial induction of such feelings, see R. R. Sears (18).

for 3 minutes while carrying through a standardized conversation with the subject. There were seven short lines in the scenario, and the observer, timing himself by a wall clock, waited 30 seconds between lines. His part was as follows:

1. (Knocks and enters at once.) Dr. Sears here? (Waits for answer.) I'd better wait for him. He said he'd be here. (Sits in rocking chair, chair 4.)
2. This where he's running the card-sorting experiment?
3. You one of his subjects?
4. How'd you do?
5. (Goes over to cards.) What do you *do* with 'em? (Gestures at cards with head but keeps hands in pockets.)
6. (After subject's description, crosses to table by window and nods head at Flipp game.) Is this part of it, too?
7. (Crosses rapidly to door.) Well, I can't wait any longer. I'll try his office. Be seeing you. (Exit.)

The experimenter returned shortly after the "stooge" had left the room and proceeded with the remainder of the experiment. Since the data from the "imitation test" are not relevant to the present topic, the details of that part of the experiment need not be described. It did not involve further success or failure.

On day 2, the experimenter was in the room when the subject arrived, and after a casual comment on the previous day's performance card sorting was started. Failure or success was induced as before. Just after the tenth trial, a loud knock at the door interrupted, and when the experimenter crossed the room and looked out he was informed by an anonymous voice (the observer) that "there is a long-distance call for you from Boston; they're waiting on the phone in your office." The experimenter excused himself to the subject, explaining again, as on the first day, that that was the end of the card sorting. An observation period of 6 minutes followed.

Another "imitations test" was performed when the experimenter returned, and then all subjects, both success and failure, were given either some further trials at card sorting (with slightly different rules) or a modification of the Dembo (14) problem that permitted a solution. On whichever task a subject worked, he received strong praise and was made to feel as phenomenally successful as possible. The experimenter then excused himself "to go get the subject's pay at the cashier's office." A final 6-minute observation period followed.

Results

A comparison of the behavior of the success and failure groups shows several decided differences between the two and at least one rather striking similarity. This latter, as will be seen, relates to the *amount* of activity following card sorting, and the differences are in the *kinds* of activity that compose the total motility pattern.

TABLE II
AVERAGE NUMBER OF 5-SECOND INTERVALS ALLOCATED TO EACH OF 3 DEGREES
OF ACTIVITY DURING THE FOUR OBSERVATION PERIODS

Group	Preexperimental			Day 1			Day 2			Post-success		
Degree of activity	3	2	1	3	2	1	3	2	1	3	2	1
Success.............	37.8	24.0	8.2	47.0	21.1	1.9	43.4	20.7	5.9	31.2	29.2	9.6
Failure.............	38.8	26.5	4.7	47.4	14.5	8.1	43.3	13.8	12.8	40.4	24.2	5.3

Amount of activity. In Table II are shown, for both groups, the average frequency of each degree of activity during each of the four observation periods. Frequency, in this case, refers to the number of 5-second intervals during which a particular response occurred. The total of all three types for each observation period is 70. The four observation periods are: preexperimental—the first 5 minutes and 50 seconds of the experiment, on the basis of which the groups were matched; this period immediately preceded the card sorting; day 1—immediately after the card sorting, with its attendant success or failure stimulation; day 2—immediately after the card sorting on the second day; post-success—immediately after the final task on which success was induced for both groups.

The two groups were matched with reference to the frequency of 3's in the preexperimental period, and therefore the average frequency of this degree of activity is approximately the same. What difference there is is in the direction of greater activity for the failure group.

A comparison of the frequency of 3's in Table II indicates that the influence of both success and failure was to increase the activity level on the first day. On the second day, both groups fell off somewhat but stayed above the original level. From these figures alone, the effects of success and failure would seem to be similar; if the measures from all three observation periods are lumped together, a χ^2 determination of the probability that the small difference between the groups is caused by other than chance factors is only .65. But the final measure (post-success) indicates a difference of possible importance. Although the frequency of 3's decreases only a slight amount in the failure group, there is a much larger drop in the success. The probability that such a difference between the groups in frequency of 3's could have occurred by chance alone is <.0001.

Both these probabilities (P's) are obtained by a χ^2 analysis in which the total number of measures, rather than group averages, was used in the computation. This method of computation is required by the nature of the present problem. Since the psychological principle that failure creates various kinds of consequences has been assumed, and since these consequences may be mutually incompatible, it is not useful to ask how many subjects portray each consequence or what the average amount of each consequence is per person. Each person might have a different one. In the intergroup comparison, then, the individual person is not the most meaningful unit; the incidence of a given behavior is what must be measured.

From a statistical standpoint, this method of computation changes the usual significance of a statement of probability. Normally, in the comparison of two groups, the question asked is one concerning the probability that the two subuniverses from which the samples were drawn were actually parts of the same total universe. In the present instance, however, the question asked is whether the difference between the two groups could have arisen by chance, i.e., what is the degree of probability that two such samples could have been drawn from a single universe.

Autism. The differences between the two groups in amount of time devoted to daydreaming and quiet thinking are shown by Fig. 3. These data are the "1" degree of activity given in Table II. The failure subjects were somewhat less inclined in this direction than the success subjects, to start with, but under the influence of the failure stimulation they increased markedly. The success subjects, on the other hand, showed an immediate sharp reduction in autism after stimulation. Both groups increased by about the same amount on day 2, but after the secondary success the failure subjects dropped back to the normal level they had shown originally, and the success subjects returned approximately to their original level. In general, it appears that failure produces an increase in autism, and success decreases it, at least temporarily. A χ^2 determination of the probability that the obtained differences between the groups are of only chance origin gives P's as follows: preexperimental = .001; day 1 < .0001; day 2 < .0001; post-success = .0001. Since the groups were not originally matched for frequency of degree 1 activity, there was an imbalance between the preexperimental measures, but in spite of this there was a complete reversal of the relationship between the groups after they had been subjected to stimulation.   The probability that the differences are nonchance in

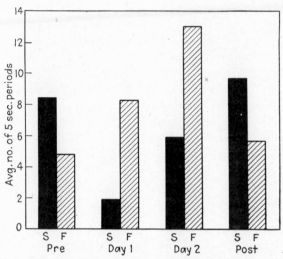

FIG. 3.—Frequency of autistic behavior during the four observation periods.

origin is actually greater, therefore, than the above values would indicate.

Choice of activities.   During the 6-minute observation periods, the subjects were free to choose any occupation that was congenial to them.   The equipment was limited largely to four games: card sorting, the Flipp game, table bowling, and dart throwing.   Actual performance at any of these would represent activity of degree 3, and, as was evidenced in Table II, there was an equal amount of this degree of activity in the two groups until the post-success period at the end.   The question must now be considered as to the kind of activity with which the two groups of subjects occupied themselves during these 6-minute periods when they were left alone.

In Table III are given the average number of 5-second periods spent in orientation toward ("2") and manipulation of ("3") the cards and the other three games. The columns labeled "Records" refer to the mimeographed record sheet, on which the experimenter had recorded the (false) card-sorting times and levels of aspiration, which was left lying on the desk while the experimenter was out of the room, and the wall chart of "Ohio high-school students."

TABLE III

AVERAGE NUMBER OF 5-SECOND INTERVALS DEVOTED TO CARDS, TO OTHER GAMES, AND TO RECORDS DURING THE FOUR OBSERVATION PERIODS

Observation period	Group	Cards	Games	Records
Preexperimental....................	Success	2.7	30.2	1.8
	Failure	1.2	29.9	2.4
Day 1.............................	Success	8.0	32.8	9.8
	Failure	22.8	24.8	4.4
Day 2.............................	Success	1.8	37.5	6.2
	Failure	10.2	30.8	3.2
Post-success.......................	Success	4.7	23.4	6.4
	Failure	8.2	26.2	2.4

Although neither group paid much attention to the cards in the preexperimental period, the frequency for the success group was greater than that for the failure group (P based on χ^2 = .01). After stimulation, however, there was a sharp change in behavior, and the groups became highly differentiated in the opposite direction. The failure subjects sorted, or at least oriented themselves toward, the cards during 22.8 of the 70 intervals, and the success group, increasing a little from the control period, had an average score of only 8.0 intervals (P < .0001). On the second day, these values were considerably reduced but were of the same relative order (P < .0001). After the final success the two groups came fairly close together again, although the success subjects still oriented toward the cards less than did the failure subjects (P = .001). It is to be noted that in all three of the poststimulational periods the greater frequency was in the failure group, whereas the success group had the greater frequency in the preexperimental period.

Not only are these differences quite reliable from a statistical standpoint but they are of great importance psychologically. In Table IV is the evidence that most of this card-oriented activity was a variety of persistent nonadjustive behavior that almost guaranteed a perpetuation of the feelings of failure. In the success group, only one fourth of the subjects sorted cards while they were alone on day 1, and only one of these sorted on day 2. But three times as many failure subjects continued to sort after the experimenter left the room on day 1, and five sorted on day 2. The total amount of sorting was much greater, of course, after failure—but the startling thing was that no success subject ever failed to finish the deck once he had started sorting, while the failure subjects finished only 14 out of 56 attempts. The probability (χ^2) that this difference between the success and failure groups was merely chance is $<.0001$. The latter group very effectually kept themselves from being successful, even though the motivation for not finishing may often have been the desire to avoid failure. In an entirely different kind of experimental situation, one involving the resumption of interrupted tasks, H. H. Nowlis (16) secured very similar results.

TABLE IV

NUMBER OF SUBJECTS WHO SORTED CARDS DURING THE LAST THREE OBSERVATION PERIODS AND THE FREQUENCY OF FINISHING AND NOT FINISHING SORTING THE FULL DECK

Group	Day 1			Day 2			Post-success		
	N	Fin-ished	Unfin-ished	N	Fin-ished	Unfin-ished	N	Fin-ished	Unfin-ished
Success.........	3	5	0	1	1	0	1	3	0
Failure.........	9	8	26	5	2	11	3	4	5

The discrepancy between the two groups in the amount of time spent on the other three games is partly a function of the discrepancy in the amount of card sorting. But again the coming together after the final success must be noted.

Social motility. A reduction in responsiveness to the external world, somewhat similar to that described in the foregoing under autism, can be noticed in the social interaction required by the "stooge's" entrance after the individual motility period on day 1. The experimenter, watching the scene, measured the total duration of the subject's responsiveness to the "stooge." This responsiveness was in the form of speech, for the most part, but included also orientation to the cards and Flipp game on those few occasions when the subject would suggest a trial for the "stooge" and then would stand and watch. Since the "stooge" said the same things to all subjects, any difference between the average duration of social interaction for the two groups must necessarily result from a difference in the extent to which the subjects responded to questions and initiated either talk or demonstrations spontaneously. The difference between the two groups in duration of social interaction is 2.02 times the standard error of the difference, the success group's time averaging 98.75 seconds of the total 180 seconds possible and the failure group's time averaging 79.08 seconds.

Contextualization. According to the law of effect, success ought to reinforce and ensure the reproduction of all forms of behavior antecedent to the success, and failure should have an extinctive effect on its antecedents. In the present experimental situation there were two kinds of behavior that not only were temporally associated with the success and failure but served to emphasize it by vivifying the context in which it occurred.

The *records*, both the subject's own and the comparative wall chart, were essential for giving the subject a feeling of success. His performance lay within a certain frame of reference and could represent *successful* performance only insofar as it was placed in context with the materials that formed the frame of reference. Actually, it must be supposed that each time a subject saw the wall chart he gained an additional reward if his score could be compared favorably with those on the wall chart. The opposite situation would be expected to operate with the failure subjects; to avoid repetitions of punishing experiences, the subjects were forced to decontextualize their performances, to keep them out of the frame of reference that led to punishment.

That there was considerable difference between the two groups in respect to their spontaneous interest in these records while the experimenter was out of the room may be seen from Fig. 4. Although the groups were almost identical under the control conditions ($P = .32$ by χ^2), after stimulation the success group spent about twice as much time examining the records as the failure group did. By χ^2 calculation, the probability that this difference could have arisen by chance is $<.0001$ for day 1, $.001$ for day 2, and $<.0001$ for the post-success period.

The *level of aspiration*, as it was set before each trial in this experiment, was closely antecedent to the occurrence of feelings of success and failure and, like the records, was an important determiner of the context or frame of reference within which a given performance would be either successful or unsuccessful. The actual stating of the level of aspiration was an instructed response, but the instruc-

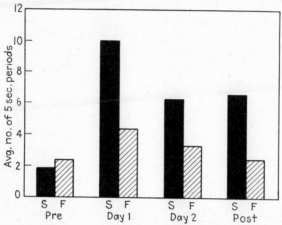

FIG. 4.—Frequency of looking at record and chart during the four observation periods.

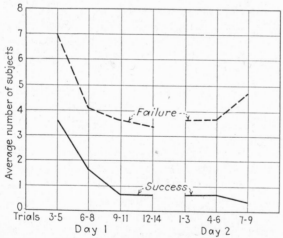

FIG. 5.—Frequency of failure to give level of aspiration, averaged in groups of three trials each.

tions were given after the first trial, and a reminder was given after the second. Thereafter the subject was forced to take the initiative in stating it. If he did not state one spontaneously by the time the experimenter had said, "Ready!" for the next trial, the experimenter

reminded the subject and asked for a statement.   The frequency
with which the subject had to be reminded, therefore, can be used as
a measure of the strength of the contextualizing process under the
two conditions of success and failure.   Again, according to the law
of effect, it would be expected that the behavior would be reinforced
by success and would suffer interference as a consequence of repeated
failures.   This expectation is borne out by the data.   Figure 5
shows the frequency with which subjects in each group "forgot"
to state a level of aspiration.   Each plotted point on the curves is
the average of three successive trials.   Trials 1 and 2 on day 1 could
not be included, because the instructions were given on those trials.
It should be noted that new instructions were given, necessarily,
each time a subject failed to give a figure, and the curves for the two
groups are as widely different as they are in spite of this extra
instigation favoring the failure group.   The reliability of this difference between the two groups can be stated in terms of the critical
ratio.   The average frequency of failing to give the level of aspiration
in the failure group was 7.5, and in the success group it was 2.1.   The
critical ratio is 3.7.

DISCUSSION

These data reveal three characteristics of the reactions to failure
that are deserving of further consideration.   First, although there
was no evidence of a decrease in object-manipulative activity, the
general motility level was less for the failure than for the success
subjects.   The frequency of daydreaming and autistic thinking was
sharply increased, and the social responsiveness was reduced.   These
changes inevitably serve to modify the effectiveness of a person's
relation to his environment.   He is less sensitive to changes, less
likely to perceive new instigators.   He is not so adjustive or so
modifiable as he would be if the failure had not occurred.   All this
reduces the possibility of his having new experiences or of initiating
new ways of behaving.   He avoids his environment.

Second, in direct relation to this, failure leads to a dogged but
ineffectual continuation of the task at which failure occurred.   What
interaction with the environment there is is in the direction of the old
activity.   But the old activity is half avoided, the card sorting is
unfinished in order to avoid the danger of failing; this effectively
precludes success, and therefore the person fails anyway.   This
persistent nonadjustive behavior, as Hamilton (9) pointed. out,

necessarily prevents the development of adjustive responses. There is no seeking for new tasks or new methods to circumvent the failure. Worse, this failure-induced behavior alienates the environment. Nonresponsive persons are neither pleasant companions nor cooperative instruments in activities that require mutual assistance.

In Hamilton's work, as well as in the present study, however, one salient characteristic of the method must be kept in mind as an important determinant of the findings. In all cases, the nature of the experimental situation forced the person (or animal) to remain in context with the source of failure. This limits the usefulness of the present results but does not nullify them. As Hamilton's 200 case histories of real people in a real community show, the exigencies of social living often impose as much restriction on motility as does any experiment. What would happen in an experiment without limitation to free ranging is a matter for conjecture at present. The fugues of real life may give some suggestion.

Finally, the process of decontextualization that failure subjects exhibit serves in still another way to reduce their adjustive effectiveness. This process splits off the activity from its social frame of reference, reduces its contact with reality, and hence decreases the opportunities for the person to check up on the task's importance by reference to reality. In a sense, decontextualization as a response to failure might be said to reduce the influence of the reality principle, to make reality testing more difficult.

These conclusions are subject to much more than the usual conventional cautions about "individual differences." What the data exhibit are trends, nothing more. There can be no such thing as a final principle concerning the influence of success and failure on motility. Or on anything else. Success and failure, as was emphasized in the introduction to this paper, are complicated states of affairs; they can represent excitors or inhibitors, completors or challengers, and obviously motility will vary with the subject's interpretation of the situation. The fact that there are clearly discernible consistencies of behavior within, and marked differences between, groups in the present data is an indication only that the experimental situation was rather generally interpretable in a single way.

REFERENCES

1. ANDERSON, H. H.   Motivation of young children: further studies in success and failure, praise and blame. *Child Develpm.*, 1936, **7**, No. 2, 125–143.

2. ANDERSON, H. H., & SMITH, R. S.   Motivation of young children: the constancy of certain behavior patterns.   *J. exp. Educ.*, 1933, **2**, 138–160.
3. BRENNER, B.   Effect of immediate and delayed praise and blame upon learning and recall.   *Teach. Coll. Contr. Educ.*, 1934, No. 620.
4. BRIGGS, T. H.   Praise and censure as incentives.   *Sch. & Soc.*, 1927, **26**, 596–598.
5. CHASE, L.   Motivation of young children.   *Univ. Ia Stud. Child Welf.*, 1932, **5**, No. 3.
6. FORLANO, G., & AXELROD, H. C.   The effect of repeated praise or blame on the performance of introverts and extroverts.   *J. educ. Psychol.*, 1937, **28**, 92–100.
7. GATES, G. S., & RISSLAND, L. Q.   The effect of encouragement and of discouragement upon performance.   *J. educ. Psychol.*, 1923, **14**, 21–26.
8. GILCHRIST, E. P.   The extent to which praise and reproof affect a pupil's work.   *Sch. & Soc.*, 1916, **4**, 872–874.
9. HAMILTON, G. V.   Objective psychopathology.   St. Louis: Mosby, 1925.
10. HURLOCK, E. B.   The value of praise and reproof as incentives for children.   *Arch. Psychol.*, N. Y. 1924, **11**, No. 71.
11. HURLOCK, E. B.   The effect of incentives upon the constancy of the I.Q.   *Ped. Sem.*, 1925, **32**, 422–434.
12. HURLOCK, E. B.   An evaluation of certain incentives used in school work.   *J. educ. Psychol.*, 1925, **16**, 145–159.
13. HUSBAND, R. W., & MILES, W. R.   On sorting packs of sixty cards with form and color as variables in two to six kinds; card sorting by reaction to the previous card.   *J. appl. Psychol.*, 1927, **11**, 465–482.
14. LEWIN, K., & DEMBO, T.   Untersuchungen zur Handlungs- und Affektpsychologie. X. Der Arger als dynamisches Problem.   *Psychol. Forsch.*, 1931, **15**, 1–144.
15. MAY, M. A., & DOOB, L. W.   Competition and coöperation.   New York: Soc. Sci. Res. Coun., 1937, *Bull.* 25.
16. NOWLIS, H. H.   The influence of success and failure on the resumption of an interrupted task.   *J. exp. Psychol.*, 1941, **28**, 304–325.
17. SEARS, P. S.   Levels of aspiration in academically successful and unsuccessful children.   *J. abnorm. (soc.) Psychol.*, 1940, **35**, 498–536.
18. SEARS, R. R.   Initiation of the repression sequence by experienced failure.   *J. exp. Psychol.*, 1937, **20**, 570–580.
19. SULLIVAN, E. B.   Attitude in relation to learning.   *Psychol. Monogr.*, 1927, **36**, No. 169.   (See, for success and failure, Pt. II, pp. 111–129.)
20. THORNDIKE, E. L.   Human learning.   New York: Century, 1931.
21. WARDEN, C. J., & COHEN, A.   A study of certain incentives applied under schoolroom conditions.   *J. genet. Psychol.*, 1931, **39**, 320–327.
22. WOOD, T. W.   The effect of approbation and reproof on the mastery of nonsense syllables.   *J. appl. Psychol.*, 1934, **18**, 657–664.

CHAPTER XIV

THE PLACE OF INDIVIDUAL DIFFERENCES IN EXPERIMENTATION

By

EUGENE SHEN

The measurement of individual differences has featured prominently in modern psychology. In the field of educational as well as vocational classification and guidance, the statistical technique of correlation and regression has provided a basis of procedure that has eliminated a considerable amount of waste and unhappiness. In the field of experimentation, however, the study of individual differences has led not so much to an enrichment of results as to a demand for more rigorous control. The investigator is usually interested in the general effects of certain experimental treatments on accomplishment or behavior and looks on individual differences as an unfortunate source of error to be eliminated as far as possible. Experimental control by individual pairing or group matching and statistical control by partial correlation or analysis of covariance are the standard means employed to achieve this end, and the validity of an experiment is judged on the adequacy of such control.

There is no doubt that the appropriate measurement of subjects can and often does increase the sensitivity of a conventionally designed experiment, but the assignment of individual differences to the role of a controlled rather than an independent variable imposes an unnecessary limitation upon the interpretation of data. Since the subjects have already been measured with respect to some character, such as ability, maturity, or previous status of achievement, one might as well evaluate, in addition to the effects of experimental treatment, the influence of subject differences and of their interaction with experimental treatment. The necessary data are, in any case, available for such evaluation, which, thus easily incorporated in the routine of statistical procedure, might reveal facts of great interest and importance.

To illustrate the need as well as the method of such statistical procedure, let us consider concrete experimental results. In the course of a comparative study on two different methods of practicing handwriting, Shyng (8) found that method *A* (free practice) was somewhat better than method *B* (tracing) for grade III but that the opposite was true for grade IV.   On further examination, it appeared that the difference between the two methods had a significant regression upon the age of the subjects.   The effect of interaction between age and the method of handwriting practice was thus forced on the investigator, who was able to draw significant conclusions by separate treatment of the age groups.   Had the experiment been confined to a single grade, the effect of age differences would not have been suspected, and facts of great interest and importance would consequently have been overlooked.

To reduce all unnecessary detail while retaining the essential points of the situation, let us take the mean gains for the different age groups as presented in the following table:

Age	Method *A*	Method *B*	Difference
7	5.65	− .44	6.09
8	3.97	− .15	4.12
9	2.95	1.70	1.25
10	1.77	3.55	−1.78
11	.25	5.75	−5.50
Mean.............	2.918	2.082	.836

Each of the age groups actually includes from 20 to 44 children, but for our present purpose we shall pretend each age to be represented by a single pair of subjects.   Variations within each age are ignored not only for the convenience of subsequent manipulation but also for the preclusion of separate tests of significance for the different groups.

A 2 × 5 factorial experimental design obviously has 9 degrees of freedom, which can be subdivided in the present case as follows:

Difference between methods......................		1
Age differences:		
Linear regression.............................	1	
Residual.....................................	3	4
Interaction between method and age:		
Linear regression.............................	1	
Residual.....................................	3	4
Total...................................		9

If we let x, y, and z designate, respectively, improvement in handwriting quality, age, and method of practice, subscripts 1 and 2 designate separate groups for the two methods of practice, and n designate the number of pairs of subjects, the total sum of squares of deviations is

$$2n\sigma_x^2 = n(\sigma_{x_1}^2 + \sigma_{x_2}^2) + n[(M_{x_1} - M_x)^2 + (M_{x_2} - M_x)^2] = 45.8524$$

of which the following is attributable to the difference between methods:

$$n[(M_{x_1} - M_x)^2 + (M_{x_2} - M_x)^2] = \frac{n}{2}(M_{x_1} - M_{x_2})^2 = 1.74724$$

To the effect of age differences is ascribed

$$2n\sigma_x^2\eta_{xy}^2 = n(\sigma_{x_1}^2 + \sigma_{x_2}^2)\eta_{xy\cdot z}^2 = \frac{n}{2}[\sigma_{x_1}^2 + \sigma_{x_2}^2 + 2r_{x_1x_2}\sigma_{x_1}\sigma_{x_2}] = 1.3307$$

of which linear regression accounts for

$$2n\sigma_x^2 r_{xy}^2 = n(\sigma_{x_1}^2 + \sigma_{x_2}^2)r_{xy\cdot z}^2 = \frac{n}{2}[\sigma_{x_1}r_{x_1y_1} + \sigma_{x_2}r_{x_2y_2}]^2 = .47432$$

The influence of interaction between age and method is represented by

$$n(\sigma_{x_1}^2 + \sigma_{x_2}^2)(1 - \eta_{xy\cdot z}^2) = \frac{n}{2}[\sigma_{x_1}^2 + \sigma_{x_2}^2 - 2r_{x_1x_2}\sigma_{x_1}\sigma_{x_2}]^2 = 42.77446$$

of which linear regression accounts for

$$\frac{n}{2}[\sigma_{x_1}r_{x_1y_1} - \sigma_{x_2}r_{x_2y_2}]^2 = 42.28232$$

The residuals can be obtained by subtraction:

$$1.3307 - .47432 = .85638$$
$$42.77446 - 42.28232 = .49214$$

As a check, the two residuals together may also be computed as follows:

$$n[\sigma_{x_1}^2(1 - r_{x_1y_1}^2) + \sigma_{x_2}^2(1 - r_{x_2y_2}^2)] = 1.34852$$

The results may be assembled in the table shown on page 262. It is obvious from the table that most of the variance can be ascribed to the linear component of interaction. But any two sources of variation may, of course, be legitimately compared and the ratio of their variances tested for significance, provided one knows exactly what is being done. Conventional statistical treatment not only neglects to study the effect of individual differences and of their interaction with experimental variants but frequently fails to reveal to the investigator what exactly is being used for an estimate of error. Let us therefore examine the conventional tests of significance before proceeding to the discussion of a more comprehensive treatment.

Source of variation	Sum of squares	Degrees of freedom	Mean square
Total	45.8524	9	
Between methods	1.74724	1	1.74724
Within methods	44.10516	8	5.513145
Age, total	1.3307	4	.332675
Interaction, total	42.77446	4	10.693615
Age, linear	0.47432	1	.47432
Interaction, linear	42.28232	1	42.28232
Residual, age and interaction	1.34852	6	.224753

The conventional test of significance for the method of paired subjects is

$$t_1 = \frac{M_{x_1} - M_{x_2}}{\sqrt{\dfrac{\sigma_{x_1}^2 + \sigma_{x_2}^2 - 2r_{x_1x_2}\sigma_{x_1}\sigma_{x_2}}{n-1}}} = \frac{.836}{\sqrt{4.277446}} = \sqrt{\frac{1.74724}{10.693615}} = .40$$

where the entire interaction variance is used for an estimate of error. If the variance between subjects were more important than the interaction variance, the standard error thus obtained would, of course, be less than that obtained from the total variance within uniform experimental treatments, and herein would lie the advantage of the method of paired individuals over that of random groups. In the present case, however, interaction is by far the most important source of variation, and $r_{x_1x_2}$ is $-.965$, so that pairing seems to have increased the standard error considerably. For if the formula for random groups is used,

$$t_2 = \frac{M_{x_1} - M_{x_2}}{\sqrt{\dfrac{n_1\sigma_{x_1}^2 + n_2\sigma_{x_2}^2}{n_1 + n_2 - 2}\left[\dfrac{1}{n_1} + \dfrac{1}{n_2}\right]}} = \frac{M_{x_1} - M_{x_2}}{\sqrt{\dfrac{\sigma_{x_1}^2 + \sigma_{x_2}^2}{n-1}}}$$

$$= \frac{.836}{\sqrt{2.20528}} = \sqrt{\frac{1.74724}{5.513145}} = .56$$

Contrary to what many investigators may think, this second test is actually the more appropriate for the present case, as Fisher has pointed out: "In cases like this it sometimes occurs that one method shows no significant difference while the other brings it out, if either method indicates a definitely significant difference, its testimony cannot be ignored, even if the other method fails to show the effect" (3, page 133).

But the method of paired individuals is a special case of the method of matched groups. To test the general significance of experimental treatment in the case of matched groups, the proper formula to use is

$$t_3 = \frac{M_{x_1} - M_{x_2}}{\sqrt{\dfrac{n_1\sigma_{x_1}^2 + n_2\sigma_{x_2}^2}{n_1 + n_2 - 3}}} = (1 - r_{xy\cdot z}^2)\left[\frac{1}{n_1} + \frac{1}{n_2}\right]$$

$$= \frac{M_{x_1} - M_{x_2}}{\sqrt{\dfrac{\sigma_{x_1}^2 + \sigma_{x_2}^2}{n - 1.5}}\,(1 - r_{xy\cdot z}^2)}$$

$$= \frac{.836}{\sqrt{2.493191}} = \sqrt{\frac{1.74724}{6.2315}} = .53$$

where the estimate of error is based upon the variance within the same methods after linear regression on age. The possible advantage of pairing individuals over matching groups as wholes is thus seen to be the elimination of the entire age variance, as distinguished from its linear component, from the error variance. If regression on age is substantially linear, further elimination of the residual influence of age will involve a loss of precision due to the necessity of basing the estimate of error upon fewer degrees of freedom. In the present case, the linear component of age variance, though slightly larger than the residual, is still very insignificant as compared with the interaction variance, so the third test gives a larger standard error than the second test.

If one wishes to test the significance of experimental treatment in general, it is obviously illegitimate to eliminate the effect of interaction from the error variance, since significance may vary from age to age. On the other hand, one is, of course, free to make a limited test just at the observed mean age, provided one is not unaware of its limited nature, in which case the following formula is applicable:

$$t_4 = \cfrac{M_{x_1} - M_{x_2}}{\sqrt{\cfrac{n_1\sigma_{x_1}^2(\text{I} - r_{x_1y_1}^2) + n_2\sigma_{x_2}^2(\text{I} - r_{x_2y_2}^2)}{n_1 + n_2 - 4}}\left[\cfrac{\text{I}}{n_1} + \cfrac{\text{I}}{n_2}\right]}$$

$$= \cfrac{M_{x_1} - M_{x_2}}{\sqrt{\cfrac{\sigma_{x_1}^2(\text{I} - r_{x_1y_1}^2) + \sigma_{x_2}^2(\text{I} - r_{x_2y_2}^2)}{n - 2}}}$$

$$= \frac{.836}{\sqrt{.08990133}} = \sqrt{\frac{\text{I}.74724}{.22475}} = 2.79$$

As can be easily seen, this test is closely related to Wilks's formula for the standard error of the means of matched samples, which has been criticized on the ground that it would require successive samples to maintain the same distribution of the matched variable (1, 2, 6, 7, 10). In the light of the present discussion, it may be observed that the crucial point is whether there is any significant interaction between the experimental and the matched variable. When interaction is negligible, test 4 will not differ from test 3 in any marked degree. If there is significant interaction, however, the result of test 4 remains incapable of general application, even for extremely large and inclusive samples such as would yield a practically constant distribution in the matched variable

We have thus far limited ourselves to an analysis of the various methods that are usually used for the evaluation of experimental difference and to pointing out what exactly is used in the estimate of error in each case. For the present data, however, these four tests of significance are all inadequate, since the effect of interaction that is by far the most important has been left out of account. If we now evaluate the linear component of interaction in terms of the residual,

$$t_5 = \cfrac{b_{x_1y_1} - b_{x_2y_2}}{\sqrt{\cfrac{n_1\sigma_{x_1}^2(\text{I} - r_{x_1y_1}^2) + n_2\sigma_{x_2}^2(\text{I} - r_{x_2y_2}^2)}{n_1 + n_2 - 4}}\left[\cfrac{\text{I}}{n_1\sigma_{y_1}^2} + \cfrac{\text{I}}{n_2\sigma_{y_2}^2}\right]}$$

$$= \cfrac{\sigma_{x_1}r_{x_1y_1} - \sigma_{x_2}r_{x_2y_2}}{\sqrt{\cfrac{\sigma_{x_1}^2(\text{I} - r_{x_1y_1}^2) + \sigma_{x_2}^2(\text{I} - r_{x_2y_2}^2)}{n - 2}}}$$

$$= \frac{2.908}{\sqrt{.04495}} = \sqrt{\frac{42.28232}{.22475}} = 13.7$$

This test of interaction, which yields by far the most significant result, is the same as an evaluation of the difference between two regression coefficients. It therefore not only follows directly from the analysis of variance but can also be easily deduced from the standard error of regression coefficients as discussed in Tippett's and other books on statistical method.

If we express the improvement of handwriting quality as a linear function of age, separately for the two methods of practice

$$X_1 = M_{x_1} + b_{x_1y_1}(Y - M_{y_1})$$
$$X_2 = M_{x_2} + b_{x_2y_2}(Y - M_{y_2})$$

the difference between the two methods may be expressed as

$$X_1 - X_2 = M_{x_1} - M_{x_2} + b_{x_1y_1}(Y - M_{y_1}) - b_{x_2y_2}(Y - M_{y_2})$$

Test 4 evaluates the difference $M_{x_1} - M_{x_2}$, and test 5 evaluates the difference $b_{x_1y_1} - b_{x_2y_2}$. Obviously, what is needed is a combination of tests 4 and 5 to evaluate the difference $X_1 - X_2$.

Since the sampling variance of $b_{x_1y_1} - b_{x_2y_2}$ is

$$\frac{n_1\sigma_{x_1}^2(1 - r_{x_1y_1}^2) + n_2\sigma_{x_2}^2(1 - r_{x_2y_2}^2)}{n_1 + n_2 - 4}\left[\frac{1}{n_1\sigma_{y_1}^2} + \frac{1}{n_2\sigma_{y_2}^2}\right]$$

the sampling variance of $b_{x_1y_1}(Y - M_{y_1}) - b_{x_2y_2}(Y - M_{y_2})$ is

$$\frac{n_1\sigma_{x_1}^2(1 - r_{x_1y_1}^2) + n_2\sigma_{x_2}^2(1 - r_{x_2y_2}^2)}{n_1 + n_2 - 4}\left[\frac{(Y - M_y)^2}{n_1\sigma_{y_1}^2} + \frac{(Y - M_{y_2})^2}{n_2\sigma_{y_2}^2}\right]$$

The difference $X_1 - X_2$ can therefore be tested by the following formula with $n_1 + n_2 - 4$ degrees of freedom:

$$t_6 =$$
$$\frac{M_{x_1} - M_{x_2} + b_{x_1y_1}(Y - M_{y_1}) - b_{x_2y_2}(Y - M_{y_2})}{\sqrt{\dfrac{n_1\sigma_{x_1}^2(1 - r_{x_1y_1}^2) + n_2\sigma_{x_2}^2(1 - r_{x_2y_2}^2)}{n_1 + n_2 - 4}\left[\dfrac{1}{n_1} + \dfrac{1}{n_2} + \dfrac{(Y - M_{y_1})^2}{n_1\sigma_{y_1}^2} + \dfrac{(Y - M_{y_2})^2}{n_2\sigma_{y_2}^2}\right]}}$$

In the present case n, M_y, and σ_y are equal for the two groups, so the computation is considerably simplified:

$$t_6 = \frac{M_{x_1} - M_{x_2} + (b_{x_1y_1} - b_{x_2y_2})y}{\sqrt{\dfrac{\sigma_{x_1}^2(1 - r_{x_1y_1}^2) + \sigma_{x_2}^2(1 - r_{x_2y_2}^2)}{n - 2}\left[1 + \dfrac{y^2}{\sigma_y^2}\right]}}$$
$$= \frac{.836 - 2.908y}{\sqrt{.08990133(1 + .5y^2)}}$$

The significance of difference as expressed by t_6 is thus a function of age and is plotted in Fig. 1. If one sets t at a value corresponding to a certain level of significance, the equation can be solved for y to determine its range of significance.   For 6 degrees of freedom, if we choose the .001 level, for example, the corresponding t is ± 5.959, and the condition for significant differences is expressed by

$$-5.959 \geqslant \frac{.836 - 2.908y}{\sqrt{.08990133(1 + .5y^2)}} \geqslant 5.959$$

$$-.345 \geqslant y \geqslant 1.054$$

$$M_y = 9.0 \qquad \therefore\ 8.655 \geqslant Y \geqslant 10.054$$

Method A is thus better for ages not older than 8.655, and method B is better for ages not younger than 10.054; between these limits the difference is not significant.

Although cases of such strong interaction may be rare, moderate effects of interaction can be much more frequently observed.   The value of t will then change more slowly.   Since linearity of regression may be true only for relatively short intervals and since the standard error increases as one gets away from the observed mean, reliable conclusions in distant regions are not frequently available. But the test may suggest a general trend and lead to fruitful further experimentation.

In case interaction turns out to be insignificant, the numerator in the formula for test 6 will remain relatively constant, whereas the denominator increases as the matched variable deviates from the observed mean.

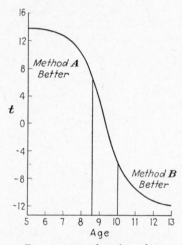

FIG. 1.—t as a function of age.

In other words, the value of t attains a maximum at the observed mean and falls off on both sides.   Whether or not interaction is significant, therefore, test 6 always reveals the range within which the experimental results are significant.

It will be further noted that test 6 does not assume perfect matching between the two groups of subjects.   Any difference between means or standard deviations will be automatically allowed for. For maximum precision, the means of the two groups should be as nearly equal as feasible, but the discarding of more than a few subjects is neither necessary nor advisable.

Since test 6 corrects for imperfections of matching, indicates the range of significance, and takes into account possible interaction between subject differences and experimental treatment, its extensive use cannot be too strongly urged. In case two different variables are used in the measurement of the subjects, the difference between experimental treatments, which is the numerator of the formula for test 6, will be a difference between two expressions of the following sort:

$$X = M_x + b_{xu \cdot v}(U - M_u) + b_{xv \cdot u}(V - M_v)$$
$$= M_x + \frac{r_{xu} - r_{xv}r_{uv}}{1 - r_{uv}^2} \cdot \frac{\sigma_x}{\sigma_u} (U - M_u) + \frac{r_{xv} - r_{xu}r_{uv}}{1 - r_{uv}^2} \cdot \frac{\sigma_x}{\sigma_v} (V - M_v)$$

where final accomplishment X is a linear function of the two new variables U and V in place of the single variable Y. The two coefficients of simple correlation in the first factor of the denominator will each be displaced by a multiple correlation coefficient, which, if the subscript designating one of the two groups is omitted, is

$$r_{x \cdot uv} = \sqrt{\frac{r_{xu}^2 + r_{xv}^2 - 2r_{xu}r_{xv}r_{uv}}{1 - r_{uv}^2}}$$

The two $(Y - M_y)^2/n\sigma_y^2$ terms in the second factor of the denominator are each to be displaced by

$$\frac{1}{n(1 - r_{uv}^2)} \left[\frac{(U - M_u)^2}{\sigma_u^2} - 2r_{uv} \frac{(U - M_u)(V - M_v)}{\sigma_u \sigma_v} + \frac{(V - M_v)^2}{\sigma_v^2} \right]$$

with the proper subscript 1 or 2 to be added. The number of degrees of freedom will be $n_1 + n_2 - 6$.

A method yielding essentially the same results has been discussed by Johnson and Neyman (5). But the exposition is based on terms and concepts that are unfamiliar to most investigators and has not led to extensive use of the method. It is hoped that the present treatment of the t test may be more easily followed. Johnson and Neyman's terms are related to the t test in the following manner:

$$\zeta = \frac{S_a^2}{S_r^2} = \frac{1}{1 + \dfrac{F^2}{(P + Q)S_a^2}} = \frac{1}{1 + \dfrac{t^2}{n_1 + n_2 - 6}}$$

$$t^2 = \frac{F^2}{\dfrac{S_a^2}{n_1 + n_2 - 6}[P + Q]} = \frac{1 - \zeta}{\zeta}(n_1 + n_2 - 6)$$

which hold in their case of two variables in the measurement of the subjects.

A further extension of the t test is to consider not merely the hypothesis

$$X_1 - X_2 = 0$$

but a whole continuum of hypotheses

$$X_1 - X_2 = D \qquad \text{or} \qquad X_1 - X_2 - D = 0$$

where D is any unspecified value. To evaluate each of these hypotheses

$$t_6 = \frac{.836 - 2.908y - D}{\sqrt{.08990133(1 + .5y^2)}}$$

and, if we choose the .001 level of significance, as before, and set t

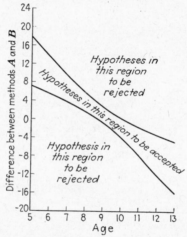

FIG. 2.—Hypothesis to be accepted or rejected according to age.

to ± 5.959, all hypotheses to be rejected may be distinguished from those to be accepted by the following condition:

$$-5.959 \geqslant \frac{.836 - 2.908y - D}{\sqrt{.08990138(1 + .5y^2)}} \geqslant 5.959$$

The hyperbolic curves bounding the regions of significance are plotted in Fig. 2.

REFERENCES

1. EZEKIEL, M. "Student's" method for measuring the significance of a difference between matched groups. *J. educ. Psychol.*, 1932, **23**, 446–450.

2. EZEKIEL, M.   Reply to Dr. Lindquist's "further note" on matched groups. *J. educ. Psychol.*, 1933, **24,** 306–309.

3. FISHER, R. A.   Statistical methods for research workers.   (7th ed.)   London: Oliver & Boyd, 1938.

4. FISHER, R. A.   The design of experiments.   (2d ed.)   London: Oliver & Boyd, 1937.

5. JOHNSON, P. O., & NEYMAN, J.   Tests of certain linear hypotheses and their application to some educational problems.   *Stat. Res. Mem.*, 1936, **1,** 57–93.

6. LINDQUIST, E. F.   The significance of a difference between "matched" groups.   *J. educ. Psychol.*, 1931, **22,** 197–204.

7. LINDQUIST, E. F.   A further note on the significance of a difference between the means of matched groups.   *J. educ. Psychol.*, 1933, **24,** 66–69.

8. SHYNG CHII JUANG.   An experimental comparison between two methods of practising Chinese handwriting.   *Jiaw Yuh Tzar Jyh*, 1935, **25,** No. 4.

9. TIPPETT, L. H. C.   The methods of statistics.   (2d ed.)   London: Williams & Norgate, 1937.

10. WILKS, S. S.   The standard error of the means of "matched" samples. *J. educ. Psychol.*, 1931, **22,** 205–208.

CHAPTER XV

INDIVIDUAL AND SEX DIFFERENCES IN SPEED OF SACCADIC EYE MOVEMENTS[1]

By

MILES A. TINKER

University of Minnesota

Notwithstanding the large amount of literature on oculomotor behavior, information concerning the angle velocity of saccadic eye movements is meager.   For the most part, the data on this subject have been obtained incidentally in such studies as those of Benedict, Miles, Roth, and Smith (1), Miles (6) and Travis (12).   Tinker (10) cites the available evidence from reading investigations.   The only systematic study of saccadic eye-movement speed as such is reported by Dodge and Cline (3).   They employed only a few measurements on their subjects and made no attempt to evaluate individual differences or the stability of the obtained means.

The rapid, sweeping movements of the eye that occur in moving from one fixation to another in the visual field are called *saccadic* because of their nature.   These movements, in which the point of regard changes from one position to another within any relatively fixed section of the field of vision, are best understood of all the eye movements.   They are illustrated by the eye movements in reading or by those employed in viewing a landscape.   Saccadic eye movements are fundamentally reactions to eccentric retinal stimulation. The eyes move so that the point of interest will be seen with the visual center of the retina.   This type of eye movement is characterized by relatively great velocity and by an absence of clear vision during the movement (2).

Saccadic eye movements reveal three distinct phases as to velocity: (*a*) at the beginning of the movement, there is a positive acceleration to the maximum velocity; (*b*) this velocity is maintained for a considerable angle of movement; and (*c*) the velocity slows down as the eye comes to rest (2).

[1] The expense of this study was met by a research grant from the Graduate School, University of Minnesota.

The purpose of this experiment is to analyze individual and sex differences in speed of horizontal saccadic eye movements. The experimental design will be such that analysis of variance may be employed in the computations.[1]

Two groups of university sophomores served as subjects. There were seven men in one group and seven women in the other. Analysis for each group was made separately and then results for the two groups compared.

The Minnesota eye-movement camera, described by Tinker (11), was used to photograph the eye movements. Seven stimulus cards were prepared, one for each of the visual excursions to be measured. There were two dots so arranged on each card that they were bilaterally symmetrical from the center of the card. Distance between dots was such that visual angles of 5, 10, 15, 20, 25, 30, and 35 degrees were subtended, respectively, for the seven cards at a reading distance of 14 inches, which was constant for all subjects.

The subjects were directed to look at the left dot and then to fixate alternately right and left as the experimenter said "right," "left," "right," etc. The shifts occurred at the rate of about 1 per second. Each subject was given a practice series to acquaint him with the camera situation and the experimental procedure. Photographs were then taken for a series of 16 shifts (8 to the right plus 8 to the left) for each of the 7 visual angles. The order of presentation for the angles is described below in the experimental design. There was a short rest between each series while the stimulus card was changed.

To provide an efficient method of statistical treatment, the 7×7 Latin square, design a, as described by Fisher and Yates (4, page 45) was employed as the experimental design. In this outline, letters A through G refer to angles 5 through 35 degrees, respectively. The rows corresponded to individuals and different orders of presentation of angles. The sequence of the angles was randomized, with the restrictions inherent in the Latin-square design. This design permits the identification of the following sources of variation: (a) between means of rows, i.e., between individuals; (b) between means of columns, i.e., between differences in the order of presentation; and (c) between means of treatments, i.e.,

---

[1] For a clear statement concerning the application of analysis of variance to psychological experiments, see Brent Baxter, Problems in the planning of psychological experiments, *Amer. J. Psychol.* (in press).

between angles.   The remainder, or the within groups, variance is the experimental error.   The significance of the three sources of variation may then be evaluated by comparing them to the experimental error.   The precision of the experiment depends on the success with which the sources of variation are identified and isolated from the error.

TABLE I

MEAN SPEED OF SACCADIC EYE MOVEMENTS FOR MEN, IN MILLISECONDS FOR VARIOUS ANGLES

Subject	Angles, degrees							
	5	10	15	20	25	30	35	Mean
A..............	27.5	39.2	50.6	56.9	64.4	75.3	87.2	57.3
B..............	24.3	31.1	42.8	53.3	58.1	68.3	83.6	51.6
C..............	23.6	33.1	39.4	51.1	57.8	68.3	80.6	50.6
D..............	26.1	37.2	46.7	55.0	71.7	77.2	91.7	57.9
E..............	24.2	40.0	52.2	63.6	74.2	74.7	87.8	59.5
F..............	28.3	40.3	51.1	64.4	75.3	93.1	98.6	64.4
G..............	32.2	47.2	58.1	79.5	78.9	92.5	94.7	69.0
Mean..............	26.6	38.3	48.7	60.6	68.6	78.6	89.2	

Timing on the records was achieved by interrupting at the rate of 90 times per second the light beam reflected from the subject's eye. This produced on the photographic record a series of dots and spaces. Each dot and also each space represented $\frac{1}{180}$ second.   The records were easily read to one half of $\frac{1}{180}$ second.   This permitted the tabulations and computations to be made, therefore, in units of $\frac{1}{180}$ second.   The final tabulations for publication were changed to milliseconds for ease of interpretation.   In reading the films, the first 10 legible records of each subject for each angle were tabulated. Occasionally the record for one sweep of the eye was illegible because of a blinking or drooping of the eyelid.   The mean of the 10 recordings was considered to be a satisfactorily stable measure of eye-movement velocity for a particular angle.   Dodge and Cline (3) have shown that highly stable means are derived from 5 to 10 sweeps. The basic data of the study are given in Table I for the seven men and Table II for the seven women.   The marked stability of the mean scores in these tables is illustrated by picking one subject at random and noting the mean deviations of the scores.   The illustrative case (subject C of Table II) is given in Table III.   It is readily seen that the mean deviations are very small in comparison with the means. It is well known from previous work that speed of saccadic eye movements is a highly stable form of response for a particular individual. The other subjects in our groups revealed a similar trend in constancy of angle velocity. Although the variation among individuals is significant (see below), it is also relatively small.

TABLE II

MEAN SPEED OF SACCADIC EYE MOVEMENTS FOR WOMEN, IN MILLISECONDS FOR VARIOUS ANGLES

Subject	Angles, degrees							
	5	10	15	20	25	30	35	Mean
A................	26.4	36.4	46.1	55.0	63.9	72.5	84.5	55.0
B................	27.2	34.4	48.9	60.3	63.9	77.2	96.4	58.3
C................	28.9	38.6	45.3	63.3	67.5	77.2	84.5	57.9
D................	24.2	32.5	39.4	44.2	53.3	59.4	64.7	45.4
E................	25.8	36.9	48.3	58.3	66.1	81.4	100.8	59.7
F................	26.9	39.4	51.7	58.9	71.1	75.6	87.8	58.8
G................	23.3	34.7	46.4	53.3	61.4	72.8	78.6	52.9
Mean............	26.1	36.1	46.6	56.2	63.9	73.7	85.3	

TABLE III

VARIABILITY IN SPEED OF EYE MOVEMENTS FOR A SINGLE SUBJECT, IN MILLISECONDS FOR VARIOUS ANGLES

	Angles, degrees						
	5	10	15	20	25	30	35
Mean................	28.9	38.6	45.3	63.3	67.5	77.2	84.5
M.D................	2.7	1.0	1.9	3.3	5.8	4.0	2.8

Application of the analysis of variance assumes that the variance is homogeneous within the various subclasses. Neyman and Pearson's L_1 test (7, page 13) was employed to test for significance of difference in variance within the classes. When the raw scores were used, some of the samples revealed heterogeneity of variance. A logarithmic transformation was then tried, and it was found that the limits of L_1 exceeded the 1 per cent level for rows, columns, and treatments both for men and for women, indicating homogeneity of variance. Consequently, the logarithmically transformed scores were used in the analysis of variance and in testing for significance of differences between means.

The normality of the distribution of the transformed scores was tested by the technique cited by Snedecor (9, page 148). Scores for both the men and the women were found to be distributed normally.

Data on the analysis of variance for the group of seven men are given in Table IV. The variance, computed by dividing each sum of

TABLE IV
ANALYSIS OF VARIANCE: SPEED OF EYE MOVEMENTS FOR MEN
(Scores are in logarithms)

Source of variation	D.F.	Sum of squares	Mean square	Variance ratio: F*
Between columns (order of presentation)...	6	.00245	.00041	1.46341
Between individuals...............	6	.10259	.01710	28.50000
Between angles..................	6	1.44463	.24077	401.28333
Within groups (error).............	30	.01789	.00060	
Total......................	48	1.56756		

* Significance of variance: At the 1 per cent level, F must equal or exceed 7.23; at the 5 per cent level, 3.81.

squares by the appropriate degrees of freedom (D.F.), is found in the column labeled "mean square." To test the significance of the variance between columns, the ratio F between it and experimental error was obtained. This is given in the last column of the table. To be significant with 6 and 30 D.F. at the 1 per cent level, F must equal or exceed 7.23; at the 5 per cent level, 3.81. In this case, there is no evidence to indicate that the variance between columns is significantly different from error. This indicates that the order in which the subjects responded to the different angles had no appreciable effect on the results. The F for individuals is so large that, with 6 and 30 D.F., it is significant at the 1 per cent level. This indicates that differences between individuals are greater than chance differences; i.e., significant individual differences are present. In a similar manner, the variance between angles is significantly different from error, i.e., there are stable differences between means for speed of eye movements.

Inspection of the sums of squares in Table IV reveals that by far the greater amount of variation may be attributed to angles, although the variation attributed to individuals is appreciable. The within-groups variation is very small. The latter indicates that the experimental design has been efficient and has yielded a precise estimate of error.

After it has been established that there are significant differences between individuals, it is desirable to compute the significance of any particular difference. The t-test, as described by Lindquist, (5, page 97), was employed for these determinations. Of 21 differences, 16 were significant at the 1 per cent level. Thus nearly all the differences between individuals are significant. When the significance of the difference between angles was determined in a like manner, it was found that all, or 21 out of 21, were significant at the 1 per cent level. In other words, the differences between angles are all highly stable.

Data on the analysis of variance for the group of seven women are given in Table V. The trends are strikingly like those in the data for

TABLE V

ANALYSIS OF VARIANCE: SPEED OF EYE MOVEMENTS FOR WOMEN

(Scores are in logarithms)

Source of variation	D.F.	Sum of squares	Mean square	Variance ratio: F*
Between columns (order of presentation).................................	6	.00552	.00092	1.95745
Between individuals.................	6	.06043	.01007	21.42553
Between angles......................	6	1.35350	.22558	479.95745
Within groups (error)...............	30	.01397	.00047	
Total............................	48	1.43342		

* Significance of variance: At the 1 per cent level, F must equal or exceed 7.23; at the 5 per cent level, 3.81.

men. The order in which the subjects responded to the angles again had no appreciable effect on the results. Variance for individuals and for angles were both significantly different from experimental error. Again, the preponderant amount of the variation is attributable to angles. Computation of the significance of the particular differences revealed that 15 of 21 differences between individuals and all the differences between angles were significant at the 1 per cent level. The trends in the two groups, therefore, are practically identical.

Computations, employing the t-test, were made to discover whether there were significant sex differences in speed of eye movements for each of the seven angles. The group means from Table I and Table II are repeated in Table VI. It should be noted that, although the differences between men and women are small, they are all in one direction. The men were slightly slower, on the average. In none of the seven comparisons was the difference significant at the 1 per cent level. For three angles (20, 25, and 30 degrees), however, the differences were significant at the 5 per cent level. The 10- and 35-degree angles reveal differences that are significant at the 10 per cent level. Nevertheless, if a fairly rigorous test of significance is maintained (the 1 per cent level), the sex differences have not been established as significant. Homogeneous sex groups give a slightly more precise estimate of error. In future work, however, mixed groups might well be employed for the sake of a broader basis of generalization.

TABLE VI

SEX DIFFERENCES IN SPEED OF EYE MOVEMENTS, IN MILLISECONDS FOR VARIOUS ANGLES

	Angles, degrees						
	5	10	15	20	25	30	35
Men.....................	26.6	38.3	48.7	60.6	68.6	78.6	89.2
Women.................	26.1	36.1	46.6	56.2	63.9	73.7	85.3
Difference..............	.5	2.2	2.1	4.4	4.7	4.9	3.9

DISCUSSION

The lack of highly significant differences between means of men and women suggest that, regardless of sex, speed of saccadic eye movements is fairly constant from group to group when averages for at least seven subjects are considered. The fact that there are significant individual differences indicates that enough subjects should be employed to stabilize the means cited as the velocity for a given angle. When the scores for men and women in our groups are combined, the mean scores should become even more stable. The averages for the total group of 14 persons are given in Table VII, and the data from Dodge and Cline are also listed for comparison. There

is fair agreement between the two sets of data, closer than might be
expected in view of the fact that individual differences are significant and that Dodge and Cline used only three subjects.   Certain

TABLE VII

Comparison of Mean Eye-movement Speeds: Tinker vs. Dodge and Cline,
in Milliseconds for Various Angles

	Angles, degrees							
	5	10	15	20	25	30	35	40
Tinker............	26.4	37.2	47.7	58.4	66.3	76.2	87.3	
D and C...........	28.8	38.8	48.2	54.8	....	80.4	....	99.9

other data fall in line with those given above.   For visual angles of
about 14 to 16 degrees, Tinker (10) obtained an angular velocity of
48 milliseconds.   Shen (8) obtained speeds of 54 milliseconds for an
angle of about 20 degrees.   Using Dodge and Cline's data, Shen
also computed the estimated velocities for small angles:

9.9 milliseconds for 1 degree   22.2 milliseconds for 3 degrees
17.3 milliseconds for 2 degrees   26.0 milliseconds for 4 degrees

Actual measurements correspond closely to these estimates.   Dodge
and Cline obtained a mean of 22.9 milliseconds for angles ranging
from 2 to 7 degrees, and Shen (8) obtained from 10 to 15 milliseconds
for a visual angle of 1 degree 15 minutes.

It is not surprising that highly significant sex differences in
velocity of eye movements were not found inasmuch as training has
little effect.   Once the eye has begun its excursion, its velocity is
practically uninfluenced by voluntary effort.   Furthermore, eye-
movement speed is remarkably constant for any individual while the
eye moves through a given angle under the same conditions of
muscular fatigue.   It is possible that the angle velocity of saccadic
eye movements is little susceptible to modification through training.

A rather interesting relationship is present between increase in
size of visual angle and change in speed of eye movements.   With
each successive increase of 5 degrees in visual angle, the time for eye
movements was increased by 10.8, 10.5, 10.7, 7.9, 9.9, and 11.1
milliseconds.   In general, the increment was fairly constant, i.e.,
about 10 milliseconds increase for each additional 5 degrees.   In
other words, there appears to be a linear function between speed and

extent of eye movement. But the apparent implication of 10 milliseconds for each 5 degrees is false. Note that doubling the visual angle does not double time of eye movements. Time for 10 degrees is only about 41 per cent greater than for 5 degrees; for 20 degrees, 57 per cent greater than for 10 degrees; and for 30 degrees, 60 per cent greater than for 15 degrees. According to Dodge (2), this lack of a one-to-one relationship between amount of movement and time taken for the movement is due to the fact that the maximum velocity of the eye during movements of large amplitude is greater than the maximum velocity during movements of small amplitude.

Summary

1. The purpose of this experiment was to study, through analysis of variance, individual and sex differences in speed of saccadic eye movements when the eye sweeps through angles of 5, 10, 15, 20, 25, 30 and 35 degrees. Seven men and seven women were employed as subjects.
2. The data satisfied the criterion of normality.
3. To secure homogeneity of variance among the samples (rows, columns, etc.), it was necessary to use a logarithmic transformation of the scores.
4. Analysis of variance for the data on men revealed:
   a. The order in which the subjects responded to the different angles had no significant effect on results.
   b. Individual differences were significant at the 1 per cent level.
   c. The differences between angles were highly significant.
   d. A large proportion of the variation was due to angles.
5. The analysis of variance for data on women showed approximately the same results as for men.
6. Although the men were consistently slower than the women in velocity of eye movements, the differences were not highly significant.
7. The mean velocities for eye movements for the 14 subjects in this study were surprisingly like those for Dodge and Cline's three subjects.
8. Although the speed of the eye is inversely proportional to the amount of movement, it is not a 1 to 1 relationship.
9. The data warrant the conclusion that individual differences in speed of saccadic eye movements and differences due to extent

of movement are highly significant but that sex differences are insignificant.

References

1. BENEDICT, F. G., MILES, W. R., ROTH, P., & SMITH, H. W. Human vitality and efficiency under prolonged restricted diet. Washington: Carnegie Institute of Washington, 1919, No. 280.

2. DODGE, R. Five types of eye movements in the horizontal meridian plane of the field of regard. *Amer. J. Physiol.*, 1902–03, **8**, 307–329.

3. DODGE, R., & CLINE, T. S. The angle velocity of eye movements. *Psychol. Rev.*, 1901, **8**, 145–157.

4. FISHER, R. A., & YATES, F. Statistical tables for biological, agricultural, and medical research. London: Oliver & Boyd, 1938.

5. LINDQUIST, E. F. Statistical analysis in educational research. Boston: Houghton Mifflin, 1940.

6. MILES, W. R. Alcohol and human efficiency. Washington: Carnegie Institute of Washington, 1924, No. 333.

7. NAYER, P. P. N. An investigation into the application of Neyman and Pearson's L_1 test, with tables of percentage L_1 units. *Stat. Res. Mem.*, 1936, **1**, 38–51.

8. SHEN, E. An analysis of eye movements in the reading of Chinese. *J. exp. Psychol.*, 1927, **10**, 158–183.

9. SNEDECOR, G. W. Statistical methods. Ames: Collegiate Press, 1938.

10. TINKER, M. A. Eye movement duration, pause duration, and reading time. *Psychol. Rev.*, 1928, **35**, 385–397.

11. TINKER, M. A. Apparatus for recording eye movements. *Amer. J. Psychol.*, 1931, **43**, 115–127.

12. TRAVIS, R. C. The latency and velocity of the eye in saccadic movements. *Psychol. Monogr.* (Dodge Commemorative Number), 1936, **47**, No. 212, 242–249.

13. WELCH, B. L. Note on an extension of the L_1 test. *Stat. Res. Mem.*, 1936, **1**, 52–56.

CHAPTER XVI

A NOTE ON PERSONALITY FACTORS AFFECTING THE REHABILITATION OF PROBLEM FAMILIES

By

RAYMOND R. WILLOUGHBY

Rhode Island Department of Social Welfare

It is frequently observed that, among a group of families in sub-marginal economic condition, some respond much more readily than do others to the help offered by social agencies. At the suggestion of the Providence Family Welfare Society, an attempt was made to investigate the causes of this difference. A full report of this study may be obtained from the Society.

Five experienced case workers, after agreeing on a definition of "maladjustment," selected from a group of approximately the same economic level 45 families whom they rated as "maladjusted" and a control group of 22 additional families rated as "well adjusted." Inasmuch as these workers had previously shown complete agreement in their ratings of three somewhat puzzling cases, it is evident that their judgments were based on similar criteria.

Three primary questions were asked about the families under consideration: (*a*) Of what does the maladjustment consist? (*b*) How may it have originated? (*c*) What modifications have been effected, and what further amelioration may be possible?

Answers to the first two questions were sought by making a statistical comparison by means of the χ^2 technique of the frequency of certain observable reactions within the experimental and control groups. Since all these families were certainly "frustrated," particular attention was given to characteristic responses to frustration, such as aggression, anxiety, and collapse. Independent rating by the writer and a colleague of the extent of these responses showed about 60 to 70 per cent agreement. It was found that extreme anxiety was significantly more frequent in the control group than in the experimental group; aggressive reactions, frequently of psychotic form and intensity, were more often shown by the maladjusted group; and collapse reactions, though the least frequent of the three types, were present in far greater degree in the maladjusted group.

A consideration of family patterns resulted in the hypothesis that, other things being equal, the husband is the first member of the group to feel pressure from the outside. If the pressure is continued for a sufficient length of time, the wife and, finally, the children will also be affected. This "normal" or usual pattern may, of course, be modified by temperamental differences and to some extent by specific environmental circumstances.

External stresses appeared to be similar in nature and degree for both the maladjusted and the control groups. As far as could be determined, the education and the vocational history of the members of the control group, although not particularly good, averaged distinctly better than was usual for the maladjusted group. There was no appreciable difference in the medical history or childhood experiences (such as abuse, divorce or desertion by parents, etc.) between the members of the two groups. The control group had a slightly higher incidence of physical illness than the maladjusted group; the maladjusted group showed a markedly larger number of mentally defective and mentally warped individuals than the control, and (as might be expected) a larger number of children whose adjustments to society were unsatisfactory. Therefore, the causes of the maladjustment seem to lie more within the individuals of the maladjusted families than with specific past or present stresses affecting them or the family as a whole. They break down under pressure more because of inherent weakness than because they are or have been subjected to particular sorts of strain.

Thus, in spite of initial determination not to be bound by traditional concepts, the very strong roles played by psychosis and mental defect in the production of maladjustment became increasingly evident as the study progressed. The odds in favor of a real difference in these variables between the maladjusted and the control families whose records were investigated are more than 100 to 1.

Because the criterion of selection was, in effect, the failure of the particular casework methods used with these families to effect any observable change in their original maladjustment, no satisfactory answer to the third question posited could be reached. However, inasmuch as the major findings point to the conclusion that mental

incapacity and psychotic tendencies are the chief factors that differentiate the families with whom treatment resulted in some measure
of success from those unresponsive to such treatment, it appears
reasonable to believe that, for the latter, supervisory and educational
techniques of the kind utilized in work with mental defectives might
prove the best solution possible.

CHAPTER XVII

VARIATIONS IN PERSONALITY MANIFESTATIONS IN MORMON POLYGYNOUS FAMILIES

By

Kimball Young

Queens College

In 1843, when Joseph Smith, the Mormon prophet, announced to his closest associates the "revelation on the eternity of the marriage covenant, including the plurality of wives," he was met by a variety of reactions. The "Principle" of polygynous "celestial marriage" ran counter to some of the deepest values of the Latter-day Saints, and it was only to be expected that many would respond negatively to such a revolutionary idea. Yet, within a few years, the pattern was accepted by nearly all the Mormons and practiced by a considerable fraction of them, but especially by those who held positions of social dominance.

This striking intrusion of a deviant sexual and familial pattern into American life, which met with tremendous resistance from the outside, affords an excellent opportunity to examine a number of points bearing on social-cultural change and on the personality manifestations that are the psychological counterparts or elements in this change. The aim of this study, in fact, is to describe and interpret certain attitudes and habits of individuals living in selected polygynous Mormon families. Such an investigation should throw light on certain interrelations of culture and personality.

Mormon polygyny affords a culture case study of a society operating under a new ideology, in which there was a radical departure from long-established mores and law. Only the broad outlines of the new pattern of plural marriage were drawn by the Mormon society; the details remained to be worked out in the course of about 50 years by the families who lived under the system, involving, as it did, for the individual member, a sharp break in social habits, attitudes, ideas, and values. However, this change in the cultural pattern permitted the individual novel expression of certain diverse biological impulses. Second, the situation allowed a wide latitude of readaptation, due, in part, to the lack of any detailed social-cultural blueprint to guide individual functioning within the new schema. And, third, it led to a variety of attempts on the part of the individual to obtain emotional security and ego satisfaction through the establishment of adequate status in terms of social interaction. Such efforts took on a variety of substitutive and compensatory forms, related to jealousy, envy, struggle for power, overt aggression, docility, and acceptance. But all these responses operated within the broad framework of the "Principle," as it was called; *i.e.*, there was more or less general acceptance of the new system, though, with respect to their emotional convictions, individuals differed considerably. In justifying the readaptation, the place of official or church sanctions and the example and stimulation of the Mormon leaders were important factors.

Thus, we see the emergence of a new pattern in which polygyny and monogamy come to exist together in this society.[1] In this development both in-group, *i.e.*, Mormon, and out-group, *i.e.*, gentile, factors operated in such a way that even after 50 or 60 years, there remained a rather wide variety of patterns within the larger cultural acceptance of the ideology and practice of polygyny. Had Mormon polygyny persisted for a longer time, there would doubtless have emerged certain standardizations in some, if not all, of these matters of everyday living. From the angle of social psychology and cultural analysis, however, the important point is that a marked variability was permitted and that gradually, through a process of trial and error, a sort of cultural and psychological norm began to be established as one form or another proved successful or otherwise. But our major concern is with the adaptation of individuals to this novel system, not the institutional development. To understand this, we must bear in mind the importance in social interaction of individual differences in drive and temperament, of noncultural personal-social relations, and, finally, of cultural patterns, both old or monogamous and new or polygynous.

---

[1] Obviously, complete polygyny would be out of the question. In Mormondom, as in other societies permitting plural wifehood, the basic pattern remained monogamous. Although no adequate figures are available, probably not more than 10 per cent of Mormon families fell into the plural-marriage class in the period of its greatest frequency—approximately 1870–1880.

There are three areas of person-to-person interaction in the family that might be discussed: (*a*) that bearing on the adjustment of the wives to the plural marriage; (*b*) that revealing the husband-and-father role and status in the polygynous family; and (*c*) that showing intersibling relations. In this paper, we shall deal only with the first and second, although some reference to the sibling contacts must of necessity be made.

MATERIALS AND METHODS

The approach may be designated broadly as that of the life history or individual case study. It is frankly qualitative rather than quantitative, and the major concern is with the processes of interaction of persons as these influence the ideas, attitudes, habits, and values involved in the social role and status of given individuals. It is the author's conviction that such materials have value for the human sciences, even though they are not in a form amenable to quantification. Our interpretation must be made in terms of the interplay of persons within given social configurations, and such interpretations are made possible, in part, by concepts developed from case-study methods as they have been worked out in social psychology, clinical psychology, cultural anthropology, and dynamic psychiatry.[1]

The basic data for this study consist of approximately 125 records of men and their families who lived at one time or another under Mormon polygyny. The material ranges from extensive interview notes and rather complete autobiographical statements and diaries to sketchy and incomplete records of interviews, brief biographies, letters, and other fragmentary sources.[2] No formal questionnaire

[1] There is an extensive literature on the case-study or individual-history method. Among others, see W. I. Thomas and F. Znaniecki, The Polish peasant in Europe and America, Boston: Gorham Press, 1918, Vol. I; John Dollard, Criteria for the life history, New Haven: Yale Univ. Press, 1935; and Kimball Young, Personality and Problems of Adjustment, New York: Crofts, 1940. Chap. XI. (The latter contains extensive bibliographic references.)

[2] In the collection of the data, the author was assisted by J. Edward Hulett, Jr., and Faye Ollerton. He wishes also to thank the Social Science Research Council and the graduate school of the University of Wisconsin for grants-in-aid during the years 1935–1939, which provided funds for some of the fieldwork involved.

In addition to the specific data compiled by the writer and his field assistants, all three workers made daily notes of their conversations and contacts with individuals who were living or had lived under the plural-marriage system. The participant-observer technique was important, and we have in this study an

was employed, but the fieldworkers followed a certain agreed-upon plan as to what pertinent data were to be collected whenever possible. Most of the autobiographical matter and the letters and diaries were, of course, written years ago, the most valuable of the documents during the very time when the practice was in full bloom. Although not always affording precise information, these data often proved most important in providing background material and revealing the "spirit" of this novel enterprise.

With respect to the nature and function of personality, the writer follows essentially the standpoint that he has indicated elsewhere.[1] With reference to our particular data, we shall discuss certain motivations of individuals as these influence their role and status in the Mormon family and in the Mormon community. In turn, these matters will be related to ego security or insecurity, degree of self-esteem, and the manifestations of aggressive or other behavior in the face of frustrations and the struggle for prestige and acceptable roles. In this analysis, attention will be given to the social-cultural configurations in which individual action takes place. Without this larger orientation, the individual's motives and satisfactions, or lack of them, mean nothing.

Role and Status of the Wives

One of the foremost difficulties that confronted a wife in a polygynous family arose out of the breakdown of certain of the basic features of monogamy. In the traditional American marriage, there had been developed a certain linkage of patriarchal control with romantic love. This implied relatively free choice of mates on grounds of mutual attraction, predicated in part on sexual appeal; it involved an idea of constancy, fidelity, complete attention of one spouse to the other, and emotional security. These, in turn, implied certain roles and statuses. Among the roles was the duty or responsibility to serve the husband, which entailed certain corresponding privileges within this framework of obligation. Thus, in the case

---

excellent illustration of the role of the interviewer and observer as an instrument not only of collection but of meaningful interpretation of the data. This is not the occasion to defend this standpoint and method, which obviously lead over from strict objectivity toward the art of handling individuals and of using inferences not always supported by completely demonstrable and self-evident data. (See Young, *op. cit.*, pp. 253–258; and G. W. Allport, Personality: a psychological interpretation, New York: Holt, 1937.)

[1] See Young, *op. cit.*, especially Chaps. IV, VII, IX, and X.

of the woman, status was assured through the performance of her major adult functions in her capacity of wife, mother, helpmate, and companion.   The husband's role was not only that of fathering his children, but of being provider and disciplinarian.   He furnished the basic economic security and authority.   The sanctions for these functions rested not only on the mores but on the law.   The legitimacy of the sexual expression and of the children, as members of family and community, was taken for granted.   Moreover, there was a cultural expectancy or approval of such emotional-aggressive expressions as jealousy and envy on the part of the wife if and when her traditional role and status were threatened.   These sentiments represented potential or anticipatory reactions toward any efforts to dislodge her from her security, possessive rights and duties, and other customary appurtenances.

This, at least, is the idealized picture of interspouse relations in monogamy.   Moreover, the powerful sanctions of the Christian church, with few deviant instances, had for hundreds of years been deeply imbedded in our cultural conditioning.   Approved marital relations of any other pattern were hard to imagine.

Within this broader cultural setting of Mormonism were other concepts and practices that must be noted if we would understand fully the meaning of plural marriage for the individuals involved. In the family life, the Mormons accepted and extended the patriarchal system.   On the religious side, the males were accorded the rights and duties of the divinely established priesthood—the lower, or Aaronic, and the higher, or Melchisedek, and women could attain salvation by becoming members of the church—through repentence, baptism, and the "laying on of hands for the gift of the Holy Ghost." For them, however, the full glory in this life and in the hereafter could be obtained only through certain sacred rituals performed "by those in authority" involving marriage for "time and eternity." These marriages linked the wife to the husband forever and made it possible for her to share in his status during this life and in the next.   But such status was not complete or satisfactory to God unless the woman bore many children not only "to people and replenish the earth" but also to afford the waiting souls in heaven an opportunity to take on the flesh and go through the "probation" of living on the earth.[1]

---

[1] It is impossible to elaborate the whole Mormon eschatology, but it is important to note the stress on large families, on many wives, and, on a projection of

Mormon polygyny was superimposed on this theological pattern. It was first enunciated in 1843 by Joseph Smith to his closest followers and members of the hierarchy, whence it spread but slowly among the rank and file of the church. "Gentile" or non-Mormon opposition to the practice, however, was a factor in driving the Mormons out of Illinois, and it was not until 1853, in the distant reaches of the Great Basin, that the "Principle" was finally publicly acknowledged. The new doctrine became integrated into the older theology. Higher glory for the man was obtainable through plural wifehood and the production of many children. Polygynous women were promised greater rewards than their monogamous sisters.

On the other hand, this novel pattern involved certain alterations in the older forms of matrimony and family life. Theoretically, the new pattern necessitated the disappearance or decline of some aspects of monogamous romantic love as a basis for wedlock. Ideally, at least, there was set up a system of equal status among two or more wives, which was applicable to emotional as well as to economic needs. But the new scheme gave no recognition to jealousy and envy—long-accepted bulwarks of monogamy. Monogamous marriage, supported as it was, of course, by outside legal sanctions, remained for the Mormons a religious sacrament. On the other hand, polygyny meant a complete abandonment of the secular, i.e., legal, sanctions of marriage, child status, and property rights. These were replaced by sacred or ecclesiastical sanctions. This loss of support from legalistic as well as traditional Christian grounds doubtless influenced the adoption of plural marriage by particular individuals. It must never be forgotten that the Mormons were a cultural island within the larger world of American society. Yet all the usual legal sanctions regarding property, contract, police power, community controls, as well as those relating more directly to marriage and childbearing and child rearing were, in large part, carried over into the Mormon pattern, since, as a cultural island, Mormondom was never fully isolated from the gentile world around it.[1] The whole course of polygyny was influ-

---

these concepts into the future life, when women would go on bearing not mundane but spiritual beings, who, in turn, would be born in the flesh.

[1] The impact of the larger America on Mormon polygyny is ably discussed with reference to public opinion by Paul W. Tappan, Mormon-gentile conflict: a study of the influences of public opinion on in-group versus out-group interactions with special reference to polygamy. Unpublished Doctor's Thesis, Univ. Wisconsin, 1939.

enced not only by the historical carry-over from gentile America but by continuing contact between the Mormons and non-Mormons.

With this brief background on the relation of plural wifehood to Mormon theology, let us examine the manner in which the new pattern worked out in the lives of given individuals.

As pointed out, in Mormondom as elsewhere, we had a combination of monogamy and polygyny. There was always the monogamous pattern as a frame of reference, competing, as it were, with the novel one. Actually, too, the wives for the most part began with monogamy in which the romantic pattern—at least as an ideal—must have had its effects.[1] This meant that the interspouse adjustment usually began in the monogamous tradition and custom, even though, as sometimes happened, the spouses recognized that subsequently the husband might add other wives to his domestic menage.

In theory, at least, when this day arrived, the first wife was supposed to give her consent to the plural marriage. (So, too, certain higher authorities in the church were to approve the same.) There are instances in which the first wife overtly encouraged the plural marriage. In many cases, however, she was informed of the matter only after complete arrangements for the additional wife had been made. In others, she was informed only after the *fait accompli;* sometimes months or years elapsed before she knew that her husband had acquired another wife.[2]

Even though the church dogma insisted on the theory of equality, in actual practice it was difficult to maintain. The first wife often attempted to keep her traditional, monogamously oriented role and status, and there usually arose a struggle among the wives for ascendancy. In some instances, there was a form of subordination of the plural wives to the first one. Such matters as the older romantic hold of the first wife, her long-accustomed habit of domination, her property rights (after all, only she was the legal wife in the eyes of the law), and her awareness of having legitimate children were important items psychologically in supporting her claims. Here we witness a good illustration of the competition of the old and

---

[1] There were some instances in which a man's initial marriage venture was marked by his marrying two wives on the same day. I have, altogether, a half dozen instances of this in my field notes. But on the whole, this procedure was unusual.

[2] These latter instances usually had some specific justification, such as the avoidance of publicity lest the federal officials arrest the husband and/or the plural wife.

new cultural patterns. In spite of preaching and theology, the first wife had the whole weight of monogamous tradition on her side. Moreover, in spite of acceptance of the "Principle" by the plural wives, most of them had been conditioned to the same monogamous frame of reference, and, in spite of their conscious protests to the contrary, they doubtless carried with them the emotional conviction of the essential moral rightness of monogamy and all that it implied.[1] Some of these matters will become more obvious if we now examine a series of instances that reveal the competition for dominance and the implications of this struggle on the sense of security or insecurity.

In the following case study, we note some features of the persistence of the highest status by the first wife.

The A family. Mr. A. was the oldest son of English converts to Mormonism. He was a hard-working, thrifty farmer who fell in love with Josephine G., the daughter of one of the Twelve Apostles—the ranking priesthood organization below the President of the Church. Her father had been a small Southern planter who brought into the church certain wealth and soon accumulated more. Josephine had a good education for her time, was socially ambitious and capable of leadership. She bore several children in rapid succession. She had complete faith in the "Principle" of plural wifehood, and during a period when polygyny was being encouraged by the official propaganda of the church, she consented to A's taking a second wife.

Aunt Ida[2] was an immigrant girl of no such background of wealth or education as Josephine's. She was provided with a home of her own adjacent to that of the first wife. The husband divided his time between the two families, and both wives bore him several children during the next decade.

During the first few years, Aunt Ida, who was some years the junior of Josephine, attempted to secure first place in the affections of the husband. But she found herself outdistanced by the first wife, who not only was an excellent manager and mother but was active in community affairs and whose prestige as a member of the G. family was always a factor in case the threat of displacement became too great. In time, the second wife gave up the overt struggle and accepted her place as subordinate. But she never "felt right" about it, nor did her children, although ostensibly they were friendly enough with their half-siblings and with Aunt Josephine.

[1] This would seem to be particularly true of those who entered into the system from monogamous family backgrounds. A small fraction of the author's family records reveal instances of wives—and husbands, too—who were brought up in polygynous families. But the number is too small to make any judgment as to whether they adjusted more adequately to polygyny than those from monogamous households. Moreover, it must not be forgotten that the majority of Mormon marriages were monogamous, so that this always remained the dominant pattern, though not officially the most desirable.

[2] The term *aunt* was almost universally applied by the children in referring to any wife other than their own mother.

The first wife had a certain protective attitude toward Ida and attempted at the conscious level of contact to show affection and to "prove" the equalitarian thesis. For instance, during the "raids" on polygynous households by federal deputy marshals, A. and the second wife were obliged to go into hiding, into what the Mormons called the "Underground."[1] During the periods of hiding—sometimes lasting for several weeks—Josephine would periodically hitch up a carriage, fill it with foodstuffs, and, at considerable risk and personal discomfort, drive long distances into the country where Ida was in hiding with friendly Saints in another village or on some remote farmstead. Although ostensibly Ida accepted this help and attention with good grace, actually it symbolized her subordinate and dependent status. For Josephine, it was proof to herself and her friends that she had the interests of the other wife genuinely at heart. In short, it fed her ego and gave her a sense of emotional satisfaction. It was the psychology of the "grand lady" who gave out largess to the less fortunate.

As the years passed and the women moved out of the childbearing period and as polygyny became officially disapproved, the two families became more adequately accommodated to each other. There had always been much borrowing and lending and mutual help. But a certain companionship emerged that had not been apparent earlier. As one of my informants, a daughter of the first wife said, "Mother and Aunt Ida used to always have a second cup of coffee along about 10 or 10:30 every morning, after father was away at the farm and the children had departed to work or school. During these tête-à-têtes they indulged in exchange of gossip, friendly discussion of their problems, and making plans for their routine duties and recreations."

In spite of this adaptation, the first wife continued to hold a high social status in the family and in the community, and, in spite of fairly equalitarian considerations as to property and personal attention from the husband, Aunt Ida and her children never did feel thoroughly satisfied about the polygynous position.

Yet, as an observer over the years, the author would say that this family was almost a model one of plural marriage. There was no serious external conflicts; the half-siblings associated together with others in the community. The author's two oldest sisters were closely associated in school and church work with daughters of both families, and his own high-school and college days were spent in social groupings in which children from both families participated without any obvious conflict.

In the A. family, the dominance-subordination relation resulted in a fairly stable situation in which the actual top status was concealed by external accommodations involving much evidence of equality as to financial support and mutual aid.

[1] The emergence of a system of hiding away from gentile territorial officials illustrates the rise of an institution. Watchers, informants, and devices for ensuring safety and secrecy became widespread during the last decade or so of polygyny. This system also afforded a situation that made possible certain advantages for the first wife, since she was not ordinarily directly involved, except perhaps as a witness in case the husband and the plural wife were arrested and haled into court.

In many cases, the legal status of the first wife, the fact that she lived in a better house than other wives, was older and more experienced, often combined to lend further support to her dominance. Though by no means a universal practice, the husband frequently brought visiting church dignitaries home to dinner or for lodging at the first wife's home. Then, too, during the "Underground," the need for secrecy as to plural marriage was increased, and this itself provided a situation favorable to the retention of first place by the legal wife. On the other hand, the "raids" enhanced the insecurity of the plural wives involved. Often these women put up with great physical discomfort and developed a keen sense of inferiority. Others proudly assumed their role as evidence that they were performing God's assignment in thus being "persecuted for the Gospel's sake."

In some instances, the ascendency-subordination relationship was more obviously accepted by the plural wife, although not without some emotional discomfort. The case of the William W. family is in point.

W.'s first wife Mary, whom he married in 1860, at the age of 29, was 4 years his senior. She was a strong, competent woman of Swiss peasant background. Six children were born during the next 12 years. During this time, W. accumulated considerable property and became locally prominent as a church leader. In 1872, he married a 20-year-old girl, Florence D. His first wife thoroughly agreed to this and always rationalized polygyny in terms of "sacrifice" for the "Principle."

Although the husband remained the patriarch of both families within the general framework of harmony, a definite superiority-dependency pattern developed. In the words of one of the second wife's daughters, it was a sort of mother-daughter relationship. The first wife set a pace in work and management that the second could not match. As a son of Florence put it, "Father obviously could do nothing about this situation. Auntie was pretty much in charge, and mother wouldn't complain, so father perhaps hardly suspected that anything was wrong." In fact, Florence in time tended to lose whatever initiative she had possessed and more and more assumed a passive role, one that, however, left her decidedly unhappy. As the son remarked, "She had no status in public. If there was ever a question of father's appearing in public with a wife, he appeared with his first wife, and Florence came with her children unattended." The informant commented that as a lad he could "never understand why he always went with his mother while Aunt Mary went with father."

In this case, the overt accommodation to superior-inferior status was so successfully achieved that none of the children probed beneath the external evidence of compatibility until they were quite mature.

In the absence of strong ambitions or aggressive desires for high status, it was possible in some instances for the various wives to work out a situation in which none of them was accorded persistent superiority. In some cases, this became almost a sister-sister relationship, in which, under the religious faith in the "Principle" and a fair degree of equalitarian treatment from the husband, there was general harmony. In such families, moreover, there was often a distinctive division of labor—each wife undertaking certain definite functions. Also, it is the author's impression from the data that, in such instances, when the families were not in too close personal contact, these relations worked out more satisfactorily, e.g., in those situations where one wife lived on the farmstead outside the village and the other wife resided in the village itself.

Thus, it is clear that in many families the first wife maintained the highest position, abetted as she was by legality of her position and that of her children and by property rights and other securities. Moreover, in spite of many protestations to the contrary—and there are many instances of such verbal contentions—the hold that this monogamous pattern had on the Mormons is further evidenced by the development of the practice of a legal marriage to the plural wife next in line if and when the first wife should die. Such a step protected her and her children as legal heirs for a share of the property of the husband and father. It also gave to this wife the traditional sanctions of legitimacy and public status. Yet the husband did not always accede to this practice.

From a social-psychological standpoint, it seems to the author that this inclination to secure a legal foundation of marriage was more than a strictly utilitarian device to protect their would-be property rights and legitimize their children. It symbolizes the fact that, in spite of verbal assertion and concrete overt efforts to adapt themselves to polygyny, they still retained emotionally many reservations about it. They found in such a legal step a support that tended to provide a needed supplement to that received from the community or from their own inner convictions. After all, such striking alterations in sexual values and in the habits of affection as are implied in polygyny are not to be acquired so quickly as the conscious declarations of adherence to the "Principle" might lead one to believe.

Status changes that arouse insecurity. The Mormon polygynous system, throughout its entire history, was a rather unstable institution. Not only was there great variation in the manner in which the interspouse relations were worked out in practice but there was never any too great assurance that a given family configuration, once in operation, would remain constant for any fixed time and place. This meant, therefore, that the individuals involved were always exposed to a certain threat to their accepted role and status, *i.e.*, psychologically to their ego security and self-esteem. Sometimes the replacement of the first wife by a second was accomplished without much overt evidence of strain. In other situations, there was a great deal of emotional distress and aggressive bitterness. Let us note some illustrative cases:

The P. family represents a mild and, on the whole, satisfactory readjustment but one in which a late plural marriage somewhat altered the security of the first wife. Mr. P., born in 1863, was the son of a fifth wife in his father's plural household. He received a good education for his pioneer community and became a bookkeeper and merchant as well as a successful farmer and stockman.

In 1886, he married his first wife, Marie R., who was 5 years his junior. Two years later, he married his second wife, but she died within less than 3 years after that marriage, leaving one child to be raised by Marie. In the late 1880's, P. married again. In 1890, in order to escape federal prosecution, he, in company with other Utah Mormons, migrated with his families to the state of Chihuahua, Mexico, where the Mormons had already set up a refugee colony for polygamists. There were no legal restrictions on plural marriages in Mexico. P. acquired considerable property through ranching and merchandising and became one of the leaders in the community. During the first decade or so after they settled outside the United States, not only did the Mormons in Mexico continue to practice polygyny but many of them took on additional wives. In 1902, P. married Annie S., a German-Swiss girl of 17 years, born, in fact, the very year that P. had married his first wife.

During these years, the first wife, who was a splendid manager and who was active in community matters, maintained her dominance as wife and helpmate. She lived in a large three-storied brick house. Because of her husband's prominence, they often entertained the leading ecclesiastical dignitaries from Salt Lake City, who occasionally paid official and unofficial visits to this remote community. P., who at first had waited on Marie, soon acquired a more demanding attitude and, though not a violent man, was a severe disciplinarian, and in his first marriages the wives acceded to his wishes. Marie said she "guessed she had spoiled him" by waiting on him too much. In addition to bearing nine children of her own, she had brought up the orphan child of the second wife and later took over the three children of the third wife, who died a year after P. had married Annie.

Although Marie consciously accepted the new marriage, as time went on she was considerably distressed to discover that her husband—in spite of obvious efforts to maintain an equality as to property and attention—was clearly much attracted to the young wife. He once confided to the author that Annie was his "favorite," that "she was so lovely, so kind, so sweet, that I could not help it." She was not only very good-looking but had youth and charm with which the first wife could hardly compete. And, as Annie herself put it, she "soon learned how to handle Brother P."

Almost from the outset, Annie came to expect a good deal of attention from her husband. Although she and the first wife got along on the surface, the latter was often grieved at his favoritism. A son of the first wife said that he had often seen his own mother "pick and shell her own garden peas, while just through the garden lot, 50 yards away, father picked and shelled peas for Aunt Annie. It hurt mother a lot, but she never complained."

Had the shift in dominance remained only evident in the interfamily configuration, the adaptation might not have been too difficult. But Annie was also envious of Marie's public role and status and in time began talking around at various gatherings of women about how well she was "managing the Bishop"—a position that P. then occupied. For instance, she told how she had "taught the Bishop to shine his own shoes" and otherwise "to wait on himself." By making use of her youth, charm, and kindliness she was able to alter a good many of the older patriarchal and demanding attitudes of her husband.

But Annie's public comments did not too greatly alter Marie's place in the community, though they did induce a sense of hurt and distress in Marie herself. On occasions when P. and Annie and their young children gathered together for an evening of reading, storytelling, and games, Marie would call her own flock around her and pop corn, make molasses balls, and entertain them. The emotional satisfaction was obvious. Marie made an intelligent adjustment, but it was purchased at the cost of emotional stress and loss of self-esteem as the accepted primary love object of the husband. To offset this, Marie's own children, though friendly with their half-siblings, always rallied around their mother to give her all the support they could.

At the age of 52, Annie died as a result of a sudden illness, and after her death P. spent all his nights with Marie but allocated certain days to Annie's children for meals and recreation.

In contrast to such a relatively mild adjustment as that just cited, we find others in which there was much overt antagonism. Sometimes this was obvious from the very inception of the plural marriage. In other cases, the conflict developed gradually. A somewhat tragic but withal amusing instance is the following.

Mr. A. A.'s first wife was strongly opposed to his taking a second wife, especially one so much younger—at least this was the rationalization. The husband provided a new home for his second wife and planned to take her there when they returned from Salt Lake City, where the couple repaired for a proper ecclesiastical marriage. On the return trip, by team, they stopped with friends of the husband who had helped promote the polygynous match. Rather late at night, the couple continued on their journey to their new home. When they arrived, they found the place locked and barred. On breaking in, they found that all the furnishings had been removed. They had to return to the home of the friend, who took them in for the balance of the night. As the husband suspected, this was more than a mere joke and had been managed by the other wife, who used this device as a form of revenge on her husband.

In a good many instances, the conflict became so intense that complete separation was the only evident solution. The following is from the life history of Mr. Z., whose first marriage occurred in 1842, when he was 20 years of age. His second marriage took place in 1862, when his first family was pretty well grown up. He writes:

"After I had entered into the Celestial order of marriage, my first wife became very dissatisfied and jealous, and wanted to take her children to live by themselves. I was sorry to have such a thing done, but as matters were getting worse, I thought it better for her, and also for me. I divided the property, and they have increased in property, having lived and worked by the cooperative principle."

In some cases, the separation led to divorce. In fact, the emergence of the institution of divorce in Mormondom requires some explanatory comment. According to the basic Mormon theology, marriage, monogamous or plural, is a holy sacrament in no way to be broken by man's own will except in carefully circumscribed situations. But in view of the fact that many polygynous matches did not work out well, the church was obliged to provide an official method of dissolving such unions through its own ecclesiastical courts.[1] Obviously, a plural wife could not seek redress in the territorial or federal courts, since polygyny had no legal sanction.

Of psychological interest, however, is the fact that, in the face of obvious conflicts in certain polygynous families, the Mormons came to accept divorce—a form of conduct almost as divergent from basic Christian values as was plural wifehood itself. Moreover, there occasionally emerged the idea that, if the plural marriage did not go, such a redress could solve the difficulties—a form of utilitarian attitude and concept quite out of line with the usual emotionalized faith in the "Principle." In the J. case, a married man of 40 years almost refused to take a plural wife when the prospective bride, a

---

[1] Just how many such "church divorces" there were of the total polygynous marriages we do not know. To discover the number would involve an extensive searching of not only the central but the local records of the Mormon church, a procedure that the church has not yet been ready to grant. In my own sample, there are altogether perhaps 10 or 12 individual cases of such church separations—out of 125 polygynous families. In one or two cases, the divorces concerned more than one wife; in one family, three wives sought and obtained church sanction for leaving their husband, but the circumstances in this family were decidedly unusual.

very attractive girl 22 years his junior, calmly told him on the day prior to the wedding that if their marriage did not work out they could easily get a church divorce, saying, "If we don't like it, we can quit." (As a matter of fact, 30 years later she did leave him, though she did not obtain a church divorce.)

Still another interpersonal pattern in plural marriage consisted in a kind of progression in the position of dominance in terms of successive marriages.

In the case of L., the father is reported to have always had a strong interest in young women. He did not marry his first plural wife, however, until he was 49 years of age, and, in the words of one informant, a daughter of the first wife, this marriage "nearly killed mother." Her affection for her husband seemed to be suppressed rather completely after that, and she remarked that she "didn't care how many women he married." Nine years later, L. was ready to try a third matrimonial venture, and on this occasion it was the second wife, Julia, who suffered intensely. But she got little or no comfort from Annie, the first wife, who took occasion to remind her how *she* felt when L. had married the second time. Julia, in turn, "never acted the same toward father again, and besides she always manifested a nasty attitude toward Luella, the third wife, who supplanted her."

In another instance, the husband took on six wives altogether and, like L., appeared to be a man easily "infatuated" by attractive young women. There was in these cases a kind of "hierarchy of heartbreak," as one informant put it, in each instance the newest wife replacing the others in the husband's affections and taking for a time the position of highest status.

It is already clear that wide divergences in the form of interspouse adjustment occurred, including both a wide variety in motivation and in occasion for getting, holding, and losing particular roles and high status. Let us examine still other devices for maintaining prestige, some culturally accepted, others not.

Additional devices for maintaining status. There were a number of accepted ways of keeping a dominant position in the household, many of them, of course, carried over from monogamy, such as the right to serve and to be a helpmate. In the traditional patriarchal family, the wife is accorded a certain status if she is a thrifty and tidy household manager. In some instances, a sharp rivalry sprang up among the plural wives in their efforts to outdo each other in these matters and thus to accumulate a certain kudos from the husband—a prestige that, as a rule, was supported by the broader community approval.

In the case of W. W., for example, the right to play the role of helpmate of the husband was for years the most concrete evidence of the second wife's status. The informant, a daughter, said that her mother "was a very fine seamstress and always made father's shirts." Regarding the division of time, she remarked, "Father divided his time between the wives by 2-week intervals. During his stay the wife he was visiting did all his washing and other services. I have seen my mother in tears because father didn't bring his laundry for her to do. She was so afraid she hadn't done it right last time."

These matters took on profound symbolic significance of security. The informant in the J. case proudly remarked, "Father always considered mother's place 'home.' He kept his clothes there." Loss of status was often indicated by some shift in just such day-by-day routine. The informant of M. M., a prominent Saint, states:

"The first wife was a very dominant person who kept her perogatives by running her husband's affairs in his absence. Also, as day-by-day evidence of her status, she acted as custodian of her husband's Sunday clothes; she did his laundry; and he always went to her house for his Sunday bath. In 1896, he married his fifth wife, described as "an entrancing widow" who had considerable money. She built a fine new home for her husband with modern plumbing and other conveniences. This fifth marriage was a severe blow to the first wife, because, among other changes, M. M. took his Sunday clothes to the new home and began to use the modern bath facilities there. Not only did the first wife lose caste by this marriage but Cecelia, the fourth, also strongly resented M. M.'s marrying the widow, since Cecelia lost her somewhat favorable status as the youngest wife."

Because of a variety of factors, such as division of time of husband among the wives and disparate households, the discipline of the children tended to be taken over by the mothers. Of course, in some families the paternal authority remained supreme and at times very severe. At the other extreme was the father who took almost no direct responsibility for controlling or training his children. Thus, one son of a polygynous family reports that each wife developed her own devices for managing the children:

There was never any corporal punishment in the R. R. families. The mothers taught the children to respect their father and never overruled any decision of his. However, the children almost invariably went to their mothers for advice counsel, or permission to do things. Doubtless this practice arose, in part, because the father was so seldom at home.

The fact that the home management and the discipline and training of the young children lay so largely in the hands of the wives gave them considerable personal satisfaction and sense of importance. There is some evidence of rivalry regarding these matters, just as there was with regard to capacity as a housekeeper. The wives often vied with each other for approval from the husband and community with respect to their children's manners, health, and willingness to work.

Note has already been made of the fact that striving for personal status and ego assurance was bound up with the struggle for economic security. Since the plural wife had no legal rights to inheritance, it became all the more essential that the wives secure land and other property from their husbands that would afford them a certain economic backlog in case of the husband's death. It was a common practice for the husband to deed a home and small parcel of land to each wife. In some families, he even gave them rather considerable properties. But in other cases, he retained a rather firm hand on the economic sources of control.

The general theory of polygyny was that the husband should provide for his wives equally in all things, physical and psychological, but it was obviously not possible to do so. Although in most of my cases, the husbands appear to have made such an effort with respect to property, the wives themselves used economic as well as other means to establish their prestige and to build up their sense of self-esteem. Not only was high status marked by living in a good house and having sufficient economic resources for the family and for occasional entertainment, but the struggle to get economic security led the wives to seek various means of money-making on their own initiative. The simplest form of this was the selling of milk, eggs, and garden produce. As a rule, this did not mean much more than pin money, but it did symbolize a certain independence. The case of Q. illustrates the matter:

Seven years after his second marriage, Q. moved both families to a 160-acre farm, where he built two identical adobe houses about 75 yards apart. Each house had a garden and chicken coop. There was a single granary, and the father and the boys operated the farm.

Each wife had her own flock of chickens, turkeys, and geese. Each also owned a number of cows; the calves and dairy products belonged to the wife whose stock produced them. Feed for the animals was taken from the common granary or barn. "It cost the wives nothing," as the informant remarked.

The energy of the wife determined the extent of her financial success from her garden, poultry, and livestock. The first wife did very well; the second was much less adequate. The former, having more ready cash, bought better clothes for her children. To this the second wife would protest. Without sufficient funds from her own enterprises, she nagged Q. until he bought her children things as good "out of his own pocket." There was no overt strife, however. Her technique consisted simply in letting her husband know that "Sally had nothing to wear to Sunday school," whereas Julia had a new dress. As a rule, Sally got the new dress.

In a number of families, a wife who was a good seamstress or milliner or weaver might set herself up in such handicraft and often was able to supplement the family's income considerably as well as to give her self a sense of freedom.

Housekeeping, management of children, and a certain amount of economic self-sufficiency constituted factors for creating and maintaining ego status. Threats to high status were, as we have seen, met in various ways; some of the devices even represented divergences from the expected polygynous patterning. In particular, the place of more or less direct sex appeal, of jealousy and envy, and of certain overt manifestations of aggression will be noted.

Although polygyny carried over from monogamy certain romantic patterns in which more or less direct sexual appeal played a part, it must be recalled that under the traditional pietistic Christian theory and under the impact of the strong patriarchal and priestly system of the Mormons, the direct sexual elements were officially, at least, somewhat disregarded. There has been much discussion of Mormon polygyny as if it represented an extension of the erotic interest of leaders and men of property in young and beautiful women. No doubt direct sexual appeal had its place, especially in those instances in which men well past 40 married young wives, but it would be a mistake to assume that plural marriage is to be explained on this basis. M. R. Werner, in fact, has aptly dubbed it "Puritan polygamy," meaning thereby that the plural households were in effect merely extensions of a strict puritanical monogamy.[1]

Although the courtship patterns ranged all the way from the mildly romantic to the highly utilitarian, in which the match was to all intents and purposes made by the parents of the girl and the would-be husband, the employment after marriage of direct sexual appeal through clothes, conversation, coyness, and the usual techniques of romantic love often set up tremendous resistances on the part of the competing wives. If this sort of thing became too obvious, it might also bring down ridicule and other forms of disapproval on the man. The impress of the official dogma was such

[1] See M. R. Werner. *Brigham Young*. New York: Harcourt, Brace, 1925. Especially Chap. VII.

that the community members—whether themselves from monogamous or polygynous households—tended to apply the official criteria
to particular cases. A young man who was kept from marrying an
attractive woman by her marriage to an older and prosperous
polygamist might easily disapprove of the very sexual romantic
reactions of this woman toward her new husband, which, had they
been applied to him in monogamy, would have been approved by
himself and by the community.

In the same manner, the use of jealousy and envy—the twin
tools of control in monogamy—became disapproved of with reference
to plural families. This type of behavior sometimes broke out
within the family circle, though with far less frequency than one
might imagine possible among people who had been brought up in a
monogamous society. The jealousy and envy tended to be suppressed, and the aggression that accumulated therefrom was usually
directed elsewhere.

In a few instances, plural wives risked using charm and romantic
appeals outside the family in order to arouse a husband's jealousy in
the hope of gaining his favor. In the case of M., the husband had
three wives. He was a rather severe disciplinarian and at times
avoided his wives. After the death of the first wife, the second,
Clara, became the dominant spouse.

Clara was an easygoing, jolly, attractive woman who enjoyed attending social
gatherings, dances, picnics, etc., in the community. Because of the husband's
rather severe and restrictive attitudes, she took to planning parties and other
affairs for the nights when he was with his other wife. She liked to go to "basket
parties" and dances, and at the basket parties she always brought her own basket
and had as gay a time as any young and unmarried woman there. She would
flirt in a mild way and always insisted that the young man who bought her
basket should take her home after the party. The husband disapproved of this,
but she persisted in such practices.

Although such conduct might amuse some of the younger members
of the community and lead to some gossip about how a certain wife
was making her husband jealous, there was always the likelihood
that the husband would take severe measures, even going so far as
to divorce the wife. Nothing of this sort happened in the case just
cited, but it was not wise procedure in such a society.

More overt manifestations of antagonism arising from jealousy
did occur within the family configuration. Sometimes the conflict
was so severe that out-and-out quarreling became the order of the
day. The R. Q. family illustrates this.

R.Q.'s first wife, Margaret, died 3 days after they arrived in Salt Lake City after a hard trip across the Great Plains. This was in 1857. On the counsel of one of the leading Mormons, R. Q. married Abbie P. a few weeks afterward. Four years later he married Anna B. In 1867, he took still another wife, Mary T.

R. Q. never had any great affection for either Abbie or Anna; they argued a good deal about their status, about the property, and over their children. The second wife was particularly quarrelsome and constantly sought special considera-tion for her own children. The informant remarks, "She used to rail at father, telling him that the other children were doing things and taking advantage of her children. . . . The wives would often wrangle so much that the father did not get along with the children unless he were alone with them. . . ."

R. Q.'s only great love was apparently for his first wife, and he became more and more introspective, less communicative, and tried to avoid these outbreaks of conflict. As the years went by, he became more and more fond of the last wife. She was quieter, more docile, a good housekeeper and managed her children well.

In some families, temper tantrums were occasionally used as power devices. Sometimes these occurred in public or among relatives and friends. The purpose was obviously to embarrass the husband and the other wife. The case of the E. family is in point.

E. had two wives, Gertrude and Christine. He married Christine approxi-mately 15 years after his first venture. Both wives had large families (12 and 9 children, respectively.) The families were well provided for economically. The second wife was constantly distressed because she could not wrest the complete dominance from Gertrude. One informant for this family reports the following:

"Once a large group of relatives came up from Ogden for the week end to the farm where Christine lived. Among them were several sisters of Christine and Gertrude. Both wives were present, and Sunday afternoon when everybody was ready to leave for home, father decided to go back to town with Gertrude [mother of informant] to spend Sunday night. This, of course, meant that Christine would have to remain on the farm. This precipitated an explosion. Christine made a terrific scene as we were about to depart. She could be heard screaming a long time after the party left. Father was about to turn back to stay with Christine when two of her own sisters intervened saying, 'Don't you dare give in to her.' They shamed him into going on to town with mother and explained that their sister had always used such means to get her own way. Mother during all this time kept very quiet and said nothing."

This is but one example of Christine's behavior. "She often made scenes like this, no matter who was around, and father, wanting to keep peace, lived most with her."

Thus, with jealousy and envy, as with other established patterns of emotional behavior, we find former practices upset by polgyny, with the result that individuals found themselves in situations for which no culturally stabilized attitudes and values had been defined. We find, too, certain forms of adaptation, which, though rare, illustrate extreme deviations in the adaptive processes.   These include invalidism, alcoholism, and outright psychopathic breakdown.

The use of invalidism as a power device of neurotics is well known, ranging all the way from the "conversion" symptoms familiar in hysteria to outright malingering.   The following case of invalidism illustrates the latter.   Although Jane, the first wife, bore nine healthy children, she was bedfast during the last 40 years of her life.

> Jane had her first baby on the Plains and was carried in the baggage wagon to a ford in the Platte River.   In crossing, the wagon overturned, injuring her and the baby.   Soon after, the infant died and was buried beside the road.   This accident made a slight cripple out of Jane, and for the next 40 years "she lay continuously on her right side. . . ."
>
> "I never saw such a home-loving man as father.   He gave mother a great deal of attention.   Every night he sat in her room and read the newspaper to her. She surely kept up with what was going on outside."

Although there may have been some anatomical basis for Jane's condition, all the evidence points to the conclusion that her invalidism was motivated psychologically.   She had a definite shock at the loss of her baby, and, though she accepted the church and the "Principle," she never made any effort to get up from her bed. The family revolved around her.   In fact, the second wife came into the household as a servant and remained to marry the husband a few years later, with Jane's full consent.   There are other examples of the use of prolonged illness as a method for getting attention, but none was quite so extended in time as this one.

The Mormon church long opposed the use of alcoholic beverages and of tobacco, tea, and coffee.   The taboo remains in effect today. In spite of the general acceptance of the "Word of Wisdom," as this doctrine was called, there was some occasional mild tippling on the part of a small minority of men.   But to find a polygynous wife who became more or less a habitual and heavy drinker and who obviously used this means to secure attention from her husband and the neighbors represents a striking deviation from the cultural norm.   Frustrated and disappointed, her status threatened, Mrs. C. went on periodic sprees as a form of aggressive demonstration against her husband and against the entire "Principle."

Also, there were some cases in which a more or less complete mental breakdown seems traceable to the inability of the wife to adapt herself to plural marriage.   Such instances are relatively

rare, however, and it has been extremely difficult to secure more
than the briefest details.   Yet in the A. T. family there seems little
doubt that the first wife's mental breakdown—predicated apparently on a definite pathic trend of some years standing—was precipitated by her husband's taking a younger and attractive wife.
The first wife went into a distinct mental decline—apparently of a
mixed type, in which there were periods of considerable lucidity
followed by periods of confusion and schizoidlike manifestations.   It
was necessary to commit her to a mental hospital.

As we look over the entire array of cases, then, we find a wide
range of adaptation.   In a large number, there is full faith in plural
wifehood.   It is well accepted, at least at the conscious level.   In
others, there is more overt resentment, exemplified in the struggle
for status, in jealousy and envy, and in open quarreling.   Finally,
there were a few extreme adaptations, such as "flight" into invalidism, alcoholism, and psychopathology.   The overt adjustments are
no different from those found in monogamy; but they have a somewhat different source and a somewhat different meaning for the
individuals concerned.   ·

It is clear that this system, in spite of its conscious acceptance, in
spite of its religio-emotional quality or faith, induced a great deal of
anxiety and disorganization in many of the participants.   For
many, the "Principle" was not sufficient to overcome the power of
long-established attitudes and values.   Yet a large number of the
participants apparently took on the new ideas and practices without
much strain, and it would be a mistake to assume that the practice
was always purchased at a high emotional price.   In the first place,
intense emotional conversion or reconditioning that characterized
full acceptance of the divine mission of Joseph Smith and Brigham
Young and all that this implied as to obedience, ritual, and everyday
living could and did carry along with it full emotional and behavioral
acceptance of polygyny.   In addition, the system may have some
biological foundations that cannot be gainsaid.   Certainly there is
no evidence that man is instinctively a monogamous animal or
innately given over to jealousy or possessiveness.   On the contrary,
there are many data from many primitives and from our anthropoid
relatives to support the idea of polygamous contacts.   One might
raise the question—the problem of sex ratios being neglected for the
nounce—whether polygyny might not provide as sound a biosocial
foundation for society as a rigidly monogamous one.   Once the

cultural patterns were well grounded, many of the distresses noted from the Mormon data might well disappear.

ADAPTATION OF THE HUSBAND TO POLYGYNY

It might be imagined that polygyny inevitably enhanced the patriarchal and priestly dominance of the male in Mormon society and that as a result there would be little or no evidence of emotional distress or of personality problems among the men of the society. From some of the details already noted, it is clear that plural marriage offered men not only some stimulation to ego security and higher status but also induced certain insecurities as well.

Factors making for ego expansion and status of the male. According to Mormon theology, a man's status here and hereafter is greatly enhanced by the taking of plural wives and the having of a large number of children. As noted in the opening section, the wife could be saved in heaven only through her husband. We shall discuss five particular activities or roles that were sources for ego expansion for the husband and father. Some of these were carried over from monogamy; others were born in part of the Mormon church dogmas, and others arose within the polygynous situation.

1. As a provider or breadwinner, the husband of a plural household carried over a conventional role from monogamy. But, although more wives and more children gave added potential labor supply for the accumulation of wealth in a pioneer community, it was equally true that multiple families laid further economic responsibilities on Mormon men. According to the official idea, the husband was expected to divide his substance equally among his families, and for the most part he did so.

Usually the father himself continued to work hard as he accumulated property and children; he might, however, take on the role of overseer and manager; and sometimes direct supervision of economic life was left to the wives and sons. This was particularly likely to be the situation in the case of men who were prominent in the church or in business. (Some of our most complete records concern these latter)

2. The role of spiritual leader of the family grew directly out of the father's status as divinely sanctioned head of the family. He provided religious and moral instruction and built up attitudes of obedience on the part of his wives and their children toward the dictates of the church. Family prayers were a very common

practice, led by the father when he was present and usually by the mother when he was not. These spiritual practices, of course, carried over from monogamy and general church patterns.

In the same way, the status of the father as ruler or authoritarian head of the household was extended from the single- to the multiple-family system. Our cases reveal a continuum from severity of discipline and punishment to mild and even indifferent discipline. The following excerpt from the interview reports shows something of this range:

"C. C. was boss." His desires were implicitly carried out by both wives, although he was not arbitrary. . . . Discipline was entirely in the father's hands, and the wives "had little to say inside or outside the house except when father was not around." His discipline was strict, systematic, and firm. The interest of the father, however, was not confined to negative controls. He took his children, especially the boys, on hunting and fishing trips; he played games with the children at home and had a real interest in them. Yet, on the whole, the children maintained high respect for their father and were not easily drawn into intimacies with him.

C. C., like many other polygynous fathers, in attempting to be fair to all his children, was forced to develop a certain psychic distance from them. He never indulged in any close confidences with any of them. He had a large family and a variety of economic responsibilities and looked on his family as a part of his large scope of duties. In sharp contrast were some instances in which the father exercised no authority at all. In general the father's role of authoritarian and disciplinarian determined his status in the Mormon household, but there is also evidence that many polygynous fathers actually lost much of the subtler power, in contrast to men who remained in monogamy.

3. With regard to property, however, the polygynous husband had a control that had a dual foundation. In official theory, he was supposed to divide his income and inheritance equally with his wives and children, but actually there was no means of coercing him to do so. Certainly the church sanctions left the matter pretty much to the husband. As indicated in the introductory section, the law never did recognize plural wedlock or provide for the inheritance of the plural wives and their children. As a result, the husband had in his hands a power device for enforcing his status, for demonstrating his headship that all the members of his family as well as the community had to recognize. Even the first wife was not always

protected, since he might refuse to support her and her children or he might deed his property to other wives before his death.[1]

The husbands usually gave the wives small parcels of land and a home in their own name, but in the case of the larger properties the man retained the legal controls in his own hands. Men sought to retain their sense of power by refusing to let their wives know about their economic condition.

In the case of M. M., for instance, the third wife pried into her husband's affairs to the extent of persuading a family friend to inquire of him how he intended to divide his property, if he was going to deed them their own home, and the like. M. M.'s reply was that his wives had homes, all right, but they weren't going to know about it as long as he lived. They weren't going to be able to tell him to "git."

4. There is no doubt that prestige and ego expansion accrued to the husband and father from his awareness of having a large number of wives and children. This fitted into the Mormon ideology, and public approval could not help influencing individual manifestations of self-esteem and status. To be the father of a large progeny was held up as an ideal throughout the entire period, and both wives and husbands gathered considerable prestige from the evidences of fulfilling these cultural expectancies. As Brigham Young remarked in a sermon in 1860 with reference to the divine obligations of wives to bear children: "It is for you to bear children, in the name of the Lord, that are full of faith and power of God—to receive, conceive, bear, and bring forth in the name of Israel's God, that you may have the honor of being the mothers of great and good men—of kings, princes, and potentates that shall yet live on the earth and govern and control the nations."

5. There is no doubt that in many instances the taking of plural wives not only was motivated by a strong sexual trend but also supplied a pattern affording ego satisfaction through giving varied sexual outlets. If we bear in mind the puritanical prudery of these people, the difficulty of securing direct evidence on this matter will be understandable. However, from a variety of data, we may conclude that many husbands got considerable personal satisfaction and sense of power from the fact that they had approved access to

[1] In order to protect the first wife, the federal laws, especially the Edmunds-Tucker Act of 1887, established dower rights for the first wife. There was considerable opposition to this on the part of the official Mormon church, since it was realized that this was a device to undermine one of the economic props of polygyny.

more than one woman.   There is no doubt that this attitude was
carried over to men who remained in monogamous relations.   It
is apparent in many jokes, in stories told about polygynous husbands,
and in the cases in which men well along in years more or less openly
sought out younger and attractive additional wives.   It was always
possible, moreover, for these more personal and biological interests
to be rationalized in terms of the "Principle," especially its stress
on the blessings here and hereafter arising from numerous progeny.
Certainly, in the anti-Mormon literature on plural marriage, the
assumption is almost universally made that this was a basic motivation not only for the inception of the practice but for its continuance.
The evidence, however, does not bear out this particularistic thesis.
Men entered into the system because of pressure or counsel from
the church authorities; they entered into it at the suggestion of their
wives or wife; they were stimulated by fathers who had eligible
daughters; and they were doubtless motivated by any number of
other considerations—such as the desire to get relief from unpleasant
matches already entered into, from the desire for children when the
first marriage had resulted in none—as well as from sexual motives.

Just what effects the multiple-wife practice had on such matters
as sexual interest, frequency of coitus, and the playing of a romantic
role in regard to physical intimacies we do not know.   Certainly
there is little evidence to support the popular notion of the Mormon
harem pictured in fiction and anti-Mormon literature.   The configuration of a sense of shame, ineptitude in love-making, taboos
of all sorts on undertaking variational practices of love-making—
these plus the obligation of earning a living, the enforced secrecy of
many of the plural marriages, and no end of other circumstances
give the quietus to such literary fantasies.   Such fictions very
possibly reveal the unconscious wishful thinking of the writers rather
than any facts obtained from polygynous practices.

Factors making for insecurities and anxieties in the male.   On the
other hand, plural marriages did not automatically confer ego
security and personal satisfaction on the men who entered into them.
Difficulties might arise from failure to play the role of adequate
provider; from loss of discipline; from distress due to jealousy and
quarreling among the wives; from conflicts between the man's
personal interests in one woman as against another and the equalitarian treatment expected; from his sense of guilt associated with
multiple wifehood.   But in the face of these difficulties, men found

a variety of outlets: in business, in church work, especially in mis-
sionary work and colonization, and in a number of more personally
dictated ways.

1. If the polygynous husband often achieved status as a good
provider and successful breadwinner, there are a number of records
that show that his failure to succeed led to a distinct lowering of
the husband's sense of self-esteem and self-assurance.   Moreover,
the failure was likely to be all the more painful because of the
official anticipation that he would make good and because he was
exposed to reactions of blame if he did not succeed.   Both wives and
children were often quick to seize upon these situations in order to
enhance their own ego status at the expense of the father.   In some
instances, failure to provide led to separation or divorce.   The
whole weight of the customary expectation that by individual initiative and effort a man could handle his own affairs bore heavily on
one who was not successful.

2. In like manner, the loss of authority or discipline over the
various families might mark a man's lowered self-esteem.   As one
informant puts it:

P. was insignificant in the discipline of the children. . . . The children of
neither family paid any attention to him.   "They went on as if he were not alive
as far as authority was concerned."   Discipline in these families devolved
entirely on the mothers.

We have already noted that the very nature of polygynous family
life tended to reduce the opportunity for the father to exercise
discipline.   In most situations, he retained a good deal of authority,
but, if he let such control slip out of his hands, he was bound to suffer
considerable emotional distress and sense of inferiority as a result.
He might want to feel that, according to the ideal expectancy of the
church and the community, he was the great patriarch, but the
day-by-day living often convinced both himself and others that he
was not.

Sometimes the jealousy, envy, and open conflict among wives
served to deplete the husband's ego.   In some instances, such as that
of Christine, cited above, the husband would have preferred to spend
more time with his first wife Gertrude, but the temper tantrums and
the open hostility of the second wife led to his giving her more time
than he really cared to.   From the remarks of our informants (his
own children), it is pretty evident that, as the years passed by, the

father found little emotional satisfaction from thus trying to pacify his plural wife.   Also, we have noted one or two cases in which the husband more or less deliberately moved away from two quarreling wives to take up residence with a third wife who was more docile and pleasant.   In the K. case, the aging father more and more gave his time to the community and the church as an escape from his carping youngest wife.   Just as in monogamy men tend to rationalize the behavior of their spouses under such a blanket stereotype as "Women are that way" or "What can you expect of women?" so, too, many of these men tried to find like justifications for the actions of their plural wives.   Such rationalizations doubtless protected them from self-blame and a certain conscious sense of responsibility for the situation.

4. Even where there was a favorite and dominant wife—consciously accepted by the family members—there still remained a problem of community approval for evidences of favoritism, such as expensive living quarters, clothes, travel, and being seen often in public with the husband.   Some of the data strongly suggest that, when a husband found himself in such a situation, he was reminded of the monogamous idea that such luxury and special attention had the appearance of keeping a mistress.   Too much conspicuous display, especially if lavished on one wife, set up a good deal of criticism in the community, and a man easily became involved in an inner conflict as to whether he should follow his inclinations toward his favorite wife or accept the community and church standards of equalitarian treatment.[1]   And it was not easy for the other wives placidly to accept such favoritism.   Hence the husband was exposed to another attack on his emotional stability from them as well as from the general public.

5. One of the most difficult topics is that of guilt feelings in these Mormon families.   Unfortunately, our data do not deal directly with these matters; hence our inferences are open to some question. Yet detachment from family conflicts or retreat into other types of activity or thoughtless day-by-day conduct furnish some clue to this.   It is well known that unsympathetic behavior is often related

[1] As a matter of fact, the Mormon church leaders all during this period inveighed in public and private against luxury and display. "Gentile" influences began to creep in, especially after the transcontinental railway line was completed, and women in families with surplus wealth were soon showing great interest in fashionable clothes.

to a sense of guilt and self-accusation.[1]   Moreover, the fact that monogamy remained the basic form of marriage, that it had all the weight of long tradition behind it, that ego security itself is so dependent on taking the conventionalized (culturalized or expected) role that calls out corresponding approvals from others—these matters are also important.   The very presence of plural wives and their children was a constant reminder of this entire cultural pattern; polygynous households existed side by side in the community with families living—with full, if not the highest, official approval—in the monogamous system.   There are a number of specific data that tend to bear out this interpretation.   In one case, L. M. refused to follow the Mormon custom of legally marrying the second wife on the death of the first spouse.   In another family, in which the husband K. K. had tried to keep a fairly peaceful situation among three wives, he grew intensely defensive when his second and third wives together only jokingly asked him if he intended to follow the usual custom of marrying the second wife legally.   K. K. stormed back: "I don't ever want to hear you girls say 'legal' again.   You're both legal in the sight of God."

Then, too, conscious and unconscious avoidance of public recognition of the plural wife or wives furnishes other evidences of a sense of guilt.   Even when secrecy—due to threat of arrest by federal officials—was not a factor, husbands often failed to take their polygynous wives out in public—to church services, to church entertainments, or to other community activities.   We have already noted that such a situation might lead to conflict for favorite status among the wives; if the husband unconsciously took the attitude—in spite of official church dogma to the contrary—that he was really legally married to his first wife only, such a struggle might actually hinder the interspousal adjustment.   For the plural wife, it might well result in the husband's secret resentment against her very striving for his attention, since it aroused in him increased guilt feelings for having married in polygyny in the first instance.

As the federal opposition to plural marriages increased during the late 1870's and throughout the 1880's, the church actually tried to stimulate more plural marriages.   This exposed the men to even greater conflicts.   On the one hand, the increased threats of arrest and imprisonment involved their sense of patriotism and law-abiding

[1] See Lois B. Murphy.   Social behavior and child personality.   New York: Columbia Univ. Press, 1937, p. 188.

attitudes as well as hindering their economic success; on the other, their desire to abide by church counsel to enter into polygyny was strong. It would be enlightening to know whether marriages contracted during this hectic period were marked by more distress and discomfort for the individuals concerned than were those contracted in the 1850's and 1860's before external pressure had become so vigorous. Unfortunately, we have no way of discovering the facts on this question.

Men often sought community outlets for their insecurities and guilt feelings in regard to plural marriage. Keeping busy with official church duties was one way. Another was that of going on missions or on colonization expeditions for the church. It is the author's impression that to be called on a mission—where the wife or wives could seldom go—many times came as a distinct relief to the husband. Of course, in some instances these men, while on their missions, met other women whom they later married; but for the time it offered them some approved way of getting out from under day-by-day problems of interwife conflict and competition.

In summary, then, we may say that living in polygyny induced problems of social-emotional adjustment for the husband and father as well as for the wives. On the one hand, it enhanced the opportunities for public approval as to role and afforded certain affectional and even directly sexual variations within the culturally approved schema. On the other, in many cases at least, it induced a sense of inadequacy in regard to property and family authority, distress at the interwife conflicts, and guilt feelings respecting the deviation from long-established monogamous standards. Without doubt, had the system developed stable institutional features, there would have been, in time, far less reason for the occurrence of some of these personality disturbances.

BIBLIOGRAPHY OF PROFESSOR TERMAN'S WRITINGS

Prepared by

GRETCHEN ANN MAGARET, *Stanford University*

and

CLARE WRIGHT, *Sonoma State Home*

1. A preliminary study in the psychology and pedagogy of leadership. *Ped. Sem.*, 1904, **11**, 413–451.

A discussion of the qualities of leadership, including a review of the literature on leadership among animals and primitive races and on children's ideals but comprising largely a report of an experiment and of a questionnaire survey with school children to ascertain the qualities by which those termed *leaders* hold ascendancy.

2. A study in precocity and prematuration. *Amer. J. Psychol.*, 1905, **16**, 145–183.

Prematuration, described here as resulting from outside interference, is discussed in its relation to education, crime, religion, unbalance, nervousness, and sex.

3. Genius and stupidity: a study of some of the intellectual processes of seven "bright" and seven "stupid" boys. *Ped. Sem.*, 1906, **13**, 307–373.

Doctoral dissertation presented to Clark University. The study is a qualitative analysis of the intellectual differences of markedly contrasting groups. The subjects came from the public schools of Worcester and were selected on teachers' judgments. Abilities studied were the logical processes, mathematical processes, language, memory, motor ability, and those abilities involved in tests of inventiveness and creative imagination, in the interpretation of fables, and in learning to play chess. The "bright" boys excelled in all the mental tasks, but the somewhat older "stupid" boys surpassed in the tests of motor ability. Also, of the subjects studied, the "stupid" were better adjusted emotionally. Individual sketches are given, and a statement is made regarding the probable effect of endowment as contrasted with training.

4. Child study: its reason and promise. *Univ. Calif. Chron.*, 1908, **11**, 145–148.

5. ANON. The teacher psychosis. *Scribner's Mag.*, 1908, **43**, 505–508.

6. Commercialism: the educator's bugbear. *Sch. Rev.*, 1909, **17**, 193–195.
7. Education against nature. *Harp. Weekly*, 1909, **53** (Nov. 20), 17.
8. Pathology of school discipline. *New Eng. Mag.*, 1909, **41**, 479–484.
9. The Binet-Simon scale for measuring intelligence: impressions gained by its application upon four hundred non-selected children. *Psychol. Clin.*, 1911, **5**, 199–206.

A preliminary report of the application by Childs and Terman of the Binet-Simon scale to 400 children, included here as part of a symposium on intelligence testing conducted by the *Psychological Clinic*. After describing briefly the extension of the Binet-Simon scale made by Terman and Childs and reporting the unit value of each test of the extended scale, the author points out that a scale for measuring mentality is a necessary prerequisite to research with feeble-minded or supernormal children and concludes by answering adverse criticism of the test made by structural psychologists.

10. Medical inspection of schools in California. *Psychol. Clin.*, 1911, **5**, 57–62.
11. Paradoxes of personality, or muckraking in the psychology of character. *New Eng. Mag.*, 1911, **44**, 371–374.
12. Relation of the manual arts to health. *Pop. Sci. Mon.*, 1911, **78**, 602–609.
13. School where girls are taught home-making. *Craftsman*, 1911, **20**, 63–68.
14. Does your child stutter? *Harp. Weekly*, 1912, **56** (May 18), 12.
15. Evils of school life. *Harp. Weekly*, 1912, **56** (July 20), 24.
16. Professional training for child hygiene. *Pop. Sci. Mon.*, 1912, **80**, 289–297.
17. School clinics, dental and medical. *Psychol. Clin.*, 1912, **5**, 271–278.
18. Survey of mentally defective children in the schools of San Luis Obispo, California. *Psychol. Clin.*, 1912, **6**, 131–139.
19. ———, with CHILDS, H. G.   A tentative revision and extension of the Binet-Simon measuring scale of intelligence. Pt. I. Introduction. *J. educ. Psychol.*, 1912, **3**, 61–74.   Pt. II. Supplementary tests. *J. educ. Psychol.*, 1912, **3**, 133–143, 198–208. Pt. III. Summary and criticisms. *J. educ. Psychol.*, 1912, **3**, 277–289.

A report of a study undertaken in 1911 in order to determine the adaptability of the 1908 Binet tests to American children, to discover necessary changes in serial arrangement of tests, to try out certain of the tests to supplement the Binet series, and to arrive at some conclusion as to the pedagogical value of the tests.   Part I reports the results of the administration of the 1908 Binet tests to 396 children aged 4 to 15, which indicated that for these California children the Binet scale was too easy at the lower end and too difficult at the upper.   Part II-1 reports the results of the administration of a generalization test consisting of a series of eight fables to 350 school children, who were instructed to write down the "lesson" the fable was meant to teach.   Part II-2 describes a completion test involving increasing degrees of mutilation. Part II-3 describes the ball-and-field test of practical judgment, illustrating four grades of performances characteristic of different chronological ages. Part II-4 presents a vocabulary test that, on the basis of the findings in the case of 161 children to whom the test was given, seems to show more promise than the scattered "definitions" tests of Binet.   In Part III, the authors submit a Stanford revision of the scale, based on the preceding papers and on the test results reported by Binet and by Bobertag.   The need for a thorough trial of this scale upon thousands of representative children is emphasized.

20. Psychological principles underlying the Binet-Simon scale and some practical considerations for its correct use. *J. Psycho-Asthen.*, 1913, **18**, 93–104.
21. A report of the Buffalo Conference on the Binet-Simon tests of intelligence. *Ped. Sem.*, 1913, **20**, 549–554.
22. The sleep of the feeble-minded. *Train. Sch. Bull.*, 1913, **9**, 150–153.
23. Social hygiene: the real conservation problem. *North Amer. Rev.*, 1913, **198**, 404–412.
24. Suggestions for revising, extending, and supplementing the Binet intelligence tests. *J. Psycho-Asthen.*, 1913, **18**, 20–33.

A paper presented before the conference on the Binet-Simon scale, held in connection with the Fourth International Congress of School Hygiene, in which are discussed problems that have been raised by the application of the scale to the group tested by Childs and to 400 additional children.   The questions of selection of a standardization population, age grouping, percentage of correct responses necessary for locating a test, criteria for eliminating and substituting tests, and the unit plan for assigning credit for single tests are treated.   The advisability of employing varying percentages of correct responses to locate tests at different points on the scale is discussed in some detail.   A number of concrete suggestions for broadening and supplementing the scale are made, including an extension of the scale at both ends, the development of other scales of the Binet-Simon type to avoid practice effects, the development of tests for mass use, the construction of graduated scales of single types of tests, and a rough scale of pedagogical tests.

25. The teacher's health: a study in the hygiene of an occupation. Cambridge: Houghton Mifflin, 1913.

A summary and interpretation of the most important investigations bearing upon the hygiene of the teaching profession, together with suggestions to the teacher himself, to school administrators, and to normal schools for safeguarding the health of the teacher.

26. Tragedies of childhood. *Forum*, 1913, **49**, 41–47.

27. ————, with Hocking, A. The sleep of school children: its distribution according to age, and its relation to physical and mental efficiency. *J. educ. Psychol.*, 1913, **4**, 138–147, 199–208, 269–282.

A summary of the available literature on the subject and the results of an investigation of 2692 children in the schools of California, Oregon, and Arizona. An Appendix gives data on the sleep of the feeble-minded.

28. Concerning psycho-clinical expertness. *Train. Sch. Bull.*, 1914, **11**, 9.
29. The effects of school life upon the nutritive processes, health, and the composition of the blood. *Pop. Sci. Mon.*, 1914, **84**, 257–264.
30. The hygiene of the school child. Cambridge: Houghton Mifflin, 1914.

Prepared as a textbook in school hygiene for normal schools, colleges, and teachers' reading circles, this book is concerned primarily with the hygiene of physical and mental growth of the child. School hygiene is envisaged as part of the program of conservation. Introductory topics considered include the physical basis of education, the laws of growth and factors influencing growth, and significance of physiological age for the teachers' understanding of children's performance. The remaining chapters are given over to certain specific problems of child hygiene: disorders of posture, malnutrition, tuberculosis, ventilation, dental hygiene, hygiene of the nose and throat, of the ear, of vision, and, finally, preventive mental hygiene. Statistics are presented showing the frequency of many of these problems in the school population, and practical suggestions are given the teacher as to means of minimizing or preventing physical defects or weaknesses in school children. The need for a vigorous reform in matters of educational hygiene is emphasized.

31. Precocious children. *Forum*, 1914, **52**, 893–898.

Three classes of precocious children should be distinguished and educational programs fitted to the needs of each group: (*a*) those who are gifted in all respects; (*b*) those who are bright but unstable, one-sided, or physically subnormal; and (*c*) those whose brightness is not real but due to an excitable imagination.

32. Recent literature on juvenile suicides. *J. abnorm. (soc.) Psychol.*, 1914, **9**, 61–66.
33. The significance of intelligence tests for mental hygiene. *J. Psycho-Asthen.*, 1914, **18**, 119–127.

In a paper presented before the Division of Mental Hygiene of the Fourth International Congress of School Hygiene, the author evaluates the mental-test movement in the light of mental hygiene, concluding that certain data needed in mental hygiene can be supplied only by further development of tests.

34. Sleep of school children. *Child*, 1914, **4**, 804–810.
35. Teeth and civilization. *Forum*, 1914, **51**, 418–424.

36. ———, with HOAG, E. B.   Health work in the schools.   Cambridge: Houghton Mifflin, 1914.

A collaboration by physician and psychologist on health supervision in the schools, written primarily for the in-service teacher.   The book is designed to acquaint the teacher with the transmissible diseases that may be found in a school population and to assist him in observing health conditions among his children, in teaching hygiene, and in safeguarding his own health.

37. ———, with WILLIAMS, J. H.   Whittier State School biennial report: psychological survey of the Whittier State School, preliminary and final reports.   Whittier: Whittier State School, 1914.

This survey, planned to ascertain the intelligence level of the boys of Whittier State School, reveals that one fourth of them are feeble-minded and only one fourth normal or above.   The necessity of considering mental defect in any attempt to deal with delinquency is therefore emphasized.

38. Review of Meumann on tests of endowment.   *J. Psycho-Asthen.*, 1914–1915, **19**, 75–94, 123–134, 187–199.

A review of "what will doubtless take rank as one of the most important events in the history of applied psychology"—the second volume of Meumann's *Experimentelle Pedagogik*.   This volume constitutes practically a source book on the psychology of endowment, including a discussion of the Binet-Simon tests, the results of experimental investigations of endowment, and Meumann's test series arranged for use in Hamburg in accordance with certain earlier recommendations by Terman and Childs.   Occasional comments by the reviewer outline areas of agreement and disagreement between Terman and Meumann.

39. The mental hygiene of exceptional children.   *Ped. Sem.*, 1915, **22**, 529–537.

Based on the results of testing 1000 children in 1914 and 1915, this paper considers the relation of school success to intelligence and emphasizes the need to recognize deviations in intelligence and to provide for the exceptionally intelligent and the exceptionally dull children in the school regime.

40. Research in mental deviation among children: a statement of the aims and purposes of the Buckel foundation.   Stanford University: Stanford Univ. Press, 1915.

41. ———, with KNOLLIN, H. E.   Some problems relating to the detection of borderline cases of mental deficiency.   *J. Psycho-Asthen.*, 1915, **20**, 3–15.

A paper presented before a meeting of the American Association for the Study of the Feeble-minded pointing out the importance of correct diagnosis of cases of border-line intelligence and comparing the accuracy of the Stanford and other revisions of the Binet scale at this level.

42. ———, with LYMAN, G., ORDAHL, G., ORDAHL, L. E., GALBREATH, N., & TALBERT, W. The Stanford revision of the Binet-Simon scale, and some results from its application to 1000 nonselected children. *J. educ. Psychol.*, 1915, **6**, 551–562.

This preliminary report of the use of the Stanford revision of the Binet-Simon scale with 1000 nonselected children discusses the procedures used in revising the scale and the preliminary results of its application, which are sufficiently encouraging to warrant the suggestion that every child should be tested at the beginning of his school career.

43. The Binet scale and the diagnosis of feeble-mindedness. *Nat. Educ. Ass. J.*, 1916, **1**, 874–879.

A clarification of the misunderstanding arising from the use of the term *feeble-mindedness* in two different senses—the psychological and the social.

44. The Binet scale and the diagnosis of feeble-mindedness. *J. crim. Law Criminol.*, 1916, **7**, 530–543.

The difficulties of diagnosing feeble-mindedness seem due largely to the nature of the phenomena dealt with rather than artificial products of the Binet age-grade method of measuring intelligence.

45. The building situation and medical inspection. In *Denver School Survey*, Denver, 1916. Pt. V.

46. The measurement of intelligence: an explanation of and a complete guide for the use of the Stanford revision and extension of the Binet-Simon intelligence scale. Cambridge: Houghton Mifflin, 1916.

The major purpose of this volume is the presentation of the Stanford revision of the Binet-Simon intelligence scale, constructed to correct as many as possible of the imperfections of the original scale. General instructions for administering and scoring the tests, together with an account of the procedure, scoring, and psychological interpretation of performance for each separate item of the scale, are given. The introductory chapters are devoted to a summary of the theory of intelligence testing, including situations in which intelligence ratings are useful, reasons why estimates are unsatisfactory; the history of both the Binet scale and the Stanford revision are discussed. Intelligence-test results are considered in relation to sex and class differences and school success. The significance of various intelligence quotients is given, with specific case histories and generalizations as to the characteristics of children at different levels of intelligence. Factors that may affect the value and correct use of the test method are outlined, and other factors frequently thought to invalidate the method are ruled out.

47. The measurement of intelligence. In *Young People's Encyclopedia*. Chicago, Hudson Bellows, 1916.

48. Review of the Vineland translation of articles by Binet and Simon. *J. Delinq.*, 1916, **1**, 256–272.

49. Some comments on Dr. Haines' comparison of the Binet-Simon and Yerkes-Bridges intelligence scales. *J. Delinq.*, 1916, **1**, 115–117.

50. ———, with others. Mentality tests: a symposium. *J. educ. Psychol.*, 1916, **7**, 348–360.

Presents the thesis that mentality testing will continue for some years to be intelligence testing and that in this field the point-scale has no advantage over the age-grade method.

51. Feeble-minded children in the public schools of California. *Sch. & Soc.*, 1917, **5**, 161–165.

52. The intelligence quotient of Francis Galton in childhood. *Amer. J. Psychol.*, 1917, **28**, 209–215.

Although Francis Galton is usually considered a genius who matured late, evidence from Pearson's *Life, Letters, and Labours of Galton* suggests that he must have had an I.Q. close to 200. Early letters written by Galton which are presented as illustrative of his vocabulary, interests, and education seem to indicate that his mental age was approximately double his chronological age. The error of Pearson and others in not recognizing the significance of these early accomplishments has been due to a failure, common also among schoolteachers, to evaluate a mental performance in terms of the mental age to which it corresponds.

53. A trial of mental and pedagogical tests in a civil service examination of policemen and firemen. *J. appl. Psychol.*, 1917, **1**, 17–29.

54. ———, with LYMAN, G., ORDAHL, G., ORDAHL, L. E., GALBREATH, N., & TALBERT, W. The Stanford revision and extension of the Binet-Simon scale for measuring intelligence. Baltimore: Warwick & York, 1917.

A summary of the data on which the Stanford revision and extension of the Binet scale rests and an analysis of the results secured by the application of the revised scale to nearly 1000 unselected school children. The data give information concerning the distribution of intelligence and throw doubt on the theories of "nascent stages" and "adolescent spurt." Other topics considered are the end of the mental-growth period, sex differences in intelligence, the relationship of social status to intelligence, and the agreement of school performance with tested intelligence. The guiding principle of the scale is to make median mental age correspond with median chronological age, thus necessitating a variable percentage passing at different age levels. The validity of the items was determined by the increase in percentage passing with age and by the criterion of internal consistency—"coherence."

55. Errors in scoring Binet tests. *Psychol. Clin.*, 1918, **12**, 33–39.

A study of errors made by five students in scoring 843 Binet tests indicates that the percentage of error can be kept low, that carelessness in computation is responsible for a large proportion of errors, that not over one half of the errors made result in incorrect mental ages, and that certain tests give more difficulty than others in scoring.

56. An experiment in infant education. *J. appl. Psychol.*, 1918, **2**, 219–228.

The introduction to a father's account of the training of his daughter who, at the age of 26 months, read as well as the average first-grader.

57. Expert testimony in the case of Alberto Flores. *J. Delinq.*, 1918, **3**, 145–164.

An analysis of the fallacies of the "expert" testimony of the prosecution given in an attempt to prove the normal mentality of an Italian criminal, who, according to three Stanford-Binet tests, had a mental age of 7½ years. Special attention is called to the responses described by the prosecution as symptomatic of normal intelligence, most of which are shown by comparison with the Binet scale to be characteristic of the subject's mental rather than his chronological age.

58. Tests of general intelligence. *Psychol. Bull.*, 1918, **15**, 160–167.

One of the series of articles outlining courses and procedures for the Students' Army Training Course, in which are discussed the need for a scientific method of rating mentality, the early work of Binet, the methods of sampling intellectual products and of standardizing tests, and the advantages of the mental-test method.

59. The use of intelligence tests in the army. *Psychol. Bull.*, 1918, **15**, 177–186.

A second article in the series for the Students' Army Training Course, outlining the advantage of the Army tests for classifying men, explaining the letter ratings obtained, and presenting evidence that the tests measure the soldier's value to the service.

60. The vocabulary test as a measure of intelligence. *J. educ. Psychol.*, 1918, **9**, 452–466.

In answer to current criticisms of the validity of the vocabulary test as a measure of intelligence, this study reports correlations between vocabulary-test score and mental age on the Stanford revision of the Binet scale and concludes that it may soon be possible to measure intellectual level almost as accurately through a vocabulary list of crucial words as by any existent intelligence scale.

61. ———, with CHAMBERLAIN, M. B. Twenty-three serial tests of intelligence and their intercorrelations. *J. appl. Psychol.*, 1918, **2**, 341–354.

A battery of tests found to correlate with other measures of intelligence and to lend themselves to the principle of serial arrangement, abandoned because of the greater promise of group tests but published in the hope that they may have some suggestive value for other workers.

62. ———, with CUNEO, I.   Stanford-Binet tests of 112 kindergarten children and 77 repeated tests.   *Ped. Sem.*, 1918, **25**, 414–428.

A study yielding a distribution of intelligence-test scores among kindergarten children, correlating these scores with teachers' estimates and school marks, determining the effect of the repetition of a test on the resulting I.Q., and throwing light upon the proper location of the tests in the lower levels of the scale.

63. ———, with KNOLLIN, H. E., WILLIAMS, J. H., *et al.*   Surveys in mental deviation in prisons, public schools, and orphanages in California under the auspices of the State Joint Committee.   Sacramento: Calif. State Printing Office, 1918.

64. ———, with WAGNER, D.   Intelligence quotients of 68 children in a California orphanage.   *J. Delinq.*, 1918, **3**, 115–121.

65. The intelligence of school children: how children differ in ability. Cambridge: Houghton Mifflin, 1919.

The purpose of the book is to illustrate the large individual differences in endowment existing among school children and to show the practical bearing of these differences on the everyday problems of classroom management and school administration.   Research studies in which the Binet tests have been used to make surveys of existing conditions and to experiment with the mental-age standard for grading are presented to assist the teacher with his problems. Special attention is called to the characteristics of superior children so that the teacher may recognize those with whom he comes in contact and make provision for an adequate educational program.

66. Some data on the Binet test of naming words.   *J. educ. Psychol.*, 1919, **10**, 29–35.

67. Condensed guide for the Stanford revision of the Binet-Simon intelligence tests.   Cambridge: Houghton Mifflin, 1920.

68. Terman group test of mental ability, for grades 7–12.   Yonkers: World Book, 1920.

69. The use of intelligence tests in the grading of school children.   *J. educ. Res.*, 1920, **1**, 19–32.

Studies of individual differences in intelligence in school classes, which indicate that only the middle 50 to 60 per cent of school children are classified as they should be, emphasize again the importance to the school of evaluating the raw material with which it works.

70. ———, with CHASE, J. M.   The psychology, biology and pedagogy of genius.   *Psychol. Bull.*, 1920, **17**, 397–409.

A summary of the literature on genius since 1914, including psychological and literary interpretations of genius; statistical, biological, and genetic studies;

social aspects of genius; psychoanalytical studies; the psychology of special talent; and, finally, the approach through the study of gifted children, with a summary of findings on a group of 59.

71. ———, with others. National intelligence tests, with manual of directions. Yonkers: World Book, 1920.

72. Intelligence tests in colleges and universities. *Sch. & Soc.*, 1921, **13,** 481–494.

73. Mental growth and the I.Q. *J. educ. Psychol.*, 1921, **12,** 325–341, 401–407.

Some of the arguments and the data relating to mental growth and the validity of the I.Q. are examined and special reference made to a monograph by Doll published the same year. Points raised by Wallin, Mateer, and Freeman are likewise discussed with a view to differentiating between mental deficiency and feeble-mindedness, emphasizing the inadequacy of the I.Q. in the diagnosis of absolute emotional or physical states and indicating the probable explanation of some differences between group test results and those obtained on the Stanford-Binet.

74. The status of applied psychology in the United States. *J. appl. Psychol.*, 1921, **5,** 1–4.

75. Suggestions for the education and training of gifted children. Stanford University: Stanford Univ. Press, 1921.

A pamphlet prepared for parents of subjects included in a survey of gifted children in California, containing suggestions for parental care based on the results of the investigation and on general psychological principles.

76. ———, with FENTON, J. C. Preliminary report on a gifted juvenile author. *J. appl. Psychol.*, 1921, **5,** 163–178.

A paper read before the American Psychological Association reporting data concerning a 9-year-old girl in the Stanford gifted-children group. Five of her poems, rated by students in advanced English classes, compare favorably with poems by well-known authors.

77. ———, with KELLEY, T. L. Dr. Ruml's criticism of mental test methods. *J. Phil.*, 1921, **18,** 459–465.

In this response to Dr. Ruml's criticism that the results of mental tests are of meager theoretical value, the authors first answer three questions posed by Dr. Ruml and then point out that the ultimate value of a hypothesis lies not in its absolute correctness but in its fruitfulness as a point of departure for experimentation.

78. ———, with WHITMIRE, E. D. Age and grade norms for the national intelligence tests, scales A and B. *J. educ. Res.*, 1921, **3,** 124–132.

79. ————, with others. Intelligence and its measurement: a symposium. *J. educ. Psychol.*, 1921, **12**, 127–133.

The definition of intelligence as the ability to carry on abstract thinking and an outline of the next steps to be taken in the measurement of intelligence.

80. Adventures in stupidity: a partial analysis of the intellectual inferiority of a college student. *Sci. Mon., N. Y.*, 1922, **14**, 24–40.

81. The great conspiracy, or the impulse imperious of intelligence testers, psychoanalyzed and exposed by Mr. Lippmann. *New Repub.*, 1922, **33**, 116–120.

An examination, in ironical style, of certain of the allegations made by Lippmann in opposition to intelligence testing.

82. A new approach to the study of genius. *Psychol. Rev.*, 1922, **29**, 310–318.

A review of the steps leading to the study of the 1000 gifted children, with a description of some of the methods being used in the research.

83. The problem. *In* TERMAN, L. M., *et al. Intelligence Tests and School Reorganization.* Yonkers: World Book, 1922, pp. 1–31.

84. The psychological determinist, or democracy and the I.Q. *J. educ. Res.*, 1922, **6**, 57–62.

In answer to Bagley, who accuses intelligence testing of operating against liberal education for all children, the author points out that the psychologist does not propose to exclude all but the most intelligent from secondary education but does demand new types of secondary education better suited to inferior intellects, so that the school may make the most of every child.

85. Were we born that way? *World's Work*, 1922, **44**, 655–660.

86. ————, with ELLIOTT, O. L., KELLEY, T. L., *et al.* Report of subcommittee of Leland Stanford Junior University Committee on Scholarship and Student Ability. Stanford University: Stanford Univ. Press, 1923.

87. ————, with KELLEY, T. L., and RUCH, G. M. Stanford achievement test. Manuals of directions for primary examination and advanced examination. Yonkers: World Book, 1923.

88. American Psychological Association. *Science*, 1924, **59**, 546–548.

89. Conservation of talent. *Sch. & Soc.*, 1924, **19**, 359–364.

90. The mental test as a psychological method. *Psychol. Rev.*, 1924, **31**, 93–117.

Presidential address to the American Psychological Association, based on the thesis that the mental test and the psychological experiment are essentially identical. Taking as a point of departure the results of a questionnaire sent to 22 past A.P.A. presidents, Terman examines the grounds for each distinction drawn between the test and the experimental method. It is concluded that the attempt to distinguish between the method of the test and the method of experiment is not warranted on either logical or historical grounds. "Objectively, the psychological test is a method of sampling mental processes or mental behavior, and so, in a sense, is any method of psychological experiment."

91. The physical and mental traits of gifted children. *Yearb. nat. Soc. Stud. Educ.*, 1924, **23** Pt. I, 155–167.

A preliminary report of some of the data obtained from the main experimental group of 643 California children of I.Q.'s of 140 and over. Summaries of the data concerning physical development, character and personality tests, and hereditary and social status indicate that the gifted group is above average with respect to health, that it tends to be superior to the control group in social and moral development, and that it has superior physical heredity and home environment. A brief review of the work of Cox on the early traits of geniuses points out the falsity of the belief that many geniuses as children were mentally slow.

92. The possibilities and limitations of training. *J. educ. Res.*, 1924, **10**, 335–343.

93. ————, with DeVoss, J. C. The educational achievements of gifted children. *Yearb. nat. Soc. Stud. Educ.*, 1924, **23** Pt. I, 169–184.

Results of the Stanford Achievement tests, administered to the experimental group of 643 gifted children, show that the gifted child tends to be superior in all school subjects and that, in relation to his ability to accomplish and to his measured educational achievement, he is underpromoted in school.

94. Genetic studies of genius. I. Mental and physical traits of a thousand gifted children. Stanford University: Stanford Univ. Press, 1925.

A study to determine in what respects the typical gifted child differs from the typical child of normal mentality. The problem is approached through the use of tests, measurements, and observational reports on about 1400 children, each ranking in general intelligence within the top 1 per cent of unselected school children of corresponding age. The data presented in this volume are concerned largely with 643 subjects for whom the results are most extensive. Information gathered includes racial and social origin, anthropometric measures, health and physical history, medical examinations, educational history, tests of school accomplishment, specialization of abilities, interests, and character and personality tests and ratings. Results indicate that the gifted child excels the average most in intellectual and volitional traits; next, in emotional and moral; and least, in physical and social traits, although it is convincingly demonstrated that the "one-sidedness" of precocious children is mythical and that the gifted child is generally superior.

95. Die Pflege der Begabung. (The conservation of talent.) *Z. pädag. Psychol.*, 1925, **26**, 137–144.

96. Research on the diagnosis of predelinquent tendencies. *J. Delinq.*, 1925, **9**, 124–130.

A discussion of personality tests for disclosing predelinquent tendencies is here given as well as some results of the application of character tests to 533 gifted and 609 unselected children.

97. ———, with Cowdery, K. M. Stanford program of university personnel research. *J. person. Res.*, 1925, **4**, 263–276.

98. Biographical note on Henry Cowell. *Amer. J. Psychol.*, 1926, **37**, 233–234.

99. Independent study plan at Stanford University. *Sch. & Soc.*, 1926, **24**, 96–98.

100. The possibilities and limitations of training. *J. educ. Res.*, 1926, **13**, 371–373.

101. The 1927 yearbook of the National Society for the Study of Education, on the possibilities and limitations of training. *Sch. & Soc.*, 1926, **23**, 404–406.

Policies to be followed in selecting materials for the 1927 yearbook are here outlined, with summaries of contributions already accepted and suggestions for possible types of investigation that might be carried on.

102. ———, with Lima, M. Children's reading: a guide for parents and teachers. New York and London: Appleton, 1926.

An experimental study of the qualitative and quantitative aspects of children's reading, based on data concerning 2000 children, secured from home, from school, and from the children themselves. Part I discusses the reading interests of children, tracing the changes in types of books enjoyed from before the age of 5 through age 16. Information on the amount and quality of reading of gifted children is included here as well as suggestions for the reading of subnormal children. Certain qualities rendering a book desirable for children are outlined. Part II, based on the results obtained in Part I, consists of an annotated bibliography of books suitable for children of different ages together with suggestions for a growing library for a child.

103. Cox, C. M., assisted by Terman, L. M., *et al*. Genetic studies of genius. II. The early mental traits of 300 geniuses. Stanford University: Stanford Univ. Press, 1926.

A study of 300 subjects from Cattell's list of the 1000 most eminent, selected upon the basis of the availability of authoritative biographical data. The method employed is that devised by Terman and used by him in 1917 in his study of Francis Galton.

104. Growth through professional reading. *Nat. Educ. Ass. J.*, 1928, **17**, 137–138.

105. Introduction to: nature and nurture. I. Their influence upon intelligence. *Yearb. nat. Soc. Stud. Educ.*, 1928, **27** Pt. I, 1–7.

106. The influence of nature and nurture upon intelligence scores: an evaluation of the evidence in Part I of the 1928 Yearbook of the National Society for the Study of Education. *J. educ. Psychol.*, 1928, **19**, 362–373.

107. Testing for the crime germ. *Sunset*, 1928, **60** (May), 24–25.

108. Ultimate influence of standard tests. *J. educ. Res.*, 1928, **17**, 57–59.

109. ———, with ALMACK, J. C. The hygiene of the school child. (Rev. and enlarged ed.) Cambridge: Houghton Mifflin, 1929.

This revised edition, appearing 15 years after the original, attempts to reflect the changes in the field of educational hygiene since the First World War. Two chapters have been dropped, those on Physiological Age and the Harmful Effects of School Life; and four chapters have been added: Mortality and Morbidity, Health of the Teacher, Hygiene of the Schoolroom, and Teaching of Physiology and Hygiene, along with new bibliographies, new materials, and a collection of teaching helps at the close of each chapter.

110. ———, with KELLEY, T. L. Ability and personality tests. *Independent Educ.*, 1929, **3**, 5–6.

111. ———, with KELLEY, T. L., & RUCH, G. M. New Stanford achievement test. Yonkers: World Book, 1929.

112. ———, with MILES, C. C. Sex difference in the association of ideas. *Amer. J. Psychol.*, 1929, **41**, 165–206.

Preparatory to setting up a word-association test to differentiate between the sexes, the authors here review the experimentally demonstrated findings in the literature, concluding that there are sex differences in the association of ideas but that their origin in primary, innate differences has not been established.

113. Talent and genius in children. *In* CALVERTON, V. F., & SCHMAL-HAUSEN, S. D. *The New Generation.* New York: Macaulay, 1930, pp. 405–424.

114. ———, with BURKS, B. S., JENSEN, D. W., *et al.* Genetic studies of genius. III. The promise of youth: follow-up studies of a thousand gifted children. Stanford University: Stanford Univ. Press, 1930.

An investigation to check on the conclusions presented in Vol. I and to help complete the picture of the typical gifted youth through new types of data not considered previously. The findings both here and in Vol. I are largely group data. This is necessary to do away with popular misconceptions and is valuable because any educational program for them must necessarily be based upon the gifted as a group. The most important single outcome is that, for the group as a whole, the picture did not greatly change in the period that elapsed between the two studies. There were, however, individual changes, and case studies illustrative of these are presented.

115. Educational psychology. *In* EAST, E. M. *Biology in Human Affairs*. New York: McGraw-Hill, 1931, pp. 94–122.

116. The gifted child. *In* MURCHISON, C. A. *A Handbook of Child Psychology*. Worcester: Clark Univ. Press, 1931, pp. 568–584.

A discussion of some of the problems involved, methods used, and results obtained in the study of children of superior general intelligence. Four approaches to the problem are outlined: (*a*) general descriptive reports; (*b*) clinical reports on a single case or a small number of cases; (*c*) statistical studies based on measurements of groups of subjects; (*d*) biographical study of the childhood of geniuses. A composite portrait of the gifted child is painted, based on results obtained in the original study of the 1000 gifted children plus other data from the first follow-up 7 years later. Information is also presented on 26 children of about average I.Q. and of superior special ability, showing that the early promise that these children gave was not in a single case fulfilled. The work of Cox is briefly reviewed to indicate the existence of important correlations between the mental abilities of childhood and later life.

117. Psychology and the law. *Los Angeles Bar Ass. Bull.*, 1931, **6**, 142–153.

An address to members of the Los Angeles Bar Association, in which it is pointed out that, since the law deals with essentially psychological problems, psychology may make valuable contributions to law, such as experimental investigations of error and its relation to testimony, deception tests, and studies of the causes and prevention of crime.

118. ———, with LIMA, M. Children's reading: a guide for parents and teachers. (2d ed.) New York: Appleton, 1931.

119. Trails to psychology. *In* MURCHISON, C. A. *A History of Psychology in Autobiography*. Worcester: Clark Univ. Press, 1932. Vol. II, pp. 297–332.

120. The measurement of personality. *Science*, 1934, **80**, 605–608.

Difficulties in the way of reliably measuring personality are here pointed out, with suggestions that an approach should be made by studying contrasting groups and that the meaning of scores yielded by personality tests be made more definite by an extensive study of extremes, with the use of both statistical and clinical methods.

121. ———, with BUTTENWEISER, P. Personality factors in marital compatibility. *J. soc. Psychol.*, 1935, **6**, 143–171, 267–289.

A preliminary report of the research on marital compatibility, outlining the purpose of the study, the use of happily married, unhappily married, and divorced groups, the types of information collected, and some of the results thus far obtained. Few large differences between the groups in mean scores on personality tests have been found, but over one fourth of the 545 test items taken singly appear to have validity as indicators of marital compatibility.

122. ———, with JOHNSON, W. B.   Personality characteristics of happily married, unhappily married, and divorced persons.   *Character & Pers.*, 1935, **3**, 290–311.

The 100 most happily married couples, 100 least happily married, and 100 divorced couples selected earlier by Terman and Buttenweiser on the basis of happiness ratings are here characterized in terms of constellations of interests and attitudes, expressed through their responses to 545 individual items on the Strong and Bernreuter scales.

123. ———, with KELLY, E. L., & MILES, C. C.   Ability to influence one's score on a typical paper-and-pencil test of personality.   *Character & Pers.*, 1936, **4**, 206–215.

Administration of the M-F test to the same group of subjects with three different types of instruction reveals that it is possible for subjects to shift their scores in a masculine or feminine direction if they are specifically directed to do so.

124. ———, with McNEMAR, Q.   Sex differences in variational tendency.   *Genet. Psychol. Monogr.*, 1936, **18**, 1–66.

A review of the literature on this subject since 1894, attempting to bring together and render comparable the results of the most important investigations bearing on its psychological aspects and to evaluate the methods that have led investigators to draw conclusions concerning sex differences in variation.

125. ———, with MILES, C. C.   Sex and personality: studies in masculinity and femininity.   New York & London: McGraw-Hill, 1936.

Presents a test of mental masculinity and femininity as a means of making the concepts of the masculine and feminine types existing in the present culture more definite and more securely based on fact.   Two forms of the test have been developed, each consisting of seven exercises: word association, information, ink-blot association, emotional and ethical responses, interests, personalities and opinions, and introvertive response.   The present volume is devoted more to the relationships obtaining between M-F scores and other variables than to the extensive experimental work that lies behind the test. To this end, M-F scores are considered in their relation to physical measurements, trait ratings, personality, and achievement measures, age, education, intelligence, and occupation.   Data are also presented on 134 cases of male homosexuality, with a tentative scale for the measurement of sexual inversion in males, derived from these results.   Three chapters are devoted to case studies.   Results of the study, or the interpretations and conclusions to which they have led, are not meant to be considered final but are significant if they point to a new application of psychometric methods in the study of sex differences in temperament.

126. ———, with MERRILL, M. A. Directions for administering the revised Stanford-Binet. Cambridge: Houghton Mifflin, 1937.

127. ———, with MERRILL, M. A. Measuring intelligence: a guide to the administration of the new revised Stanford-Binet tests of intelligence. Cambridge: Houghton Mifflin, 1937.

The theoretical background of the new revised Stanford-Binet and a practical guide to its administration. The reasons for its construction, the population on which it has been standardized, and units in which the results may be expressed are considered. Only the most essential facts of the statistical treatment are given here, with a more detailed treatment reserved for a separate publication. The necessity of adhering to a standard procedure, of establishing rapport, and of correctly appraising the results obtained is stressed. Because of the special difficulties encountered, an additional section is devoted to the testing of preschool children. An Appendix gives tables for securing the I.Q., once the detailed instructions for establishing the mental age have been followed.

128. Psychological factors in marital happiness. New York & London: McGraw-Hill, 1938.

The results of an investigation of factors correlated with marital happiness based on a study of 792 married couples. The approach to the problem is from three directions: (*a*) from the point of view of personality, including attitudes, interests, likes, dislikes, and opinions; (*b*) from the point of view of background and personal history; and (*c*) from the point of view of specific sexual adjustments. The relative contributions of these three factors to marital happiness are determined, and it is found that the influence of the sexual factors is at most no greater than that of the combined personality and background factors. The validity of the data is assured by special precautions taken in regard to the anonymity of the subjects. A scale for the prediction of marital happiness is drawn up from items found to be discriminating for the experimental group. In addition to determining factors positively correlated with marital happiness, the study discredits many current views on causation in this field.

129. Educational suggestions from follow-up studies of intellectually gifted children. *J. educ. Sociol.*, 1939, **13**, 82–89.

130. The effect of happiness or unhappiness on self-report regarding attitudes, reaction patterns, and facts of personal history. *Psychol. Bull.*, 1939, **36**, 197–202.

Presents evidence to show that the domestic happiness or unhappiness of married subjects does not have a halo effect invalidating self-report regarding attitudes, reaction patterns, and facts of personal history when these data are gathered in the manner described in *Psychological Factors in Marital Happiness*.

131. The gifted student and his academic environment. *Sch. & Soc.*, 1939, **49**, 65–73.

An address to members of the Association of American Universities, which begins by summarizing recent follow-ups of the gifted children with reference to studies of their college achievement and concludes with pleas for a special university for the most gifted students of the best institutions and for financial support from members of the association for research on the abilities of their students.

132. ———, with JOHNSON, W. B.   Methodology and results of recent studies in marital adjustment.   *Amer. sociol. Rev.*, 1939, **4**, 307–324.

Critical comment on six of the leading studies of factors correlated with marital happiness that have appeared in the last decade, describing the methods by which the problem has been approached and emphasizing in particular the desirability of collaborating studies of marriage by investigators of different points of view and training.

133. Frank Angell: 1857–1939.   *Amer. J. Psychol.*, 1940, **53**, 138–141.

A tribute to Frank Angell, head of the psychology department at Stanford from 1892 until his retirement in 1922, including, in addition to biographical data, descriptions by certain of his former students of Angell's advanced courses and of his opinions regarding the goal of science and particularly the place of psychology among the sciences.

134. Intelligence in a changing universe.   *Sch. & Soc.*, 1940, **51**, 465–470.

A critical review of a symposium of the same title appearing in a special issue of *Educational Method* for November, 1939.   Attention is called to the possibility of interpreting differently arguments used by four of the seven contributors in support of their opposition to intelligence testing.

135. Personal reactions of the Yearbook Committee (Nat. Soc. Stud. Educ.)   *Yearb. nat. Soc. Stud. Educ.*, 1940, **39** Pt. I, 460–467.

A comparison by the chairman of the 1928 Yearbook of the evidence on nature and nurture as it stood in 1928 and as it stands today.

136. Psychological approaches to the biography of genius.   *Science*, 1940, **92**, 293–301.

Presidential address to the Pacific Division of the American Association for the Advancement of Science, outlining the Stanford studies of genius, both in terms of the life histories of eminent characters and by the study and follow-up of intellectually superior children.

137. ———, with JOHNSON, W. B.   Some highlights in the literature of psychological sex differences published since 1920.   *J. Psychol.*, 1940, **9**, 327–336.

Comments on the literature on sex differences in two aspects of personality, social attitudes, and emotionality, suggesting the hypothesis that sex differences in personality and behavior may parallel sex differences in physical homeostasis.

138. ———, with ODEN, M.   The significance of deviates.   II. Status of the California gifted group at the end of sixteen years.   III. Correlates of adult achievement in the California gifted group. *Yearb. nat. Soc. Stud. Educ.*, 1940, **39** Pt. I, 67–74, 74–89.

Two separate follow-up studies of the 1922 gifted group show that, although a considerable proportion of the subjects have not yet lived up to their ability, the accomplishments of the group as a whole have been as good as could reasonably have been expected, considering that most of its members are still under 30 years of age.   A separate study of selected groups of successful and unsuccessful gifted boys shows that, at least under the conditions obtaining in this group, excess in I.Q. above 140 or 150 adds little to one's achievement in the early adult years, such achievement being determined rather by the factors of social adjustment, emotional stability, and the drive to accomplish.